Modern Business Law

By the Same Author

- Business and Industrial Law
- Mercantile Law
- Organisational Behaviour (UPTU)
- Principles of Management
- Business and Corporate Law (UPTU)
- Organisational Theory and Behaviour (Text and Cases), 2nd Edition

Modern Business Law

Dr. B.S. Moshal
Associate Professor
Department of Commerce
Zakir Husain Post Graduate Evening College
(Delhi University)
Founder Director, D.C.A.S
(I.P. University)
Former Visiting Faculty ICAI

Ane Books Pvt. Ltd.
New Delhi ♦ Chennai

Modern Business Law

B.S. Moshal

Published by

Ane Books Pvt. Ltd.

4821, Parwana Bhawan, 1st Floor, 24 Ansari Road, Darya Ganj,
New Delhi - 110 002, Tel.: +91(011) 23276843-44, Fax: +91(011) 23276863
e-mail: kapoor@anebooks.com, Website: www.anebooks.com

Branch Office:

- Avantika Niwas, 1st Floor, 19 Doraiswamy Road, T. Nagar,
Chennai - 600 017, Tel.: +91(044) 28141554, 28141209
e-mail: anebookschennai@gmail.com, rathinam@anebooks.com

ISBN : 978-93-8116-244-6

Printed at : R.K. Digital Process, New Delhi.

Dedicated to my

Parents & Guru

Preface

This book has been designed primarily to cater to the needs of B.Com. (H) students of Delhi University, as being prescribed in New Semester System. The contents of this book are perfectly in tune with revised syllabus of this course. It may also be profitably used by the students of other professional courses.

In this book, attempts have been made for presenting contents of the various relevant provisions of the different Acts in more effective and simplified manner.

The use of class teaching language and citation of suitable examples and leading cases make the subject matter more understandable and interesting. While writing the book due care has been exercised in providing precise and easy interpretation of the various provisions in points.

Although, a few authors have made an impressive attempts to write the subject, but the subject-matter of law needs regular updating. Thus, the concept of 'latest is the best' holds good.

The subject-matter of the book has been organised into four major parts. The first part, which consists of fourteen chapters deals with formation of contract, essentials of a valid contract, its performance and special contracts of indemnity and guarantee, bailment and agency. The second part comprising of four chapters on Indian Sale of Goods Act, is related to the formation and performance of the contract of sale. Part third on Limited Liability Partnership Act provides detailed information regarding the various provisions related to the formation, fucntioning and structure of LLP instruments, their use and regulation in practice. Fourth part of this book contain legal provisions of Information Technology Act.

In completing this book I feel privileged to acknowledge moral support, help and guiding inspiration provided by enlightened friends and colleagues including Dr. R.B. Solanki (Ambedkar College) Sh. C.S. Pant (D.S. Eve.), Dr. G.C. Kasturi (R.C.) Dr. N.K. Agrawal (SOL.) Mrs. Kalpana Bhola (J.D.M), Sh. Mod. Naqi (Z.H.) and Dr. S.K. Tandon (D.C.A.C.). I also express my sincere thanks to the publishers Sh. Sunil Saxena and Sh. Jai Raj Kapoor of Ane Books Pvt. Ltd. for getting the book published.

I shall be obliged to solicit and take care of the comments, suggestions and quaries from the readers.

Dr. B.S. Moshal

Contents

PART 1 INDIAN CONTRACT ACT, 1872

Part 1

Indian Contract Act 1872

Chapter 1

Contract; Definition, Essentials and Types

Learning Objectives

- Develop Conceptual clarity about the terms, contract and agreement.
- Understand essentials of a valid contract.
- Remember various types of a contracts.
- Be clear about formation of a contract.
- Understand legal consequences of offer acceptance, agreement, promise, and obligations.

INTRODUCTION

In order to conduct business operations, many transactions are made by the parties. Mostly these transactions are made in the form of contract. In these transactions certain rights and obligations are created. The rights of one party would be a obligations of other party and vice-versa. It is therefore to regulate and settle these transactions Indian Contract Act 1872 has been enacted. The law of contract deals with those transactions or promises which create legal rights and obligations. This act lays down legal rules relating to promises, their formation and enforceability. In case of non performance of the promise by one party, it also provides legal remedies to an aggrieved party.

Indian Contract Act came in to being in September 1872. The act is extended to the whole of India except the state of Jammu and Kashmir. It contains 266 sections. Out of these, sect 1 to 75 are related to formation and performance of the contract. Sections 124 to 238 deal with some special contracts such as agency, bailment guarantee etc. Section 73 to 123 and section 239 to 266 have been repealed and merged in to Indian Sale of Goods Act and Indian Partnership Act.

In brief Indian Contract Act can be studied in following phases:

1. Formation of contract and essentials of a valid contract.
2. Performance of a contract or promises made in a contract.

3. Special contracts including contracts of indemnity and guarantee, bailment and agency.

The contract Act has the following limitations.

A. Firstly Indian contract act creates right 'in personam', which is available only against particular party or particular person. (Parties or person making a contract). For example, A lends sum of Rs. 10,000 to B. In this transaction A gets right to recover the money only from B and not from any one else. Secondly the Law of contract is not the whole law of agreements or the whole law of obligations. Agreements and obligations which are not contractual in nature do not come with in the purview of this act. For example A borrows sum of Rs. 5000 from his friend B. If A does not repay money B gets right to sue upon him. But if A invites B his friend for a dinner at his home. B agrees to it. And if B does not turn up for dinner A has no legal remedy against him. It is because in this case relationship created between A and B is personal and social in nature not covered by Indian Contract Act. According to Salmond, Law of contract is the law of those agreements which creates obligations and those obligations which have their source in agreement. In other words, provisions of this Act are applicable only on those obligations which are contractual and legal in nature.

CONTRACT DEFINED

It is clear that the legal provisions of Indian Contract Act are applicable only on those transactions which are made in the form of contract.

Therefore, it is necessary to define and understand the meaning of the term contract.

Generally contract may be defined as an agreement which creates rights and obligations between the parties. These rights and obligations must be of such a nature that these can be claimed in the court of law.

In the words of Sir William Anson "contract is a legally binding agreement made between two or more persons by which rights are acquired by one or more to acts or forbearamces on the part of other".

Salmond has defined contract "as an agreement creating and defining obligation between the parties". According to section 2 (h) of the Indian Contract Act "contract is an agreement which is enforceable by law".

Analysis of the above definitions of contract reveals that contract has three major components

(a) Agreement.
(b) Obligation.
(c) Enforceability.

(a) *Agreement:* In order to form a contract at first instance there must be an agreement between parties.

(b) *Obligation:* Agreement made between the parties must give a rise to rights and obligations. These rights and obligations must be legal in nature. Such obligations form a central part of a contract.

(c) *Enforceability:* Rights and obligations created in agreement must be contractual in nature. In other words, these must be legal in nature which can be claimed in the court of law. It is the legal consequences involved in these obligations and rights which make them enforceable in the court.

Agreement defined: Agreement a foundation stone of a contract. The contract is formed only on the basis of agreement. It is a combined effect of offer and acceptance. One party makes an offer for doing or not doing, anything and other party accepts it. Agreement is formed between them.

Agreement = offer + Acceptance.

According to section 2 (e) agreement is a promise or a set of promise forming consideration for each other.

The offer itself is of no legal consequences unless it is accepted. On acceptance the offer is converted in to binding promise. The party making an offer becomes promisor and acceptor becomes promisee. As a legal consequence of acceptance, the acceptor becomes promisor and offeror becomes promisee. In this way there is a mutual exchange of promises between offeror and acceptor resulting in formation of an agreement.

It is, however to be noted that in an agreement the promisee is always in a position of benefit. It is because the promisor has to perform the act for the benefit of promisee.

Example: A offers to sell out his bike to B for Rs. 30,000 B, accepts the offer. Agreement is formed between A and B. In this agreement A is a promisor for transferring the possession and ownership of the bike to B. B, is a promisee in the position of benefit. On acceptance of the offer B also becomes promisor for making payment of Rs. 30,000 to A who has come in a position of promisee.

Agreement creating rights and obligations between the parties become enforceable subject to fulfillment of some conditions. These conditions are mentioned in section 10 of Indian Contract Act.

ESSENTIALS OF A VALID CONTRACT

An agreement to be enforced in the court has to satisfy certain conditions. On satisfying these, the agreement becomes a contract, and those conditions become essentials of a valid contract. According to section 10 of Indian Contract Act, "all agreements are contracts if they are made by free consent of parties, competent to contract, for a lawful consideration and with a lawful object and are not expressly declared to be void". In brief essentials of a valid contract are as under:

1. *Agreement:* To form a contract, there must be an agreement between the parties. Agreement is created by offer and acceptance. It is a result of mutual exchange of promises between the parties. One party makes a promise for doing or not doing anything to another and that another makes similar promise to first one.

Agreement is created by lawful offer and valid acceptance. It is only by an agreement a contractual relation is established between the parties.

2. *Creation of legal relationship:* Agreement made between parties must create legal relationship. Legal relationship consists of rights and obligations which can be claimed by the parties in the court of law. Sometimes, there may be an agreement between the parties. Which creates relationship other than legal one such as social, personal and religious etc. Such, agreement is not enforceable, thus will not become a contract.

Example: A invites his friend B to his birthday party. B accepts the offer. But he fails to turn up for the party. This agreement creates social and personal relationship between A and B. It can not be enforced in the court. Thus A has no legal remedy against B.

The very base of a contract is a legal relationship.

Example: A borrows sum of Rs. 500 from his friend B for three months. B gets legal right to sue upon A if he fails to return money. It is because this agreement creates legal relationship, which can be enforced in the court.

The parties make an agreement with an intention to create legal relationship.

BAL FOUR VS. BAL FOUR (1919) 2 K.B 571: In this case a husband just makes a promise to pay his wife monthly allowance of £ 30 for her maintenance. Later on they separated and husband failed to pay stipulated amount to his wife. She filed suit for that allowance. But it was held by the court that such arrangements are not contracts or do not result in a contract. Because parties did not intend to create legal relationship. And finally the suit was dismissed.

3. *Lawful consideration:* Agreement is a mutual exchange of promises between parties. Each party making a promise gets something in return of his promise. It constitutes a consideration for his promise. An agreement to be enforced must be supported by lawful consideration. The consideration may be defined as a price for which, a promise of the promisor is bought. Generally, consideration will be given by the promisee But in some cases even if it is given by other party on behalf of promisee it is valid.

According to English Mercantile Law consideration may be defined as any benefit, interest or right which one party gets at the cost of loss, detriment or obligation on the part of other party.

Any act or promise or abstinence will constitute lawful consideration which is legal, moral and not against the public policy.

4. *Contractual capacity:* Parties making an agreement must have contractual capacity. Lack of contractual capacity would invalidate contract. Contractual capacity of the party means he or she must be legally competent for making a contract.

Section 11 of Indian Contract Act states that "every person is competent to contract who is of age of majority, of sound mind and is not disqualified from contracting by any law to which he is subject".

In other words, the person to have contractual capacity must satisfy the following conditions

(a) He must be of a major age and not a minor.

(b) He must be of a sound mind and not lunatic, idiot or drunkard

(c) He must not have been declared disqualified by law from contracting such as insolvent, convict and alien enemy etc.

Agreement made by the parties not fulfilling the above conditions cannot be enforced in the court of law and will not become contract.

5. *Free consent of the parties:* State of mind of the parties is involved in making offer and giving acceptance for it. As soon as offer is accepted it becomes a binding promise having a legal consequences. Thus both the parties entering into agreement must have their consent for it and that consent must be free. Consent may be defined as an identity of two or more minds on a particular subject matter. Two or more persons are said to have consent if they agree upon same thing in the same sense. And their consent is said to be free if it has not been induced by any one of the following factors

(a) Coercion (b) Undue influence (c) Misrepresentation

(d) Fraud (e) Mistake.

When consent is caused by any of the first four factors the contract becomes voidable and if it is induced by mistake it would be void and cannot be enforced in the court of law.

6. *Lawful object of agreement:* Agreement is made for some object or purpose such object is formed on the basis of promises made by the parties. These promises are made either for doing or not doing any thing. The object of an agreement must be to do some act which is legal. Contrary to it, agreements made for doing some thing illegal, immoral or against public policy, cannot be enforced in the court of law.

Example: A and B make an agreement for smuglling out some goods from India to another country. This agreement cannot be enforced in the court. Similarly A in consideration of Rs 1 lac from B makes promise to kill C. This agreement has been made for doing some illegal act and therefore cannot be enforced.

7. *Agreement, not declared expressly void:* There are certain agreements which have been expressly declared void by the law. Thus an agreement made by parties should not fall in that category. If it is so it would also meet same fate and cannot be enforced in the court of law.

Briefly, agreement expressly declared void are agreements in restraint of marriage, trade, legal proceedings and wagering agreements etc. In spite of having all other features of regular agreement these cannot be enforced.

8. *Certainty in the meaning of agreement:* Agreement made by the parties must be certain or capable of being made certain in its meaning. It is because agreement would result in creating rights and obligations between the parties. These rights and obligations will be claimed in the court of law. Agreement with uncertain meaning will bring uncertainly in the rights and obligations created by it. And uncertain rights and obligations cannot be enforced in the court of law.

Example: A, is a dealer of kerosene oil and coconut oil. B makes an agreement with him for buying 10 lts of oil. Meaning of this agreement is uncertain and therefore it cannot be enforced.

Example: A, has agriculture land in Delhi. He makes an agreement with B for selling entire produce of wheat crop of next year @ Rs. 1000 p.q. Although on the face of it, meaning of agreement seems to be uncertain, but it can be made certain on the production of wheat crop next year.

9. *Other legal formalities:* Agreement to be enforced, needs to satisfy other conditions of being in writing, registered and duly stamped. Generally Indian contract Act does not make any discrimination between written and oral agreement. Oral agreements are as good as written agreement. Reasons being that oral or verbal agreements creates similar rights and obligations between parties as being created by written agreements And oral agreements can be enforced in the same manner as written agreements. But some agreements to be enforced in the court need to be made in writing and got to be registered with appropriate legal authority and must have adequate stamp duty.

Example: All insurance agreements, arbitration agreements, and those related to transfer of immovable properties, negotiable instruments like cheque, Bill of Exchange and Promisory note, Articles of association and Memorandum of association must be made in writing and must be registered. Some of these must carry required stamp duty such as Promissory Note, and Agreements for transferring immovable properties etc.

To acquire status of a valid contract, the contract must possess above mentioned features. The contracts meeting above requirements are known as regular or valid contracts.

CLASSIFICATION OF CONTRACTS

Contracts made by the parties can be classified in to different types on the following bases.

A. Formation of Contract.
B. Performance of Contract.
C. Extent of Validity of Contract.

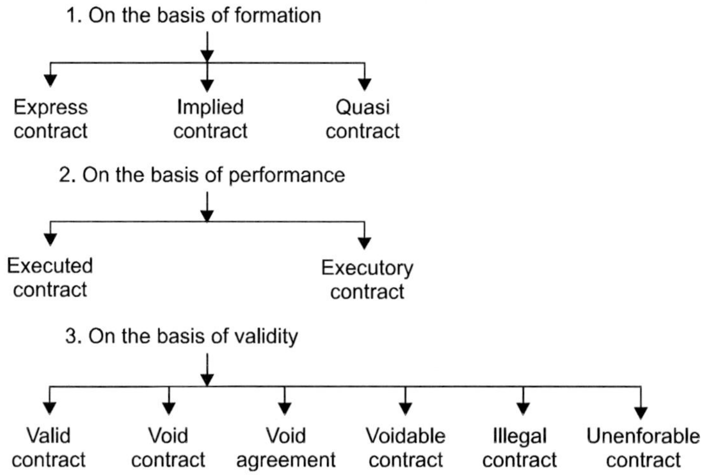

Fig. 1 Classification of Contracts

1. On the basis of formation, contracts may be grouped in to three groups.

A. *Express contracts:* Generally the contracts are made in this form. These contracts results from express agreements. Express agreement is formed by making offer and giving acceptance in the words spoken or in writing. According to Section 9 of Indian Contract Act "in so far as the proposal and acceptance of any promise is made in words, the promise is said to be express. An express promise leads to the formation of express contract".

Example: A, who is in front of B makes an offer to sell out his bike to B by the words of mouth. B gives his acceptance verbally. Express contract is formed between them. Similarly B sends offer for selling out his bike to B by post and B gives his acceptance by sending letter by post. It would also result in express contract.

B. *Implied contract:* Implied Contracts are formed on the basis of implied promises on the part of parties. Implied promises are those which are not made by the parties in writing or by the words of mouth. Rather these promises are inferred from the conduct of the parties or from the circumstances. In a implied contract, one of the party conduct himself or does some act which is being accepted by other party either by his conduct or course of his dealing or circumstance. Thus in implied contract, making of an offer and giving acceptance to it is manifested by the act on the part of party

Example: City transport company has plied various buses on the different routes. A, a commuter is standing at a particular bus stop on a particular route. Bus bearing specific number meant for that route comes to halt at that stop. A, gets in to the bus and travels on that route for his destination. He is bound to pay freight charged by the company for that distance. Contract between city transport company and A is implied in nature.

C. *Quasi-contracts:* Quasi-contracts are based on the principle of justice and equity. In spite of not having any contract between parties, the rights and obligations are created. These are resembling to rights and obligations as created by a formal contract. In such contracts, obligations between parties are created by operation of law rather than offer and acceptance. The legal base of quasi-contract is that a person shall not be allowed to enrich himself unjustly at the cost or expense of other. If he does so he comes under legal obligation to pay cost or expense without any formal contract.

Example: A has lost his dog. B finds it and takes it into custody. He spends on the maintenance of the dog. On tracing real owner, B can claim reimbursement of expenses incurred by him without any contract. Similarly A is under legal obligation to take reasonable care of the dog. Such rights and obligations which are quite resembling with that of formal contract are considered as quasi-contracts.

Section 68 to 72 of Indian Contract Act deal with the cases of quasi-contract.

2. On the basis of performance, the contracts may be grouped up as under:

A. *Executed contract:* Contract consists of certain legal obligations. On the complete discharge of these obligations, the contract is said to have been executed. In other words, executed contract is one that has been performed. It means, both the parties have fulfilled their respective promises, which they have made in contract. Nothing more remains to be done either by the parties.

Example: A makes an agreement for buying one hundred cotton bales from B @ Rs. 5000 per bale. B delivers these cotton bales to A and in return of it A makes payment to B. This contract becomes executed one.

B. *Executory contract:* Executory Contract is one that has not been yet performed. In other words, parties having made promises for doing or not doing any thing have not fulfilled their respective promises.

Till such promises are fulfilled the contract remains to be executory one. Not only this, but also if one party has performed his promises and an other party has yet to perform his promise, the contract remain executory in spite of partial performance.

Example: A makes an agreement for buying a car from car dealer. A has made payment. The car has been delivered to him. But ownership of that car is yet to be transferred to him. The contract remains executory.

3. On the basis of extent of validity the contract may be classified as under:

A. *Valid contract:* Contract is said to be valid if it satisfies all conditions required for its enforceability. In other words, valid contract is enforceable in the court of law. Lack of any element as prescribed by section 10 would change legal status of a contract and it may not be permitted to be enforced.

B. *Void contract:* A contract which ceases to be enforceable by law becomes void. No party has right to claim it in the court of law. The contract may become void either from beginning when it was made or may lateron discovered to be void.

Example: A was elected as a managing directions of X Company. by its board of directors. After six months it is found that one of the directors who have elected A has not purchased qualification share. He was not a bonafide director. Thus service contract made with A is discovered to be void.

Some times validity of a contract may adversely be affected by supervening impossibility or by the element of free consent.

Example: A makes an agreement with B for buying 500 quantal of wheat @ Rs. 1000 p.q. But before the date of performance the Central Govt enacts new legislation debarring an individual to buy more than 10 quantal at a time. The contract becomes void on account of supervening impossibility which arises after the formation of a contract.

Example: A, by causing consent of B by coercion makes agreement with him for buying his bike for Rs. 50,000. Lateron, B who is an aggrieved party declares it as void this contract becomes void due to lack of free consent.

C. *Void agreement:* Agreement which is not enforceable by law is void agreement. In other words, if an agreement lacks any one of essentials of a valid contract except free consent it becomes void. Such agreement does not create any legal rights and obligations between the parties and can not be enforced in the court either by the parties. Void agreements do not have any legal consequence and it is null and void in the eyes of law. Not only this, but also such agreements remain void from the time at which these are made for example agreement with a minor, agreement without lawful consideration, agreement having uncertain meaning or declared as void by law etc.

Major points of distinction between void agreement and void contract are that void agreement is void from the beginning, but void contract becomes void later on.

Similarly, void agreement does not create any legal right and obligation between the parties while as void contract creates such rights and obligations.

D. *Voidable contract:* According to section 2 (i) "An agreement which is enforceable by law at the option of one or more parties, but not at the option of other or others is a voidable contact". In a voidable contract consent of one of the parties has been caused by other party either by using coercion, or undue influence or misrepresentation or fraud. Such contract lacks element of free consent. Voidable contract has the following features.

(a) Consent of one of the parties is not free. It has been caused by using coercion, undue influence, misrepresentation or fraud.
(b) It is voidable only at the option of aggrieved party whose consent had not been free but not at the option of other.
(c) Voidable contract remains valid till so far, it has not be declared void by an aggrieved party.
(d) Aggrieved party can avoid it, can enforce it and if other party compels him to perform he can seek protection on the ground of his not having free-consent.

Example: A, by causing consent of B at gum point makes an agreement with him for buying his bike for Rs. 50,000. This contract is voidable at the option of B only (whose consent had not been free) He can declare it as void or can enforce it against A or if A compels him, he can seek protection.

D. *Illegal contract:* Every contract carries some object or purpose. It is formed on the basis of promises made by the parties in that contract. The contract is said to be illegal if its object is illegal. Illegal agreement has the following features.

(a) The contract becomes illegal if it is made for doing something illegal, immoral or against public policy. Such contracts defeat provisions of law.

Example: A, in consideration of Rs. one lac from B agrees to kill C. Contract is illegal.

(b) Illegal contracts are necessarily void contract not creating any legal rights and obligations between the parties.
(c) Illegal contracts cannot be enforced either by the parties.
(d) Any transaction or agreement which is based on illegal contract would also be void having no legal substance.

E. *Unenforceable contract:* Sometimes, a contract may be good in the eyes of law. But due to some technical reasons it may not be allowed to be enforced in the court. Technical reasons affecting validity of contract may be that contract is not made in writing or is not registered or has no adequate stamp duty on it. Such contracts are good in substance. But due to non-fulfillment of prescribed legal formalities these can not be claimed in the court. As soon as the technical reason is looked into and rectified such contracts may be allowed to be enforced.

Example: A makes out promissory note in favour of B for Rs. 1000. It has stamp duty of Rs. 5 only. While as as per requirement of law it must have stamp duty of Rs. 10 such promissory note is invalid But if stamp duty is raised up to required level it may be allowed to be enforced.

Table Distinction between void, agreement and voidable contract

Base	*Void agreement*	*Voidable contract*
Definition.	Agreement not enforceable by law is void agreement.	Agreement which is enforceable by law at the option of one party only is voidable contract.
Cause.	Agreement becomes void if it lacks any one of the essentials of a valid contract.	Agreement becomes voidable if the consent of one of the party had not been free (Except mistake)
Time	Void agreement is void when it is made	Voidable contract becomes void only when it is declared to be so by an aggrieved party.
Right	In void agreement if the party has suffered any loss he cannot claim any compensation.	If aggrieved party in voidable contract caused by fraud suffers any loss he has a right to claim compensation from other party.

Table Distinction between void and illegal agreements

Base	*Void agreement*	*Illegal agreement*
Cause	Agreement becomes void if it lacks any one of the essentials of a valid contract. Such as agreement with minor, agreement without consideration and agreements, having uncertain meaning etc.	Agreement becomes illegal if the very object or purpose of it is to do some act which is illegal or immoral or against public policy.
Scope	void agreement is wider in scope, because it also includes illegal agreement.	Illegal agreement are used in a narrow sense and less wider, because agreement becomes illegal when its object is illegal.
Time	Though void agreements are void from the beginning, Sometimes, valid contract may become void or may be discovered to be void later on.	Illegal agreements are void from the begining.
Punish-ment	Void agreements do not attract any punishment for the parties.	In a illegal agreement if the party has done act which is illegal, immoral or against public policy, he may be prosecuted or punished.
Effect	Void agreement has no effect on other transaction or agreement which is based on it.	In case of illegal agreement, any transaction or agreement based on illegal agreement will also be affected and will be void.

Review Questions

1. Define the term contract. Explain essentials of a valid contract.
2. 'All contracts are agreement, but all agreements are not contract'. Comment.
3. Distinguish between agreement and contract.
4. All agreements enforceable by law are contract. Comment.
5. 'Law of Contract is not a whole law of agreement nor the whole law of obligations'. Comment.
6. Distinguish between
   (a) Void agreement and voidable contract.
   (b) Void agreement and illegal agreements.
   (c) Express and Implied contract.
   (d) Agreement and contract.

7. Write notes:
   (a) Quasi-contract.
   (b) Void agreement.
   (c) Illegal agreement.
   (d) Voidable contract.

Practical Problems

1. A has applied for a license of liquor. In the meanwhile he starts selling liquor. What is the legal position of A in the eyes of law.
2. A, borrows sum of Rs. 1000 from his friend B. for three months At the expiration of that period A refused to repay. Can B sue upon his friend B for the recovery. (Yes)
3. A makes a promise to his friend B for giving him a ring on his coming birthday. A fails to do so. Can B sue upon him. (No)
4. A was appointed managing director in a X Coy. by board of directors of the company. After three month it was discovered that one of the directors of the coy who was member of selection committee has not purchased qualification shares. Can A claim benefits mentioned in a service contract which is void.? (Hint Yes).
5. A in consideration of Rs one lac from B agrees to kill C. B, borrows this amount from D. Who knowingly lends money to B. Can D recover this amount from B (Hint No, agreement based on illegal agreement is also void).

Chapter 2

Offer and Acceptance

Learning Objectives

- Get a clarity about the basic concepts of offer and acceptance.
- Examine legality of a valid offer.
- Remember legal provisions regarding communication of offer, acceptance and revocation.
- Understand the factors which make acceptance valid and effective.
- Analyse both offer and acceptance separately and jointly.

INTRODUCTION

Offer and acceptance are the two basic elements which comprise an agreement. One person makes an offer to another person, when the other person accepts that offer, it becomes a binding promise or an agreement. The person making the offer is a promisor and the other person becomes the promisee. The point to be noted here is that an offer gets legal sanction and acquires legal consequences when it is accepted. It means that every agreement is an accepted offer or proposal.

OFFER

Offer is one of the essential elements of a contract. Making an offer is giving a proposal for doing or not doing a thing. The term proposal has been defined under section 2(a) as 'when one person signifies to another his willingness to do or to abstain, from doing anything with a view to obtaining, the assent of that other to such act or abstinence, he said to make a proposal'

Offer has Following Elements

(a) In an offer one party expresses his willingness for doing or not doing a thing.

(b) The person giving an offer expresses his willingness to another person whom he wants to give his offer.

(c) Offer is made with a view to know assent of the other person to the proposed act or abstinence (will he accept offer?).

According to the definition of proposal given in the Act it is clear that the mere expression of willingness for doing any thing will not constitute offer.

Example: A desires to sell his bike to B for Rs 30000—it does not constitute an offer, because A has merely expressed his desire. On the other hand if A asks B would you buy my motorbike for Rs 30000 this makes an offer, because in this expression A wants to get B's consent for the proposed act.

Thus the expression of willingness for 'doing' or 'not doing' any thing will constitute offer if it is followed by the intention of getting the assent of the other party to such act or abstinence.

An offer may be made for 'doing' (positive act) or 'not doing' any thing (negative act).

Example: A cricket star makes a promise to X Sports goods company not to use bats manufactured by the coy other than X Sports goods coy. The offer is made for not doing something.

The person who makes an offer is known as offeror and the other person to whom to the offer is made is known as the offeree.

Classification of Offer

(i) *Specific offer:* Sometimes an offer is made to a particular person, party or organisation, such offer is known as a specific offer. The specific offer can be accepted only by that particular person or organisation.

Example: A makes an offer for selling out his car to B for Rs 1,00,000. Similarly, A offers to supply fifty cotton bales to B @ Rs 500 per bale to X & coy.These are specific offers.

(ii) *General offer:* It is an offer which is made to a group of people or public at large. Such offer can be accepted by any member of that group or public.

Example: A, is student of B.com (H) has lost his bag in a class. He offers to pay Rs 500 to whosoever who gets it and gives it back to him. This is general offer, any student of that class may accept it.

(iii) *Cross offer:* Two parties exchange identical offers with each other. They are ignorant about each others' offers. Such offer is known as a cross offer. Such offers do not amount to valid acceptance for each other and therefore may not result in a binding contract with each other.

Example: A makes an offer to sell out his bike to B for Rs 20000. B is ignorant of this offer and makes a similar offer for buying A's bike for Rs 20000. These two offers are known as cross offers and none of these will constitute as an acceptance.

(iv) *Counter offer:* Incomplete and conditional acceptance of an offer is known as a counter offer. In other words, the acceptor, instead of accepting the offer as such along with all its terms and conditions deviates from it. Such acceptance becomes a counter offer.

Example: A makes offer to B for selling 100 quintals of wheat @ Rs 1000 per quintal on cash down basis. B gives his acceptance stating that he will make 50 per cent payment on cash down and remaining by instalment or B gives his acceptance for buying 80 quintals only. In both these cases, acceptance given by B is known as a counter offer.

Essentials of Valid Offer

The offer to be legally valid must be subject to certain rules which are prescribed in Indian contract Act.These rules are as under:

(i) *Offer must create a legal relationship and consequence*: The whole concept of 'contract' is based on legal relationships or obligations of legal consequences. Thus the formation of a contract which starts with an offer, its acceptance followed by the legal relationship and its consequences means the party making an offer must have a clear intention to establish the legal relationship with other party. He should ensure that the offer made by him gives a rise to legal foundation. Lack of such intention on his part may invalidate the offer. Similarly if the party is engaged in creating a social relationship through an offer and its acceptance then such offer will have no legal value in the eyes of law.

Example: A promises to pay a particular amount per month to his mother on completion of his graduation and subsequently getting a suitable job. On his failure to do so his mother will not get legal right to sue upon him for the recovery of that payment. It is because mother and son were engaged in creating social and personal relations. Thus the promise on the part of the son will have no legal consequence.

(ii) *Offer may be express or implied:* The offer may be made either by the words of mouth or in writing. Such an offer is known as an *express offer*. On the other hand if the offer is inferred, or indirectly understood either from the conduct of parties or from the circumstances. Such offer is known as implied offer (implied by conduct of parties or circumstances).

Example: Delhi Transport Corporation has plied many buses in different routes of Delhi. A who is a commuter, is standing in a particular bus stop. A bus comes and A gets into it. He is bound to pay the prescribed freight for specified destination travelled by him. In this case Delhi Transport Corporation has made an implied offer which is being accepted by A and it results in an agreement between them.

(iii) ***Offer may be specific or general:*** The offer being made to a particular individual or organisation is known as aspecific offer. It can be accepted only by that individual or organisation. On the other, if an offer has been made to a group of people or public at large, such offer is known as general offer. General offer can be accepted by any member of that group or public.

(iv) ***Offer must be communicated:*** An offer is made with a view to create, legal relationship so it must be communicated to the person to whom it is made. In other words it must be brought to the notice of that person, so that he may do what is necessary at his end to accept it. With out communication an offer is incomplete so it can not be accepted.

Lalman Shukla Vs. Gauri Dutt (1913 all L.J.389). In this case G sent S, his servant, in search of his missing nephew. Meanwhile G made an announcement that anyone who traces his missing nephew and brings him back home will be suitably rewarded. S found the boy and brought him back. He claimed for reward. It was held that he cannot claim a reward because he reached out and brought that boy home in ignorance of that reward (there is no communication of offer to S he can not accept it and it would not result in agreement between S and G).

(v) ***Offer must be distinguished from a mere expression of intention or invitation:*** Sometimes, one party merely shows his intention for making an offer or invites other party for making it. Such intention or invitation for making an offer will not be considered as a valid offer. Such as pricelist, advertisement for vacant position, goods price marked in showroom, customer enquiries and quotations etc. cannot be stated as offers.

Example: A bookseller has published a pricelist for the various books being sold by him. But legally he is not bound to supply any particular book at the price mentioned against it. It is because the price list is a mere declaration of his intention and not an offer.

Example: In a showroom of readymade garments a particular shirt is displayed which is price marked, again, in this case the showroom owner has not given any offer for selling that shirt at the price marked on it because he is not making an offer, rather desires to sell that shirt for the marked price.

Harvey vs. Facie (1893 A.C 552). This case explains a distinction between an offer and an invitation to offer. In this case, the plaintiffs telegraphed to the defendant writing that will you sell us bumper hall pen. Telegraph lowest cost price, the defendant replied by telegram, 'lowest cost price for bumper hall pen $ 900'. The plaintiff immediately sent this last telegram stating, 'we agree to buy bumper hall pen for $900 asked by you'. The defendant however refused to sell pen at that price. The plaintiff contended that by quoting their minimum price in response to the enquiry, the defendant has made an offer to sell at that price, but the judicial committee turned down the suggestions. Their lordship pointed out that in their first telegram the plaintiff has asked two questions, as to the willingness to sell and second as to lowest price. They reserved their answer as no willingness to sell, thus they had made no offer, the lordship were of the opinion that the mere statement of lowest price at which vendor should sell contained no implied contract to sell at that price to the person making the enquiry.

Following this case, it was held in another case where the owner of property says that he will not accept less that Rs 6000 as price – so he does not make an offer but mearly invites to make an offer **MAC PHERSO VS. APPANNA (1951, A.S.C 184).**

(vi) *Offer may be conditional:* While making an offer the offeror may impose conditions for the acceptor, such conditional offer is valid subject to the following conditions:

(a) Offeror can not impose any such condition the non-fulfillment of which would lead to acceptance of that offer.

Example: A offers to sell out his bike to B stating that if B does not reply with in a week, he will assume that he has accepted the offer. This is not a valid offer, because failure on the part of B to reply would result in an acceptance.

(b) The terms and conditions imposed by the offeror must be mentioned in the offer in such a way that a person of a reasonable prudence may find indication for those conditions and those conditions must be readable with reasonable eye sight.

Example: A has delivered some woollen clothes for dry cleaning purpose to B and B issued receipt to A for it. At the back of receipt some terms and conditions are laid down. In the absence of the indication B is not suppoed to go through them and they are not binding on him. But if at the bottom of receipt it is mentioned that 'for conditions see reverse side, B is bound by these conditions even if these are mentioned in the language other than known to him, he is expected to take the help of the person who knows that language. Finally if those condition are not readable because of printing defect B is not bound by those conditions.

REICHADSON VS. ROWN TREE (1894, A.C 217). In this case, the passenger booked his passage on a ship and received a ticket, it was folded in such a way that no writing was visible until it was opened. It was held that the passenger is not bound by conditions which limited ship-owners liabilities to $50 in case of any loss.

Standing Offer or Tender

Standing offer is an offer which is continuous in natrue. It is made for supplying certain goods on a particular price up to a specified period of time. It is also known as a tender, In this offer it is not necessary to mention the quantity of the goods to be supplied over that period of time. Such type of offer is suitable for those who need regular supply of specified goods or services for a particular period of time.

On the acceptance of a standing offer or tender, order may be placed as and when the goods and services are required. In this regard it is to be noted that each a time distinct contract is made for the goods and services By giving notice of revocation to the offeror standing offer may be put to an end for the remaining period.

Ganilatif Vs. Manilal (1916, 18 Bombay, L.R 227). In this case A agrees to supply coal to B in any quantity upto 1000 tonnes @ 150 per tonne as and when required by B over a period of 12 months. This is a continuous offer or tender. Each order placed by B will amount to the acceptance of offer. A can revoke this offer regarding future supply at anytime by giving notice of revocation to B.

It is also to be noted that in a standing offer the offeree has a right not to place any order even after having the approved this tender, it is because a tender becomes an offer only when it is approved. The agreement is formed, when an order is placed to the party accepting the tender according to the terms of a tender.

ACCEPTANCE

Introduction

Offer has no legal consequence or value unless it is accepted. It is only by acceptance that the offeror and the acceptor come into a legal relationship and formation of an agreement becomes complete on the acceptance of offer.

Meaning

According to section 2(b) a proposal or offer is said to have been accepted when the person to whom the proposal is made, signifies his assent to the proposal. In otherwords, when a person to whom the offer is made gives his assent for the act or abstinence accordingly, it amounts to an acceptance.

Sir **William Anson** has rightly defined relationship between offer and acceptance by clarifying their legal consequences. According to him 'acceptance is to offer what is a lighted match is to a train of gun powder'

According to this statement it is clear that an offer has little or no legal consequances. Once it is accepted it creates binding legal relationship between an offeror and acceptor. The legal consequence of a valid acceptance cannot be undone. Though an offer or proposal lays down the foundation of a contract but it becomes complete only through a valid acceptance. On the other hand if the offer has lapsed or revoked before acceptance it has no legal consequences. Thus an offer is considered a lighted match and its acceptance is considered a train of gun powder. The gun powder will explode when it gets lighted, so offer without an acceptance will not form an agreement. Similarly a train of gun powder will not explode without a lighted match, and once an offer is accepted it becomes a promise which cannot be withdrawn or cancelled.

Rules Regarding a Valid Acceptance

An acceptance to be legally valid and effective must be subject to the following rules:

(i) ***Acceptance must be absolute and unconditional:*** Offer may be made for a specific quantity, volume and price. It may also contain terms and conditions. It is necessary for the acceptor that he must give his acceptance for the entire quantity & volume offered. Similarly he must accept each and every terms and conditions, of the offer If he deviates on minor conditions the acceptance will not be legally effective. In this regard the general rule is that the offer must be accepted and the acceptor must not impose any condition for the offeror. Partial and conditional or qualified acceptance will not be valid. Thus an offer must be accepted without any variations, conditions and reservations.

Example: Ram offers to supply 100 tonnes of wheat to Shyam @Rs 1000 per tonne Shyam gives his acceptance for buying only 50 tonnes of wheat at that rate. Acceptance is partial therefore it is not valid. Similarly if Shyam gives his acceptance for entire quantity but puts condition that the payment will be made after a month. This acceptance is conditional and therefore is not valid.

Routledge Vs. Grant (1828, 4 bing 653). In this case, a party offered to purchase another's house with vacant possession from 25, July. The vendor of the house sent his acceptance suggesting possession from 1 August. It was held that the acceptance is not valid; therefore it will not conclude to valid contract.

(ii) ***Acceptance must be given in a prescribed mode or manner:*** While making an offer, the offeror may prescribe a particular mode or manner of acceptance and the acceptor must abide by it. If the acceptor does not follow that perticular mode for sending his acceptance, the offeror that further insist the acceptor to abide by it. But if still it is not followed, the offeror can reject that acceptance.

On the other, if no mode is prescribed, by the offeror then the acceptor can follow the usual mode of acceptance.

Example: A offers to sell out his car to B and asks him to send his acceptance through a registered post. B accepts the offer and sends his acceptance through e-mail. A may further insists upon B to use the prescribed manner for sending his acceptance. On this if B fails to comply with prescribed manner A can reject the acceptance.

Section 7(2) of the Indian Contract Act states that acceptance must be expressed in some usual manner, unless the proposer prescribes the manner in which it is to be accepted.

Example: A sends an offer by ordinary post to buy a television set from B. On acceptance B may also send his acceptance by ordinary post because no manner or mode was prescribed.

SURINDERNATH VS. KEDARNATH (1936 A.I.R, Cal 87). In this case an offer was made to a person to sell a house at Rs 7000 and it was specifically mentioned that in case the offer is accepted he should write to X at his address. The intended purchaser sent his representative to X, in place of writing him for accepting the offer, here this acceptance was not given in the prescribed manner, so it was held that the acceptance is not valid

(iii) ***Time of acceptance:*** To make it valid acceptance, it must be given with in stipulated period of time if any. When no time is specified, acceptance must be given within reasonable period of time.

Reasonable time in each case is a question of fact which varies from person to person depending on the intention of party, nature of transaction and circumstances. In case acceptance is not sent within the prescribed time or reasonable time (which is applicable), the offer is deemed to lapse.

Example: A is a student of B. Com. He placed an order in the last week of June with X bookseller of Meerut for the supply of books on Business law, Accounting and Economics. Time has not been stipulated and bookseller is supposed to supply these books within reasonable period of time. According to circumstances, the intention of the party and nature of transaction, he must supply these books, latest by middle of July. It is because by this time academic session starts and the student may be in need of these books.

RAMSGATE VICTORIA HOTEL COY. VS. MONTEFIORE 1866 L.I.R EX 109). In this case, a person applied for certain shares in a joint stock company in the month of June. But the company made an allotment in the month of November. That person refused to accept the shares, so allotted on the plea of delayed acceptance. He was allowed to withdraw the offer.

(iv) ***Acceptance must be communicated:*** As the offer needs to be communicated, so does the acceptance. Acceptance to be legally effective must be communicated and brought to the knowledge of the offeror. Even if the acceptor has accepted the offer but if it is not communicated properly it would not result into an agreement.

In this regard it is however to be noted that mental acceptance is no acceptance. If the offeree mentally accepts the offer or decides to accept it but does not communicate it, it will not be considered as legally effective acceptance.

BROGDEN VS. METROPOLITAN RAILWAY COY (1877, A.C 66). In this case the manager of railway coy received a draft agreement relating to the supply of coal. He wrote the word approved 'on it and put it is his drawer'. Its was held that here was no contract because the acceptance has not been communicated.

Thus mere mental expression to an offer, not backed by spoken or written words or conduct of the party will not constitute acceptance.

Powell Vs. Lee (1908, 99 LT 284). In this case, P applied for the post of principle of a school. Management of the school decided to appoint him but the announcement was withheld. One of the member of management informed P about the decision. But later on the management changed decision. P filed suit for breach of contract, but the suit was rejected on the ground that the management of the school has never communicated their decision to P, thus there is no contract.

(v) ***Acceptance may be express or implied:*** The acceptor may give his assent for the proposed act by the words of mouth or in writing. Such acceptance is known as express acceptance. In addition if the acceptance is directly understood either from conduct of the party or from circumstance, it is known as implied acceptance. In other words when party does some act as being intended by the offeror, it amounts to implied acceptance.

Carlill Vs. Carbolic Smoke Ball Coy. In this case carbolic smoke ball coy, has been producing smoke balls. The company made an announcement whosoever buys these balls from the market and uses in the given direction, even then if he or she gets influenza the coy will suitably reward him. Lady Carlill got these balls purchased and used them in the given direction. But unfortunately got influenza, she claimed reward. It was held that there is contract between the coy and Carlill through implied acceptance on the part of Carlill and therefore she can claim reward.

(vii) ***Acceptance must be made before offer is revoked:*** Acceptance implies mental readiness of the person for proposed act or abstinence. Therefore, it must be given before the offer lapses or is withdrawn or cancelled. Once the offer is dead due to any reason it is dead for ever, and to revive it, such offer is to be made afresh.

Example: A made an offer to B for selling 100 cotton bales @ Rs 2000 per bale and prescribes week time for acceptance. B fails to accept it on time, the offer is lapsed. Afterwards B gives his acceptance, such acceptance is not legally valid.

(viii) ***Acceptance is not implied from silence of the party:*** Acceptance of offer is not implied from silence. The offeror cannot impose condition on offeree that his silence will amount to acceptance. It is very clear that it should be given either by spoken words or in writing or by performing any act which amounts to implied acceptance. Thus silence on the part of offeree regarding the offer in no case may amount to acceptance. But in practice, this rule is subject to following exceptions:

(a) When offeror has been dealing with offeree in the past and the offeree has given reasons to understand that his silence amounts to acceptance.

(b) Communication of acceptance has been dispensed with by the offeror as per conditions of offer. So silence on the part of offeree may amount to acceptance.

(c) Where performance or fulfillment of all terms and conditions of the offer without communication of acceptance is regarded sufficient acceptance.

(d) Where the offeree gets reasonable opportunities to reject the offer. But takes the benefits of that offer it will also amount to acceptance of offer. The acceptor need not do any thing for it.

Example: A subscribes particular magazine for a period of one year. At the end of the year contract automatically comes to a end. But the company continued to supply that magazine to A. And he gets benefit of this offer and continues to accept it, without giving any intimation to the coy. A, would be liable for paying subscription.

Example: Ram offers to sell out his house in Delhi to Shyam, if he comes to Delhi, gets house repaired and starts living in that house. Shyam does all these, without communicating acceptance to Ram. There is a contract between Ram and Shyam.

COMMUNICATION OF OFFER AND ACCEPTANCE

It is very necessary to know that whether the offer and acceptance has been properly communicated because without communication of offer it can not be accepted. Similarly acceptance to be legally valid and effective must have been communicated properly. Communication of offer and acceptance can be made either by spoken words or in writing or it may be inferred from the conduct of the party. According to section 3 of Indian Contract Act 'that the communication of proposal, the acceptance of proposal, and the revocation of proposal and acceptance respectively are deemed to be made by any act or omission of the party proposing, accepting or revoking by which he intends to communicate such proposal, acceptance or revocation or which has the effect of communicating it'.

Communication of Offer

Offer is communicated to the party to whom it is made. Unless it is communicated it cannot be accepted. According to section 4 of the Act 'communication of offer is complete when its comes to the knowledge of the person to whom it is made'. It means even if the letter of offer has reached to offeree, unless he goes through it the communication will not be complete.

Example: Ramesh makes an offer to his friend Mahesh in Bombay for selling his car to him. The offer is sent though registered post and reaches to Mahesh. But Mahesh did not open it and go through. It's communication is not complete.

Communication of Acceptance

According to section 4 of the Act, 'communication of acceptance is complete

(a) As against the proposer, when the letter of acceptance is put in a course of transmission, so as to be out of the power of the acceptor and
(b) As against the acceptor, when it comes to the knowledge of proposer'.

Example: A applied for 100 equity shares of X and Coy. Face value of each share was Rs 100 per share. The Coy demanded Rs. 10 per share on application and Rs 20 per share on allotment. Remaining balance would be obtained through various calls. In the meeting of broad of directors 100 shares were alloted to A and a letter of allotment was sent to him for demanding allotment money. The letter was duly stamped and correctly addressed. In the meanwhile the Coy went into liquidation and official receiver found that a sum of Rs 9000 was due on the account of A to whom 100 shares were allotted. He sent a notice for the recovery of the amount along with interest. A pleaded that he never received letter of allotment. But it was held against A, who is a proposer that communication of acceptance is complete and he is bound to pay. But he cannot claim rights of a shareholder because letter of allotment had not been reached to him.

Thus communication of acceptance against the coy in not completed therefore he cannot be treated as a share holder.

ADAM VS. LIND SELL, (1818 1.B & Alal 68). In this case A proposes to sell a house to B at a certain price thorough a letter which was posted on 10 March. it reaches to B on 12 March. Communication of offer was complete when B received a letter on 12 march. B sent his acceptance through post on 13 March which was received by A, on 15 March. Communication of acceptance as against A is complete on 13 March and as against B on 15 March.

Revocation of Offer

Offer is made with an intention of seeking the assent of offeree for proposed act or abstinence. But before it is accepted by offeree, the offeror can withdraw it, or can cancel it or the offer may be lapsed on account of other reasons, it is known as revocation of offer.

Briefly revocation of offer means withdrawl, cancellation or lapse of offer. According to section 6 of this Act offer can be revoked under the following circumstances.

(a) ***By notice:*** Offer can be revoked by giving a notice to this effect. Such notice will be given by the offeror. The offeror after having made offer, can withdraw or cancel it. But such notice of revocation must be given before the communication of acceptance is put in the course of transmission. After that point of time notice of revocation will have no legal value.

(b) ***By lapse of time:*** The offer must be accepted well in time as prescribed by the offeror. And if no time in prescribed, acceptance must be made with in reasonable period of the time. On the expiration of stipulated or reasonable period of time, the offer is lapsed.

(c) ***Death or insanity of offeror:*** In case of death or insanity of offeror, the offer is revoked, provided information regarding death or insanity reaches to offeree before he puts letter of acceptance in a course of transmission. If it reaches after words, there is a binding agreement which may be enforced, against the legal representative of deceased offeror.

(d) ***Non fulfillment of prerequisite conditions:*** when the offeror has put some conditions, which are prerequisite to acceptance. Such conditions must be fulfilled before accepting offer. Non fulfillment of such conditions will lead to revocation of an offer.

Example: A offers to sell his house to B who stays in Bombay, provided B comes Delhi and starts living in that house. To accept the offer B has to come Delhi and start living in that house. If he does not do so the offer given to him will automatically be revoked.

(e) ***By counter offer:*** To form an agreement the acceptor must give absolute and unconditional acceptance. Contrary to it, partial or conditional acceptance becomes counter offer and leads to revocation of offer.

Example: Ram offers to sell his bike to Shyam for Rs 20,000 on the basis of cash down payment, Shyam accepts the offer on a condition that he will make payment in two instalments, such acceptance is a counter offer and initial offer is revoked.

(f) ***Non-compliance of prescribed mode or manner:*** Sometime the offeror may prescribe particular mode or manner in which offeree must send his acceptance. Non compliance of prescribed mode may lead to rejection of acceptance provided the offeror once insists upon offeree to use prescribed mode only.

Communication of Revocation

According to section 4 of this Act communication of revocation is complete

(a) As against the person who makes it when he puts letter of revocation in a course of transmission for sending it to another party. and

(b) As against the person to whom it is made, when the letter of revocation reaches and comes to the knowledge of that person.

Example: A, makes an offer to B for selling 200 cotton bales @Rs 2000 per bale on 1st March. It reaches to B on 2nd March B, accepts it and sends his acceptance on 5th March which reaches to A on 6th March. A revokes his offer on 4th March, communication of revocation is complete against A on 4th march and against B it will be complete when it reaches to B.

Review Questions

1. What do you mean by the 'term offer'? Explain the rules regarding a lawful offer?
2. 'Binding relationship between two parties is the result of a valid offer and acceptance', comment?

3. Define the term 'acceptance'. Explain requirements of a valid acceptance.
4. What is revocation of offer? Explain those circumstances under which offer can be revoked.
5. Explain rules regarding communication of an offer and communication of acceptance. Give suitable examples.
6. Comment on the following:
   (a) An offer is quite different from a mere expression of intention and an invitation to offer.
   (b) Acceptance is to an offer, what a lighted match is to train of gun powder.
   (c) There cannot be a contract to make contract.
   (d) Mere mental acceptance is no acceptance.
   (e) An offer cannot be accepted, without communication and without communication of acceptance, there cannot be an agreement.
7. 'Acceptance cannot implied from silence' explain this rule and discuss the various exceptions to this rule with suitable example?
8. Write notes on:
   (a) Communication of acceptance
   (b) Standing offer
   (c) Counter offer
   (d) Revocation of offer

PRACTICAL PROBLEMS

1. A desires to sell his horse to B for Rs 5000 B accepts the proposal of A is this agreement, (no, mere expression of desire made by A is not valid offer).
2. Ram makes an offer to Shyam for selling 200 tonnes of wheat @ Rs. 1000 p.t. Shyam accepts the offer, prepare a letter of acceptance and forgets to post it, does it constitute agreement if not so why/? (hint communication of acceptance)
3. A offer to sell out to his house to B who is staying in Bombay for Rs 5 lacks provided B comes to Delhi, repaires the house and starts livening in it. B accepts to buy house from Bombay itself. Is acceptance valid? (No)
4. Ramesh visits showroom of maruti car in Delhi, he finds that particular car which is price marked and is displayed in showroom. Asked showroom owner to sell that car for the price mentioned on it. Can Ramesh compel showroom owner to sell that car for that price? (it is not offer, but intention to make an offer)
5. A has agricultural farm in Delhi. He offers to sell out 50 tonnes of wheat to B at the price of Rs 1500 p.t on cash down basis. B accepts the offer and

states that payment will be made through instalments. Is acceptance valid/ (Hint-No condition has been put by B)

6. Mohan applied for 200 shares in particular company. The company allotted shares after more than six months from submitting application by Mohan. Mohan refused to accept delivery of shares on the plea that his offer has lapsed after a reasonable period of time. Has he right to do so discuss. (Yes)
7. A has lost his pet dog. He made an announcement that whosoever traces his dog and gives this information to him he will be suitably rewarded. B finds the dog in ignorance of the reward, he hands over dog to A. Can he claim for reward. Substantiate your answer with reasons
8. Ram sends an offer for selling his bike to Shyam on 4th march. It reaches to Shyam on 6th of March. Shyam gives acceptance and puts it a letterbox at 10.a.m on 10th March. Immediately after that he receives letter of revocation from Ram. Is there any agreement between Ram and Shyam (communication of acceptance)
9. A reputed pharmaceutical company in Delhi is manufacturing drug to be used as anti malaria drug if used in the given direction. The company made an announcement that any one who uses that drug in the given direction and even if he gets contacted with malaria the coy will pay Rs 2000=/ to him as compensation. Manoharlal purchased drug and used it in the given direction. But he contacted with malaria, he claimed reward, Is he entitled to reward ? give reason and discuss entire case
10. A was appointed as managing director in X coy by board of directors, after 6 months it was found that one of the directors in the board had not purchased qualification shares. What's the legal status of agreement made by the coy with A. Is he entitled to all benefits mentioned in the agreement? why give reason?
11. Manohar offers to give some presentation to shoran on his marriage. But he failed to do so. Can shoran has any legal remedy against Manohar (No)
12. B has given woolen garments for dry-cleaning to shopkeeper. The shopkeeper issued a receipt for that. In the back of that receipt terms and conditions were laid down in Bangali language. B does not know that. Is he bound by that condition? give reasons? (Yes)
13. A sends telegram to B would you sell your car 'quote lowest price B replied that 'lowest price is Rs 20000 A sent another telegram stating that I would buy your car for that price. B refused to sell the car. Can A compels him? give reasons (No).
14. Ram borrows a sum of Rs 1000 from his friend Shyam for three month. At the expiration of that period Ram refused to repay. Can Shyam sue upon him for recovering that amount? (Yes)

■■■

Chapter 3

Consideration

Learning Objectives

- Understand the concept of consideration in the context of validity of a contract.
- Examine, essentials of a lawful consideration.
- Remember the rule of 'No consideration, no contract along with exceptions to it.
- Analyse the role of stranger to consideration and stranger to contract regarding validity of a contract.
- Analyse case study of 'Chinaiya Vs. Ramaiya' and find out the guideline given by the court.

INTRODUCTION

Consideration is one of the essential element of valid contract. Every agreement must be supported by lawful consideration as to get legal validity.

Agreement is a mutual exchange of promises. One party makes a promise for 'doing' or 'not doing' any thing to an other party. And another party also makes similar promise. In such mutual exchange, every promisor gets some thing in return of his promise from another party. Whatever he gets will constitute consideration for his promise.

Example: A offers to sell his car to B for Rs. two lacs. B accepts the offer. There is a mutual exchange of promises between them. A is a promisor for handing over possession and ownership of that car to B. In return of his promise he gets right to recover Rs. two lacs from B which constitute consideration for his promise. Similarly B is a promisor to pay two lacs to A. And in return of it he will get possession and ownership of that car which will constitute consideration for his promise.

CONSIDERATION DEFINED

Consideration is regarded as a price for which promise of the promisor is bought. The term consideration has been defined by British court in one of the leading **CASE RE CURRIE VS. MISA (1875. L.R, 10 EX 153)**

"A valuable consideration in the sense of law may consist either in some right, interest, profit or benefit accruing to one party or some forbearance, detriment, loss or responsibility given, suffered or undertaken by other".

It is clear from the definition that in agreement right, benefit or interest got by one party will constitute consideration for his promise. It is at the cost of loss or responsibility or detriment on the part of other party.

According to section 2 (d) of this Act, "when at the desire of promisor, promisee or other person has done or abstained from doing, does or abstains for doing or promises to do or to abstain from doing something, such act, abstinence or promise is called consideration for the promise".

In the words of PATTERSON, J. "consideration means something which is of some value in the eyes of law, moving from the plaintiff. It may be some benefit to the plaintiff or some detriment to the defendant".

Example: A promises to compensate B for the losses which he may incur in the suit filed by C against him. B pays Rs. 10,000 to A. In this example A is benefited by Rs. 10,000 which is consideration for his promise to B who loses this amount. Similarly B gets right to be compensated by A which is an obligation of A. and consideration for B.

RULES REGARDING CONSIDERATION

An analysis of the above definitions of consideration reveals some legal requirements of a valid consideration. These are as under.

1. *Form of consideration:* The consideration will always be in the form of some act or abstinence or a promise for doing or not doing something.

Example: In return of Rs. two lacs from a Sports Goods company a super star of cricket makes a promise not to use bats other than manufactured by that company. In this case consideration for the company is in the form of abstinence. A superstar has promised to abstain from using other bats.

It is however to be noted that any act, abstinence or promise may result in benefit, right or interest for one party and loss and obligation for another party.

2. *Consideration must be moved or given at the desire of promisor:* In agreement there are two parties i.e. promisor and promisee. The consideration is generally given by the promisee to promisor. According to this rule any act or promise will be valid consideration if such act has been done or promise is made at the desire or request of the promisor.

In other words, if the act is done voluntarily or at the request of the person other than promisor, it will not constitute valid consideration.

Example: A buys a book for his friend B. Later on B promises to pay Rs. 100 to A. Since A has bought a book voluntarily without the desire of B, it cannot be valid consideration for the promise of B.

DURGA PRASAD VS. BALDEV (1880, 3, All, 221). In this case, Deputy Collector has requested A, who is an influential person of that area to develop market in that area. A did so at the desire of Deputy Collector. On the development of market B promised to pay commission to A in return of some space in that market.

It was held that to get space in the market will not constitute consideration for B's promise. It is because market has not been developed at the desire of B. Rather it is developed at the desire or request of Deputy Collector.

3. *Consideration may be past, present or future:* Promisor makes a promise and consideration is given to him for his promise. If these two act of making promise and getting consideration are done simultaneously, the consideration is known as present consideration.

Example: A buys a book on Business Law from the bookseller and makes payment of the price simultaneously. In this agreement consideration given to bookseller is present consideration.

In addition, if the consideration has been given to the promisor before he makes a promise. It is known as past consideration. But even in case of past consideration desire or request for that act which constitute consideration must have been made by promisor.

Example: A buys a book on Business Law for his friend B at his request on Ist January. Later on after two months B promises to pay Rs 100 to A. In this case, consideration for the promise of A is past considertion.

Similarly, consideration may be in the form of promise to be performed in future. Such consideration is known as future consideration or executory consideration. In other words when consideration is to be moved at some future date it is known as future consideration.

Example: A makes an agreement for buying raw material from B. on 1st January. The raw material is to be supplied by B on 20th Jan. and payment is to be made by A on 15th March. In this agreement consideration is future consideration for both parties.

It is however to be noted that according to English Mercantile Law consideration may be present and future consideration only. And past consideration is not recognised by English Law.

4. *Consideration may be moved or given by promisee or any other person:* Generally in every agreement consideration is given by promisee to the promisor. But it is not necessary. Any other person on behalf of promisee may give consideration. Such consideration will also be valid. According to Indian Contract Act it is not important that who has given a consideration, because it can be given by any person who is not even party to a contract. But the English law differs on this point. According to it consideration must be given by the promisee himself.

In this regard, question arises that who may be that person who is not party to a contract, but gives consideration to promisor. The court has given following two guidelines in the case **'CHINAYYA VS. RAMAYYA'**.

(i) If there is a contract between A and B, no other person gets any right unless he is made party to contract.

(ii) Stranger to consideration, but party to a contract can sue upon that contract. It is also known as 'Doctrine of constructive consideration'.

In other word, if some one does not know anything about consideration or he has not given consideration, but he is party to a contract will get rights in that contract.

Example: A distributes his property between his two sons C and D makes agreement with them that they will bear all expenses of his daughter's marriage.

In this case C and D are promisors and the daughter is a promisee. Though the daughter has not given consideration to C and D (She is stranger to consideration), yet she can claim expenses of her marriage from them because she is party to a contract.

CHINAYYA VS RAMAYYA, (1881, 4 MAD, 137). In this case A transfers part of his property to his daughter B and makes agreement that she will pay a particular amount, out of that property annually to his brother C. Later on B refused to pay stipulated amount to C on the plea that there is no consideration form C for supporting B's promise. But it was held that it is not necessary that consideration should have been given by the C. (promisee) It has been given by A on behalf of C. Thus B is bound to pay.

It is however to be noted that any person can claim his right in a contract only if he is a party to that contract, irrespective of the fact that he is stranger to consideration.

5. *Consideration need not be adequate:* In agreement promisor makes promise for doing or not doing something. Such promise will have some value. He gets consideration for his promise, that will also have some value. According to Indian Contract Act it is not necessary that the value of promise should be equal to the value of consideration. Even if the value of consideration is less that value of promise, the contract is valid.

Inadequacy of consideration does not invalidate contract provided the consent of the party getting lesser consideration has been free.

Example: A has got house in Delhi which is valued at Rs. 10 lacs. He makes agreement to sell out this house to B for Rs. 5 lacs. Agreement is valid provided consent of A has been free.

Thus, in a contract, presence of consideration is necessary (Barring exceptions given under Section 25) But its adequacy is not needed for making contract valid one. Whileas, inadequacy of consideration may be taken in to account to ensure that party has free consent for the contract. Therefore, the concept of consideration is a mere technicality for validity of contract. Its presence is essential, but its inadequacy does not matter.

6. *Consideration must be real and not illusory:* Inadequacy of consideration does not affect validity of contract, But whatever consideration is being given it must be real. In other words, it must have some value in the eyes of law. It must not be illusory, fictitious, fraudulent, uncertain and illegal.

Example: A in consideration of some money from B promises to bring gold for him from sun or convert copper in to gold with the help of magic. The consideration is illusory and fictitious on account of impossibility and uncertainly

Example: Ram borrows sum of Rs. 5000 from his friend Shyam for six months. After three month Ram promises that if Shyam returns money immediately he will allow discount of Rs. 500 to him The promise of Shyam for allowing discount is not backed by consideration having real value. It is because consideration must be something more than what the promisee is already bound to do.

The performance of a act by a person who is legally bound to perform, the same cannot be a consideration for a contract.

RAMACHANDRA CHINTAMAN VS. KALU RAJU, (1877, 2 BOM.362). In this case it was promised by the party to pay an additional amount to the lawyer above his service charges, if the suit was successful. Held the promise is void, since the consideration being illusory due to pre-existing legal obligation on the part of the lawyer to render required services under the original contract.

7. *Consideration must be lawful:* Agreement to be enforced in the court must be made for lawful consideration. Any act which is illegal, immoral and against public policy will not constitute valid consideration for the contract.

It is to be noted that in a contract if any part or whole of consideration is illegal, the contract is void if illegal part cannot be separated from legal part.

Example: A agrees to supply 100 cotton bales of quality X and 50 cotton bales of quality Y. to B at certain rate. But sale and purchase of Y quality of cotton bales is prohibited. In this case sale of X quality cotton bales can be separated from the sale of Y quality cotton bales. Former part is legal and later par is illegal.

NO CONSIDERATION, NO CONTRACT

To form a valid contract, there must be an agreement between the parties. That agreement must be enforceable by law. In order to enforce agreement in the court it must be supported by lawful consideration. Contrary to it any agreement which lacks consideration cannot be enforced in the court and therefore will not become a contract. In the words of Salmond, "a promise without consideration is a gift, and a promise made for consideration is a bargain".

Section 25 of Indian Contract Act states that, "subject to certain exceptions, agreements without consideration are void". Leaving aside these exceptions, agreement to be enforced needs consideration. Under exceptional situations which are contained in section 25, the agreement or promise without consideration is valid in the eyes of law. These exceptions are as under:

1. ***Any agreement, which satisfy the following conditions can be enforced by law without consideration:***

(a) Agreement between the parties must be made in writing.
(b) Agreement must be registered.
(c) Agreement must have been made on account of natural love and affection between the parties.
(d) Agreement must be made between the parties, standing in near relationship.

Example: A agrees to transfer part of his property to his son. This agreement is valid provided it is made in writing and made registered. It is assumed that father has done it on account of natural love and affection for the son and both are having near relationship. Agreement is valid without consideration.

Rajlukhee Debee Vs. Bhootnath (1900, 4 CWN, 488). In this case, there was a marital disagreement and discard between husband and wifc. Husband executed registered document in favour of his wife agreeing to pay for her maintenence. But there was no consideration from the side of his wife. It was held that agreement was void for the want of consideration. It was not made out of natural love and affection.

2. ***Promise to compensate for past voluntary services:*** A person renders some services or does some act for other person voluntarily in the past. Another person who gets benefit of these services or act makes promise to compensate wholly or partially, such promise is valid without consideration. (Services rendered in the past voluntarily do not constitute consideration)

Thus in order to make such promise legally binding the following conditions must be satisfied.

(i) Services must have been rendered voluntarily.
(ii) These services must have been rendered for the promisor only and he must have got benefit of these services.
(iii) The promisor must have been in existence at that when services were rendered.
(iv) The promisor must have clear intention to compensate the promisee for those services rendered by him.
(v) The service rendered by the promisee must be legal.

3. *Promise to repay time-barred debt:* While lending money, relevant provisions of Banking, law, Money lenders Act and Indian Limitation Act are applied. Provisions of Indian Limitation Act provide time period (if not determined by debtor and creditor) with in which, the lender must give notice of demand or must have got debt recovered. Failure to do so will make that debt time-barred. On being debt time-barred the creditor of such debt has no legal authority to recover it. But if the debtor of such debt makes a promise to repay part or whole of it to the creditor, Such promise is valid without consideration provided the following conditions are satisfied.

(i) Promise made by debtor should be in writing
(ii) It should be signed by the promisor or by his agent
(iii) There must be express promise to pay.

Example: A has borrowed sum of Rs. 10,000 from B for the period of 2 yrs. Till the expiration of that period neither A served notice of demand to B nor B repaid the deb. Debt becomes time barred which A cannot legally recover. B makes promise to repay Rs. 5000 after a month. This promise is valid without consideration provided B makes it in writing and signs on it with a clear intention of making partial payment.

4. *Completed gifts and donation:* Explanation 1, to section 25 states that "nothing in this section shall affect the validity as between donor and donee of any gift actually made. In case of completed gift or donation the rule of 'no consideration and no contract' does not apply. In this connection the following points must be taken care of".

(i) Promise to donate money or give some gift to any charitable organisation or friend is not valid without consideration.
(ii) But, if money has been donated or goods have been gifted, these cannot be taken back on the plea that there was no consideration.
(iii) Although promise to donate money is not valid, but if the promisee of such promise undertakes some liability on the basis of such promise, the promisor is bound to donate money.

KEDARNATH VS. GAURI MOHAMMED (1886, 14Cal, 54). In this case KadarNath was a secretary of Town Hall. He approached Gauri Mohammed to give some donation for the construction of Town Hall at Howrah. Gauri Mohd. promised to give Rs. 100 as donation. On the faith of this promise Kedarnath engaged contractors and thus incurred liability to pay them. Gauri Mohd refused to pay donation. It was held that since Kedarnath has incurred liability on the basis of promise to donate, made by Gauri Mohd, thus he is liable to pay to the extent of liability subject to maximum amount of Rs. 100

5. *Contract of a agency:* According to Section 185 of this Act contract made for creating relationship of agency between parties does not require any consideration. Without consideration such contracts are valid. Thus a promise made by the person to act as an agent of another person is enforceable without consideration. Similarly if the person makes an agreement with another to appoint him as his agent for a particular period of time. It is also a valid agreement.

Example: A appoints B as his agent for the period of one year on the basis of 10% commission on sale. There is no consideration for supporting A's promise. As an exception, such promise is valid.

6. Remission by the promisee of performance of the promise: Promise made by the party for accepting lesser performance for the whole promise is valid without consideration. Similarly, an agreement to extend time of performance of a contract does not require any consideration.

According to Section 63 of this Act, "a creditor can agree to give up part of his claim and there need be, no consideration for such an agreement".

Example: A owes Rs. 5000 to B. B makes an agreement with A that in receiving Rs. 4500 from A it will be treated for the discharge of whole debt. Agreement is valid, B has a right to give up a part of claim in favour of A.

Example: Ram agrees to deliver raw material to Shyam on 12th March and Shyam is to make payment on 20th March. Ram supplied raw material on time but Shyam is unable to pay on time. Ram extends date of payment by month. This promise is also valid without consideration.

STRANGER TO CONSIDERATION AND STRANGER TO CONTRACT

It has been made clear by the court in 'Chinayya Vs. Ramayya' case that the consideration may also be given by some one else on behalf of promisee. In this case it was held that contract cannot confer rights or impose obligations on any person other than the party to it. And more over it is cardinal rule of law that only the person who is party to a contract can sue upon that contract.

The party who does not know any thing about consideration or who has not given consideration or who is stranger to consideration. But if he is party to contract he will get the rights. Contrary to it, the person who is not a party to contract or who is stranger to it cannot sue upon that contract. Thus stranger to consideration can sue upon while stranger to contract cannot.

Dunlop Pneumatic Tyre Co. Vs. Selfridge & Co. (1915, A.C. 847). In this case a dealer buys tyres from Dunlop Coy and sold them to a retailer on the condition that he shall not sell the tyres below the listed price of the company. If this condition is violated he will be penalised with £5 for each tyre sold below the list price. But retailer, in one case did not comply with this condition. Dunlop Company sued him for breach of contract. It was held that there is no contract between Dunlop company and the retailer. Thus the company does not get any right and cannot sue the retailer for breach of contract.

DOCTRINE OF PRIVITY OF CONTRACT

This doctrine states that to get rights and obligations in a contract one must be party to it or there should be privity of contract between that person and another party. One cannot sue upon simply because contract is made for his benefit or consideration has been given on his behalf. On the other, if that person is stranger to consideration but stays in the privity of contract, he will gets the rights in that contract.

In the above case since there is no privity of contract between Dunlop company and a retailer, thus the company was not allowed to sue the retailer for breach of contract.

In practice there are certain exceptions to this doctrine. Under these exceptional situations, person who is stranger to a contract made for his benefit can sue upon that, contract. These exceptions are as under.

1. *Beneficiary of a trust:* Trust is an arrangement whereby some property is handed over to trustees by the owner. This property is to be managed by the trust or trustees for the benefit of party known as beneficiary. In this arrangement of trust, the beneficiary can sue to enforce his rights under the trust, though he is not a party to a contract.

UMANATH BAKSH SINGH, VS. JANG BAHADUR (AIR, 1938, P.O, 245). In this case A appointed his son B his successor and was put in possession of his entire estate and made an agreement with him that B would give certain sum of money to C, an illegitimate son on attaining majority. It was held that trust was created for the benefit of C and therefore he is entitled to maintain a suit for the recovery of that benefit.

2. *Marriage settlement, partition or other family arrangement:* Agreements may be made with regard to marriage of a family member, partition of properties and other family arrangements. In such agreement provision may be made for the benefit of a particular member. Such person, who is beneficiary in the agreement can maintain a suit, though he is not in privity of a contract.

Example: Agreement was made by the family members for setting aside particular part of property of family for meeting marriage expenses of female member. Such female member gets right to sue for that benefit, without being party to a contract.

ROSE FERNANDEZ VS. JOSEPH GONSLAVES (1950, A.I.R BOM, 97). In this case, father of a girl made an agreement with joseph for the marriage of her daughter. Later on Joseph refused to marry. It was held that after attaining age of majority she can maintain a suit against Joseph for breach of promise of marriage, though she was not a party to a contract.

KHWAJA MOHD. VS. HUSSAINI BEGUM (1910, 32 All 410). In this case a muslim lady filed suit against his father in-law to recover Rs. 15000 being the arrears of allowance (Petel box Expenses) payable to her by him under an agreement made between him and father of that lady at the time of her marriage. It was held that she was entitled to recover the money, though she is stranger to contract, made by her father and father in-law.

3. *Contract made by an agent:* Agent makes an agreement on behalf of his principal. His main role is to bring third party into contractual relationship with the principal. In all such contracts made by agent, there is no direct privity of contract. But as an exception, principal gets rights in such contract, can file suit against third party or can be sued by third party.

Example: A is an agent working on behalf of his principal B. A makes an agreement for selling goods on behalf of B. to C. Later on C refuses to pay to B. B, though is not a party to a contract made between A & C, but as an exception he gets right to sue upon C for the recovery of sale price.

4. *Estoppel to acknowledgment:* When a party acknowledges or admits liability in a contract to third party. Lateron if he denies or refuses it on any ground, he will be stopped from doing so . His liability would continue towards third party, though there may be no privity of contract between party admitting liability and third party.

Example: Ram gives sum of Rs. 1000 to Shyam to be paid to Mahesh. Shyam informs to Mahesh that he is holding that amount to pay him. Lateron Shyam refuses to pay. Shyam will be stopped from denying his liability to pay and Mahesh is entitled to recover it from Shyam.

5. *Charges created on immovable property:* Agreement creating charge on immovable property in favour of third party for his benefit can be enforced by third party. Although third party is stranger to contract but can sue upon that contract.

Example: A Public Limited Coy issues debentures and created charge on its immovable property in favour of debenture holders. These debenture holders are beneficiary and in case company fails to repay them, they can maintain suit against coy for enforcing charge created on immovable property.

6. *Agreements relating to land:* The owner of land is subject to certain rights and obligation to some authority of land. Buyer purchases that land and gives notice to the authority that owner of a land is bound by those rights and obligations. Although, buyer is stranger to a contract between seller and land authority but he will be subject to those right and obligation.

Example: A, possesses, piece of land on lease basis which he gets from Delhi Development Authority. He is subject to some rights and obligations to Delhi Development Authority B. buys this piece of land from A and gives notice to the authority that he will be bound by those rights and obligations. Lateron if that land becomes free hold A will get benefit of it, though he was not party to a contract entered in to between A and Delhi Development Authority.

Review Questions

1. Define the term consideration. Explain various rules regarding lawful consideration.
2. 'No consideration and No contract' Discuss this rule and explain various exceptions to this rule.
3. What do you mean by Doctrine of Privity of Contract. Explain various exceptions to this doctrine.
4. 'Agreement without consideration is void'. Are there any exceptions to this rule discuss them.
5. Discuss, consideration as an essential element of valid contract.
6. Stranger to consideration but party to a contract can sue upon that contract. Explain it by giving suitable examples.
7. Under what circumstance can stranger to a contract enforce it.
8. Can consideration be given by a person other that promisee.
9. Comment on the following
   (a) Inadequacy of consideration does not invalidate the contract.
   (b) Consideration must be given at the desire or request of promisor.
   (c) Stranger to contract cannot sue upon that contract.
   (d) Law does not confer rights and obligation on the person who is not a party to contract.
   (e) Valid consideration is legal and real.
   (f) Past consideration is as good as present and future consideration.
   (g) Insufficiency of consideration is immaterial, but agreement without consideration is void.
   (h) Stranger to contract can enforce it provided it is made for his benefits.
10. Can gratuitous promises be enforced. Give suitable examples.

Practical Problems

1. A buys book for his friend B without his request. Lateron B promises to pay the price of the book. Is the promise of B is valid. (No)
2. Ram has lost his bag in the college. He makes an announcement that whosoever finds the bag and returns it to him will be suitably rewarded. Shyam made a search voluntarily for a bag without any intention of getting reward. He found it and returned it to Ram. Has he got legal claim for reward. (No)
3. A developed a shopping Mall in Delhi at the request of B who is a Municipal Corporator. C makes agreement to pay Rs. 5000 p.m to A for some space in that Mall. Judge the validity of an agreement made between A and B.

4. Mahesh has got a house in Delhi costing Rs. 10 lacs. He makes agreement for selling this house to Ramesh for Rs. 5 lacs. Is this a valid agreement? (Hint: consent of Mahesh should be free).
5. A gives sum of Rs. 5000 to B to be given to C. B informs C that he is holding that money which is to be paid to him. Lateron he refuses to pay it to C on the plea that he has no obligation to pay. Can C, recover this amount from B. (Yes).
6. A makes trust arrangement with B, C. & D. (Trustees) and transfers a part of his property to the trust. As per agreement it is to be managed for the benefit of E. Can E enforce his right for the benefit? (Yes).
7. Manohar made a promise to donate sum of Rs. 5000 to the secretary of RamLila committee. New Delhi. The secretary of committee hires a contractor for constructing stage for RamLila and incurs a liability of 2000 He does it with a hope that he will get donation from Manohar. Is Manohar liable to pay donation? If yes to which extent he is liable? (Hint he is liable to pay Rs. 2000 only).
8. A pays sum of Rs. 2000 as donation to a charitable institution. Can he take this money back on the plea that there has been no consideration from the side of that institution? (Hint: No).
9. Ram borrows a sum of Rs. 10,000 from B for one year. After three month, B promise to allow a discount of Rs. 1000 if Ram repays that money immediately. Is the promise of B is valid (No, preexisting obligation on the part of Ram to repay).
10. There is a constant quarrel and marital discord between husband and wife. As a part of settlement the husband agrees to pay sum of Rs. 5000 p.m. as maintenance allowance to his wife provided she stays separately. Does a wife has claim to get that amount (No).
11. Ram borrows Rs. 5000 from Shyam @ 10% interest for one year. He fails to repay and makes an agreement with Shyam that if Shyam does not move to court Ram will pay higher rate of interest i.e. 15% p.a. Ram agrees to it. Can Ram enforce the promise made by Shyam (Hint: Yes).

Chapter **4**

Contractual Capacity

Learning Objectives

- Note the various ingredients of incapacity to contract.
- Remember legal position of minor's agreements.
- Examine those situations in which minor's agreements are enforceable and minority does not matter.
- Analyse legal qualification of various special parties in the light of contractual capacity.

INTRODUCTION

Contractual capacity is an essential ingredient of a valid contract. According to Section 10 of this act, parties making an agreement must have the contractual capacity. Contractual capacity means they must be legally competent for making a contract.

Meaning

The legal competence of the party is determined by Section 11 of this Act.This section states that 'every person is competent to contract who is of a age of majority according to law to which he is subject, and who is of a sound mind and is not declared disqualified from contracting by law to which he is subject'.

Briefly speaking the age, soundness of mind and legal qualification of a person constitute his contractual capacity.

To have a contractual capacity, one must fulfil the following conditions:-

Elements

(i) ***Age:*** The person to have a contractual capacity must be of a major age and not a minor.

(ii) ***Soundness of mind:*** The person must be of sound mind to possess contractual capacity and must not be lunatic, idiot and drunckard.

(iii) ***Legal qualification:*** Contractual capacity implies that the person must not have been declared disqualified by law for making contract.

1. FACTOR OF AGE

Section 11 of this Act provides that an age of majority of a person is determined by law to which he is subject.

According to Section 3 of the Indian Majority Act 1875, every person in India who has completed 18 years of his age becomes major. This rule is subject to the following exceptions:

(i) When the guardians of the minor are appointed by the court, such minor will have to complete 21 years of his age, to become major.

(ii) When the property of minor has been handed over to court of ward' for its management, minority will continue till completion of 21 years of age.

Legal Position of Minor's Agreements in India

Generally it is assumed that mental faculties of a minor are a in developing state. He is not mature enough to understand what is good and what are its implications on his interest. In the light of it, law protects a minor, so that any person by making an agreement with him cannot exploit him.

The Indian Contract Act 1872, has also granted privileged position to a minor with regard to agreements made by him. In any agreement he does not incur personal liability. He is allowed to get benefit in an agreement entered into by him. Not only this, but entire Judicial mechanism helps him; Judges are their councellors, Jury are their servants and law is their guardian. But at the same time, it is ensured that while protecting interest of minor, unnecessary hardships should not be created for the persons who deal with a minor.

Legal position of minor's agreement can be understood clearly with the help of following instances:-

(i) ***Agreement made by minor is absolutely void and inoperative:*** A Minor does not have the contractual capacity. When he makes agreements, such agreements are void and cannot be enforced in the court of law. Even if he has got some benefit in that agreement, before declaring that agreement as void, he may not be compelled to return that benefit.

Mohiri Bibi Vs. Dharmodas Ghosh (1930, 30 cal is 539 1 A 114). In this case, a minor has borrowed Rs 8000 from a moneylender and executed a mortgage bond of Rs 20,000 in his favour. Later on, the minor filed a suit for setting aside the mortgage on the plea that he is a minor. It was held that the agreement of mortgage is void ab-initio and the money lent by mortgagee could not be recovered.

(ii) ***Minor can be a promisee or beneficiary:*** Although, an agreement entered into by a minor is void, but he can be a promisee or beneficiary in an agreement. Simple rule of law is that a minor cannot be stopped from getting benefits in an agreement. By being in position of a promisee means to be in the position of getting benefit. When the minor is promisee or is to get some benefit in the agreement, he can enforce agreement against other party in the court of law.

Example: A is a minor. He draws a cheque in favour of B. B cannot recover the payment of that cheque from the bank. But, if B draws a cheque in favour of A, who is a minor, A can get payment of this cheque from Bank.

There is nothing in law, which debars a minor from becoming a promisee or beneficiary.

Colletor Of Meerut Vs. Hardian (1954, All 156). In this case, minor purchased certain property and has paid price for it to a vendor. Vendor declined to give possession of that property to a minor. It was held that minor has performed his obligation in the agreement. He is allowed to enforce it against the vendor. The minor was given decree for possession of the property purchased.

(iii) ***Rule of Estoppel is not applicable in case of minor:*** Rule law of Estoppel is a branch of law of evidence. According to rule of estoppel, when the person has made any statement by the words spoken or in writing or by his conduct, which induced other persons to believe that a particular event has happened. Later on if the person denies happening of that event, he will be stopped from doing so.

But in case of minor, this rule is not applicable. A minor who makes an agreement by representing himself to be a major and gets a benefit in that agreement can still plead his minority for declaring agreement as void.

Gadigeppa Bhimappa Mets Vs. V. Balangowda Bhiman Gowda (AIR, 1931, Bom 561). In this case, a minor who represented himself to be a major and induced another for making an agreement. The court was of the opinion that where an infant represents fraudulently or otherwise that he is of age and thereby induces another to enter into contract with him then on an action founded on the contract, the infant was not stopped from setting up infancy.

(iv) ***Doctrine of restitution is not applied against minor.*** Accordingly to this doctrine if a person obtains property or goods by making false representation he can be compelled to restore it to the person from whom he has obtained it. But earlier this rule was not applicable on minor. As it was held in **Mohiri Bibi Vs. Dhamodar Ghosh** case that section 64 and 65 of the Indian Contract Act which deals with restitution will not be applicable on minor's agreements.

With the passage of time many developments took place and it was made clear that the law gives protection to a minor but does not give him the liberty to cheat others.

R. Leslie Vs. Sheill (1941, 3, K.B, 607). In this case **Sheill**, a minor misrepresented his age and made an agreement for selling his property to **Leslie**

and received Rs 10,000 as consideration from him. Out of this amount he spent Rs 6000 in purchasing a car and the balance on a pleasure trip. When he attained majority LESLIE applied to the court for the performance of this contract. It was held that an aggrieved party had no legal remedy against the minor because, agreement was void ab-initio. But on account of misrepresentation the court was at its discretion to order him to handover the car to the aggrieved party.

However, the situation was changed after the enforcement of the Specific Relief Act 1963.

Section 33 of this Act provides:

(a) Where void or voidable contract has been cancelled at the instance of a party there to, the court may require him to restore such benefits which he may have received from the other party and to make any compensation to him which Justice may require.

(b) Where defendant successfully resists any suit on the ground that the agreement sought to be enforced against him in the suit, is void by reason of his not having been competent to contract. Under section II of this Act the court may if the defendant has received any benefits under the agreement, from the other party requires him to restore the benefit obtained by him under the agreement, but only to the extent to which he or his estate has benefited thereby.

Sub Section (i) of the above provision states that 'he who seeks equity must do equity' Under this rule courts have discretion to require minor plaintiff to return benefits obtained under void agreement. But the court will not compel minor to restore benefit, where other party was aware of infancy or where false representation did not influence decision of other party.

According to sub-section (2) of the above provisions where the minor is defendant successfully resist any suit on the ground that contract is void by reason of his being a minor he may be required to return benefit obtained by him by the court. But court will allow restitution only to the extent to which he or his estate has been benefited.

(v) *Agreements for basic necessities of life:* Although agreements entered into by minor are void. But if he makes an agreement for buying goods of basic necessities of life on credit such agreements carry different legal consequences. In these agreements, the person who has supplied those goods will be reimbursed provided:

(a) Goods were of basic necessities of life for a minor.

(b) Re-imbursement will be made only for reasonable cost of those goods and not a contracted price.

(c) Such reimbursement will be made only from property of a minor if any. But minor will have no personal liability.

The goods of basic necessities of life of a person will differ from person to person depending on social status and economic position of that person. It is to be noted that the goods which are of a basic necessities of life for one person (high income bracket) may be goods of extra comfort for another person (low income bracket).

On the basis of decisions of the courts from time and again the following have been considered to be necessaries of life:

(a) Fund supplied to a minor for the marriage of a female member in the family.

(b) Funds required for performing funeral obsequies of the father of minor.

(c) Expenses incurred in connection with litigation regarding his property.

(d) Funds required for the education and training of a minor.

In addition to these necessaries it would also include, items of food, clothings, shelter, education and training, medical treatment etc.

Roberts Vs. Gray, (1913, I K.B 520). In this case, a minor who was intended to become a billiards player entered into contract with R, a famous billard player. He agreed to pay him fees to learn the game and play matches with him during his world tour. It was held that G was liable to pay, as it was an agreement for necessaries related to education, training and employment.

(vi) *Ratification of minor's agreement is not allowed:* Agreements made by a minor during minority are void. On attaining age of majority he cannot ratify those agreements for making them valid. Ratification implies subsequent authorization of the act done earlier.

Example: A, who is a minor makes promissory note in favour of B. Such Promissory note is void. After some time A attains age of majority and gives new promissory note in place of old one. Second promissory note is also invalid, because it is a subsequent approval of first one.

Ramaswamy Vs. a Chettiar (1906, 16 Mc, J 422). In this case, a minor borrowed a sum of money and executed bond for it. After attaining majority he executed second bond in respect of original bond and interest therein. It was held that second bond was not maintainable, since it was without consideration.

(vii) *Agreements made by the guardian of a minor:* Agreements made by a minor are void. But if the guardians of a minor make an agreement on behalf of a minor, such agreement is valid provided:

(a) Agreement has been made for the benefit of a minor.

(b) It was made on behalf of a minor.

(c) It was made by the guardian within the scope of authority given to them.

It is however to be noted that a guardian cannot purchase an immovable property on behalf of a minor without the consent of the court.

(viii) ***Minor cannot be declared insolvent:*** Agreements made by minor are void. In these agreements, he does not incur personal liability. At the most, in some cases he may be compelled to return benefit or pay reasonable cost only from the property if any. Thus he cannot be adjudicated as an insolvent by the court.

(ix) ***Minor as agent:*** A minor can be appointed as an agent. He can work on behalf of principal. It is because the main job of agent is to bring third party into contractual relationship with his principal. As soon as relationship is established, his role is over. And third party can sue upon the principal for that transaction, made by the agent. Thus minor agent binds principal without incurring any liability.

Example: A appoints B as his agent. B is a minor. He was appointed for selling goods. He sells goods to C. C refuses to pay to B. A can file suit against C for the payment of price.

(x) ***Minor as shareholder:*** A minor cannot be shareholder in a Joint Stock Company because he is not legally competent for making a contract. But if he has been allotted shares due to some mistake, both he and the company may continue to enjoy a benefit of such holding. But he would not be liable to pay calls, which are due on his holding.

Minor can become a shareholder in a company, through his guardian who will act as his trustee. Trustee's name will be recorded in the Register of member, and he shall be a member of the company for all purposes.

PALANIAPPA VS. OFFICIAL LIQUIDATOR. In this case shares were allotted by a company to a minor under an application signed by his guardian. When company went into liquidation, neither minor, nor his guardian was found liable for paying unpaid call. It is because the name of a minor was written in the register of members. By being incompetent to contract he cannot be sued.

(xi) ***Minor as a partner:*** Relationship of a partnership arises out of a contract and minor has no capacity to contract. Therefore he cannot become partner in a partnership firm. But if all partners do agree, he can be admitted to the profits or benefits of the firm. His liability for the acts of the firm will be limited upto his share which he has got in assets and profits of the firm.

(xii) ***Surety for a minor:*** A person who stands guarantor for the debt borrowed by the minor is known as surety. Though the creditor cannot sue upon minor, but directly he can file suit against surety. The liability of surety arises out of a different contract which he makes with creditor.

KASHIBA VS. SRIPAT (1894, Bom, 697). In this case it was held that contract between surety and third party (creditor) is a direct and independent contract, thus the minor will be saved from his liability.

2. SOUNDNESS OF MIND

To have contractual capacity one must be of a sound mind. According to Section12 of this Act 'a person is said to be a sound mind for the purpose of making contract, if at the time, when he makes it he is capable of understanding it and forming a rational Judgement as to its effects upon his interest'.

To determine soundness of mind for making a contract one has to ensure that,

(a) The person at that time of making contract is capable of understanding the contract.

(b) He is also capable of understanding implications of that contract upon his interest. He knows it that how that contract can affect his interest.

Section 12 of this Act further states that 'a person who is usually of unsound mind, but occasionally of sound mind may make contract when he is of a sound mind'.

Soundness of mind of a person is adversely affected by certain factors including use of intoxicants and mental disease etc. These factors are as under:

(a) ***Lunacy:*** Lunacy is a mental disease which is curable. In this disease mental faculties of a person start working above or below the normal prescribed range. So long as these faculties operate with in a prescribed range, the person is of a sound mind. When those faculties starts moving out of range, he becomes of unsound mind.

It is however to be noted that the lunatic, when he is of sound mind he has a contractual capacity. All agreements made by him are valid and enforceable except those made by him when he becomes of a unsound mind.

(b) ***Idiocy:*** It is also a mental disease which is not curable. In this disease the mental faculties of a person have not been developed since birth or he has lost his mental faculties for ever due to some accident or shock etc. Such person will never come to the state of understanding contract and its impact on his interest. Idiots do not have a contractual capacity and therefore agreement made by them are absolutely void. Such person can be beneficiary in a agreement for supplying necessaries of a life to him or to his dependents and money is recoverable from his property if any.

(c) ***Drunkards or intoxicated person:*** A person who takes any intoxicants like alchohol, marijuna and cannabis, etc., he is temporarily incompetant for making an agreement. The mental faculties of such persons are clouded for sometime. Thus so long as he remains under the influence of intoxicant or drug he has no contractual capacity. Agreement made by such person are void. But for the supply of necessaries, reasonable cost of it can be recovered from his property and he has no personal liability for it.

3. LEGAL DISQUALIFICATION

In addition to the above, there are certain parties whose contractual capacity has been restricted by law to which they are subject. Such incompetancy may arise by the status of a person. And law may debar him from making an agreement. The following persons have been included in this category.

(i) *Alien enemy:* A person who lives in and is a citizen of foreign country is known as an alien. He may be friend or enemy to the citizen of our country. Alien friend can make an agreement with Indian citizen. But if war is declared between the two countries, the citizens of those countries become alien enemy to each other. And agreements made with alien enemy are void.

In other words, after the declaration of war citizens of those countries become alien enemy and agreement cannot be entered into by them. When they make agreements, such agreements are void. But agreements made before the declarations of war will be either declared as void or may be suspended so long as war continues. Such agreements can be revived, when the war is over and can be re-enforced in the court of law with prior approval of the Central Government.

(ii) *Foreign sovereign and ambassadors:* Ambassadors, High Commissioners or foreign diplomatic staff do represent their country. Therefore they have been provided some immunities. They can make an agreement with Indian citizen and can enforce those agreements against Indian citizens in India. But Indian citizen to sue upon them for the rights arising out of an agreement has to seek prior permission of Central Government.

It has been done with a view to ensure that for personal gain no one is allowed to spoil relationship of the country with the country to which that diplomatic official belongs.

ENGELKE VS. MUSMAN (1928, A.C, 433). In this case Engelke was in the diplomatic staff of foreign Embassy. He was tenant of Musman, Engelke did not pay rent regularly and it causes into arrears. It was held that he cannot be sued upon for the recovery of rent, because he was protected under diplomatic immunities.

(iii) *Married woman:* Indian constitution does not discriminate between man and woman, and grants equal rights to them. But after marriage, status of woman is slightly changed. With regard her contractual capacity the following guidelines should be taken care of:

(a) Married woman has no right to make agreements regarding joint property of husband and wife, unless she is authorised to do so by her husband.

(b) Married woman is free to make any agreement to deal with her personal property such as bank balance in her name and jewelleries, etc.

(c) On the failure of husband, to fulfil the basic necessities of her life, she becomes 'agent of her husband by necessity'. For the supply of such basic necessities she can make agreements binding on the property of her husband.

(iv) ***Corporation and joint stock company:*** Corporation is a body corporate which is brought into existence by passing special legislation in parliament. Joint Stock Company comes into being after fulfilling legal formalities prescribed in the Indian Company Act. Once such corporation or company comes into existence, legal status is granted to them, and they are considered as separate legal entity. Such corporation or company can enter into an agreement, can sue third party or can be sued upon. Not only this, but also they can own properties and transfer it.

Since Corporation or Company has no physical existence, some official is to be authorised for using these rights on behalf of the corporation or company. contractual capacity of such corporation or company will be limited upto the provisions of the law which brings them into existence. Any agreement or any other act beyond the provisions of that Act would be ultra vires and void.

Similarly the corporation or company exists only in the eyes of law, thus no agreement of personal nature can be entered into on behalf of the corporation.

(v) ***Insolvent:*** Generally, when the assets of a person fall short of liabilities and liabilities cannot be paid fully. Such state of affair is known as insolvency. The person is declared as an insolvent by the court, his property handed over to the 'Official Receiver'. The insolvent cannot make any agreement regarding that property. The Official receiver realises the property and distribute the cash among creditors ratably. It is only when the court issues' order of discharge' in favour of that person he becomes competent to make agreements.

(vi) ***Convict:*** A convict is a person who has been found guilty for some legal offence. He may be prosecuted and may be sent to imprisonment. So long as he remains in the imprisonment he has no contractual capacity. On his release from imprisonment on bail or 'parole', he becomes competent for making agreement, when such convict is finally released from imprisonment he becomes competent. But in case of barbaric offences such person may be declared disqualified for a particular period of time, even after being released from imprisonment.

However in England Barristers are not permitted to enter into agreement relating to their profession. They cannot be sued upon or cannot file a suit against the client for theirs dues. But in India an advocate can sue upon his client for the recovery of fees and other dues.

Review Questions

1. Define the term 'Contractual Capacity' Explain its elements in brief?
2. 'Agreements entered into by a minor are void'. Discuss exceptions to this rule.
3. Explain legal position of minor's agreement in India.
4. What is soundness of mind. Discuss the contractual capacity of various categories of people whose mental state is affected either by illness or by intoxicants.

5. Explain with suitable example, the law relating to validity of contract made by a minor.
6. Comment on the following:
   (a) Minor is not allowed to cheat others.
   (b) Agreements for minor's benefit can be enforced by him.
   (c) Minor as an agent.
   (d) Lunatic can make agreements.
7. Discuss the legal competence of the following for an making agreement.
   (a) Corporation
   (b) Married woman
   (c) Alien enemy
   (d) Insolvent

PRACTICAL PROBLEMS

1. Ram is a minor. He falsely represents himself to be a major makes agreement with Shyam, gets benefit in that agreement and finally sets aside it as void. Can Ram be compelled for returning the benefit to shyam (Yes, Specific Relief Act).
2. A 'who is a minor' had borrowed a sum of Rs. 5,000 from B. He has spent that money for paying fee towards a computer course being pursued by him. Is A liable to repay? (Yes from his property for basic necessaries).
3. A shoe merchant has supplied 10 pairs of shoes to C who is minor at a particular price. Is he entitled to recover that price? (Yes, but reasonable price for 2, 3 pairs of shoes from the property if any).
4. A is a lunatic. He has a wife and two children. He makes an agreement to borrow a sum of Rs. 5000 from B. The money is utilised on fooding and clothing of his family members. Can B recover this amount? (Yes from the property).
5. Mahesh, who is a minor makes an agreement for borrowing Rs 10,000 from Ramesh. To borrow this amount he is signing mortgage deed of his property for Rs. 20,000. Later on he wants to get his property free from mortgage. Can he do it without returning Rs. 10,000 to Ramesh? (Yes, as per section 64,65 of Indian Contract Act).
6. A is a minor. His guardian opens a bank account jointly in the name of minor. Discuss the legal status of this account.
7. Ram is a minor. His father was a partner in a partnership firm. He dies. Shyam and Manohar agree to give his share to his son, Ram. What is the limit of liability of Ram for the acts of the firm?

8. X, a minor, has been allotted shares in a Joint Stock Company by mistake. Is he liable to pay calls which are due on shares? (No)
9. A is a minor draws cheque of Rs. 2000 in favour of B. After attaining the age of majority he replaces the cheque and instead gives new cheque for it. Can B get payment of the cheque? (No)
10. A foreign diplomatic official got a house in rent from an Indian citizen in Delhi. He refused to pay the agreed amount of rent to the Indian citizen. Can he sue upon the foreign diplomat? What is the legal remedy available to him? (No, without permission of Central Govt. he may approach to House of Parliament).
11. A got married with B and A does not fulfil the basic necessities of his wife. Can she make a binding agreement on the joint property? (Yes Agency by necessity).
12. A is Managing Director of X corporation. He is authorised to make an agreement on behalf of the corporation. He makes an agreement beyond the powers of Managing Director mentioned in the Act. Is this agreement binding on the corporation? (No Ultra vires).
13. A minor falsely represents himself to be a major, enters into an agreement for selling his property to B. A receives Rs. 20,000 a part of price in advance out of this amount he buys car for Rs .15,000 and spends remaining amount on a pleasure trip. After A gets the majority age, B files suit against him for transferring possession and ownership of that property. Will he succeed? or will he get Rs. 20,000 back from A? (Hint: Refer to R Leslie Vs Shell). He cannot succeed, the court may allow him to repay Rs. 15,000 to B).
14. Y, a minor, who wanted to become a professional magician, makes an agreement with a musical company and agrees to pay a certain sum of money for attending classess of music. Is he liable to pay the fee? (Yes from his property as a case of basic necessaries).

■■■

Chapter 5

Free Consent

Learning Objectives

- Examine the consequences of free consent and lack of consent in the formation of a contract.
- Get familiar with the concept of 'consensus-ad-idem, in the formation of contract.
- Analyse the consequences of various elements of free consent.
- Make distinction between fraud and misrepresentation and coercion and undue influence.
- Understand the role and consequences of various types of mistakes on the validity of a contract.

INTRODUCTION

Free Consent is equally important for the validity of a contract. Formation of an agreement involves two parties. One party makes an offer on particular subject matter to another party and that another party accepts it. Both the parties must ensure that they have consent on that subject matter of an agreement and that consent is free. Without free consent of the parties an agreement does not acquire legal sanctity and consequences.

Generally, consent of the parties means, both of them have understood subject matter of an agreement in the same sense. Other way, around both of them have identical minds on that subject matter.

Section 10 of this Act states that, all agreements are contracts if they are made by the free consent of the parties. According to section 13 of this Act, "two or more persons are said to consent when they agree upon same thing in the same sense"

Section 14 of this Act states that,' Consent is said to be free when it is not caused by

(i) Coercion-application of physical force
(ii) Undue influence- use of mental pressure
(iii) Misrepresentation- innocent false representation.
(iv) Fraud-cheating or deceiving
(v) Mistake -wrong impression about anything.

However, it is to be noted that, the use of any one of the four factors to seek consent will make that contract voidable one. While as, use of mistake in causing consent will make contract void. But when the parties make fundamental mistake regarding subject matter or identity of party or a nature of agreement. Either there will be no agreement or agreement will be void. Simple rule is that a contract does not arise in the absence of consent. This point was made clear in the following case.

Cundy Vs. Lindsay. In this case, while placing an order for the goods, with Cundy, Blenkiron an individual closely imitated address and signature of well known firm Blenkiron & Coy. Cundy sent goods to him thinking that the order came from Blenkiron & Coy. Who in turn sold them to Lindsay. Cundy on discovering his mistake filed a suit against Lindsay for the recovery of goods. It was held by the House of Lords that as Cundy thought that he was dealing with Blenkrion & Coy and knew nothing about Blenkiron and had no intention to deal with him. Thus there was no contract between Cundy and Blekiron.

Boulton Vs. Jones (1857, E.R.232). In this case, A sold his business to B without disclosing this fact to his customers. C sent an order for goods to A. B received order and without intimating change of ownership supplied the goods to C. It was held that there was no contract between B and C, because C intended to make contract with A only and not with B.

In practice it is difficult to distinguish between case of fundamental error or mutual mistake. It is made clear that fundamental error means there is no consent of parties, thus there is no agreement. But in case of mutual mistake on the part of the parties agreement will become void.

Example: A has got two scooters i.e. Vespa and Bajaj. He made an agreement for selling a scooter to B for Rs.10, 000 believing that he is selling Vespa but B thought that he is buying Bajaj scooter. Agreement between A and B is void on account of mutual mistake regarding identity of subject matter.

ELEMENTS OF FREE CONSENT

1. Coercion

Coercion implies use of some kind of physical force by doing some act forbidden by law to seek consent of other party. For example one may put an other into physical injury to cause his consent or may threat to retain physical possession of his property.

According to Section 15 of this Act, coercion is, "committing or threatening to commit any act forbidden by Indian Panel Code or unlawful detaining or threatening to detain any property, to the prejudice of any person, whatever, with the intention of causing any person to enter into an agreement".

On the basis of above definition of coercion, the following features of it may be pointed out as under:

1. *Coercion includes:* Coercion includes committing or threatening to commit any of the following acts.

(a) To commit any act which is forbidden by Indian Panel Code or any act which is punishable under I.P.C.
(b) Threatening to commit such forbidden or punishable act.
(c) Unlawful detention of the property of that another person.
(d) Threatening to detain that property of another person.

Example: A is seeking consent of B for an agreement at revolver point or A has fired one round and then forcing B to sign on agreement. A withholds possession of Bs car unless B gives his consent for agreement. In all these cases coercion has been used for causing consent of other party.

2. *Intention of the party:* Committing or threatening to commit forbidden acts will amount to coercion provided those acts would have been done with a view to cause consent of other party for an agreement. Thus intention of the party doing those act is very important for determining use of coercion. By committing such act another party must have been compelled to give his consent for an agreement. Then only it will amount to coercion.

3. *Direction of coercion:* It is not necessary that the act of coercion must be directed against the person whose consent is being caused for agreement. It may be directed upon any other person even who is not a party of agreement. Coercion may be directed upon A to cause consent of B.

BANSRAJ VS. THE SECRETARY OF STATE (1939, A.W.R 242). In this case, the Government imposed a threat of attachment against the property of A for the recovery of a fine due from B, the son of A. A had to pay fine. It was held that payment of fine was induced by coercion and therefore A was entitled to recover the money paid to remove wrongful attachment.

4. *Place of coercion:* The explanation of section 15 of this Act makes it clear that, it is not necessary that the place at which the act of coercion is done is subject to Jurisdiction of Indian Panel Code. Even if coercion is used in the aeroplane going in the sky or ship going in the ocean, it will amount to coercion. It cannot be pleaded that in the sky or ocean, the provisions of Indian Panel Code are not applicable.

Case: A and B were on the board of ship. A caused B to make a contract by an act of criminal intimidation. Later on B did not perform contract. A sued B at Calcutta for breach of contract. B's argument that the contract was caused by coercion was accepted and it was held that it was immaterial whether at the place of making a contract Indian Panel Code was applicable or not.

5. *Threat to commit suicide amounts to coercion:* Although, as per the provisions of Indian Panel Code it is only an attempt to commit suicide, which is punishable. But in many decisions of the courts it was held that if the person seeks consent of another for agreement by threatening to commit suicide it will also amount to coercion.

Chikkam Amiraju Vs. Chikkam. In this case a person threatened to commit a suicide if his wife and son did not contract with his brother to release certain disputed property in his favour. The court held that the contract was caused by threat to commit a suicide, which amounts to coercion.

6. *Effect of coercion:* According to section 19 of this Act, if one person seeks consent of another by using coercion such contract is voidable at the option of aggrieved party whose consent had not been free. He can repudiate or avoid a contract, or he can enforce it against another party. And if other party compels him to perform it he can refuse it on the plea that his consent has been caused by coercion.

Generally, burden of proof that consent was obtained by coercion lies on the party who alleges coercion. And who wants to set aside contract on the plea of coercion.

Duress and coercion: In English Mercantile Law, the term 'duress' has been used for coercion. Duress is defined as causing or threatening to cause bodily violence or imprisonment with a view to obtain the consent of other party for a contract. Main point of difference between duress and coercion is that duress does not include unlawful detaining property of other to cause his consent. Secondly coercion may be used by any person even by a person stranger to contract, but duress must be used by the party to the contract.

2. Undue Influence

Undue influence implies unfair use of dominating position to cause the consent of other party for a contract. In undue influence some kind of mental and moral pressure is brought upon the party to cause his consent.

According to section 16(1) of this Act, 'a contract is said to be induced by undue influence where the relation subsisting between the parties are such that one of the party is in a position to dominate the will of other and uses the position to obtain an unfair advantage over the other'. According to this definition it is clear that undue influence involves the following elements.

(i) Two parties making a contract are some how related to each other.

(ii) One of the party is in dominating position who can dominate or influence will of other party for making contract.

(iii) The party who is in dominating position gets unfair advantages of his position by causing the consent of other party.

Example: A who is a doctor makes an agreement with B who keeps poor eyesight and health to pay for his professional charges. The amount to be paid by B is unreasonably very high. In this example, the doctor who is in a dominating position must have used his position to get unfair advantages by causing consent of B for the agreement.

Legal presumption of undue influence: According to section 16(2) of this act it is legally assumed that under the following situations one party who is in dominating position must have caused undue influence to cause the consent of other for the agreement.

(i) *Relationship of real and apparent authority:* One party holds real and apparent authority over other party. They make an agreement. It will be legally assumed that the party who is in a superior position, in terms of authority must have used undue influence for causing the consent of other party. Pre-existing relationship of authority means the relationship of superior and subordinate.

Example: A and B are working in the same department. A is a section officer and B is an assistant. Both of them enter into contract. It will be legally assumed that A who is in a superior position to dominate will of B must have exercised undue influence to cause the consent of B for a contract.

(ii) *Fiduciary relationship:* Fiduciary relationship is a relationship, which is based on a mutual trust and confidence between two parties. In such relationship one of the parties is thought to be in a dominating position. When parties standing in fiduciary relationship make an agreement, legally it will be presumed that the party in a dominating position must have caused the consent of other through undue influence.

Some of the cases of fiduciary relationship are as under:

(a) Father and Son / Guardian and Ward
(b) Teacher and disciple
(c) Doctor and Patient
(d) Advocate and Client
(e) Trustee and Beneficiary

RHODES VS. DATE (L.R.I, Ch.257). In this case the court has made it clear that the doctrine of undue influence applies to all varieties of fiduciary relations in which domination may be exercised by one person over another. A test is to be applied whether one party is able to dominate the will of other.

(iii) *Mental distress:* Sometimes, mental capacity or a strength of a person may be adversely affected either by age, illness or other bodily and mental strain. Such person is said to be in a mental stress. Any one who makes an agreement with such person is assumed to have exercised undue influence to cause his consent for an agreement. In these cases, status of a party is enough to prove the existence of undue influence.

Example: An old man of 80years who is being looked after by his relatives may be influenced by the relative for making a agreement regarding the property of old man.

Similarly the person who meets with an accident and gets serious injury, is in a dire need of money to get necessary treatment makes an agreement for borrowing money. He may also be easily influenced by the money lender for paying higher rate of interest.

(iv) *Inadequacy of consideration:* Though, it is not necessary that value of consideration given to the promisor must be equal to the value of a promise made by him. If he gets consideration of lesser value than the value of promise. In this case, it will be assumed that consent of the party getting lesser consideration has been caused by exercising undue influence. Thus inadequacy of consideration is also considered as an evidence of use of undue influence.

Burden of proof: In all above cases, cited under section 16(2) there is a legal presumption that the party in a dominating position must have used it, in an unfair manner to cause the consent of another. In these cases, burden of proof for not using undue influence lies on the party who is in a dominating position. He can rebute the presumption by showing that

(i) He had made full disclosure of facts relevant to the contract to that another party.
(ii) Consideration was adequate and transaction is not unreasonable.
(iii) The weaker party was in a position to receive independent advice and his consent was free.

Effects of undue influence: Where the consent is caused by exercising undue influence, contract is voidable at the option of aggrieved party whose consent had not been free. Such contract may be set aside by an aggrieved party. He can also enforce it against another party. And if he is compelled to perform it he may refuse it on the plea that his consent has not been free.

According to section 19A, of this Act, if the party who is entitled to avoid the consent has received any benefit there under may be called upon to restore it upon such terms and conditions, as the court may consider just and equitable.

Unconscionable transactions: Where the party in dominating position, makes an agreement with weaker party to make exhorbitant profit, such agreements are known as unconscionable transactions or agreements. In these transactions the party in dominating position makes unreasonable profit from weak position of another party. In such agreements, the burden of proof is shifted to the dominant party. He has to prove that he did nothing to dominate the will of other party.

Mostly, money lending transactions and gifts belong to this category. But to declare transaction unconscionable the parties of a transaction must have unequal position so that one can dominate the will of other.

Sometimes, high rate of interest may be charged by the moneylenders. If he is in a position of dominating will of the borrower and uses his position to get unfair advantage, the transaction may be declared as unconscionable one, and the court may intervene. In one of the case, where a poor widow borrowed Rs.1500 from a money lender @ 100% interest per annum, for filing a suit to establish her right to maintenance. The rate of interest was reduced to 24% per annum by Madras High Court. This relief was granted only on the basis of undue influence.

The court while dealing with the cases of undue influence normally takes four factors in to consideration:

(i) Whether the transaction is righteous i.e. whether it is an act a right minded person could be expected to carry out.

(ii) Whether it manifest so much improvidence as to suggest the idea that executant was not master of himself and not in a state of mind to sit and weigh as to what he was doing.

(iii) Whether intention of making the gift originated with the donor.

(iv) Whether it was a matter, which requires legal advice.

Pardanashin women: Any women who observes 'parda' system is known as pardanashin woman. She does not come into contract with any person, other than her family members. She remains with in four walls of the house and does not interact with outside world. Due to lack of outside exposure, the law grants protection to her. Thus anyone making a contract with pardanashin woman, can enforce such contract provided he proves that,

(i) She was in receipt of independent advice.

(ii) She has free consent for that contract.

(iii) She understood the nature of the contract as explained by another party.

Such protection is also granted to illeterate and ignorant women who are equally exposed to the danger and risk of unfair deal.

Table Distinction between Coercion and Undue Influence

	Coercion	*Undue Influence*
Meaning	It includes committing or threatening to commit unlawful act or unlawful detention or threatening to detain property of others, to cause his consent	A person in dominating position gets unfair advantage of his position to cause consent of other person.
Contents	It implies use of physical force or threat to cause consent	It involves use of moral or mental pressure to cause consent.

Pre existing Relationship	It is not required for using coercion	Pre-existing relationship between parties is required to use undue influence.
Party of contract	It is not necessary for the party to direct coercion against the other party of contract and he may use it against the person who is stranger to contract	Party using undue influence and against whom it is used, both of them must be parties of contract.
Burden of Proof	In coercion an aggrieved party who is entitled to set aside contract has to prove the act of coercion	In undue influence burden of proof shifted on dominant party making unfair use of his position and getting consent of other party.
Restoration of benefit	In the use of coercion if an aggrieved party repudiates contract he has to restore benefit received in that to other party (section 64)	In case of undue influence the court is at a discretion to direct an aggrieved party to return whole or part of benefit received, to other party (section 19A)

3. Misrepresentation

While making contract, one of the party may make any statement regarding the subject matter of a contract. Such statement, if turns to be untrue it amount to misrepresentation. It is a misstatement of material facts.

Misrepresentation of facts is always innocent in nature. The party making untrue statement believes that the statement is true, but in reality statement turns to be incorrect. The party making misrepresentation has no intention for making untrue statement. And at the same time he may not have sufficient ground to believe that the statement was true.

According to Section 18 of Indian Contract Act misrepresentation means and includes the following:

(i) ***Assertion of facts:*** The positive assertion in a manner not warranted by information of the person making it which is not true, though he believes it to be true. In other words, in misrepresentation, the person asserts on untrue statement, however innocently. And he has no sufficient ground to believe that it is untrue. But really it turns to be untrue.

Example: A has a Maurti Car. He believes that his car runs 20 Km by using one litre of petrol. He make this statement to B believing that it is true. B makes an agreement to buy the car. And it appears that the car hardly gives mileage of 12 Km with one litre of petrol. It amounts to misrepresentation on the part of A, by making positive assertion of facts.

(ii) ***Breach of duty:*** Any breach of duty which without an intention to deceive, gains an advantage to the person committing it or any one claiming under him, by misleading another to his prejudice or anyone claiming under him.

There are certain case in law, where one party is under legal obligation for making full and correct disclosure of material fact related to contract to another party. In such case, if the party makes breach of duty however, innocently without an intention to deceive other; it amounts to misrepresentation on his part. It happens in all contracts of 'utmost good faith'.

In these contracts, one party knows material facts related to subject matter of a contract, which other party does not know and has no reasonable means to know. The party having knowledge of a material facts is under legal obligation to make full and correct disclosure of those facts to other party. These contracts include, contracts based a fiduciary relationship, insurance contracts, contracts to buy shares in joint stock company, partnership contracts and contracts related to family matters etc.

Example: A makes a contract with Fire Insurance Company to get his house insured against the risk of fire. This is a contract of utmost good faith. In this contract A is in a position to know each and every material facts about the house, which insurance company does not know or does not have reasonable means to know. Thus A is under legal obligation for making full and correct disclosure of these facts to insurance company. If he does not do so however, innocently which means innocent breach of duty and it amounts to misrepresentation.

(iii) ***Untrue statement made innocently:*** Causing, however innocently, a party to an agreement to make a mistake as to substance of the thing which is the subject matter of the agreement.

Sometimes, the person innocently makes untrue statement regarding particular subject matter before another person. That another person makes mistake on the basis of that statement and enters into a contract for buying that subject matter. Later on, it appears that contract was made on the basis of untrue statement. The person making such untrue statement however, innocently will be liable for misrepresentation.

Example: A & B are sitting in coffee house. A however innocently says to B that his house is fit for dwelling purpose. B, makes mistake on the basis of this statement and buys A's house. Later on it appears that there are big cracks on the walls and foundation of the house is very weak. A will be liable for misrepresentation.

DERRY VS. PEEK (1889,14 App. Cas 337). In this case, In the prospectus of a company there was an assertion that it had statutory powers to run its tramways by steam, provided the consent of Govt. is obtained. The director issued prospectus stating therein that the company has a right to use steam power. They believed that the company would be given permission for using steam power. The permission was refused and company had to wound up. It was held that the directors were liable for misrepresentation.

Effects of misrepresentation: In a contract, when consent of the party is caused by misrepresentation made by another party. Such contract is voidable at the option of an aggrieved party whose consent was caused by misrepresentation. He has the following rights:

(i) He can avoid or rescind the contract.

(ii) He can insist on the performance of a contract with a condition that he shall be placed in the same position, as he would have been if there had been no misrepresentation.

Example: A had rented his house to B and has given a notice to him for vacating the house. Believing that it will be vacated soon he makes a statement to C that his house is free from tenancy. C is induced to make mistake and finally he makes the agreement for buying that house. It is found that house is not vacated. This contract is voidable at the option of C and he can insist on A to perform the contract by getting house vacated and making it free from tenancy of B.

In case of misrepresentation, the aggrieved party can avoid the contract provided he proves that he had no reasonable means of knowing truth.

Example: A owns a factory of plastic goods at Okhala. He gives statement to B that his factory produces 100 units of particular plastic item. He does it however, innocently. By mistake B gets induced to buy his factory. After buying factory it appears that factory can produce only 700 units of that plastic item. There is a misrepresentation. But B has no right to rescind or avoid a contract, because by inspecting production records of the factory he would have discovered truth of statement made by A.

Thus an aggrieved party whose consent has been caused by misrepresentation loses the right to avoid or rescind contract under the following situations.

(i) Aggrieved party has reasonable means for discovering truth of a statement.

(ii) Right to avoid or rescind a contract must have been used with in reasonable period of time. In case of undue delay he may lose his right.

(iii) If the parties cannot be restored to their original position, the contract cannot be rescinded.

(iv) If third party has purchased goods in good faith for valuable consideration which were brought in by using misrepresentation the aggrieved party will lose the right to avoid or rescind the contract.

4. Fraud

An intentional misrepresentation of the facts amounts to Fraud. Fraud is always committed with a view to deceive or cheat another person. Thus, when one person does any thing or makes false statement knowingly to induce other for causing his consent, it is known as fraud.

According to section 17 of Indian Contract Act, "fraud means and includes any of the following acts committed by a party to a contract or with his connivance or by his agent with intent to deceive other party thereto or his agent to enters into a contract".

(i) The suggestion as to a matter of fact, of that which is not true, by one who does not believe it to be true.
(ii) The active concealment of a fact by one having knowledge or belief of the fact.
(iii) A promise made without an intention of performing it.
(iv) Any other act fitted to device other.
(v) Any such act or omission as the law specially declares to be fraudulent.

Elements of fraud: According to the definition of fraud the following elements are included in a fraud.

1. ***False representation:*** Most important element of fraud is false representation or untrue statement made by the party intentionally. The party, while making agreement, makes untrue statement regarding subject matter of a contract with an intention to cause the consent of another party, it amounts to fraud. The person giving untrue account of material facts has a knowledge of it, he does it to cheat or mislead another party. Thus, to constitute fraud, false statement must be accompanied by intention to mislead.

Example: A has purchased second hand scooter from B. He makes an agreement to sell it to C by saying that it is brand new scooter. A has committed a fraud with C by causing his consent for the agreement.

2. ***Active Concealment of facts:*** A person may also commit a fraud by hiding certain material fact related to subject matter of contract. It also amounts to fraud if he does it to deceive other by causing his consent.

Example: A buys a second hand car from car dealer. He gets it repaired and painted it, as it looks new one. Later on he agrees to sell it to B as a new one car. A has made willful concealment of material facts regarding the car, it amounts to fraud. He has done it by covering up defects of old car by getting it painted.

However, if some businessman makes any untrue statement in making self praise or commendation of his own goods it will not amount to fraud. It is because businessmen are supposed to speak optimistically about their products.

Example: A is a manufacturer of Coloured Television sets. He gives an advertisement that television set manufactured by him is the best available in the market. Such statement will not amount to fraud, because it is a mere expression of opinion for making self praise of his own goods.

3. ***Making promise without an intention to perform:*** When a person makes a contract with another person, without an intention of performing it. It will also amount to a fraud. It is because the promisor carries an intention to deceive other party by making such contract right from the beginning.

Example: A buys some goods from B on credit. A carries an intention of not making payment to B. I t will amount to fraud, because A has made a promise with an intention not to perform it.

4. ***Any other acts fitted to deceive:*** In order to extend coverage of fraud this clause has been added. According to this clause, acts other than covered under section 17, if performed with an intention to mislead other, it will also amount to a fraud. It makes clear that all other acts which are not covered under section 17 will also be considered as fraud if such acts are done to deceive another.

5. ***Act or omission declared fraudulent by law:*** In addition, law has declared many acts or omission as fraudulent. If these are done it will also amount to fraud. Such acts or omissions have been cited in Insolvency Act, Indian Company Act and Transfer of property Act etc. Under section 55 of Transfer of Property Act, transferor of immovable property is required to disclose to the buyer or transferee all material defects in a property to be sold and non-disclosure of such defects amounts to a fraud.

Briefly speaking to constitute fraud the following conditions must be satisfied:

(i) Untrue or misleading statement has been made or any other device or technique is used or act is performed.

(ii) Knowledge: Such misleading statement or fraudulent act or technique must have been used knowingly.

(iii) Intention: Intention of giving misleading statements doing acts or using technique must be to deceive another person.

However, mere non-disclosure of the facts or mere expression of opinion or statement by a businessman in making self praise of his goods will not amount to fraud.

Silence as fraud: Mere silence or mere non-disclosure of facts normally does not constitute fraud unless party keeping silence is under legal obligation to speak or his silence is equivalent to speech.

According to section 17, "mere silence as to fact likely to affect the willingness of a person to enter in to a contract is not fraud unless the circumstance of the case are such that regard being made to them, if it is duty of a person keeping silence to speak or unless silence is equivalent to speech".

Example: A and B are traders. A enters in to an agreement with B for buying some raw material. B has got private information regarding change in the price level of that raw material. He does not disclose it to A, because it may affect A's willingness to make an agreement. Such non disclosure on the part of B will not amount to fraud. So, as per law, that a person before entering in to a contract or while entering into it need not disclose material facts which he knows to the other party. But he must refrain from making active misstatement.

Thus generally silence, maintained by the party on material facts of subject matter does not amount to fraud. But this rule has certain exceptions. Under these situations, silence maintained by the party will amount to fraud. These situations are as follows:

(i) ***Party keeping silence is under duty to speak:*** In a contract of utmost good faith, one party who has complete knowledge of subject matter is under legal obligation to make full and correct disclosure of that information to the another party. That another party may not be knowing it or may not have reasonable mean to know it. So if the party under legal obligation does maintain silence it will amount to fraud.

Duty to speak and make disclosure of material facts arises when parties entering into contract repose trust and confidence on each other. It happen in all contracts based on fiduciary relationship. Obligation to speak and making disclosure arises in the following contracts.

(i) Contracts of insurance
(ii) Contracts of Allotment of shares in Joint Stock Company
(iii) Contracts of family settlement
(iv) Partnership Contracts.
(v) Contract between parties having fiduciary relationship
(vi) Contracts of marriage
(vii) Contracts of transferring immovable property.

(ii) ***Silence maintained by the party is equivalent to speech:*** In all such cases, where silence maintained by the party is equivalent to his speech. Such silence will also amount to fraud.

Example: A makes an agreement for buying B's motorbike. While making an agreement A says to B that if you do not refuse I believe that motorbike is in operational condition. B keeps silent. Later on it appears that motorbike is out of operation. B's silence is equivalent to his speech, thus he will be liablc for a fraud.

(iii) ***Half truth:*** While making an agreement when one party discloses a portion of information or relevant fact, in the mean time he stops to disclose remaining facts. Disclosure of half truth amounts to fraud. It has been treated worse than misleading statement, by the court. Thus silence regarding unspoken facts will amount to fraud.

Effects of fraud: When the consent of a party has been caused by fraud, such contract is voidable at the option of an aggrieved party. Aggrieved party has the following legal remedies:

(i) He can avoid or recind the contract.
(ii) He may insist on other party to perform a contract on the condition that he must be placed in that position, as there would have been no fraud.
(iii) Aggrieved party can also claim for compensation if he has suffered any loss due to fraud.

Table Distinction between Fraud and Misrepresentation

	Fraud	*Misrepresentation*
Meaning	It includes any act, technique or misstatement to deceive other	It includes misstatement of facts made honestly believing it to be true.
Intention	In case of fraud, intention of a party making it is to cheat another	There is no such intention on the part of the person making misstatement.
Nature	It is intentional in character and is made deliberately.	It is however innocent in nature.
Remedy	Aggrieved party can avoid the contract and claim for compensation for the loss	Aggrieved party can avoid the contract
Silence	Under certain circumstance, silence maintained by the party amounts to fraud i.e. duty to speak, and if silence is equivalent to fraud.	But silence maintained by the party does not constitute misrepresentation.
Discovery of truth	In case of fraud aggrieved party can avoid contract and except in case of silence as fraud he has to prove that reasonable means for discovering truth was not available	In case of misrepresentation aggrieved party can avoid or recind a contract provided he had no reasonable means to discover truth.
Criminal Act	Fraud is a civil wrong or criminal act which is punishable under Indian Panel Code	But misrepresentation does not amount to criminal act.

5. Mistake

Last element which affects the free consent of the party is the mistake. The consent cannot be said to be free if it is caused by mistake.

Mistake may be defined as a wrong impression or erroneous opinion in the mind of a person about any subject matter, event or it may concern something.

According to section 20of this Act, "where both the parties to an agreement are under mistake as to the matter of fact essential to an agreement, the agreement is void". Thus it is clear that in case the consent of the party is induced by mistake the contract becomes void.

In the words of Salmond error in consensus prevents existence of any contract. It means, in some cases of fundamental error, a contract does not even exist between parties.

Surat Chander Vs. Kanai Lal (1921, Cal. 786). In this case Surat Chander was induced to sign a sale deed by Kanai Lal on representation that it was power of attorney. It was held that there was no contract due to error in consensus.

Mistake may be of two types.

(i) Mistake of Law, and

(ii) Mistake of fact

Mistake of Law again can be of two types:

(i) Mistake of Law of own Country

(ii) Mistake of Law of Foreign Country.

Mistake of law or own country: Sometimes the person may carry wrong impression in his mind regarding related provisions of law of his country. He may commit a mistake on the basis of that wrong impression and makes a contract. Such contract is binding. It is because, being citizen of the country he is expected to know the law of that country related to him. There is a general rule of law that 'ignorance of law is no excuse' and a person must be punished if he breaks the law- no matter he knows or does not know the law.

Example: A lends money to B and does not know law of limitation Act under which debt becomes time barred. Till the expiration of particular period of time he did not recover or made a notice of recovery of debt. That debt becomes time barred. So A cannot claim innocence of not knowing relevant provisions of the Act. Had he known it, he would have recovered it. The law will not excuse him for his ignorance.

But mistake related to law of foreign country renders a contract as void. According to section 21 of this Act, a mistake as to a law not in force in India, has the same effect as the mistake of fact has and, on account of mistake of fact contract becomes void.

Mistake of fact may also be of two types:

(i) Bilateral mistake

(ii) Unilateral mistake

Bilateral mistake: When both the parties of a contract are under mistake and mistake is related to material facts of subject matter of a contract, such mistake is known as mistake of fact. The contract affected by mistake of fact is void. Thus the contract will become void on account of mistake of fact provided the following conditions are satisfied.

(i) Both the parties of a contract must be under mistake

(ii) Mistake must be of a facts.

(iii) Mistake must be of a material fact of subject matter of a contract.

Bilateral mistakes of fact, related to material facts of subject matter of contract, are as under and the contracts are void under these situations

(a) *Existence of subject matter:* Both the parties of a contract are mistaken regarding existence of subject matter, the contract is void on account of mistake of fact. Such mistake occurs if at the time of making contract, the subject matter of contract ceases to exist, but the parties do not have knowledge of it.

Example: A agrees to buy some cargo from B which is being brought by a ship of B. But at the time of making a contract ship was sunk in the ocean. This fact was not known to them. The contract between A and B is void.

(b) ***Identity of subject matter:*** Identity of subject matter is also a material facts. When both the parties of a contract make mistake regarding identity of a subject matter, such contract will also be void.

Example: A has two cars Maruti 800 and Honda City. He makes an agreement for selling a car to B. A believes that he is selling Honda City and B thinks that he is making a contract to buy Maruti 800. Both of them are mistaken on the identity of subject thus the contract is rendered to be void.

(c) ***Ownership of subject matter:*** Where both the parties of contract commit a mistake regarding ownership of subject matter. Such contract is void due to bilateral mistake of fact.

Example: A has purchased a machine 10 years back on higher purchase basis. He is yet to pay last instalment. Believing that he has become owner of the machine he makes a contract to sell it to B. B thinks that A has been using that machine for the last 10 years, therefore he will be real owner of that machine. The contract is void.

(d) ***Quantity of subject matter:*** The quantity of subject matter to be supplied is also an essential fact of a contract. Therefore common mistake on the part of both parties will render such contract as void.

HANKEL VS. PAPE (1870, L.R.6 EX 7). In this case A inspected 50 rifles in a shop. Later on he telegraphed "send three rifles", But due to a mistake of the telegraph department it was made as, "Send the rifles". The shopkeeper sent 50 rifles. But A refused to accept delivery. It was held that, the contract is void because both the parties are under mistake regarding quantity of subject matter.

(e) ***Price of subject matter:*** When there is mutual mistakes on the part of both the parties regarding price of a subject matter, the contract is void. It is because price is also a material fact related to subject matter.

Example: A buys certain grocery items from B. While preparing a bill, the price of a particular item has been added twice by mistake. Contract is void on account of bilateral mistake of fact.

DAGADU VS. BHAN. (1904,38, BOM.42). In this case, A agreed to hire B's auditorium at Rs 800. But while writing an agreement the figure was written as Rs.1000 by mistake Agreement is void.

However, it is to be noted that when both parties of a contract make mistake regarding value of subject matter, the contract will not be void. It is because value of a particular subject matter differs from person to person depending on ones outlook, attitude, interest and hobby etc.

UNILATERAL MISTAKE

Mistake regarding subject matter on the part of one party only, is known as unilateral mistake.

According to section 22 of this Act, "a contract is not voidable merely because it was caused by one of the party to it being under mistake as to a matter of fact"

In other words, while entering in to a contract one of the party carries erroneous opinion about essential facts of subject matter. But another party understood those facts correctly. The contract will not be void.

SMITH VS. HUGHES (1871). In this case, a party bought oats from a vendor. A sample of which has already being shown to him. He erroneously thought that the oats were old. However the oats were new one. It was held that he had to suffer due to his own mistake and he could not avoid the contract.

Exceptions: But this rule is subject to certain exceptions, which are as under. In these exceptional cases, though the mistake is unilateral but agreement would be void.

(i) ***Mistake regarding nature of contract:*** When the party of a contract gives his consent under a mistake as to nature and character of a written document, such mistake may render the contract void.

In this regard, it is made clear that according to the judgement of Supreme Court if there is a fraud about character of document agreement is void.

Example: A is an old man who is being looked after by his relative B who has also been managing A's property. B states to A that part of his property is being given on lease to C and asks him to sign a document, which is in fact a gift deed in favour of B. A signs on it by mistake. Such deed is void, because there is fraud about a character of document.

(ii) ***Mistake regarding identity of a party:*** When one of the party of a contract is under mistake regarding an identity of another part, which is essential for performing a contract. Such contract is also void. Thus mistake regarding identity of party renders contract void provided such identity is essential for the performance of a contract.

Example: A agrees to sell his motor bike to B on credits believing that he is C. Contract is void, because A is under mistake regarding B's identity and identity of B is essential for performing a contract i.e. recovery of price from him.

LAKE VS. SIMMONS (1927, A.C. 487). In this case, a woman by falsely representing her to be the wife of well known Baron. She obtained two pearl neckless from a firm of jewellers on the pretex of showing them to her husband for the approval. She pledged them with a pawn broker who in good faith paid the $ 10000. It was held that here was no contract between the Jweller and woman thus even an innocent buyer did not get good title and must return them to the jwellers.

In this connection Sir William Anson has rightly pointed out that, "If a man accepts a offer which is plainly meant for another or if he becomes a party to a contract by falsely representing himself to be another, the contract in either case is void".

Effects of mistake: When the consent of the party is caused by mistake for a contract. Such contract is void and the following legal remedies are available to the parties.

(i) Any person, who gets any advantage in such contract, is bound to restore it or to make compensation for it to the person from whom he has received it (Section 65).

(ii) A person to whom money has been paid or any thing delivered by mistake must repay or return it to the party delivering it (Section 72)

REVIEW QUESTIONS

1. Define free consent and explain various elements of free consent in brief.
2. Free Consent is one of the essential of a valid contract. Comment.
3. Explain with suitable examples that how free consent and its various element affect validity of contract.
4. What is coercion? Explain various elements of coercion.
5. Distinguish between coercion and undue influence.
6. Define undue influence. Discuss those situations in which it is legally assumed that one party must have exercised undue influence to cause consent of another party.
7. What is misrepresentation? Explain various components of misrepresentation with suitable examples.
8. What do you mean by fraud? Explain contents of fraud with suitable examples.
9. Distinguish between fraud and misrepresentation.
10. What do you mean by 'Silence as fraud'. Explain its exception.
11. Define mistake. Discuss various types of mistakes and explain the effect of mistake on the validity of a contract.
12. What is mistake of fact? Under which situations contract becomes void on account of bilateral mistake regarding material facts of subject matter.
13. Define unilateral mistake. Discuss the circumstances in which contract becomes void by unilateral mistake.
14. Comment:
    (a) Making untrue statement regarding subject matter of contract is not fraud.
    (b) Unilateral mistake does not affect validity of contract.

(c) Mere silence on the part of the party is not fraud.
(d) Fundamental mistake regarding subject matter may not give a rise to contractual relation.
(e) Place at which coercion is used may not necessarily be with in the juridiction of IPC to prove it as coercion.
(f) Mistake of law is no excuse.

15. Write notes:
    (a) Pardanashin Woman
    (b) Contract of utmost good faith
    (c) Effects of fraud
    (d) Unconscionable transaction.
    (e) Bilateral mistake
    (f) Free Consent
    (g) Duress and Coercion

PRACTICAL PROBLEMS

1. A makes an agreement with B for buying his house and seeks the consent of B by threatening to file a suit against him .Is this a valid contract? (Hint; Yes
2. A kidnaps B's son and demands a ransom of Rs10, 000. B agrees to pay this amount to A. Does it amount coercion on the part of A. (Yes).
3. Ram sold his business to Shyam. Ram did not disclose it to his customers. Manohar sent. an order of goods to Ram. But Shyam received an order and without informing change of ownership he supplied goods to Manohar. Is there a contract between Manohar and Shyam. (Hint; No, because of fundamental error about identity of the party
4. X has two horses, one is black and another is white. He makes an agreement to sell one horse to Y. X believes that he is a making an agreement for selling white one, while as Y thinks that he is buying black horse.
   Is there any contract between X and Y (Hint; Yes, but the contract is void on account of bilateral mistake regarding materiel fact i.e. identity).
5. A has delivered some goods to B by mistake. Can he recover those goods from B. (Yes under section 72). B has consumed those goods. What legal remedy is available to A.
6. A has agricultural land in Delhi. He makes statement to B that he produces 100 tonnes of wheat per harvest from this land. B, by mistake enters into an agreement with A for buying that land on the basis of that statement. Later on it appears that hardly 50 tonnes of wheat can be produced in that land. Is contract between A and B valid. Can B avoid this contract? (Hint; Contract is voidable But B can avoid it because he had no reasonable means for discovering truth of the statement).

7. A applies for a loan to a banker at a time when there is stringency in the money market. The Banker declines to sanction the loan except at an exceptionally high rate of interest. A accepts the loan on those terms. Is the contract induced by undue influence? (Hint, No).
8. A agrees to buy some raw material from B at a particular price. B has got private information regarding change in the price level of that raw material. He does not disclose it to A, because it may affect A's willingness to make contract. Is this contract valid (Hint: Yes).
9. A has advanced money to B during his minority. Upon B becoming of major age A obtains a bond from B by using influence of B's parents for a greater amount than the sum due in respect of his advance. Can A enforce the loan? (Hint; No, because ratification of minor's agreement is not allowed).
10. A is already indebted to B, the money lender of his village. A seeks fresh loan from him. B grants loan at unreasonably high rate of interest. Is there any use of undue influence? (Yes, unconscionable transaction).
11. Manohar is manufacturing coloured Television sets. He gives an advertisement in the newspaper that the television sets being produced by him are the best available in the market. However he knows that there are many other companies, which are manufacturing television set better than produced by him, Does it amount to fraud? (No, Businessmen are supposed to make self commendation of their products).
12. A is enfeebled by disease of age is induced by B who is his attendant to pay B unreasonable amount for his professional services. Can B enforce agreement) (No. use of undue influence).
13. A young widow was forced to adopt a boy, under threat of preventing the dead body of her husband from being removed and getting cremated. Can widow set aside adoption deed? (Yes, use of coercion).
14. A enters into an agreement with B believing that he is C for selling goods on credit. Is there is any agreement between A and B. Can A enforce the agreement? (No).
15. Life Insurance Agent gives proposal to B for getting his life assured for a specific amount. B just thinking that he is 18 years old fills up it in the column of age. But actually he is 19 years old. Can L.I.C avoid this contract? (Yes, misrepresentation, innocent breach of duty).
16. A purchased shares in a company on the basis of information given in the prospectus. The prospectus contained a false statement that B was a director of the company. A never heard of B earlier. Can A recind the contract? (No, because false statement given in the prospectus is not a material fact for making contract of buying shares).
17. A threatened his wife and son to commit suicide if they did not agree to transfer A's house to his brother C. His wife and son agreed to it. Later on they file a suit to set aside the contract. Can they do it? (Yes).

■■■

Chapter **6**

Legality of Object

Learning Objectives

- Get familiar with the various objects of a contract.
- Examine legality of object.
- Be clear about legal object and lawful consideration.
- Develop conceptual clarity regarding Public Policy and agreements opposed to it

INTRODUCTION

Every contract is made for a object or purpose. The object of a contract is formed on the basis of promises made by the parties. The contract to be legally valid, must contain lawful object. When the contract is made for doing some thing illegal defeating provisions of the law such contract is not valid in the eyes of law.

According to section 10 of this act "all agreements are contract if they are for lawful consideration and with a lawful object. Lawful object means, intention to do something permissible with in the provisions of law".

However it is to be noted that in many cases the consideration and the object of a contract may be the same. But in all cases it is not necessary. But the object and consideration of an agreement must be lawful.

Example: A in consideration of Rs. one lac from B agrees to kill C. The object of this agreement is killing of C, which is illegal and punishable under Indian Penal Code.

Example: A, B and C agree to smuggle out some goods to D outside India. Again agreement is illegal.

According to section 23 of this act, consideration or object of an agreement is unlawful under the following situations.

1. IT IS FORBIDDEN BY LAW

There are many acts, which are forbidden, i.e. punishable under Indian Panel Code or under other laws. Thus if the object or consideration of any agreement is to do any of such act which is in contravention of provisions of the law such agreements are void on account of being illegal one.

Example: A is working at a higher capacity is some Govt. organization. In consideration of Rs. 50,000 he ensures employment to B in this organization. Agreement is void because of its illegal object.

Biggs Vs. Lawrence (1789, 3, T.R.454). In this case, a dealer agrees to sell certain goods to the buyer, knowing well that the goods are to be smuggled out of the country. It was held that the contract is unlawful.

2. IT DEFEATS THE PROVISION OF ANY OTHER LAW

If it is of such a nature that if permitted it would defeat the provision of any other law: it will be illegal one. When the agreement made by the parties is of such a nature that if it is permitted to continue it may lead to violation of the some provision of the law of land. Such agreements in fact involve indirect violation of the provisions of law. These agreements do not defeat the provisions directly, rather provisions of the law get defeated, when such agreements are allowed to continue.

Example: A has got house in Delhi. He pays house tax every year, which is calculated on the basis of rental value of that house. A, rents out his house to B for Rs. 5000 as rent per month and makes another agreement with B that of Rs. 5000, Rs. 2000 will be considered rent and remaining amount has been charged for other amenities. If this agreement is allowed to continue the house rent comes down from Rs. 5000 to Rs. 2000 and simultaneously rental value of the house is reduced which ultimately reduce amount of house tax to be paid to Municipal Corporation. Thus the agreement is void, because of unlawful object.

Example: Agreement by the person who has been declared insolvent to pay full amount to any of his creditor in preference to other creditors is void on account being unlawful under Insolvency Act.

Napier Vs. National Business Agency Ltd. (1951, 2 ALL.E.R.264). In this case, X agrees to enter Y's service in consideration of a weekly wage of Rs. 100 and weekly expense allowance of Rs 20. Both parties are aware that the expense allowance is a device to conceal the revenues. It was held that agreement is void, because it defeats the provisions of law.

3. IT IS FRAUDULENT

Fraud is considered as civil wrong or tort, which is punishable under the provisions of law. Thus any agreement made with a object of defrauding or deceiving anothers will be void on account of illegality of object.

Scott Vs. Brown. In this case T agrees to buy shares at premium in a Joint stock company through a broker S who has given as impression to the public that shares were useful of being purchased at a premium. Later on he found that broker has sold his own shares to him and not purchased any shares from the market. It was held that agreement was aimed at cheating the public and therefore is void.

Example: An agreement between A and B to defraud Govt. department by submitting tender in their names though they were both partners in transaction, is void as object is fraudulent.

4. IT INVOLVES AN INJURY TO A PERSON OR PROPERTY OF OTHER

Agreements made with an object or consideration of putting some person in to criminal or wrongful harm or damaging his property or reputation is void. It is because in all such cases intention is to harm to someone or his property.

Example: A promise to repay his debt by doing manual labour daily for a particular period of time and agrees to pay interest at an exorbitant rate in case of default. Such agreement is void, because consideration is illegal as it imposes slavery on the part of A.

Example: A in consideration of Rs. 10,000 from B agrees to publish defamatory material against C. agreement is void, because it involves injury to the reputation of C.

5. IT IS IMMORAL

When the object or consideration of an agreement is considered as immoral in the opinion of the court, such agreement will be void on account of unlawful object.

Among others, the immoral acts involve interference in a marital relationship, and the act of promoting or encouraging prostitution.

Example: A lets his house to B a prostitute knowingly that she will display her character there. Agreement is void A cannot recover rent from B.

Example: P had advanced money to D a married woman to enable her to obtain divorce from her husband. D agreed that as soon as she gets divorced she will marry with P. agreement between P and D is void on account of immorality.

6. IT IS AGAINST PUBLIC POLICY

The term public policy has not been defined under this Act. But in the name of public policy freedom of making a contract has been restricted by law only for the good of public.

Any agreement which goes against public policy and adversely affect public welfare, public decency, public cause and interest will be void.

It is therefore desirable to invoke 'doctrine of public policy' only in those areas where the damage to public interest and welfare is substantial. An attempt to enlarge scope of public policy will result in curtailment of individual's freedom to contract.

The courts have declared the following agreements oppose to public policy.

(i) ***Trading with alien enemy:*** In the event of war declared between two countries, citizens of those countries become alien enemy to each other. Taking into account national interest, no one is allowed to make an agreement with the citizens of enemy country. It is because it may help that country. The contracts made with that country before declaration of war will remain suspended till war continues. When the war is over such agreements can be enforced only with the permission of Government.

It is however to be noted that an agreement, which promote or encourage hostility with a friendly country is also considered oppose to public policy and therefore is void.

(ii) ***Trafficking in public office:*** Agreements, which interfere with the functioning of the public office and encourage corruption and inefficiency, are considered against public policy. Thus such Agreements are void on account of illegality of object. The word trafficking is used in the sense of doing business with public office for private again.

Example: A is a manager in public sector bank. He makes an agreement with B that in consideration of money he will provide employment to him in the bank. Such agreement is void, because in public office if there is any employment opportunity, every one who so ever is eligible has a right to avail it.

Example: A is a businessman who is to pay Rs. 2 lacs income tax for a particular financial year. He makes an agreement with some official in Income Tax depts. As a result of that agreement, A will pay Rs. 50,000 income tax and remaining part will be shared by A and income tax officer. Such agreement being opposed to public policy is void.

(iii) ***Interfering with course of justice:*** Impartial and independent functioning of judiciary is necessary. No one is allowed to interfere with an administration of justice. In every situation, it is ensured that law takes its own course. Any agreement which Interferes in the administration of justice either by influencing judge or the process of judgment is void as being against public policy. Agreements interfering with course of justice include following:

(a) *Stifling prosecution:* when some one commits a legal offence, he must be suitably punished under the provisions of law. An agreement, which protects the person from being prosecuted or reduces quantum of punishment in consideration of money is void.

General rule of law regarding it is "in public interest criminal should be prosecuted and punished. Any agreement not to prosecute the offender or to withdraw a pending prosecution is void if the offence is of a public nature"

BHAWANIPUR BANKING CORPORATION LTD. VS. DURGESH NANDANI (1941, A.I.R., P.C., 95). In this case, a mortgage was executed by Durgesh as a part of consideration for a promise by the bank to withdraw the criminal proceedings instituted against her husband by the bank. It was held that mortgage deed was void.

(b) *Reducing period of limitation:* agreement made by the parties which reduces period of limitation with in which an aggrieved party can enforce his right, is void. It defeats the object of law of limitation. According to law an action against the party making breach of contract must be taken with in three year from the date of breach. An agreement which makes this period shorter less than 3 years will be void.

(c) *Maintenance and champerty:* These two terms are related to promotion of litigation between the parties.

Maintenance includes those agreements, which are made with a view to promote litigation in which a person has no interest of his own.

On the other, Champerty includes an agreement whereby one party agrees to assist another in recovering property in a suit and to share such proceeds.

In England both agreements of maintenance and agreement of champerty are void if they are found against public policy.

NUTHAKI VENKATSWAMI VS. KATTA NAGI (1962, A.I.R. A.P. 457). In this case it was decided that an agreement to transfer ¾ share in the property if recovered has been held champertous and therefore void.

(iv) *Marriage brokerage agreements:* Marriage, being matter of one's life must be founded on mutual understanding between the parties. When the marriage is procured by some middleman, in consideration of money, such agreements are considered against public policy and thus are void.

Agreements to pay money as marriage brokerage that brings two parties in to matrimonial relationship are void, because these agreements hinder exercise of free choice by the parties.

PITAMBER VS. JAGJIVAN (13, BOMBAY 131). In this case a Purohit was promised Rs. 200 as consideration for procuring wife for a defendant. It was held that agreement is invalid and the money could not be recovered.

(v) *Agreement creating interest against professional duty:* In every profession the person who is engaged in it is subject to some obligations and duties. He is supposed to perform these to the best of his knowledge and capacity. Any agreement made by him, which goes against his duty and brings some personal gain to him, is void.

Example: A and B are partners in a partnership firm. A has been authorised to manage business of the firm. A makes secret profits in the business for him. Agreement of earning such profits is void because it creates interest against duty of a partner for not making personal gain.

(vi) *Agreement interfering with parental duties:* Parents and guardian have an authority and duty over their children. They are supposed to use it for the maximum welfare of their child. The authority of the parents cannot be transferred absolutely to another person. Agreements made for restricting parental authority or transferring such authority or interfering with such authority are void on account of being against public policy.

Example: A agrees to place his daughter at the disposal of B to be married according to her choice. This agreement is void and illegal because it interferes with a parental duty of A to find out suitable husband in the best interest of his daughter.

However, agreements of adoption duly made under Hindu Adoption and Maintenance Act are valid as an exceptions

(vii) *Agreements restraining personal freedom:* Article 21 of Indian constitution has guaranteed personal freedom to the citizens. Any agreement which takes away such personal liberty partially or completely is void being as oppose to public policy.

HARDWOOD VS. MILLARS TIMBER AND TRADING COY (1917, I.K.B., 305). In this case, A has borrowed some money from B who is a money lender and entered into an agreement with him that he will not change his residence, and employment or will work for the money lender at reduced salary. It was held that agreement is void and illegal, because it interferes with personal liberty of the person.

(viii) *Agreement interfering with marital duty:* After the marriage husband and wife owe certain duties to each other. Agreement which stops them from performing marital duties is void on the ground of being against public policy. Some of these agreements are as under.

(a) A promise by a married person to marry during the lifetime of the spouse or after his or her death.

(b) An agreement in contemplation of divorce e.g. an agreement to lend money to a woman in consideration of her getting divorce and marrying the lender.

(c) An agreement that husband and wife will always stay at the wife's parent's house or the wife will never leave her parental house.

UNLAWFUL VS. ILLEGAL AGREEMENTS

Unlawful agreement does not create any rights and obligations between parties and therefore cannot be enforced in the court of law. It is absolutely void and does not have any legal sanctity and consequences. In such agreements only the parties making agreements are affected.

On the other, illegal agreement is one, which cannot be enforced in the court and does not have any legal consequences. In such agreements not only the immediate parties are affected but collateral transaction which is based on illegal agreement will also be void.

Example: A in consideration of Rs. One lac from B agrees to kill C. For making payment to A, B borrows this amount from D and D knowingly lent the amount to B that it is to be paid to A who is to kill C. agreement between A and B is void and illegal. Another agreement between B and D is a collateral transaction based on first one will also be void.

All illegal agreements are unlawful, but all unlawful agreements are not illegal. Distinction between unlawful and illegal agreements can be made on the basis of the intention of the competent authority of making law.

When the law is made for protecting public and public interest any agreement which defeats provision of such law is illegal agreement on the other hand, if law is made for protecting revenue and administrative convenience and any agreement which violates the provision of such law is unlawful agreement.

Example: A agrees to sell 20 carets of liquor to B at a specified price. A does not possess licence for it. Such agreement is illegal and void. It is because sale of liquor without license is illegal and the object of prohibition is to protect the public.

Example: A has purchased a DDA flat. He constructs second floor on it without permission of DDA. He is liable to pay penalty. Such agreement is unlawful and void because it makes breach of law, which intended to protect revenue and administrative convenience.

CONSEQUENCES OF ILLEGAL AGREEMENT

(a) When the object of an agreement is to do some thing illegal which defeats provisions of the law, such agreement is void ab-initio. Such agreements do not create any right and obligation between parties and cannot be enforced in the court either by the parties.

(b) No legal remedy is available to any party and nothing can be recovered under illegal agreement. In other words, no action can be taken for the recovery of money paid or for the breach of agreement.

In the example given above if A kills C and B does not pay to A. A has no legal remedy for recovering Rs. one lac from B. and if B has paid money to A and A did not kill C, B can not recover this amount from A.

(c) Collateral transaction based on illegal agreement will also be void.

(d) Any party who has done illegal act will be prosecuted as per relevant provisions of the law.

REVIEW QUESTIONS

1. 'Agreement can be enforced only with lawful object and consideration' comment.
2. Discuss those situations under which object is considered to be unlawful.

3. Define illegal agreement. Explain its effect with suitable examples.
4. What is Public Policy? Explain the agreements, which are declared against public policy.
5. Comment:
   - (i) Every illegal agreement is unlawful, but every unlawful agreement is not illegal.
   - (ii) Consideration and object of agreement must be lawful to be enforced in the court.
   - (iii) No action is allowed in an illegal agreement.
6. Write notes on the following:
   - (a) Maintenance and Champerty.
   - (b) Illegal agreements.
   - (c) Agreements oppose to public policy.
   - (d) Effects of illegal agreement.
   - (e) Agreement of marriage brokerage.

Practical Problems

1. X is a section officer in a bank. He makes a promise in consideration of Rs. 20,000 from Y, to procure suitable employment for him in the bank. Is agreement valid? (Hint: No).
2. A rented out his house to B at a rent of Rs. 10,000 per month. In order to reduce municipal taxes A makes another agreement with B for reducing rent to Rs. 5000 and remaining amount will be charged for other services. Explain the validity of second agreement.
3. A borrows some money from B and makes an agreement that he will remain in employment with him unless he pays back money to B. Is it a valid agreement? (No).
4. Manohar agrees to kill Shyam in consideration of Rs. one lac from Hari. Hari borrows this amount from Shohan who knowingly lent money to Hari. Can Shohan recover this amount from Hari? (No).
5. A lent a sum of Rs. 50,000 to B who is to seek divorce from her husband and agrees to marry A. Can A recover this amount from B. (No).
6. Mohan has rented his house to a prostitute at certain amount of rent. Mohan knew that the prostitute will display her character over there. Can he claim rent from her. (No).
7. A in consideration of Rs. 10,00 from B enters into an agreement with him for publishing same objectionable material against C. Can A recover this amount from B? (No).

8. A is a businessman. He has a tax liability of Rs. 2 lacs in Income tax deptt. makes an agreement that he will deposit Rs. 50,000 as a tax and remaining balance will be shared equally by them. Is agreement valid? why? (No).
9. A has got a claim of Rs. 20,000 against B, he files suit against B for the recovery of his claim. C makes an agreement with A to help him financially. And in consideration of such promise A also makes a promise to give him ½ of proceeds recovered from B. A wins cause and refuses to pay any thing to C. can C recover his share from A? (Yes).
10. A has two daughters. After the marriage of second one he makes an agreement with her husband that both of them will stay with him and look after him so long he is alive. Is it a valid agreement? (No).

■■■

Chapter 7

Agreement Expressly Declared Void

Learning Objectives

- Understand the basic concept of agreements which are expressly declared void.
- Get knowledge about agreements in restraints of marriage, and legal proceedings.
- Examine agreements in restraint of trade.
- Understand difference between wagering agreements and other agreements.

INTRODUCTION

In general, an agreement becomes void if does not satisfy any one of the essentials of a valid contract. Such as agreements with minor, agreement without consideration, agreement with illegal object and agreement by the parties having no contractual capacity, etc.

Void agreements do not create any rights and obligations between parties and cannot be enforced in the court either by the parties.

In addition, there are many agreements, which have also expressly been declared as void by the law. Thus if agreement made by the parties falls in this category, such agreement will also become void. These agreements are as under:

1. Agreement in restraint of marriage (section 26).
2. Agreement in restraint of trade (section 27)
3. Agreement in restraint of legal proceedings (section 29)
4. Agreement meaning of which is uncertain (section 29)
5. Agreement by way of wager (section 30)
6. Agreement to do impossible act (section 56)

1. AGREEMENT IN RESTRAIN OF MARRIAGE (SECTION 26)

Every individual is at a liberty of getting married and enjoy marital status. For every reason law gives due recognition to such status.

An agreement which prevents the person from getting married or puts any hindrance in the process of marriage is void. Restrictions on marriage may be either absolute or partial in nature. In both the cases agreement will be void. When the person is prevented from marrying at all it is known as general restraint. On the other when he is restrained to marry particular person or person from particular community such restraint is particular. But the restraints will be void in both the cases.

This rule is subject to following exceptions:

(i) A promise to marry a particular person does not imply restraint of marriage.

(ii) Penalty imposed upon marriage under the provisions of law does not amount to any restraint.

(iii) Agreement, which prevents a minor from getting married, is valid.

However it is to be noted that in English mercantile law it is only an absolute restraint which is void and partial one is valid.

Lowe Vs. Peers (1768, 98, E.R. 160). In this case, P promised to marry with Miss L and in default he will pay her $ 1000. Later on, he got married with some one else. Miss L sued upon P for the recovery of that amount. It was held that the contract was in restraint of marriage and thus void.

2. AGREEMENT IN RESTRAINT OF TRADE (SECTION 27)

As per the Indian constitution every citizen has a right to start and conduct any lawful trade, industrial work or vocation. He can earn profit out of it. Thus an agreement which prevents the person from carrying such business is void. Not only this, but also an agreement that creates any hindrance in that process is void.

According to section 27 of this act, "every agreement is restraint of trade is to that extent void"

Example: A and B are doing business of timber at Kirti Nagar. Both of them are rivals to each other. To protect him from this rivalry A agrees to pay a sum of money to B provided B closes his business from this area. B closed his business but A refused to pay him. Agreement is void, ab-initio and therefore money cannot be recovered.

Agreement in restraint of trade may be either absolute or partial. But in both cases agreement will be void. However it is to be noted that if an agreement is divisible and partial restraint is upon particular part of an agreement only that part will be void.

There are certain exceptions to this rule. Some of them are statutory in nature and others are arising out of judicial interpretation of section 27.

(i) ***Sale of goodwill:*** Goodwill is known as name and fame of the firm. It refers to capacity of the firm to earn super profits on and above reasonable rate of return of the industry to which the firm belongs.

According to section 27(I), one who sells the goodwill of a business may agree with the buyer to refrain from carrying on a similar business, with in specified local limits so long as the buyer or any person deriving title to the goodwill from him carries on, a similar business therein.

In other words, when the owner of a business has earned a goodwill and makes an agreement for selling it to other. The buyers of the goodwill may prevent the seller from being in similar business. Such agreement as an exception is valid provided;

(a) Seller of goodwill is being prevented from doing similar business of which he is selling goodwill.

(b) Seller is prevented from carrying similar business with in specified local limits only.

(c) Such restraints have been imposed on the seller only for a reasonable period of time, e.g. so long as buyer derives benefits of goodwill.

Example: A is doing a business of steel goods at Moti Nagar, Delhi. A makes an agreement for selling goodwill of his business to B for Rs. one lack. In that agreement B prevents A from doing business of steel goods for two years in Moti Nagar. Such agreement is valid because restraints have been imposed on A only for Moti Nagar. He can do similar business in other local areas of Delhi; Secondly restriction is imposed for a particular period of time e.g. two years, which seems to be reasonable one.

(ii) ***Restrictions under partnership act:*** The Indian Partnership Act also provides certain exceptions to the rule of 'agreement in restraint of trade is void'.

These are as under:

(a) At the time of admission of a partner in the firm he makes an agreement with the firm that so long as he remains partner will not conduct similar business. Such agreement is valid through it restricts right of partner for doing business. Section 11(2) of Indian partnership act.

(b) Agreement made by outgoing partner for not doing business similar to that of firm for reasonable period of time with in specified local limits is also valid. Section 36(2) Indian Partnership Act.

(c) In anticipation of dissolution of the firm, agreement made by the partners for not carrying a business similar to that of firm for a particular period of time and with in specified local limits. Such agreement is also valid. Section 54 Indian Partnership Act.

(d) Any partner or firm on sale of goodwill enters into an agreement with the buyer for not doing business similar to that of firm for a particular period of time with in local limits. Such agreements are valid. Section 55(3).

Exceptions under judicial interpretation:

(i) *Trade combinations:* In practice, many agreements are made by the firms doing similar business. Agreements made with a primary objective of regulating business or conditions of a business are valid. Reasons being that such agreements are in the interests of all firms belonging to that business.

Such agreements may take a form of trade association, chamber of commerce and pools, etc. These are made by the firms voluntarily for reducing cut throat competition by dividing market, fixing prices and standardising goods. These agreements restrict liberty of the firms in conducting business, but by being in a larger interest these are valid as an exceptions.

On the other hand, agreements made by the various firms doing similar business with a view to create monopoly in the market are void. It is because monopolistic practices in the market may lead to exploitation of customers.

Example: There are four dealers of Maruti car in Delhi. They make an agreement for distributing entire market of Delhi among them. Each of them will function with in boundaries of the market allotted to him. An agreement among them is valid, because they made it to regulate the market of their product.

Example: In anticipation of huge sale of sweets during Diwali festival all sweet meat makers of Delhi make an agreement that they will not sell sweet below Rs.100 per kg. This agreement tends to create monopoly in the market, thus it is void.

Agreement tend to create monopoly are governed and regulated by the provisions of the Monopoly and Restrictive Trade Practices Act 1969.

(ii) *Sole selling agreements:* In practice manufacturers appoint agents for selling their products. They may give this right only to a particular agent on distributor who may be refrained from dealing in goods of other manufacturers. Such agreements are valid, though freedom of sole selling agent or distributor is restricted. These agreements are considered part of common commercial practice among businessmen for promoting their business.

Example: Tata Tele services Ltd appoints A as their sole selling agent, making an agreement with him that he will not deal in the goods of other Teleservice companies. Such agreement is valid.

It is however, to be noted that such agreements should not create hardship either for manufactures or purchasers by creating monopolistic trends in the market. In such cases, such agreement may be declared void.

S. Kallu Vs. Ramsaran Bhagat. In this case a person agreed to buy all combs manufactured by all the manufacturers in Patna. Such agreement was declared to be oppressive and monopolistic. Thus it is void.

(iii) *Service contracts:* When the person is appointed as an employee in a particular organisation. As a matter of condition of service agreement he may be restricted by his employer from doing similar job outside. Such agreement is valid. For instance doctors of government hospitals are usually debarred from conducting private practice, so long as they remain in the employment with Govt. hospitals.

But such restraint on the employee is valid only during his employment. When he leaves the organisation or is terminated from the service he may be engaged in similar job outside the organisation.

It is to be noted that the service restraint put on the employee must be reasonable one, which differs from case to case depending on nature of job and other factors.

Lumley Vs. Wagner (1852, I.D.M.C., 604). In this case Miss Wagner agreed to sing at the theatre of Mr. Lumley for three months and will not sing elsewhere. It was held that she can be restrained from singing elsewhere during the period of three months.

Charlesworth Vs. Mcdonald (1898, 23, Bom.103). In this case, M agreed to work with Dr. C. at Zanzibar for a period of three years. The contact provided that during the term of agreement M will not practice on his own account at Zanzibar. However after one year of service, M left the service and started his own practice at Zanzibar. It was held that agreement was valid and Dr. C was entitled to get injunction, restraining M from practicing at Zanzibar during the period of agreement.

3. AGREEMENT IS RESTRAINT OF LEGAL PROCEEDINGS (SECTION 29)

Jurisdiction of court or law cannot be restricted by any agreement. Every one who is entitled to a legal course can adopt it. And let the law take its own course.

Thus any agreement, which interferes with the course of justice or prevents the person from taking legal course, is void. Similarly, any agreement which limits time period with in which one can enforce his right arising out of contract is void.

According to section28 (a) of this Act, 'every agreement by which any party thereto is restricted absolutely from enforcing his rights under or in respect of any contract, by the usual legal proceedings in the ordinary tribunal's or which limits the time with in which he may thus enforce his rights is void to that extent'.

It is clear that the access to normal course of law for enforcement of agreement cannot be denied to themselves by the parties.

However it should be noted that restraints to legal proceedings must be absolute. If it is partial agreement will not be void.

Following are the exceptions to section 28.

(i) *Arbitration of present dispute:* When some dispute is going on between the parties. They make an agreement that instead of going to the court, they refer is to an arbitration. Such agreement is valid, though they cannot agitate for the same dispute in the court.

(ii) *Arbitration of future dispute:* In anticipation of some dispute, the parties enter in to agreement that in case any dispute arises, it will be referred to an arbitration. Such agreement is valid.

However an agreement that the validity of an award shall not be objected on any ground, by any party entitled to, in an appropriate court is void.

4. AGREEMENT MEANING OF WHICH IS UNCERTAIN (SECTION 29)

To enforce an agreement in the court it's meaning must be certain or capable of being made certain. Any uncertainty in the meaning of agreement will create uncertainty regarding rights and obligations. Such uncertain rights and obligations cannot be claimed in the court of law.

Thus, an agreement, which is ambiguous or vague in it's meaning, creating confusion about basic nature of it, cannot be enforced in the court of law.

Example: A agrees to buy 10 liters of oil from B who is a dealer of kerosene oil and mustard oil. Agreement is void on account of uncertain meaning.

Example: A has got agricultural land in Delhi. He agrees to sell entire crop of wheat next year to B at specified rate. Agreement is valid, because it's meaning would become certain with the passage of time when the crop of wheat will mature.

Montreal Gas Coy Vs. Vasey (1900, A.C. 595). In this case, Gas coy agreed with Vasey that at the expiration of Vasey's existing contract of service, the company would favourably consider the renewal of the contract. It was held that agreement was void, it is because there is uncertainty in the meaning of agreement, and thus no obligation will arise.

Example: A agrees to sell his motorbike to B for a price which will be determined by C, agreement is valid, because the price can be very well determined by C.

5. AGREEMENT BY WAY OF WAGER (SECTION 30)

Wagering agreement is one in which money is to be paid by one to another party or vise versa on the happening or non-happening of future uncertain event. If the event turns in one way one party is to pay to another and on the turning of event in another way, another party will pay to first one. But in every case, whether event happens or does not happen, payment of money is to be made.

In the words of William Anson, wager may be defined as, 'a promise to give money or moneys worth upon the determination or ascertainment of an uncertain event'.

In wagering agreement either of the party is to win or to lose. Thus if one loses another will win or vice versa.

Essential of wagering agreement:

(i) *Mutual gain or losses:* There are two parties in wagering agreement. One of the parties will win and another party will lose. Their gain or loss depends on the happening or non-happening of future uncertain events. That party will lose if event happens who has promised payment of money on the happening of the event and vice versa.

Example: Cricket match is going on in Pakistan, between India and Pakistan. A agrees to pay a sum of Rs. 20,000 to B if India wins and if India loses B will pay same amount to A. This is wagering agreement made by the parties for their mutual loss or gain.

(ii) *Uncertain event:* The performance of wagering agreement depends on happening or non-happening of a future uncertain event. The event is not uncertain because it is to happen in future, but it is more uncertain because its result is not at all known to the parties. Both the parties of an agreement keep on guessing about happening or non- happening of future event.

(iii) *Interest of the parties:* Parties of wagering agreement do not have any interest on the happening or non-happening of that event. They simply look at the possibility of happening of the event for their gain or loss. They contemplate the determination of the uncertain event as sole condition of their contract.

(iv) *Control over the event:* In wagering agreement, there is no control of the parties, on the happening of the event. Event is an independent one, which may or may not happen, but its own way. There is no influence of the parties on it. If any of the party has a control over the event, it will not be considered as wagering transaction.

According to section 30 of this act 'Agreement by way of wager are void. And no suit shall be brought for recovering anything alleged to be won by any wager or entrusted to any person to abide by the result of any game or other uncertain event on which any wager is made'.

Effect of wagering agreement:

(i) Wagering agreement are void. Therefore the winner cannot recover amount which other party had to pay.
(ii) Agreement by way of wager is just void and unenforceable. The collateral transaction based on such agreement are not affected and thus are valid.

However in the state of Maharastra and Gujarat, such wagering agreements are not only void, but illegal also.

Example: A agrees to pay Rs. 5000 to B if cricket player Dhaumi makes out century in the match going on between India and West Indies. A borrows this amount from C who knowingly lent this amount to him. In the state of Maharastra and Gujarat C cannot recover this amount from A, but in other states he can recover it.

The following transactions are included in wagering agreement:

(i) *Speculative transactions:* These transactions are made in stock exchanges. These transactions are related to purchase and sale of shares and other securities of the companies. In these transactions, parties are intended to buy or sell securities with a prime motive of making profit out of changes in the market value of these securities. In speculative transactions, payments of price, delivery of securities and transfers of ownership do not take place. Simply on the date of settlement of transaction, a difference in market value of the securities is calculated and paid either to the party. Though such transactions are allowed in stock exchanges, but are void.

Example: A agrees to buy 100 shares of X coy at the price Rs. 250 per share from B on 1st of January. On due date of transaction no real sale or purchase takes place, rather difference between agreed price and market price is calculated and paid to the party accordingly.

(ii) *Transactions of lotteries:* A lottery is a game of chance. An agreement to buy a lottery ticket is void. Thus if some one buys lottery ticket and wins the prize. Legally he cannot recover it from the party conducting the business of lottery. But in fact various state Govts. have permitted government deptt. or other agencies for conducting this business. Still transactions of lottery remain void. Only effect of such authorisation is that persons conducting business of lotteries are not to be prosecuted.

(iii) *Horse race and gambling transaction:* These transactions are also included in wagering transactions and therefore void. Gambling is an offence under Indian Panel Code, thus any transaction on gambling will be void.

So far as, transactions of horse race are concerned, agreement to pay less than Rs. 500 to the winner of the horse race is void. But to subscribe Rs. 500 or more to the winner of the horse race is valid.

(iv) *Crossword puzzle:* In a crossword puzzles winning of the puzzle may be the matter of chance and involves manipulation of words and does not require special skills. Such puzzles are considered as lottery transaction and thus are void.

However the following transactions are resembling with wagering transactions, but are not of a wagering nature.

(i) *Purchase of shares and debentures:* Transaction of real and genuine sale and purchase of shares and other securities in stock exchange is not of wagering nature. In these transactions shares are actually delivered, ownership in transferred and payment of price is made. These transactions are absolutely valid.

(ii) *Competition and crossword puzzles:* To win a prize in any competition including athletic competition or debate competition, etc. or cross word puzzle is a valid transaction. It is because such competitions do require special skill and talent on the part of participants. Thus if someone wins a prize, he can legally recover it from the party organising such competition.

(iii) *Insurance contract:* Insurance contract is a contract whereby the insurance company in consideration of payment of premium from the insured promises to compensate his losses arising out of insured cause. These contracts are valid.

Such contracts differ from wagering agreements on the following grounds.

(a) In insurance contract the party (insured) has insurable interest on subject matter. It is only to protect such interest he makes an agreement. But in wagering agreements parties have no interest on the event. They are only interested in winning.

(b) In insurance contract, on the happening of uncertain event actual losses of the party are compensated by the insurance company. But in wagering agreement only stipulated amount will be paid to the winning party.

(c) Insurance contracts are considered in the interest of the society and therefore encouraged. But wagering transactions do not serve any interest of the society, rather encourage gambling.

(d) In insurance contract, the amount of premium is determined on scientific way, keeping in view degree of risk involved. But in a wagering agreement, to determine amount of loss or gain has no basis at all.

ALMAI VS. POSITIVE, GOVERNMENT SOCIETY LIFE ASSURANCE COMPANY (1889, 23, BOM. 191). In this case, Almai insured the life of Mrs. X, a wife of his employee for a term of 10 years and for Rs. 25000 with a insurance coy. The policy was assigned to Almai. Mrs. X died a year later. A filed suit for the recovery of the amount of policy. It was held that it was a wagering transaction, because A had no insurable interest in the life of Mrs. X, therefore A cannot recover the amount.

AGREEMENT TO DO IMPOSSIBLE ACT (SECTION 56)

Section 56 of this act states that 'an agreement to do an act impossible in itself is void'.

When the parties make an agreement to do something impossible, such agreement has been expressly declared void by law.

Example: A, in consideration of Rs. 10,000 agrees to discover treasure with the help of magic. Agreement is void due to impossibility of act.

Impossibility may arise in the contract, after its formation, due to change in law or any other reason, beyond the control of parties. Such impossibility is known, as supervening impossibility and the contract affected by it, will be void.

When one party makes a promise for doing something which he knew or must have known with reasonable diligence that is impossible and promisee did not know it. Such promisor must pay compensation to the promisee for any loss, which he suffers, because of non- performance of contract.

Example: A contracts to marry B who is already married to C. and being prohibited by law to practice polygamy. A must pay compensation to B for a loss caused to her by non-performance of a promise.

Right of restitution in void contract: According to this right, when contract becomes void, the party who has received any benefit under it must restore it to the other party. In case, restoration is not possible he must compensate to another party. This right is claimed by the party from whom other party has got benefit. It is based on the principle of justice and equality.

Section 64 and 65 of this act deal with this right. According to section 64, a party who is entitled to avoid contract if does so, he shall restore any benefit received by it to the person from whom it was received.

Section 65 gives a right of restitution to the party concerned under the following situations.

(a) *When an agreement is discovered to be void:* when parties make an agreement but it is not enforceable, such agreement does not become a contract. Thus in such an agreement one party who has received some benefits must return it or compensate other party.

(b) *When a contract becomes void:* A contract has been entered into between the parties. But due to impossibility of performance arising after a formation of contact it cannot be performed. Such contract becomes void. A party who has received any benefit under it he must restore it to the party from whom such benefit has been received.

However when the agreement has been expressly declared void by the law under various sections, no restitution is allowed in these cases.

Example: A agrees to sell his car to B for Rs. onc lac. B pays Rs. 50,000 as an advance. Before sale takes place the car has been stolen. The contract becomes void on account of impossibility of performance. Thus A should return Rs. 50,000 to B.

Example: A in consideration of Rs. 10,000 from B agrees to discover treasure by magic. B has paid Rs. 2000 as an advance. A fails to discover treasure. B cannot recover money given in advance, because this agreement has expressly been declared void by law.

REVIEW QUESTIONS

1. Discuss agreements, which have been expressly declared as void by the law.
2. 'Agreements in restraint of trade are void', explain exceptions to this rule.
3. 'Agreements interfering with legal course are void'. Explain exceptions to this rule.
4. Distinguish between wagering agreements and insurance contracts.
5. What do you mean by the term 'wagering agreement'. Discuss various wagering transactions with suitable examples.

6. Comment on the following:
   (a) Agreement in restraint of marriage are void.
   (b) Meaning of an agreement must be certain.
   (c) transactions which resemble with wagering transaction are valid.
   (d) Agreement in restraint of legal proceeding are void.
   (e) Void agreement are different from void contracts.
7. Write short note on:
   (a) Wagering agreement.
   (b) Right of restitution.
   (c) Uncertain agreements
   (d) Characteristics of wagering agreements.

Practical Problems

1. A agrees to marry B and non-else except her. If A defaults he will pay a sum of Rs. One lac to B. Later on, A got married with someone else. L. filed a suit for the recovery of that amount. Will he succeed to get it? (No, agreement is void).
2. A and B are doing business of computer spare parts in Delhi separately. They are rivals to each other. In order to reduce cut throat competition they agree to divide market of Delhi in two parts and allot these parts to themselves. Later on A sells computer spares in one of the areas of the market belonging to B. suggest legal remedy to B.
3. Ram made an agreement with B to sell all his produce at a specified rate with a condition that B was bound to accept the whole quantity. Is it a valid agreement. (Yes).
4. Ram and Shyam are two rival shopkeepers in a particular colony of Delhi. They make an agreement that if Ram closes his shop from the colony, Shyam will pay him Rs.20000. later on Shyam refused to pay. Can Ram recover this amount from Shyam (Hint: No, agreement is void ab-initio).
5. While admitting A into partnership as a partner the firm makes an agreement with him that so long he is a partner in the firm he will not do business similar to that of partnership firm. Is it a valid agreement? (Hint: yes, exception to the agreements in restraint of trade are void).
6. A was employed with B as an assistant. B makes an agreement with him that so long as he is working with him, he will not be allowed to get engaged in similar work, but A takes up a similar kind of job outside on part time basis. Suggest legal remedy to B.
7. All dealers of a particular commodity in a particular market enter into agreement that they will not sell the product for less than agreed price. Is it a valid agreement? (No it tends to create monopoly)

8. Manohar was appointed as an agent for selling the goods produced by Sohan. On a condition that Manohar will not deal in goods of any other manufacturer. Is such restraint valid? (Hint: Yes, the principle can put such restraints on his agent).
9. A agrees to pay Rs. 5000 to B if it rains today. And if it does not rain B will pay some amount to A. Is it valid agreement.
10. Ram agrees to pay a sum of Rs. 1000 to the winner of horse race at Racecourse Delhi. Examine validity of this agreement.
11. A agrees to discover treasure with the help of magic and B pays Rs. 2000 to A for his promise. A fails to do so. Can B recover this amount from A? (No agreement is void ab-initio).

■■■

Chapter 8

Quasi-Contracts and Contingent Contracts

Learning Objectives

- Try to understand logic behind quasi-contract.
- Compare quasi-contract with other contracts.
- Examine various types of quasi-contracts.
- Get familiar with contingent contracts.
- Compare contingent contract with wagering agreements.
- Analyse an enforceability of contingent contracts.

MEANING AND DEFINITION

Quasi-contract implies creation of legal rights and obligations between parties without making any formal contract. In quasi-contracts, the parties do not go into the process of offer and acceptance, rather a relationship resembling with that of a contract is established between them from the circumstances or by operation of law. The law imposes such obligations on the parties, which are similar to that created by contract. Thus such cases are known as quasi-contractual obligations or quasi-contracts.

Briefly speaking, a quasi-contract is created by law or circumstances. The obligation created by quasi-contracts can be enforced in the court in similar manner as in case of a formal contract. It is therefore quasi-contracts are known as 'relations resembling those created by contracts' in Indian contract Act.

The term 'quasi-contracts' has been used in English law. In the words of Pollock,

'Quasi-contracts are a contract in law but not in fact, being the subject matter of fictitious extention of the sphere of a contract to cover obligations which do not, in reality, fall with in it'.

This definition makes it clear that quasi-contracts are simply an extention of formal contract.

WHY QUASI-CONTRACTS

The concept of Quasi-contracts is based on the principle of equity and justice. According to this principle, nobody will be allowed to be enriched at the expense or cost of another person. If he gets benefit unjustly he must pay its cost to the person from whom he derives it.

Sometimes he may not so easily be paying its cost, in such situations law will impose obligation upon him to pay the cost.

Lord Mansfield has rightly pointed out that 'law as well as justice should try to prevent unjust enrichment of one person at the cost of another; in one word, the gist of this kind of action is that the defendant, upon the circumstances of the case, is obliged by ties of natural justice and equality to refund the money'.

Lord Wright has stated that, 'it is clear that only system of law is bound to provide remedies for cases of what has been called unjust enrichment or unjust benefits, that is, to prevent a man from retaining the money of or some benefit derived from another which is against conscience that he should keep'.

On the basis of these statements it is clear that;

(a) If the person has got payment of money or any other benefit unjustly under any circumstances. He must not retain it.
(b) Such benefit or payment should be returned back to the person from whom it has been received.
(c) In case benefit has been consumed, its cost should be paid or should be compensated for that loss.
(d) Both parties should be put in equal footing. One should not unjustly get benefit and another unjustly should not suffer a loss.

Section 73 of thus Act provides that, 'when an obligation resembling those created by contract has been incurred and not been discharged, any person injured by the failure to discharge is entitle to receive same compensation from the party in default as if such person has contracted to discharge it and has broken his contract'.

From the above, it is clear that, when the person fails to discharge his obligation arising out of Quasi-contract, another party will get legal remedies as if the contract in broken.

TYPES OF QUASI-CONTRACTS

The Indian Contract Act provides for five types of quasi-contracts, which are contained in section 68 to 71 of this Act.

1. ***Supply of necessaries to the person having no contractual capacity or to his dependent:*** Agreements made by the person who has no contractual capacity are void. These agreements cannot be enforced in the court of law. But agreements made by such person to procure necessaries for him or for his dependent carry different legal consequences. And supplier of necessities is legally entitled to recover the cost of such supplies provided:

(a) Articles supplied or money paid is basic necessity of life.
(b) It was supplied to him or to the person whom he is bound to support.
(c) Reasonable cost of such supplies is recoverable and not a contracted price.
(d) Necessaries should have been supplied with an intention of getting payment for it.

Example: A is lunatic having no contractual capacity. B 'a grocery merchant' has supplied grocery items for five months to fulfil the basic needs of the family of such person. Agreement is void, but B is entitled to recover reasonable cost of these items from the property of lunatic if any.

Nash vs. Inman (1908, 2 KBI). In this case, a minor studying at Cambridge was supplied with clothing including eleven waistcoats. He already had sufficient clothing with him. It was held that waistcoats were not basic necessities of the life. It is because he was adequately provided with articles of that kind. Thus he is not liable to pay for them.

To determine the basic necessities of life, facts of individual case, such as social status and financial position will be taken care of.

2. *Reimbursement of payment made by a person who is interested but which another person is legally bound to pay (section 69):* In many cases it happens that one party makes a payment, because he is interested in that payment. But liability for making that payment lies on another person. Thus on making such payment, the person liable to pay has to reimburse it to the person who has made the payment.

For making that person liable, the following conditions must be satisfied.

(a) Plaintiff must have some interest in making the payment. That interest must be legal, recognizable and bonafide.
(b) Plaintiff must have made payment for protecting his bonafide interest. And payment should have been made by him to another person or organization.
(c) But that payment must be liability of defendant. He should be bound to pay. Such liability may be either contractual or statutory in nature

Example: A has got a house in Delhi. He has rented it to B. Regarding that house; municipal taxes have not been paid by him. And due to huge arrears of taxes Municipal Corporation has proposed auction of that house if arrears are not paid by a stipulated date. On being aware of this fact, A makes payment of the arrears.

Though there is no formal agreement between A and B, but B is legally bound to reimburse A.

In this case B was under legal obligation to pay municipal taxes. But A who is a tenant in that house has interest in protecting it from being auctioned. It is therefore to protect this interest he makes payment. He is entitled to recover it from B.

3. *Obligation to pay for non-gratuitous act or service (section 70):* Sometimes, a person may render some services or do some act for another person. That person does such act voluntarily with an intention of getting its return. Thus the person who gets benefit of such acts or services is liable to compensate the person doing such act or rendering services. But the following conditions must be satisfied.

(a) The service rendered or act done by the party must be lawful. It is clear that for unlawful act, no payment can be recovered.

(b) Services must have been rendered voluntarily with out any request. The intention of the person rendering services must be to get compensation for those services. If he renders services gratuitously, he is not entitled for the payment.

(c) The person for whom services have been rendered or act has been done must have got its benefit. If he is not benefited he is not bound to pay for.

Example: A's house is in fire. B who is passers by helped A in extinguishing fire with out A's request. B did it with an intention of getting compensation for his services. A is under legal obligation to compensate B for the services rendered by him.

However, section 70 of this act is not applicable on the person having no contractual capacity. If such person gets benefit of services rendered by other, he is not bound to pay.

4. *Rights and duties of the finder of lost goods (section 71):* A person who finds goods lost by another person. On his being taken custody of those goods, certain rights and obligations are created on his part without any formal contact. These rights and obligations are against the person who has lost goods or who is owner of the goods. Such rights and obligation are resembling with that of a formal contract and can be enforced in a similar manner. Obligations of finder of goods are as under:

(a) To take reasonable care of goods, as he would have taken in case of his own goods.

(b) To make reasonable efforts for tracing owner of those goods.

(c) Not to make use of those goods.

(d) On finding real owner to return goods to him.

Rights of finder of goods:

(a) To make claim for expenses paid by him for the maintenance of goods.

(b) To keep possession of goods.

(c) To claim for reward if any.

(d) To exercise lien over the goods for expenses and reward.

(e) To sell goods under certain circumstances.

Example: A has lost his pet dog. Not being able to find it out he announces that whosoever finds it and returns it back to him, he will suitably reward him. D found that dog and took custody of it. By making reasonable efforts he could find owner of that dog. On tracing him B claimed expenses which he incurred for the maintenance of dog and reward. A is bound to pay both expenses and reward to B.

5. *Liability of person to whom money is paid or things delivered by mistake or under coercion:* (under section 72) where the person has delivered some goods or has made payments of money to another person either by mistake or under coercion. Such person is under legal obligation to return it to the person delivering. In case he has consumed it, he will pay compensation.

Example: A Railway company refuses to deliver certain goods to the consignee, except upon the payment of illegal charge of carriage. And the consignee was bound to pay such charges to get goods released from the Railway company. He is entitled to recover these charges from Railway coy.

Money paid under mistake is recoverable. Mistake may be mistake of the fact or law. It implies equitable restitution. When the person makes payment believing that it is due, but in reality it is not. He has right to recover it.

SALES TAX OFFICER VS. KANHAIYA LAL MUKUNDWALA SARAF (1959, S.C.J. 53). In this case levy of sales tax imposed on forward transaction having been held to be ultra vires by Allahabad high Court. The respondent claimed refund of money paid under mistake of law. It was held that the party paying such levy is entitled to get the refund.

However it is to be noted that for applying section 72 of this act undue pressure on the party is enough to prove coercion. And an interpretation of this term is not same as it is under section 15 of this act. In other words co-ercison, in this context, has been used in more popular and practical way.

Section 72 of this act does not apply on the following cases:

(a) Natural obligation demands that if it discharged, party discharging it has no right to recover it. Repayment of time barred debt is a suitable example of it.

(b) When the party makes payment by making deliberate disregard to law, such payment cannot be recovered. For example if the party makes the payment voluntarily and Knowingly well that the contract is void he can not recover such payment.

CONTINGENT CONTRACTS

MEANING AND DEFINITION

Contract is a mutual exchange of promises between the parties. These promises are got to be performed on the due dates. But in many cases the performance of a contract instead depends on the happening or non-happening of some future uncertain event. Such contracts are known as contingent contract.

According to section 31 of this act, 'A contingent contract is a contract to do or not to do some thing, if some event, collateral to such contract does or does not happen'.

It is clear from the above definition that contingent contracts are conditional in nature. The condition is related to the performance of such contract. In other words, the performance of a contract is dependent on the happening or non-happening of future uncertain event.

However it is to be noted that the collateral event must be independent and ancillary to the contract. It should not be a performance of promise by the promisor or consideration given to him.

Example: A agrees to pay sum of Rs. 20000 to B, if his house gets a fire. Contract between A and B is a contingent contract. The performance of it depends on breaking of fire in B's house.

FEATURES OF CONTINGENT CONTRACTS

(i) It must satisfy all essential conditions of a valid contract, such as consideration, contractual capacity and free consent etc.

(ii) The performance of a contingent contract depend on the happening or non-happening of an event in future.

(iii) That event must be uncertain, and contingency will arise only if it's happening or non-happening is quite uncertain.

(iv) That event must be collateral to the main contract. Collateral event means, neither it is performance of a promise on the part of a promisor nor it constitutes any consideration for the promise of the promisor. Rather the event is independent and ancillary to a contract.

In the example of contingent contract given above, payment of money by A will be made on breaking of fire in the house of B. fire in B's house is not a consideration for A's promise and nor it is a performance of a promise on the part of A. It is an independent event which is ancillary to the contract between A and B.

RULES REGARDING CONTINGENT CONTRACT (SECTION 32 TO 36)

1. *Contingency on happening of an event (section 32):* The contract, which is contingent on the happening of the future uncertain event, will be performed only when the event occurs. It's performance is conditional on the happening of an event. Thus it cannot be enforced unless such event occurs. Due to any reason if the happening of that event becomes impossible or it does not occur, such contract becomes void.

Example: A agrees to sell some goods to B, which are being brought by ship coming to Bombay. But the ship sinks in the ocean. Agreement becomes void, because happening of an event upon which performance of contract depends has become impossible. And this agreement will be performed only if ship returns to Bombay.

2. *Contingency on non-happening of an event:* when the performance of contingent contact depends upon non-happening of future uncertain events; on the occurrence of that event, agreement becomes void. The obligation to perform it will arise only when that event does not happen or it's happening has become impossible.

Example: A promise to pay sum of Rs. 2000 to B if B's ship does not return from United Kingdom. On the return of ship agreement becomes void. The liability of A to pay will arise only when ship does not return on it has sunk in the ocean, as to make it impossible to return.

3. *Contingency of human conduct:* when the performance of a contingent contract depends upon the happening of the future uncertain event which is contingent on the behavior or conduct of the third party at the specified time. When that third party does any act, which renders happening of that event impossible; such contract will become void.

Example: A agrees to rent out second floor of his house to B, provided D.D.A gives him permission for constructing second floor. D.D.A refused to give him the permission, contract becomes void. The performance e.g. renting out of second floor of the house depends on the construction of that floor. Which is contingent on the permission to be given by D.D.A and on the refusal, of permission such contract becomes void.

4. *Contingency on the happening of an event with in stipulated time:* The contract, which is contingent on the happening of some future uncertain event within stipulated time. Such contract can be enforced only if that event happens with in that stipulated period of time. In case happening of such event becomes impossible even before that time, such contract becomes void.

Example: A has taken final examination of graduation. Provisionally he has been allowed to appear in bank examination subject to passing of examination of graduation within two months. If he fails in that examination even before two months, he ceases to be eligible for that job. And if the result is not declared within two months, his eligibility for a job comes to an end.

5. *Contingency on non-happening of an event with in the stipulated time:* Contrary to earlier one, when the performance of a contract depends on non happening of some event with in stipulated period of time, if the event occurs with in that, contract becomes void. And the contract can be enforced if till the expiration of that time, that event does not occur. When, before that time happening of that event becomes impossible, the contract can be enforced.

Example: A agrees to pay a sum of Rs. 5000 to B if B's ship does not return to Bombay with in three months. When the ship returns to Bombay within that time the promise of A becomes void. But if ship sinks into ocean before that time or does not return to Bombay A will be liable to pay.

6. *Contingency on the happening of impossible event:* Contingent contract to do or not to do some thing if an impossible event happens is void. It is insignificant that the impossibility was known or not known to the parties at the time of making a contact. Impossible event cannot happen, thus contract based on it will also be void.

Example: A agrees to pay Rs. 20000 to B if he discovers treasure with magic. This agreement is void, because its performance is based on happening of impossible event.

Table Difference between wagering transaction and contingent contract.

	Wagering agreements	*Contingent contract*
Meaning	It implies promise to give money upon the determination of an uncertain event.	It is a contract to be performed on the happening or non happening of some uncertain event, collateral to it.
Validity	Wagering agreements are void.	Contingent contracts are valid subject to conditions.
Mutual Promise	It consists of mutual promises. money will be paid either in case and either to party.	It is to be performed on happen ing or non happening of some uncertain event.
Interest of Party.	in wagering agreements parties do not have any interest on the happening or non-happening of that event.	in contingent contract, one or both the parties may have some interest on the event.
Nature of event.	In wagering agreement future event is determining factor	But in a contingent contract future event Is collateral to a contract.

REVIEW QUESTIONS

1. What is a quasi-contract? Explain behind quasi-contract.
2. Discuss the various types of quasi-contracts with the help of suitable examples?
3. Quasi-contracts are not formal contracts, but these are the obligations created by law?
4. In certain cases, law imposes an obligation and allows an action to be taken on it, as if it arises out of a contract. Explain it with examples?
5. Discuss rights and duties of finder of goods.
6. 'A person shall not be allowed to enrich himself at the cost of others'. Comment.

7. Does the law of contract impose any obligation on the person enjoying benefits of a non-gratuitous act of another person done for the former? Explain it by citing suitable examples.
8. Comment on the following:
   (a) Quasi contacts are based on the principal of equity and justice?
   (b) Obligation resembling that of a formal contact carry some legal consequence.
   (c) Gratuititous acts are to be compensated.
   (d) Money paid by mistake is recoverable.
9. What is contingent contract? Explain essential features of contingent contract.
10. Discuss the rules regarding contingent contract?
11. Performance of contingent contract depends on happening or non-happening of some future uncertain events.
12. Distinguish between wager agreements and contingent contract.

PRACTICAL PROBLEMS

1. A in consideration of Rs. 10000 from B promises to bring gold for him from the sun. Examine validity of this agreement.
2. A has offered his bike to B. A makes an agreement with C that if B refuses to buy his bike he will sell it to him at particular price. Is it a valid agreement?
3. A, who is a minor, purchases grocery items regularly for three months from a grocery merchant on credit. Later on A refuses to pay the bills. Suggest legal remedy to grocery merchant.
4. Ram hails from lower income class. He buys 5 pairs of Woodland shoes from Shyam on credit @ Rs. 2000 p.p. can Shyam recover this amount from Ram?
5. X, a minor, had been studying at Cambridge brought 10-waistcoats on credit from a merchant. In fact X had adequate stock of such clothing with him. Is he liable to pay for waistcoats?
6. An insurance company makes payment of claim to the policyholder on fire insurance policy. While making the payment the company was under mistake to believe that goods have been destroyed by insured cause. Infact, goods were stolen. Is company entitled to recover this payment from the policyholder.
7. A agrees to sell a part of specific crop of wheat to be grown on his agricultural land to B at a specific price. Crops were being delivered after two months. But before delivering B paid a part of the contracted price. The crop of wheat was destroyed. Examine the legal consequences of an agreement between A and B.

8. Fire broke out in the godown of Ram. Shyam who was passing over rendered his services in extinguishing that fire. He did it with an intention of getting compensation for it. Has he a legal right to recover it from Ram?
9. A has lost his horse. B finds it and takes it into his custody. By the time he could trace owner of the horse. B incurred some expenses on the maintenance of that horse. Explain rights and duties of B with regard to that horse.
10. A stays in the house of B regarding that house municipal authorities made an annocement that if the taxes are not paid by the stipulated date, the house will be sold in auction. A makes payment can he recover it from B?

■■■

Chapter 9

Discharge of Contract

Learning Objectives

- Develop conceptual clarity about discharge of contract and it's consequences.
- Examine various modes of getting a contract discharged.
- Analyse, discharge of contract by breach of contract.
- Remember meaning and nature of supervening impossibility
- Learn how contract is discharged by supervening impossibility and compare it with other similar situations when contract is not discharged.

INTRODUCTION

Formation of a contract results in the creation of certain rights and obligations on the part of the parties. These rights and obligations can be claimed in the court of law. These are also known as contractual relationship between the parties making a contract. The rights on the part of one party becomes obligations for another and vice versa.

MEANING

Discharge of a contract implies termination of the contractual relationship between the parties. On the termination of such relationship the parties are released from their obligations in the contract. And in this way contract comes to an end. In other words, a contract is said to be discharged, when rights and obligations created by it comes to an end.

Broadly the contract may be discharged either by the act of the parties or by operation of the law. The parties of a contract may be released from the obligations either by fulfilling or discharging them or the law may exempt them from their obligations in the contract.

MODES OF DISCHARGING CONTRACT

The contract may be discharged in any one of the following ways which are known as modes of discharging contract.

1. By Performance.
2. By Mutual Agreement.
3. By Supervening Impossibility.
4. By Operation Of Law.
5. By Lapse Of Time.
6. By Material Alteration.
7. By Breach Of Contract.

1. Discharge of Contract by Performance

This is the most popular and usual way of discharging contract. The contract is a mutual exchange of promises between two parties. They make a promise either for doing or not doing any thing. Both the parties are promisor's as well as promisees. When both the promisor do what they have promised to do, the contract is said to be performed. And this way both parties get released from their obligations in that contract and contract comes to an end.

Example: A agreed to supply 200 cotton bales to B at particular price. On due date A delivers cotton bales and makes payment. Both of them get released from their obligations in the contract and contract comes to an end.

Performance of a contract may be of two types:

(a) Actual performance
(b) Attempted Performance

(a) *Actual performance:* Generally at the time of making a contract, parties to it decide about the point of time on which both parties will perform their respective promises. In actual performance, both the promisors perform the acts, which they have promised to perform on the decided point of time. Actual performance brings the contract to an end.

Example: Ram agrees to deliver 50 tonnes of wheat to B. on 1st September at a particular price. B was to make payment on 5th September. A delivers wheat to B on the due date (1st Sep). And Simultaneously B makes payment on 5th Sep. the contract is said to be discharged by actual performance.

(b) *Attempted performance or tender:* When the promisor is ready and willing to perform his promise, but he cannot do it, because the promisee does not accept the performance – this is known as attempted performance and it is legally treated equivalent to actual performance except in case of payment of money.

Section 38 of this act provides that 'where a promisor has made an offer of performance to the promisee, and the offer has not been accepted, the promisor is not responsible for non- performance, nor does he thereby lose his rights under the contract'.

Example: Ramesh was to supply 50 tonnes of coal to Mahesh on 15th Oct and Mahesh is to pay for it on 20th Oct. On the due date of performance Ramesh made an offer to supply coal to Mahesh But he refused to accept delivery of specified quantity of coal. It amounts to attempted performance and Ramesh gets released from the obligation of supplying 50 tonnes of coal to Mahesh. But his rights against Mahesh will remain intact, e.g. he can proceed against Mahesh for breach of contract.

Example: A has borrowed sum of Rs. 10,000 from B for two months. On the due date, A makes payment, but B does not accept it. In this case A will not be released from his liability of making that payment to B. however, he will not be liable for paying any interest on that after two months.

Essentials of Valid Attempted Performance or Tender

An attempted performance, to be legally valid must meet the following requirements.

(i) *It must be unconditional:* while making an attempted performance, the promisor cannot put any condition, regarding that, for the promisee. Conditional offer to perform is not valid.

Example: A agrees to supply 100 tonnes of wheat to B and subsequently, B was to make the payment. A offers to deliver wheat to B provided he makes half of the payment in advance. Such attempted performance is conditional and thus is not valid.

(ii) *It must be made at reasonable place and time:* Attempted performance to be legally effective, must be made with in usual business hours and at a reasonable place.

Example: Ram agreed to supply 100 tonnes of iron-ore to B. on 1st January. On the due date of supply he took stipulated quantity of iron-ore to B's residence at 12.00 midnight. Place and time of supply is not reasonable, thus making attempted performance is invalid.

(iii) *Reasonable opportunity to ascertain capability:* the person to whom attempted performance is being made, should be given reasonable opportunity to ascertain that the person giving attempted performance is able and willing to fulfill whole of the promise, then and there. A person offering to perform the promise must have necessary stock of goods to be delivered along with required manpower.

(iv) *Inspection of goods*: when the attempted performance is made to supply the goods, the promisee should be given reasonable opportunity to ascertain that the promisor really possesses the goods of contracted quality.

Example: A agreed to supply 100 cotton bales of X trademark to B on 2nd of Feb. A attempts to supply these to B on the due date. B is not willing to accept delivery. He should be given reasonable opportunity to inspect quality of cotton bales to be delivered.

(v) *Proper person:* In case of valid attempted performance it must have been made to the promisee or any other person duly authorized by him.

(vi) *Joint promisees:* In case there are two or more than two joint promisees, an attempted performance can be given to any one of them. It is not necessary that it should be given to all promisees.

Example: A made a promise to supply specific quantity of wheat to B and C. On the due date he can offer to supply either to B or to C.

2. Discharge of Contract by Mutual Agreement

A contract is formed when the parties are mutually agreed. In a same way both the parties of a contract by mutual agreement can discharge that contract.

Section 62 & 63 of this act provide for the following methods of discharging a contract by mutual agreement:

According to section 62 of this act, 'if the parties to a contract agree to substitute a new contract for it or to rescind or alter it, the original contract need not be performed'.

(i) *Novation:* Under the method of Novation, existing contract is replaced by new one either between same parties or between new parties. It discharges an existing contract and brings new contract in to existence.

Example: A borrows sum of Rs. 10000 from B on promissory note for six months. On the due date A is unable to pay and makes out another promissory note along with the amount of interest. It amounts to novation and existing promissory note is terminated and new one of Rs. 10,000 + interest is made.

Example: A owes Rs. 5000 to B and B also owes same amount to C. on the due date they agree that A will pay Rs. 5000 to C. In this case, two agreements, one between A and B and another between A and C have been replaced by third agreement which is between A and C (new parties) will exist.

(ii) *Alteration:* Parties of an agreement are at liberty to alter or change any one or more terms of it. mutually. When they make any change regarding any terms of contract by mutual consent, such contract need not be performed and is discharged. Mutually agreed alteration discharges the original contract and the parties become legally bound by new contract. In this context, new contract means the contract with altered terms and conditions.

Example: A agrees to sell his bike to B for Rs. 50,000 on cash down payment. Before the due date of performance A and B mutually agreed that B will make payment in instalments. Thus original agreement of making cash down payment is discharged. And now A and B are bound by the new agreement in which payment will be made in instalments.

(iii) *Rescission:* When the parties of a contract, by mutual agreement cancel all or some of the terms of a contract, it is known as recission. As a result of rescission the contract, whose terms have been cancelled is discharged. In brief rescission means cancellation of terms of a contract.

Rescission may be either partial or absolute. In a absolute rescission entire contract is cancelled and need not be performed. But in partial rescission, some of the terms may be cancelled, but contract will be performed with remaining terms.

Example: Ram agreed to supply 100 units of plastic goods to Shyam at a particular price. Later on they agree that Ram will supply only 50 units of plastic goods to Shyam. It is known as partial rescission. On the other hand if they agree that Ram will not supply any unit of plastic goods to Shyam. It is absolute rescission, which leads to termination of the whole contract.

Rescission of a contract takes place under the following circumstances:

(a) Rescission may take place by mutual agreement between the parties of contract.
(b) When one party of a contract fails to perform his promise, another party can rescind the contract without losing his rights for breach of contract.
(c) In voidable contract, an aggrieved party whose consent had not been free has a right to rescind contract.

(iv) *Remission:* Sometimes, the promisor may perform only a part of his promise and promisee accepts it for the performance of the whole promise. It is known as remission and that contract is discharged.

In other words, remission means acceptance of lesser performance than what was actually due is a contract. Section 63 of this act provides that "a party may dispense with or remit, wholly or in part the performance of the promise made to him. He can also extend the time of such performance or accept, instead of it any satisfaction, which he deems to be fit".

However acceptance of lesser performance does not require any consideration.

Example: A has borrowed sum of Rs. 10,000 from B for two months. B promises that if A refunds Rs. 9000 immediately after a month he will accept it for the settlement of whole debt. Agreement is discharged on account of remission on the part of B.

Kapur Chand Godha Vs. Nawab Himayatali Khan (1963, 2, S.C.R, 168). In this case, M was to pay a sum of Rs. 27 lacs to K. Since Hyderabad had been taken over by the Indian Government, a committee was appointed to clear the matters. It offered Rs. 20 lacs to K who accepted it in full satisfaction of the claim of Rs. 27 lacs. Lateron K filed a suit for the recovery of the balance. The Supreme held that K could not do so as he had accepted Rs. 20 lacs in full satisfaction.

(v) *Waiver:* In a contract, every party is at liberty to give up some of his rights in favour of other party. When a party agrees to give up his rights the another party will get released from his obligation and the contract comes to an end. But the waiver on the part of one party must result in release of the other party from obligation. Then only the contract will be discharged. It is because waiver of rights by one party means discharge of the other party from his obligations.

Example: A draws a Bill of Exchange on B, who accepts it and gives it back to A. Lateron A indorses it in favour of C who further indorses it to D. while indorsing it to D, the C waives right to get notice of dishonour in favour of indorsee. Thus if B/E gets dishonoured, C will become liable without getting notice of dishonour.

3. Discharge of Contract by Supervening Impossibility

Contract is made between parties either for doing or not doing some act. The act, for which promise has been made, must be capable of being performed. When the parties enter in to an agreements for doing some thing impossible, such agreement is void ab-initio.

In many occasions, the contract at the time of formation is capable of being performed. Subsequently after the formation, its performance becomes impossible or illegal. Such impossibility may arise due to the reasons beyond the control of both parties. This kind of impossibility which crops up in a contract after its formation is known as 'Supervening Impossibility' and the contract is discharged.

An impossibility whether it is there at initial stage of making a contract or arises subsequently after the formation of a contract will render contract as void.

At the initial stage of formation of contract such impossibility may be known or unknown to the parties. If an impossibility was known to the parties that agreement is void ab-initio. In case the parties were not aware of impossibility and come to known about it afterwards, such contract becomes void.

Example: A agrees to sell his motor bike to B for a specific price. Lateron they come to know that motor bike has already been stolen. Contract is void.

However, the contract becomes void on account of subsequent impossibility provided the following conditions are satisfied.

(a) The act which is to be performed in a contract must have become impossible.
(b) Impossibility should have been caused by circumstances beyond the control of parties.
(c) Impossibility must not be the outcome of some acts on the part of the parties.

In this regard, section 56 of this act provides that, 'A contract to do an act, which after the contract is made, becomes impossible or by reason of some event which the promisor could not prevent, unlawful, becomes void, when the act becomes impossible or unlawful'.

A contract is discharged due to supervening impossibility under the following situations.

(i) *Destruction of subject matter:* Every contract has same subject matter. When the subject matter is destroyed due to any cause beyond the control of the parties, before the performance of a contract; such contract is discharged on account of supervening impossibility.

Taylor Vs. Caldwell (1863m 122, A.R, 299.): In this case, a music hall was let out on rent for a series of concerts on certain days. The hall gets destroyed by fire before the date of first concert. The plaintiff filed a suit against the defendant for damage arising out of breach of contract. It was held that the contract had become void and defendant was not liable to pay compensation.

(ii) *Discontinuation of particular state of thing, which is essential for performance:* When the contract is made by the parties, on the ground that, certain state of things will continue till the performance of a contract. But that state of things gets changed or discontinued due to any reason beyond the control of the parties; such contract becomes void on the basis of supervening impossibility. It is because, the very object of contract is defeated, due to discontinuation of that state of things.

Krell Vs. Henry (1903, 2, K.B, 740). In this case, Henry hired a room from Krell for two days to witness the coronation procession of King Edward VII. Owing to king's illness, the procession was cancelled. It was held that Henry was excused from the obligation of paying rent for the room. As an existence of coronation processeian was necessary to continue for the performance of a contract. But it was discontinued, due to the reasons beyond the control of both parties.

(iii) *Change of law:* Change of law, after the formation of a contract, if renders perfomance of contract unlawful; such contract is discharged on the ground of supervening impossibility. However, change of law should go in to the root of contract as to defeat its object.

Example: A entered in to an agreement with B for selling 100 tonnes of wheat at specified price to him on 15th of March. But, before due date of delivery the Government of India has passed an ordinance debarring the individual from supplying more than 5 tonnes of wheat. The contract between A and B comes to an end due to reason that its performance has become unlawful.

However legal intervention on the part of the Government which is of a temporary nature and which does not adversely affect foundation of a contract will not render it as void.

Satyabrata Ghose Vs. Mugneeram Bangur & Coy. (A.I.R., 1954, S.C. 44.). In this case the company started a scheme for developing a land in to housing colony. S was one of the purchasers of the land. The coy. undertook the construction of roads and drains necessary for making land suitable for residential purpose. But before any thing could be done regarding transfer of land to S, the State has acquired substantial part of that land for military purpose. The requisition order was temporary and therefore it was held that the contract will not be discharged due to supervening impossibility.

(iii) *Death or personal incapacity of the party:* In a contract of personal nature, if the promisor dies or becomes incapable of performing contract, such contract will be discharged. Such personal contracts are formed, on personal considerations and may require personal skill and talent to perform the contract. So death of promissor may create vacuum and contract can not be performed.

Robison Vs. Davison (1871M L.R.6, EX 269). In this case, an artist promised to perform some concert for a certain price. Before she could do so, she was taken seriously ill. It was held that she was discharged from her obligation due to physical incapacity.

(iv) *Declaration of war:* On the out break of war between two countries, the citizens of those countries cannot make any contract. If they make contract it will be void ab-initio. The contracts, made by the parties before the declaration of war will remain suspended during the war. When the war is over an enforceability of such contracts depends on the discretion of the Central Government. The Govt may either abrogate them or may allow to enforce them on some conditions.

Example: Ram agrees to supply some raw material to Shyam in another country at a specific price. Before due date, war is declared between the countries. It makes contract void, because Ram can not deliver that raw material to Shyam.

Exceptions to doctrine of supervening impossibility. In a contract when the person makes promise for doing or not doing any thing, he must perform it. But on becoming performance impossible, due to reasons beyond his control, the contract is discharged. There are certain situations, resembling to supervening impossibility, but are not included in supervening impossibility.

Under these situations, contract will not be discharged and the parties are liable to perform it. Though the performance may be more difficult, expensive, less profitable or cumbersome, But the parties concerned have to perform it. These situations may be considered as an exceptions:

(i) *Difficulty of performance:* Generally, difficulty is no excuse for performance. When the performance of the promise becomes more expensive, difficult and cumbersome due to any reason, the promisor has to perform it. He can not seek any excuse on the ground of performance becoming difficult.

Example: A agreed to supply huge quantity of iron-ore to B at a particular price. Before due date, due to steep hike in the prices of petroleum products, cost of transport has been doubled. But A has supply iron-ore inspite of increased transportation cost.

BLACKBURN BOBBINNS COY. LTD. VS. ALLEN & SONS (1918, 2, K.B, 467). In this case, A sold certain quantity of Finland timber to B to be delivered between June and September 1914. No delivery was made before August when war brokeout and transport was disorganized so that A could not bring any timber from Finland. Held impossibility of getting timber from that country could not excuse performance.

(ii) *Commercial difficulties:* When the performance of a promise becomes costlier, non profitable and more risky, such contract will not be discharged. Such difficulties are known as commercial difficulties. These may arise due to sudden change in price line, economic policies of the Government, not-availability of raw material, deep drastic change in exchange rate and outbreak of war, etc.

Example: A agreed to supply certain goods to B. Before due date, due to sudden outbreak of war, the market price of goods shot up. And supply of goods has become costlier. But A is liable to supply even if he suffers a loss.

(iii) *Strikes, lockout, riots and civil disturbances etc:* When the performance of a contract becomes very difficult or practically impossible due to strike of labourers, lock out in the business premises, or riots etc, the contract will not be discharged. These events have not been included in section 56 of this Act

HARI LAXMAN VS. SECRETARY OF STATE OF INDIA (1928, 30, BOM. L.R. 49). In this case, the lessor of certain salt pans failed to repair them, as per the terms of the contract on the ground of strike of workmen. It was held that, a strike by workmen was not sufficient reason to excuse performance, of a contract.

(iv) *Difficulty arising out of conduct of third party:* When the party of a contract relied on third party for the performance of his promise. Failure of third party or his inability will not be considered sufficient ground for discharging a contract.

Example: A is a wholesaler of some goods which are manufactured by B.A agreed to supply some goods to C. which he will procure from B. But goods have not been manufactured by B. Even then A is liable to supply these goods to C. Failure on the part of B for producing those goods is not sufficient ground to discharge the contract.

ALLOPI PARSAD VS. UNION OF INDIA (1960, S.C. 588). In this case, A was acting as an agent of Government of India for procuring edible oils for the use of Army personnel. The rates of oil were fixed by the Govt. But due to out break of IInd world war, there has been steep rise in the price of oils. A maintained a supply at higher prices. But it was held that A was not entitled to claim more than the price as fixed by the Govt.

(v) *Partial impossibility:* When the contract has been entered in to for achieving single oobjective and achievement of which becomes impossible, that contract will be discharged. But in many case, the contract may be made for achieving more than one objectives. In case one object fails cotract will not be discharged. Rather the parties will perform it for achieving another object.

H.B. Steam Boat Coy Vs. Hutton (1903, 2, K. 683). In this case, stream Boat Coy agreed to let a boat to Hutton to view; (i) the navel review at the coronation of king Edward VII and (ii) to cruise round the fleet. Due to illness of king, the navel review was cancelled, but the fleet was assembled and the boat could have been used to cruise round the fleet. It was held that the contract is not terminated, because it will continue for another object.

4. Discharge of Contract by Operation of Law

Contract may also be discharged by operation of law. In these cases, law comes in to force and the parties are released from their obligations in the contract. These cases are under.

(i) *Death of promisor:* After having made a contract, if the promisor dies, the contract of a personal nature comes to an end. It is because such contracts require special skill and talent on the part of promisor to perform the promise. Thus in case of his death, contract is discharged.

Example: A, who is singer has agreed to perform certain programmes on a particular date. But before that date A dies, such contract which is of a personal nature will come to an end.

However in case of other contracts, if the promisor dies, his legal representative will be called upon to perform the promise. But his liability will be limited only to the extent, he inherits properties from such deceased promisor.

(ii) *Insolvency:* In case the person is declared as an insolvent by the court of law, he is released from performing his part of contract by law. His rights and liabilities are transferred to the official Assignee or official Receiver appointed by the court.

After getting certificate of discharge he is discharged from all obligations prior to his declaration as an insolvent. And he gets new lease of life.

(iii) *Merger:* Two parties make two contracts on the same subject matter. In one contract the party get superior rights. And in another contract he gets inferior rights. When these two contracts merge or coincide on that same subject matter, the contract containing superior rights will exist and another contract which carries inferior rights will vanish and discharged by operation of law.

Example: A acquires a piece of land from Delhi Development Authority for doing some industrial work on lease basis for 10 years. Before 10 years A could manage the fund, and by making another agreement he buys that same piece of land on ownership basis. Thus agreement of lease and agreement of ownership merge on that particular piece of land. An agreement of lease will be discharged by law and agreement of ownership will remain in force.

5. Discharge of Contract by Lapse of Time

While making a contract, the parties prescribe a time with in which it is to be performed. When no time of performance is fixed, the contract must be performed with in reasonable period of time. Reasonable period of time is a matter of fact which differs from case to case depending on nature of agreement, circumstances and intention of the parties.

Thus the contract must be performed with in stipulated period of time or reasonable period of time. Till the expiry of such times, if the contract is not performed it will be discharged.

Relevant provision of Indian Limitation Act provide that "a contract should be performed with in a specified period i.e. period of limitation. If the contract is not performed and if no action is taken by the promisee with in the period of limitation, he is deprived of his remedy at law". In case of contracts, the period of limitation is three years. After the expiry of this period the court will not allow to enforce the contract and it will be discharged.

Example: Ram agreed to supply raw material worth Rs. 10,000 to Shyam on credit. The period of credit has not been fixed. In this case, Ram must file suit for the recovery of payment with in three years. In case, Ram fails to do so, at the expiry of three years period, that amount will become time barred and Ram will not be legally entitled to recover it.

6. Discharge of Contract by Material Alterations

Sometimes, the contract and its terms and conditions may be contained in a particular document. When the promisee or his agent make any material alteration without the consent of other party in that document of contract, such contract is treated to be discharged. Such alteration to be legally effective must satisfy the following conditions

(a) Alteration or change in the document must be related to a contract.

(b) Consent of other party has not been taken for such alteration, it is unilateral in nature.

(c) Alteration made with regard to a contract must be material alterations.

Material alterations include all those alterations which in a significant way affect rights and duties of the parties in that contract. Such as change in the name of payee, change in the date of payment, and change in the amount which is payable, etc.

After the material alterations, the contract no longer, continues to be the same, thus no party can sue upon it.

However, alterations which are not material and do not affect rights and duties of the parties or which are made to carryout common intention or protect common interest will not affect validity of a cotract. Such alterations may include correction of clerical mistake, correction of spelling of the name or place etc.

It is to be noted that the party who makes material alterations in the document of contract will have no right to claim performance of contract as it stood before alteration.

Example: A borrows a sum of Rs. 10,000 from B, for one year at 10 per cent interest per annum. All these terms are put in a document which is known a promissory note. B, who is having promissory note makes a change in the rate of interest by increasing it to 15 per cent without consent of A. This alteration is material one and affect right and duties of the paties. Thus the contract of promissory note is discharged. Since B has made material alteration, he is deprived of his right to claim interest of 10 per cent. However the altered promissory note may be used as an evidence by B for proving debt covered by it.

In one of the leading cases, **ANANTH RAO VS. KANDIKANDA (1920):** It was held that the document, though altered, could be used as proof of the transaction and the creditor might be allowed to claim refund of money actually advanced by him.

Therefore, the promissory note becomes invalid due to material change in it made by one of the paties without the consent of other. Nevertheless, such promissory note may be used as a proof of debt covered under it.

7. Discharged by Breach of Contact

Contract can also be discharged by not performing it. Breach of contract means refusal of performance on the part of the parties. When a party to a contract refuses to perform it, or does not perform it or makes himself unable to perform it, other party may put such contract to an end.

Example: A, enters in to a contract with B for supplying spare parts of a machine on particular date at specified price. On the due date of performance A fails to supply. B, has a right to put this contract to an end, thus the contract comes to an end because A fails to perform it. It amounts to breach of contract.

Breach of contract may be of two types.

(i) Actual Breach
(ii) Anticipatory Breach

Actual breach: Generally, the time of performance of a contract may be determined by the parties at the time of making a contract. In such case, the parties must perform their promises on that time. Failure on the part of the party to perform his promise on due date is regarded as actual breach of contract.

Thus, actual breach of a contract occurs when the party does not perform his promise on due date or refuses to performs it on that date. On such refusal, another party of a contract is entitled to treat the contract discharged and can move against the paty making breach of contract.

Example: Mahesh agreed to supply one hundred cotton bales to suresh on 10th march at specified price. On 10th March he refused to supply. Suresh has a right to treat this contract as discharged and sue upon Mahesh for breach of contract.

CORT VS. AMBERGATE RAIL COY. (1851, 17, Q.B. 527). In this case Cort contracted with Railway company to supply 3000 tonnes of railway timber at a certain price. to be delivered in instalments. After supplying 1787 tonnes, the Railway coy. asked to Cort not to supply more. It was held that Cort could bring an action for breach of contract.

Anticipatory breach of contract: When, before due date of performance of a contract the promisor refuses to perform or disabled himself from performing his promise; it is known as anticipatory breach of a contract. In anticipatory beach the promisor refuses to perform before due date of actual performance. The promisor either informs the promisee regarding his refusal or may do some act which is in consistent with the contract or which renders him disabled from performing his promise.

Example: A, agrees to marry B on 1st January. Before this date A gets married with C. As a result of it, he has disabled himself from getting married with B, before due date. It amounts to anticipatory breach of contract.

Review Questions

1. What is discharge of a contract? Discuss various ways in which the contract gets discharged.
2. Explain the various modes of discharging a contract by mutual agreement and give suitable examples.
3. Define the term 'supervening impossibility'. Discuss various circumstances under which contract is discharged due to supervening impossibility.
4. Explain various exceptions to supervening impossibility.
5. What is material alteration? How does the contract comes to an end by material alteration.
6. Define attempted performance. Explain requirements of a valid attempted performance.
7. Impossibility of performance is as rule, not an excuse for non-performance of contract. Discuss it with suitable examples.
8. Explain different ways in which the contract is discharged by operation of law.
9. Comment:

   (a) Discharge of a contract releases the parties from their obligation.

   (b) Performance as a usual mode of discharging contract

   (c) Difficulty of performance may not lead to discharge of contract.

   (d) Attempted performance is equivalent to actual performance.

   (e) Impossibility which is known to the parties at the time of making a contract is one and same thing as subsequent impossibility.

10. Write notes on the following:

(a) Merger	(b) Supervening impossibility
(b) Material alterations	(d) Breach of contract
(d) Rescission	(f) Discharge of contract by lapse of time.

Practical Problems

1. A borrows a sum of Rs. 10,000 from B for one year @ 10 per cent per annum A did not make demand for repayment before the expiry of one year and B did not repay it. Can A recover this sum from B after the expiry of that period of time? (No, debt has become time-barred).
2. Ram agrees to supply some furniture to Shyam in two instalments. Shyam was to pay stipulated price to Ram on a particular day. Identify rights and obligations of Ram and Shyam.
3. Akhilesh, agreed to supply 200 tones of coal to a Railway company at specified price. On the due date of performance Akhilesh took required quantity of coal to the godown of Railway coy, but they refused to accept delivery. Is Akhilesh released from his obligation of supplying coal. What is the legal status of his rights against Railway coy?
4. X, owes Rs. 5000 to Y. On due date he offered to repay this amount to Y., but Y refused to accept payment. Is X released from his obligation of repaying that amount to Y (No; monetary obligation).
5. S, a singer, makes a contract with R to sing at his mugical theatre every night for one month. R has agreed to pay her Rs. 2500 for each night show. On 15th night S willfully absents from the mugical show. Can Y put this contract to an end; (Yes breach of contract by S).
6. X and coy was in agreement with Russell, a citizen of foreign country for supplying certain goods at a particular price on 25th December. But before due date of supply war is decleared between two countries. Is X and coy legally bomd to supply the goods. what will be legal position of this contract when the war is over?
7. A, an eminent piano player, promised B to perform at a concert. In the morning of that day A informed B that she is too ill to attend the concert. Explain legal status of this contract.
8. Manohar hired a room at Connaught place in some hotel to witness Republic Day parade on 26th Janruary. But due to some emergency the parade show was cancelled. Examine legality of this contract.
9. A, is a wholesaler of particular item of plastic goods to be manufactured by B.A enters in to a contract for supplying 50 items of plastic good to C who is a retailer. But due to labour strike B could not manufacture plastic goods.

Is A liable to supply that quatity of plastic good to C? (Yes, otherwise he will be liable for breach of contract).

10. Contract was entered in to between London based merchants, for the sale of certain goods which were to be imported from Algeria. Due to riots and civil disturbances the goods could not be imported. Is seller liable for the supply of those goods? (Yes; commercial difficulty).
11. A, borrows Rs. 2000 from B and writes a promissory note in his favour for three months, After three months A goes to B and expresses his inability to repay that amount and gives new promissory note to him. Is old promissory note cancelled or discharged?
12. Mahesh took piece of land from Delhi Development Authority on lease basis for 10 years. At the end of 5th year of lease he makes another agreement with D.D.A for buying the same piece of land. Explain this contract with the help of 'rule of merger'.
13. Y, draws a bill of exchange on Z for Rs. 10,000 at three months. Z accepts the bill and returns it back to Y. Y, who is a drawer makes change in the amount of that bill and raises it to Rs. 20,000. Can Y claim this amount from Z? (No, material alteration).
14. Suresh is sugar mill owner at Lucknow. He makes an agreement for supplying 200 tones of sugar to Mahesh in Delhi on 25th December. In the meanwhile, the Central Government has brought a notification that no one can transact for more than 5 tones of sugar. Explain legal remedies available to Mahesh if any?

■■■

Chapter **10**

Performance of Contract

Learning Objectives

- Understand basic concept of performance of contract.
- Examine performance of joint promises.
- Remember rules regarding appropriation of payment.
- Get familiar with that who can perform and who can claim performance.
- Examine time as an essential factor for performing contract and its implications appropriation of payment
- Learn basic concept of reciprocal promises and their performance.

INTRODUCTION

Contract is a mutual exchange of promises between parties. They make promises for 'doing' or 'not doing' something. After having made such promises, they are legally bound to fulfil what they have promised to perform. If they do so, it is known as performance of a contract. Subsequently, on the performance of a contract the parties are released from their obligations and the contract comes to an end.

Briefly, performance of a contract means fulfillment of legal obligations created by a contract. And the performance of a contract is a natural mode of discharging a contract. According to section 37 of this Act, 'the parties to a contract, must either perform or offer to perform their respective promises, unless such performance is dispensed with or excused under the provisions of the Act'.

As per the interpretation of this section, the performance of a contract may be of two types actual performance and attempted performance. In actual performance, both the promisors of a contract do an acts which they have promised to do. And it leads to peaceful ending of a contract. Sometimes, one of the promisor may be ready and willinging to perform his promise, but fails to do so, because another party does not accept it. It is known as attempted performance.

Legally valid attempted performance releases such promisor from his obligation in that contract. But his rights against another party will remain intact.

Example: A agrees to supply 100 bags of tea to B @ Rs. 500 per bag on a particular date. B was to pay subsequently after the supply of tea. On due date A supplies tea and B makes payment. It lead to actual performance of a contract and the contract comes to an end. But, if on due date, A takes the contracted quantity of tea to B's godown and B refuses to accept the delivery. Thus, it is regarded as attempted performance and as a result of it A gets released from the obligation of supplying tea to B.

However under both ways of performance, the promisors get released from their obligations in that contract and the contract comes to and end. It is to be noted that in case of attempted performance for the payment of money the promisor, making it, does not get released from the obligation of making payment. But from the date of attempted performance he would not liable for any interest.

With regard to performance of a contract, many questions arise as to – who must perform the contract, who can demand such performance and what should be the time and place of performance. The Indian Contract Act contains various provisions to deal with these questions.

WHO MUST PERFORM CONTRACT

Contract is nothing but a bundle of promises. These promises are made by the promisors and these are made for doing or not doing something. The promisors are under legal obligation and they have to fulfil that obligation, unless it is dispensed with by law. The liability of performing a contract basically lies on the promisors. Section 37 to 41 of this Act lays down the basic rules regarding legal status of the person who is to perform the contract. The contract may be performed:

(i) *By the promisor himself:* Simple rule of law is that the person who makes a promise must perform it. Sometimes, law may permit him to get his promise performed through another person.

But in case a of contract of personal nature, which is based on personal considerations and which requires special skill and talent to perform, must be performed by the promisor himself. In case of his death, such contract will come to an end. Section 40 of this Act provides that, 'where the contract is of a personal nature only the promisor can perform it and no one else'.

Example: A, who is painter, enters into a contract for preparing painting piece for B at a particular price. This contract is of a personal nature and therefore A must perform his promise, he cannot get it performed by anyone else.

But in case of general contract the promise may be either performed by promisor himself or he may get it performed by another person.

(ii) ***By the agent of promisor:*** In case of a contract of impersonal nature, the promisor may appoint someone as his agent for performing his promise. Such agent will act on behalf of a promisor and the promisor will be bound by the acts of his agent. If an agent does not perform the promise according to the terms and conditions of a contract, ultimate liability will be on the part of promisor. Section 40 (Para 2) states that the promisor himself or his agent may perform the contract.

Example: A, appoints B as his agent for selling goods. B enters into a contract with C for selling goods on credit. C makes default in payment. This contract is binding on A, therefore he can sue upon C for the recovery of payment.

(iii) ***By legal representative:*** According to section 37 (Para II) of this Act, 'A contract which involves the use of personal skill or is founded on personal considerations comes to an end on the death of the promisor. As regards any other contract, the legal representatives of the deceased promisor are bound to perform it, unless contrary intention appears from the contract. But their liability under a contract is limited to the value of property they inherit from the deceased'.

Example: A borrowed sum of Rs.10, 0000 from B for two years. After one year A dies and C, who is a legal representative inherits property of Rs. 60, 000 from him. On the due date of repayment B will call upon C to repay. But the liability of C is limited upto the value of Rs. 60, 000. He cannot be liable for more than that.

(iv) ***By third person:*** The promise may also be performed by a stranger on behalf of promisor, provided promisee agrees to it. When the promisee accepts performance of promise by third person later on he cannot enforce it against the promisor.

According to section 41 of this Act, 'Performance by a stranger accepted by promisee produces the result of discharging promisor'.

Kapur Chand Vs Mir Nabab Himayat Ali Khan. In this case, A, who has to recover Rs.15, 000 from B, accepts Rs.11, 000 from a third person C in full settlement of account with B. It was held that A cannot enforce this contract against B.

WHO CAN DEMAND PERFORMANCE

Contrary to the obligation of performing contract, the right to claim lies with anyone of the following.

(i) ***Promisee:*** There is direct privity of contract between promisor and promisee. Therefore, the promisee, in a natural way, has a right to demand performance of the contract.

(ii) ***Legal representative:*** In a contract, in case of death of promisee, right to demand performance is shifted to his legal representative; unless contrary intention appears from the contract or the contract is of personal nature.

Example: Y agrees to marry Z. Before the marriage Y dies. Contract comes to an end. Because it is of personal nature and legal representative of Y cannot demand performance of contract from Z.

(iii) *Third person:* The general rule of law in that a person can not acquire rights under a contract to which he is not a party. But this rule is subject to following exceptions. Under these exceptional situations, stranger to a contract can demand performance of a contract.

(a) Third person, who is beneficiary in a agreement of trust can demand performance of a contract.
(b) If the party, as per rule of estoppel, is stopped from denying his liability toward third party, third party gets right to demand performance.
(c) In a contract of family settlement, if the provision is made for the maintenance of female member or for her marriage expenses, she has right to demand performance, though she is stranger to a contract.

PERFORMANCE OF A JOINT PROMISES

When two or more person jointly make a promise for doing or not doing some thing to two or more persons such promise is known as joint promise, promisors become joint promisors and promisees are known as joint promisees

Joint promises may take any of the following forms:

(a) Two or more promisors jointly make a promise to the promisee.
(b) One promisor makes a promise to two or more promisees.
(c) Two or more promisors make a joint promise to two or more promises.

Rules regarding performance of joint promises:

(i) *Joint liability:* When two or more promisors make joint promise for doing or not doing some thing; both the promisors are jointly liable to perform it. In case of death of any one of them, his legal representative along with remaining promisors will perform the promise. When both of them or all joint promisors die, their legal representatives will be called upon to perform the promise jointly.

Example: A and B have borrowed sum of Rs. 10,000 from C. On due date both A and B are jointly liable to pay. If A dies, his legal representative with B and if both of them die, their legal representatives will jointly repay the amount to C.

(ii) *Individual liability:* When two or more joint promisors make promise and there is no express contract contrary to it, both of them are individually liable to perform. So in addition to joint liability they are individually liable to promisee. Hence liability of joint promisors is 'Joint and several'. In case of individual liability, the promisee of a joint promise can compel any one of the joint promisors to perform whole of the promise.

Example: A and B are joint promisors to repay Rs. 5000 to C. He can compel either A or B to repay entire amount.

(iii) ***Right of contribution:*** Joint promisors have joint and several liability. Any of them can be compelled to perform whole of the promise. When one of the joint promisors has been compelled to perform entire promise, he has a right to claim contribution or share of other promisors, unless contrary intention appears from the contract.

Example: X, Y, and Z are joint promisors. They have promised to pay sum of Rs. 20, 000 to R. On the due date R compels X to pay entire amount. Later on, X has a right to claim respective share or contribution of Y and Z.

However, it is to be noted that ratio of contribution may be decided by them. In case it is not decided they are expected to contribute equally.

(iv) ***Default in making contribution:*** When any one of the joint promisors could not contribute his share, remaining joint promisors will bear the loss arising from such default. The loss will be shared by them equally.

It is to be noted that this principle is also applied in case of recovery of loan from the legal representatives of deceased debtor, who become joint promisors by operation of law after the death of debtor,

(v) ***Release of one of the joint promisors:*** According to section 44 of this Act, "a release by the promisee of any one of the joint promisors does not discharge other joint promisors from liability. The released joint promisor also continues to be liable to other joint promisors".

Application of this section does not allow that released joint promisor to gain any thing out of it. Rather, after release he will be liable for his share or contribution to other joint promisors who will perform the promise.

Rights of Joint Promisees

In case of joint promise, all joint promisees have a joint right to demand performance of a contract. Unless it is agreed, one promisee cannot claim performance of a joint promise.

According to section 45 of this Act, 'When a promise is made to a several persons jointly, then, unless the contrary intention appears from the contract, the right to claim performance, rests with all promisees jointly and a single promisee can not demand performance. When any one of the promisee dies, right to claim performance rests with the legal representative of such deceased person jointly with the surviving promisees. When all the promisees are dead, the right to claim performance rests with legal representatives of all promisees jointly'.

Thus, so long as, all joint promisees survive, they have joint right to claim performance. In case of their death such right is shifted to their legal representative and they can jointly claim performance.

TIME AND PLACE OF PERFORMANCE

Generally, while making a contract, the parties, by mutual agreement decide about time and place of performance. And both the parties are expected to perform their respective promises accordingly. When time and place, are not determined, they should perform their promises within a reasonable period of time and place. Reasonable time and place is a matter of fact which varies from situation to situation depending on intention of the parties, nature of contract and circumstances of the case.

In order to facilitate performance of contract without any dispute, certain rules are laid down regarding time and place by the Indian Contract Act. These are as under:

(i) ***Time is not prescribed and performance is not to be applied:*** Time of performance has not been stipulated and the promisor has to perform his promise without the request or application of promisee. In such case, the promisor must perform his promise within reasonable period of time. Reasonable period of time depends upon the—intention of the parties, nature of contract and circumstances. (Section 46).

(ii) ***Time is specified, performance is not to be applied for:*** When a promise is to be performed on a certain day, the promisor may undertake to perform it without application or request by the promisee, in such a case, the promisor may perform the promise at any time during usual business hours on such day. (Section 47)

Example: A agrees to supply 200 bags of sugar to B on 1st October at a particular price. A should deliver these bags to B during usual business hours on 1st Oct.

(iii) ***Application for performance by promisee:*** When date of performance is specified and the promisor has to perform his promise on the application or request of promisee. Thus it is the duty of promisee to apply for performance on that day. He must apply during usual business hours.

Example: A agreed to supply 50 bags of tea to B on 8th September. As per the terms of a contract B would apply for performance. Thus on due date, with in usual business hours, B must inform A regarding time and place of supply of tea bags to him.

(iv) ***No application of performance and no place is fixed:*** When, the place of performance is not fixed and promisor has to perform his promise without application or request of promisee. Thus, it is a duty of promisor that he must contact with promisee as to decide about place of performance and accordingly perform the promise. (Section 48).

In case, the place of performance is fixed in a contract, promisor is bound to perform at that place. The place which is fixed in a contract must be reasonable for both the parties. Place of performance implies both place for delivery of goods and place of payment.

Example: Ram entered in to a contract for supplying 100 quintals of jute to Shyam on 5th September at a specific price. On due date of performance, Ram must apply to Shyam for determining reasonable place and must deliver the jute to him at that place.

(v) ***Promisee prescribes the manner and time of performance:*** According to this rule, the promisor must perform his promise in any manner and at any time, being prescribed by the promisee. (Section 50)

Example: B owes to A, Rs. 10,000. A asks B to deposit this amount in A's bank account. B deposites the amount in A's account. After some times bank fails and A has no information regarding transfer of money to his account. There has been good payment by B and in this way he is discharged from his obligation.

In another case, A owes Rs. 5000 to B. B agrees to accept some goods supplied by A in the deduction of the debt. The delivery of goods will be considered as a part of payment.

Time as the Essence of a Contract

It is usual on the part of the parties to decide about the time of performance at the time of making a contract. In this case, the promisor must perform his promise with in such stipulated time. In other cases, reasonable time must be followed for the performance.

The time of performance stipulated by the parties does not become an essence of a contract unless the parties have an intention to do so.

According to section 55 of this Act, 'when the party to a contract, promises to do certain things at or before the specified time and fails to do any such thing at or before the specified time the contract or so much of it, has not been performed, becomes voidable at the option of the promisee, if the intention of the parties was that, the time should be of essence of the contract'.

The contents of this section make it clear that when the parties decide about time of performance and have a intention to make it essence of a contract, such stipulated time becomes the essence of a contract. And the promisor must fulfil his promise with in that stipulated time. It he fails to do so, the contract becomes voidable at the options of promisee.

It was held in, **Hitkari Singh Vs. A.I.R. (1952, J.K.10)** that, 'in mercantile contracts, where once a particular time is specified, the presumption is that the time is of the essence of the contract, unless a contrary intention appears from the terms of the contract and other surrounding circumstances'.

Thus time is an essence of a contract, provided:

(a) Time of performance has been decided about by the parties
(b) Parties are intented to make it the essence of a contract, either by the words of mouth or in writing.
(c) Surrounding circumstances are also in favour of making it as the essence of a contract.

It is to be noted that when time is an essence of a contract and promisor fails to perform his promise on time, such contract becomes voidable at the option of the promisee.

Keeping in view the various judicial decisions, stipulated time is considered as essence of contract under the following situations:

(a) When the parties of a contract have expressly agreed that stipulated time will be the essence of a contract.

(b) In a contract of sale, stipulated time for the delivery of goods and payment of price has been considered as the essence of the contract.

(c) Again, in a contract of sale, time of shipment is of the essence of the contract.

Wasoo Enterprises Vs. J.J. Oil Mills (1968). In this case, the goods were to be shipped by August 1954. On the failure, to ship in August, time was extended to 10th September. Even then the supplier failed to ship the goods. The buyer repudiated the contract. It was held that time was of essence of the contract. Thus supplier is liable for breach of contract.

(d) In all commercial transaction, time of performance, as determined by the parties is considered as an essence of the contract.

When the stipulated time is not the essence of a contract and the promisor fails to perform his promise on due date, the promisee can only claim for compensation, if he has suffered any loss.

Even if the time is an essential factor in a contract, the promisee is free to accept delayed performance. If he wants to claim compensation for delayed performance, he must give notice of his intention to the promisor.

PERFORMANCE OF RECIPROCAL PROMISES

Generally, a contract is a mutual exchange of promises. The promise made by one party forms consideration for the promise of another party. Such promises are known as reciprocal promises. According to section 2(f) of this Act, 'when one party gives a promise in consideration of other party's promise, both the promises are called reciprocal promises'.

Example: A promises to deliver raw material to B, B promises to pay for that. There is a mutual exchange of promises between A and B. These are known as reciprocal promises, because one promise forms consideration for another promise.

Lord Mansfield, in **Jones Vs. Barkly**, case has classified reciprocal promises as under.

(a) *Mutual and dependent:* Such promises are interdependent. The performance of one promise depends on the prior performance of other promise. In other words, performance of one promise depends on other.

(b) *Mutual and concurrent:* when both reciprocal promises are got to be performed simultaneously with each other, these are known as mutual and concurrent promises.

(c) *Mutual and independent:* Such promises are independent but forms consideration for each other. These promises are performed independently without waiting for other.

Rules regarding performance of reciprocal promises: Section 51 – 54, 57 and 58 deal with the performance of reciprocal promises.

(i) *Simultaneous performance of reciprocal promises:* When a contract consists of reciprocal promises to be performed simultaneously, no promisor needs to perform his promise unless promisee is ready and willing to perform his promise. This is so, because both the promisors have to perform their promises simultaneously with each other. (Section 51)

Example: A agrees to deliver 200 tonnes of rice to B. and B is to make payment on delivery. Thus A has to give delivery and B is to make payment. A need not give delivery unless B is ready and willing to pay.

(ii) *Order of performance:* when the parties making reciprocal promises, determine the order of performance expressly, they must perform in that order. (Section 52).

Example: A makes promise to build a house for B at fixed price. A must build house first for B as to get payment from him. A can claim payment from B only when the house is built, because order of performance of both promises is determined.

(iii) *Effect of one party preventing another from performing promise:* In a contract consisting of reciprocal promises, if one party prevents another from performing a promise the contract becomes voidable at the option of the party so prevented. He can claim compensation if he has suffered any loss (Section 53)

Example: A promises to sell standing timber to B. As per the terms of a contract A will cut and cord the timber, where upon B will take it away and pay for it. A cords only a part of timber and neglects to cord the rest. In this contract, B may avoid contract and claim compensation from A.

(iv) *Effect of default as to promise to be performed first:* When the contract consists of reciprocal promises, such that one promise can not be performed or its performance can not be claimed till other promise has been performed. In case of default on the part of promisor who is to perform first, he can not claim performance from another promisor and if other promisor has suffered a loss due to non-performance, he is entitled for compensation (Section 54).

Example: B, a ship owner agrees to convey A's cargo from Calcutta to Mauritius for a certain amount of freight. A fails to provide cargo to B. B is entitled to avoid contract and claim compensation for the loss it any.

(v) *Reciprocal promise to do some thing legal and also some other thing which is illegal:* When a person reciprocally promise first to do certain things which are legal and secondly to do certain other things which are illegal. The first set of promise is a contract and second set is void agreement.

Example: A and B agree that A will sell a house to B for Rs. 50,000/- and also that if B uses it as gambling house A will further pay him Rs. 75000/- The first set of reciprocal promise for selling a house is a valid contract, but the object of second one is illegal therefore if it is void.

This rule is applicable, where reciprocal promises can be separated out. Legal part of promise can be enforced provided it can be separated from illegal part of the promise.

APPROPRIATION OF PAYMENT

Appropriation of payment implies to apply or use particular payment for discharging debt. It is related to time and place of performance of a contract. The person may borrow money from the creditor many times. Each borrowing may be of distinct amount and repayable on different dates. It means various debts are different in terms of amount as well as date of payment. In such case, if the borrower makes payment which is not sufficient for discharging all debts. The question arises, how to apply or use that payment and against the discharge of which debt it should be used.

In this regard, the following rules, which are give under section 59 to 61 of this Act are followed:

(i) *By express instructions of debtor:* While making payment, generally, the debtor gives necessary instructions to the creditor for the application of that amount. In such case appropriation must be made according to those instructions. It has been rightly pointed out by Lord Camp bell, in '**RAFT VS. LUMELY**' case that 'there is an established rule of law that, when money is paid, it is to be applied according to express will of the payer, not of the receiver'.

(ii) *Implied by intention of debtor and circumstance:* In case the debtor does not give express instructions for the application of payment, it can be used according to an intention of debtor and the circumstances.

Example: A owes three debts to B. One of Rs, 5000 for two months, another of Rs. 2000 for one year and third one of Rs. 1000 under Bill of Exchange which is due on 5th January. A makes payment of Rs. 1000 to B on 4th January, but does not give any instruction for application of that payment. In this case, it is implied, both from intention of A as well as circumstance that the payment must have been made by A to discharge that Bill of Exchange which falls due on 5th January.

(iii) *Discretion of creditor:* When the debtor does not give any instruction and nothing is indicated by his intention and circumstances, the creditor has a discretion to apply such payment for discharging any lawful debt due against the debtor. The creditor can apply such payment, even for discharging debt which, otherwise has become time-barred under the provisions of Indian Limitation Act.

Example: Ram owes several debts to Shyam, which are of distinct amount and payable on different dates. One of the debts has become time-barred which Shyam can not legally recover it from Ram. On a particular date Ram makes a payment, does not give any instruction and its application is not implied from intention of Ram and circumstances. In this case, Shyam has a right to apply this payment for discharging even that time-barred debt.

(iv) *Order of time:* When the parties do not make appropriation and it is not implied from the circumstances, the payment shall be applied for discharging debts in order of time. The debt which falls due first will be discharged first. But, if two or more debts fall due on same date, the amount of payment shall be applied to those debts in the ratio of principal amount.

Example: A owes many debts to B. Two debts fall due on the same date prior to others. The principal amount of these two is Rs. 5000 and Rs. 10,000. A pays Rs 4000. In the absence of all other rules this amount will be applied against these two debts in the ratio of 1:2.

ASSIGNMENT OF CONTRACTS

Assignment of a contract is a process, whereby rights and liability of a contract are transfered to a third party. As a result of assignment, such third party can bring an action, against another party of a contract at his own. Though, Indian contract Act does not contain any provision to deal with assignment of a contract. But generally, the following rules are followed by the courts of law

(i) *Assignment may take place by the act of the parties of a contract:* By making agreement of assignment they can transfer contractual rights and liability to a third party. Assignment of contract, by the act of the parties is subject to the following rules.

(a) According to section 40, of this Act, contractual obligations involving personal skill or ability can not be assigned, e.g. contractual obligation by a singer to sing, or by film actor to act or a contract of marriage, etc.

(b) In a contract, promisor can not assign his liability or obligation without the consent of the promisee. On giving such consent by the promisee, it becomes case of novation. The promisee is entitled to know that, in a contract who is to provide satisfaction to his right.

Example: A owes Rs. 2000 to B. A can assign his liability of paying the debt to C, only with the consent of B and C. This is so because B as a promisee has a right to know that who is to pay him.

(c) Rights and benefits under a contract can be assigned, except in a contract which involves personal skill and ability. But such assignment must be subject to all equities between original parties of a contract. Such as, an actionable claim (right to take legal action) can be assigned only by making an instrument in writing. And it is in the interest of assignee to give notice of assignment to the debtor, though it is not legally required.

KEMP VS. BAERSELMAN (1906, 75 L.J.K.B., 873). In this case, B agreed to supply eggs to a cake manufacture. The eggs were to be delivered at three different places and payment to be made through Bill of Exchange drawn upon him. The business of cake manufacturer was taken over by a company in which he was main shareholder. B refused to deliver eggs to the company. It was held that the contract was based on personal considerations, therefore it can not be assigned.

(ii) *Assignment by operation of law:* In many instances, rights or benefits in a contract automatically devolve upon third party by operation of law. As it happens in case of death or insolvency of the party, the rights and liabilities are transfered to their legal representatives (Except in case of a contract of personal nature) or official assignee. (in case of insolvency).

CONTRACTS WHICH NEED NOT BE PERFORMED

According to Indian Contract Act, in the following cases, a contract need not be performed.

(i) According to section 56 of this Act, when the performance of a contract becomes impossible due to any reasons beyond the control of the parties, such contract becomes void and need not be performed.

(ii) When the parties of a contract, substitute to new contract, or alter it or cancel it by mutual agreement, such contract need not be performed. (Section 62).

(iii) When the promisee of a contract accepts lesser performance of the whole promise or extend the time of performance, such contract is discharged. (Section 63).

(iv) When the party who is entitled to rescind the contract or at whose option the contract can be declared as void, avoids such contract, it need not be performed. (Section 64).

(v) When the promisee neglects or refuses to afford the promisor reasonable facilities for the performance of his promise, such contract comes to an end. (Section 67).

REVIEW QUESTIONS

1. What do you mean by 'performance of a contract'? Explain actual and attempted performance.
2. Explain who can demand performance of a contract and from whom it can be demanded?
3. Discuss the rules regarding performance of a joint promises.

4. Explain the various rules regarding time and place of performance of a contract.
5. Explain time as an essence of a contract. Discuss the various instances in which time is considered as an essential factor of a contract.
6. Can rights and liabilities of a contract be assigned? Discuss the rules regarding it.
7. Define reciprocal promises with suitable examples. Explain various legal provisions related to the performance of these promises.
8. What is appropriation of payment? Explain the legal provisions regarding it.
9. Comment on the following:
   (a) Performance is a natural mode of discharging a contract.
   (b) Contract of a personal nature cannot be assigned.
   (c) Time as an essence of a contract.
   (d) Contract for doing something impossible need not be performed.
   (e) Joint promisors are liable Jointly and severally.

Practical Problems

1. A, who is a painter, agrees to make a painting for B. Before the due date, A dies. Can B claim performance? (No)
2. Ram borrows a sum of Rs. 20,000 from Shyam for six months. Two months, after having borrowed the money, Ram dies. Manohar, who is a legal representative of Ram inherits a property worth Rs. 15,000 from him. Examine the legal consequences of this contract.
3. X and Y jointly promise to pay Rs. 5000 to Y. Before the due date X dies and Y becomes insolvent. What is the legal remedy available to Z?
4. A owes Rs. 10,000 to B. B asks A to deposit the amount in the account of B. A does so. Before B knows about the transfer of money to his account the bank fails. Can B recover this amount from A? (No)
5. A agrees to get B's house repaired, provided B vacates the house. But B does not vacate the house and as a result of it A fails to repair his house. Is A liable for breach of contract? (No)
6. A enters into an agreement with B for selling his house to B at Rs. 50,000. But if B uses this house for gambling purpose he shall pay Rs. 75000 for it. Can B avoid both sets of promises? (No)
7. In a contract, A has to recover Rs. 25000 from B. Later on, A accepts a sum of Rs. 15000 from C in full settlement of account with B. Can A claim the remaining balance from B? (No)

8. Manohar was to deliver 200 bags of cement to Sohan on 5th September. As per the terms of a contract Sohan would apply for performance. On the due date Sohan forgets to apply for performance. Can the contract be enforced? (No)
9. A was to supply 100 cotton bales to B on 10th October. Both the parties are intented to make it an essential factor of a contract. A fails to deliver cotton bales. What is the legal remedy available to B. Explain if time fixed by the parties of contract is not an essence of a contract can B avoid that contract. (No)
10. X owes several debts of distinct amount and payable at different period of time to Y. One of the debt has become time barred. Meanwhile X makes payment at random and does not instruct Y for applying it. Y gets an opportunity and uses this payment for discharging the debt which has become time barred. Is appropriation of payment valid? (Yes).
11. A agrees to marry B. Before marriage A becomes unsound mind. Can B claim compensation from the legal representative of A ?
12. Ram agreed to supply eggs to Shyam who manufactures cakes. Eggs were to be supplied at different places and payment was to be made through Bill of Exchange drawn upon Shyam. The business of Shyam was taken over by newly formed private company in which Shyam is main stockholder. Ram refuses to supply eggs to the Company. Can the company take any legal action against Ram? (No)

■■■

Chapter 11

Breach of Contract

Learning Objectives

- Understand meaning and concept of breach of contract
- Compare legal consequences of actual breach and anticipatory breach of contract.
- Get familiar with legal remedies of an aggrieved party in breach of contract.
- Develop clarity about damages and their types.
- Examine suitability of each legal remedy.
- Analyse rule of 'quantum meruit' and its applications.

MEANING AND TYPES OF BREACH OF CONTRACT

Formation of contract results in creating contractual obligations between the parties. These contractual obligations are to be fulfilled by the parties on the due date as per terms and conditions of a contract. When the party does not fulfil his obligation or refuses to fulfil it or disabled himself from fulfilling it is known as breach of contract. Such contract comes to an end, and another party gets certain legal remedies to be used against party making breach of contract.

Breach of contract may be of two types: (a) Actual breach (b) Anticipatory breach.

Actual breach of contract takes place when the promisor fails to perform his obligation or refuses to do so on the due date of performance.

Example: A was to deliver 100 bags of sugar to B on 5th September at a specific price. On the 5th September A does not make supply or refuses or becomes untraceable. It amounts to actual breach of contract and the contract is discharged.

In ***Anticipatory breach*** of contract, the promisor either refuses to perform or makes himself unable to perform a promise before due the date of performance. Anticipatory breach of contract takes place before the date of actual performance. The promisor may either inform promisee that he is not going to perform his promise or does any act, which is inconsistent with terms and conditions of a contract.

According to section 39 of this act 'when a party to a contract has refused to perform or disable himself from performing his promise in its entirely, the promisee may put contract to an end; unless he has given his acquiescence in its continuance by words or conduct'.

In other words on the refusal of promisor if the promisee condones breach of contract or waives his rights the contract will continue.

Anticipatory breach of contract also takes place if the promisor does an act, which renders performance of his promise impossible or illegal.

Example: A enters into an agreement to marry B on 15th January. But on 15th December he marries C. This act on the part of A has rendered the performance of his promise illegal; thus A will be liable for anticipatory breach of contract by impossibility.

On anticipatory breach of contract the promisee or aggrieved party has the following options:

(a) The promisee can wait till the due date of performance. And on that date, anticipatory breach will be automatically converted in to actual breach and the contract will be discharged.

During intervening period between anticipatory breach and actual breach if supervening impossibility takes place and contract is discharged; the promisee or aggrieved party loses his right to claim for compensation.

Avery Vs. Bowden (1885,5 E&B, 714). In this case B chartered A's ship and agreed to load it with a cargo at Odessa with in 45 days. On the arrival of the ship at Odessa, B was unable to supply cargo. A did not accept the refusal and continued demanding the cargo. Before the expiry of 45 days war was broken and performance of the contract became impossible. It was held that, contract was discharged and A is not entitled to sue upon B for compensation.

(b) On getting information regarding anticipatory breach, the promisee can immediately rescind or avoid the contract. And without waiting till due date of performance he can use legal remedies against the promisor e.g. sue upon the promisor for compensation or specific performance etc.

HOCHSTERV VS. DE, LA, TOUR (1953, 2E & B, 678). In this case, defendant agreed to engage the plaintiff as his attendant on a continental tour, which he will start from June 1st for three month at a particular salary. The defendant later on changed his mind and informed plaintiff before June 1st that he would not require his service. It was held that the plaintiff can put contract to end even before 1st June and bring a suit for compensation. He was not bound to wait till the date of performance.

LEGAL REMEDIES FOR BREACH OF CONTRACT

There are two parties in a contract. They make mutual exchange of promises between them. These promises are known as contractual obligations. When a party does not fulfill his promise or refuse to perform it, breach of contract takes place. In that contract, another party is technically known as aggrieved party. Such aggrieved party has got various legal remedies, which he can use against the party making a breach of contract.

These legal remedies are as under:

- Rescission of the contract.
- Suit for damages.
- Suit for Specific performance.
- Suit injunction.
- Suits upon 'Quantum Merit'

1. Rescission of the Contract

When a party makes breach of contract by not fulfilling his obligation, the aggrieved party has a right to rescind such contact. To exercise this right, the aggrieved has to file a suit for rescission of a contract. On granting rescission, the aggrieved party gets released from his obligation in that contact. He is no more liable to perform his promise. The net legal effects of rescission are as follows:

(a) Aggrieved party is discharged from his obligation in that contract.

(b) Right of restitution comes in to force and the party who has got benefit in that contract will be liable to restore it or give it back to the party from whom he has received it. (Section 64)

(c) It would also clear the way for aggrieved party to use other legal remedies against the party making breach of a contract.

Example: Manohar was in an agreement with Sohan for supplying 200 bags of cement on 5th January. On the due date Manohar does not supply bags of cement to Sohan. It amounts to breach of contracts by Manohar. Sohan, before taking any legal remedy against Manohar, has to get himself absolved from his obligation of making payment. It is only by getting rescission from the court he gets free from his obligation and it also clears the way for using other legal remedies against Manohar.

2. Suit for Damages

On making a breach of contract by a party, the aggrieved party may suffer monetary loss. In the event of breach he may be put in a disadvantageous position or in a position of discomfort. In such case, the aggrieved party has a right to claim for compensation. The basic idea of providing compensation to the aggrieved party is to put him in the same financial position, as he would have been if the contract had been performed.

However due to breach of contract the aggrieved party may suffer variety of losses such as loss of profit, loss of reputation, loss of payment of expenses and loss due to change in price line etc. Not only this, but aggrieved party may also exaggerated his losses as to get benefit of the situation.

Thus in this regard the courts make judicious assessment of the losses suffered by an aggrieved party and grant compensation accordingly. The amount of compensation granted by the court is technically known as 'damage'

In one of the leading case, the court has observed that, 'the role of common law is that where a party sustains loss by reason of breach of contract, he is to be placed in the same situation, with respect to damages as if the contract has been performed'.

According to section 73 of this act, 'when a contract has been broken the party who suffers by such breach is entitled to receive from the party who has broken the contract compensation for any loss or damage caused to him there by'

(a) Which naturally arose out of breach of contract.

(b) Which the party knew when they make contract to be likely to result from the breach of it.

(c) Such compensation is not to be given for any remote and indirect loss or damage sustained by reason of the breach.

In this connection there had been very interesting case in which certain rules regarding damages were made clear.

Hadley Vs. Baxendale (1854, 9, EX, 341). In this case, the plaintiff had delivered a crankshaft to the manufactures who were to make a new shaft on the basis of old one. The servant of plaintiff had informed the carrier that the working of the mill was stopped and the crankshaft must be sent to the manufactures immediately. The carrier made delay in sending crankshaft as a result of which new shaft was received very late and the mill could not work. The plaintiff filed a suit against the defendant claiming damage for the loss of profit, because of the stoppage of the mill due to non-availability of crankshaft. Defendant pleaded that these were remote damages and they were not liable to pay.

Justice B. Alderson observed that, 'where two parties have made a contract, which one of them has broken, the damage which the other party ought to receive in respect of such breach of contract should be as such as fairly and reasonably be considered either arising naturally, that is, according to the usual course of thing from such breach of contract itself or such as may reasonably be supposed to have been in the contemplation of both parties, at the time they made contract as the probable result of breach of it'.

This decision lays down the following two rules

(a) Only those losses may be compensated which are fair, reasonable and directly and naturally arising out of breach of contract.

(b) Indirect or remote losses such as loss of profit may be compensated provided such loss would have been in contemplation or consideration of both parties at the same time of making the contract.

Example: A agreed to supply spare parts of machine to B on 5th September at a particular price. A fails to deliver spare parts on due date. There is a breach of contract and filed B a suit against A for the compensation of losses. B claimed that due to non-delivery of spare parts, the machine could not function, as a result of which the following losses were incurred.

(a) Depreciation on machine
(b) Fixed expenses such as salary paid to permanent to permanent staff, rent of premises and other rate and taxes.
(c) Loss of profit which would have been earned through contract which could not be done due to non functioning of machine.

In this case, taking note of **HADLEY VS. BAXENDALE,** compensation may be granted to B only for depreciation, fixed expenses and salary paid to permanent staff. The loss of profit from Govt. contract is a remote and indirect loss there fore it can be compensated provided A and B could have considered it at the tine of making contract.

Types of damages:
Damages can be of the following types:

- Ordinary Damages.
- Special Damages.
- Exemplary or Vindictive Damages.
- Nominal Damage.

(a) *Ordinary damages:* When breach of contract takes place, the aggrieved party is entitled to claim for compensation for the losses caused to him. Ordinary damages are those damages, which will be sanctioned by the court for those losses, which do arise in the natural and ordinary course from the breach of contract. These damages are granted for the losses, which are directed and general in nature. The calculation and quantum of ordinary damages depend upon the circumstances, which were prevailing at the time of breach of contract.

According to section 73 of this Act, general damages is referred to, 'compensation for any loss caused to him thereby which naturally arose in the usual course of things from such breach'.

Natural and direct losses resulting from breach of contract may, vary situation-to-situation depending on nature of transaction and prevailing circumstances. The following examples may help in understanding such losses.

Difference between contract price and market price: *Example:* A agrees to sell 200 bags of cement to B on 5th September at Rs. 500 per bag. B is to make payment on the delivery of cement bags. Before due date the price of cement has increased to Rs. 600 per bag. A refused to supply cement to B. There is breach of contract B is entitled to claim for compensation for the loss arising out of change in price, e.g. Rs. 100 per bag of cement (Rs. 2000).

Principal amount & interest for delayed payment: *Example:* X borrows sum of Rs. 1000 from Y @ 10 per cent interest per annum for one year. On due date X fails to repay. As a result of it Y could not fulfill his obligation and totally ruined. X liable only for the payment of Rs. 1000 plus interest @ 10 per cent for delayed payment.

Medical expenses and financial losses caused by death: *Example:* A's wife brought tin fish from the merchant. After consuming it the poisoning was caused and she died. A is entitled to recover from the merchant @ expense for employing servant during her illness (b) medical expenses (c) Financial loss caused by the death of his wife.

Cost of hiring another ship: *Example:* A, hires B's ship for going to Mumbai and boarding cargo on 1st January which is to be brought to Calcutta at particular fright. B does not send his ship to Mumbai and made a breach of contract. A is entitled to receive compensation for such troubles and expenses which will be incurred by him for hiring another ship.

Cost of rebuilding the house, loss of rent and compensation to third party: *Example:* A entered into an agreement for constructing house for B. and to give complete possession on 1st January. B makes agreement with C for renting out that house to him from 2nd January; this fact is very much in the knowledge of A. the house was badly constructed and collapsed before 1st January. B is entitled to get compensation for (a) Cost of reconstructing the house. (b) Loss of rent (c) compensation, which B was to pay to C for not renting out the house.

Not responsible for the losses due to closure of the mill: *Example:* A made a contract for supplying 100 cotton bales to B at a particular price. A knows nothing about the nature of business, being contracted by B. As a result of non-availability of cotton bales B's mill is closed. B entitled to get compensation for the loss expenses, price difference to be incurred for arranging supply from other sources. But A is not liable to pay compensation for the loss caused by closure of the mill.

Losses arising out of breach of conditions and warranties in a contract of sale: *Example:* A agrees to sell washing machine on a warranty of particular quality to B. B who relies on that warranty sells it to C. But C does not find the machine of that quality on which warranty has been given. B pays compensation for breach of warranty to C. later on; B is entitled to recover it from A.

(b) *Special Damages:* Special Damages are granted by the court for compensating special losses caused to the party due to breach of contract. Special losses are those losses, which do arise from special circumstances, which are attached to a contract. These special circumstances, which may cause special loss to the party in case of breach of contract, must have been informed to another party at the time of making a contract.

According to section 73 of this act, special losses refer to those that may be caused by breach of contract, 'which the party knew, when they made a contract, to be likely to result from breach of it'.

Thus the special damages imply:

(a) Compensation for special losses arising out of the breach of contract.
(b) These special losses do arise from the special circumstances, which were attached to the contract.
(c) These losses must have been in consideration of the parties at the time of making a contract. It means such probable loss must have been properly communicated to the other party.
(d) Special losses are in addition to ordinary losses. Special losses are remote and indirect in nature, not directly arising from breach of contract rather, these are arising out of special circumstances attached to the contract.

The basic nature of special losses can be understood on the basis of the following examples.

Loss of profit: *Example:* A was in agreement to supply spare parts of machine to B latest by a particular date. While making agreement B has properly informed to A that in case he does not get that part of machine on time, in addition to other losses, he will also suffer a loss of a particular amount per day due to non execution of government contract. A fails to deliver part of machine on time. B is entitled to claim for compensation both for ordinary losses and special loss, e.g. loss of profit regarding non-execution of government contact.

Loss of income: *Example:* Ram, who is a taxi driver gives his taxi to Shyam for getting it repaired and informs him that unreasonable delay in repairing will result in loss of income of Rs. 100 per day. Shyam makes unreasonable delay in repairing. He is bound to pay compensation for the loss of income, which is a special loss.

(c) *Exemplary or vindictive damages:* When the amount granted by the court is more than ordinary and special losses it is known as Exemplary or Vindictive damages. Such damages are granted by the court, for the disapproval of conduct of the party making a breach of contract.

These damages are the exceptions to the general rule that damages are not to be in the nature of punishment but only compensation for the losses incurred by the party.

Exemplary damages are generally awarded to deter the person from making breach of contract on the one hand and on the other, the idea of awarding such damages may also be to compensate the aggrieved party to some extent, for mental pain, loss of reputation and sense of humilation etc.

These damages are awarded by the court, under the following situations:

(a) When there is a breach of contract of marriage, aggrieved party is entitled to claim such damages. The quantum of damage depends on the extent of mental injury and loss of reputation caused to him.

(b) When a bank, wrongfully dishonours a customer's cheque drawn upon it on the plea of insufficient credit balance in his account, the customer is entitled to claim exemplary damages for compensating the loss of credit.

Western Vs. Olathe State Bank (1925,78, col.217). In this case, a banker agreed to advance money to Western's trip to California, by putting credit balance in his account. But the bank wrongfully failed to put that amount in the credit of customer's account. As a result of it, the cheques drawn by the customer were dishonoured. It was held that Western was entitled to claim for exemplary damages for humiliation and mental suffering.

It is interesting to note that, in such cases, the rule of determining damages is, 'the smaller the cheque, the greater the damage'.

(d) *Nominal damages:* Nominal damages are awarded, when the court is of the opinion that aggrieved party has not suffered real loss due to breach of contract. The basic idea of granting such damages is to bring the party making breach of contract to record and to recognize the right of aggrieved party. In other words, such damages are awarded just to establish the right to decree for the breach of contract.

According to the recent decision of Delhi High Court that no damage can be allowed under section 73 of this act unless the aggrieved party has suffered some loss.

Union Of India Vs. Tribhguwan Das Ji Patel. (1971, A.I.R. Delhi 120). In this case, T agreed to supply sleepers to Railway Administration. As per the terms and conditions of the contract, T was required to pay damages to the Railways on his failure to supply, regardless of the fact that whether the railways suffer any loss or not. T failed to supply and Railways did not suffer any loss. Thus Delhi High Court disallowed the suit filed by the Railways for compensation.

How to calculate damages: In order to calculate amount of damage, to be sanctioned to the aggrieved party, the courts normally follow the following guidelines.

(i) Damages are allowed only to compensate the aggrieved party for the losses, which are direct, fair, natural and reasonable.

(ii) Remote or indirect losses of aggrieved may also be compensated provided such losses were in contemplation or consideration of the parties at the time of making a contract.

(iii) Only in a very specific cases, exemplary damages may be granted for compensating loss of reputation and mental suffering.

(iv) While calculating the amount of damage the court takes into account that the aggrieved party is being put in such a financial position, in which he would have been, if the contract had been performed.

(v) The court will also recognize that there is duty on the part of aggrieved party to mitigate the loss arising out of breach of contract. He cannot claim compensation for that amount of loss which would have been mitigated by making reasonable efforts.

(vi) The aggrieved party is also entitled to get the cost of getting decree for damages.

(vii) Damages can also be recovered for physical inconvenience and discomfort.

(viii) While calculating amount of damage in case of breach of contract of sale, generally the difference between contract price and market price is taken into consideration. And any change in the price taking place after date of breach will not be considered.

Jamal Vs Moola Dawood & Sons. In this case, A agreed to sell 23500 shares to B, to be delivered and paid for on 30 Decemember 1911. On that date, B refuses to accept delivery. The market price, on the date of breach was such as to cause loss of Rs. 109218. But A sold those shares much later and suffered a loss of Rs. 79862. but the court allowed damage of Rs. 109218 to A.

Liquidated damage and penalty: The concept of Liquidated damage and penalty is relevant in connection with calculation of damage. Sometimes, the parties while making a contract, may fix the amount of damage, which may be either Liquidated damage or penalty depending on the manner of fixing it.

(i) When the amount of damage to be paid to the aggrieved party has been fixed by the parties, on the basis of probable losses which may arise out of breach of a contract, such amount is known as liquidated damage.

(ii) When the parties fix the amount of damage to be paid not on the scientific basis, but with a view to put some kind of punishment on the party who will make breach of contract, such amount is known as penalty.

These two terms are used in English Mercantile Law. The courts in England, usually allow 'Liquidated damage' without any regard to the actual loss suffered by the party due to breach of a contract. And the court will make assessment of actual loss and grant damage for compensating that loss.

The distinction between penalty and liquidated damage has been made clear in the following case.

Dunlop Pneumatic Type Vs.New Garage And Motor Coy. (1914, A.C. 79). 'The essence of penalty is payment of money stipulated as 'in terrorum' and the essence of liquidated damage is a genuine covenated pre estimate of damage'

But, Indian courts do not recognize difference between liquidated damage and penalty. Rather, in case of breach of a contract, the court makes assessment of actual loss and grants compensation for it. While granting damage, amount fixed by the parties will be taken as maximum limit of damage.

According to section 74 of this Act, 'when a contract has been broken, if a sum is named in the contract as the amount to be paid in case of breach or if the contract contains any other stipulation by way of penalty, the party complaining breach is entitled, whether or not actual damage or loss is proved to have been caused thereby, to receive from the party who has broken the contract, reasonable compensation not exceeding the amount so named, as the case may be, the penalty stipulated for'.

Stipulation regarding payment of interest: when the creditor charged, increased rate of interest from the date of default such stipulation for increased rate of interest will be regarded as penalty. And if the debtor makes default in repaying the debt, such increased rate will be disallowed by the court provided increased rate of interest seems to be unreasonable.

Example: A borrows sum of Rs. 20000 from B @ 10 per cent interest per annum for 2 years. A signs promissory note with a stipulation that in case of his default in repaying that sum B will be allowed to charge @ 50 per cent interest from the date of default. The stipulation of increased rate of interest seems to be unreasonable thus B will be allowed to get compensation as court regards reasonable.

In connection with a stipulation for increased rate of interest, the following rules should be taken care of

(a) Unless, the parties make express or implied agreement interest cannot be recovered as a damage.
(b) Stipulation for increased rate of interest will be regarded as penalty. Thus only reasonable amount of compensation may be granted by the court in such cases.
(c) Increased rate of interest, which the party is supposed to pay from the date of default must be unreasonable in the eyes of law.
(d) When the contract provides that the amount should be paid without interest by a particular date and on default it will be payable with reasonable rate of interest, it may be allowed by the court.
(e) Payment of compound interest on default is allowed provided it is not at an increased rate.

3. Suit for Specific Performance

When, breach of contract takes place and aggrieved party suffers a loss. These losses may be of such a nature that damage granted for these by the court may be inadequate. It is because such losses can not be measured in terms of money. In such cases, the aggrieved party is entitled to claim for order of specific performance. Specific performance means actual carrying out of a contract as agreed.

The order of specific performance is an order issued by the court directing upon the party making breach of contract and instructing him to perform what he has undertaken to perform. Such order is a discretionary order, which is allowed by the court in a limited number of cases.

The rules for granting order of specific performance are contained in chapter II of specific Relief Act 1963. These are as under:

The order of specific performance, at the discretion of the court may be granted in the following cases:

(a) Where monetary compensation is not an adequate remedy for breach of contract.
(b) Where there is no standard for ascertaining the actual damage, caused by non-performance of promise by the party.
(c) When it is probable that compensation in terms of money on non-performance of contract cannot be obtained.
(d) In a contract of sales of goods such order can be granted for specific goods, which are unique, rare and cannot be easily purchased from the market, such as rare articles and antiques etc.

But order of specific performance will not be granted in the following cases:

(a) Where monetary compensation is an adequate remedy for the breach of contract.
(b) Where the court cannot supervise performance of contract, particularly when it is of continuous in nature.
(c) To enforce a contract of personal nature based on personal consideration and which requires special skill and talent to perform it, such as contract of marriage, contract with singer and painter etc.
(d) Contracts made by a company beyond its powers as laid in its Memorandum of Association.
(e) Contracts, which are made by trustees which amount to breach of trust.

4. Suit for Injunction

In a contract if the party has made a promise for not doing something, and that party makes a breach of contract by doing that thing. To prevent such party from doing that act an order of injunction may be claimed by an aggrieved party.

It is an order, passed by the court of law, directing upon the party and refraining him from performing what he has promise not to perform.

An injunction is a preventive relief, which is provided to an aggrieved party where damages would not be an adequate relief. It is a negative form of order of specific performance.

The power of the court for granting injunction is discretionary in nature. The court may grant such order either on temporary basis or for a indefinite period of time.

Example: Super star of a cricket makes an agreement with some sports goods company for not using the bats except manufactured by that company. On some occasions the company finds him using cricket bats manufactured by some other company. There is a breach of contract on the part of superstar of cricket.

To grant damage for compensating losses of the sports goods company is an inadequate remedy. Thus the company may get an injunction from the court for preventing cricket star from using bats of other company.

LIMLEY VS. WAGNER (1852, 5 De, GM & coy 604). In this case, W agreed to sing at L's theatre during certain period of time to sing nowhere else. Later on W made an agreement with Z to sing at his theatre and refused to perform the contract with L. it was held that W could be restrained by injunction from singing at Z's theatre.

5. Suit upon Quantum Meruit

In a contract the promisor may be in the process of performing his promise. Before he completes it, the promisee makes a breach of contract. Among other remedies, the aggrieved party can also claim for quantum Meruit.

Quantum Meruit is a Latin dictum, which means" as much as earned or merited". That means under Quantum Meruit aggrieved party can also claim for the reasonable cost of work done by him in the contract.

This legal remedy is claimed by an aggrieved party where in the performance of a contract, he has done some work or rendered some services. In case other party makes a breach of contract he can recover reasonable cost of work done or services rendered.

According to section 70 of this Act an aggrieved party can claim right of Quantum Meruit under the following situation:

(a) ***Breach of contract:*** One party is in the process of performance of a contract, but other party makes a breach of such contract. In such case if an aggrieved party has done some work or has rendered services, he is entitled to claim reasonable cost of work done services rendered.

Example: In an agreement A was to construct three storeyed building for B. He was to make payment of particular amount at the completion of each storey. A completed first storey of the building, but B fails to make stipulated payment. Among other remedies, A can also claim reasonable cost of constructing first storey of building.

(b) ***When contract is discovered to be void:*** when the person has done some work or rendered services in a contract, which was discovered to be void. Another person who gets benefit of such work or services must pay its cost to the person who has done the work in that contract.

Example: A was appointed as CEO of a company by the board of directors. After six months, it is found that one of the directors of the board who was a member of selection committee has not purchased qualification shares and therefore he was not a bonafide director. Thus service contract of CEO was discovered to be void. But he is entitled to get all benefits under that contract for a period of six months.

(c) ***Something done Voluntarily, but with an intention of getting consideration:*** When the person delivers some goods or renders some services for another person with an intention of getting consideration for it. The person who gets benefits of such services or goods is bound to pay reasonable cost or compensation to that person.

Example: A's godown gets into fire. B who is passersby helps A in extinguishing that fire. B has an intension of getting something in return of his services. Thus he is entitled to get reasonable compensation for his services.

(d) ***Divisible contract:*** Where a contract made by the parties is divisible. And a party to that contract has completed a part of his obligation, even if he has made breach of contract he can claim right of Quantum Meruit.

The right of Quantum Meruit is subject to following limitations

(a) A person who has made breach of contract is not allowed to claim right of Quantum Meruit.

(b) In a contract which is not divisible into part and lump sum payment is to be made for the complete work the party making part performance is not entitled to claim this right.

REVIEW QUESTIONS

1. Define the term 'Breach of Contract'. Explain how the contract is discharged by Breach. Give suitable Example.
2. Discuss the various Legal remedies, which are available to an aggrieved party in case of Breach Of Contract.
3. What are Damages? Discuss the various types of damages, which can be claimed by an aggrieved party for compensating his losses.
4. Explain various rules regarding calculation of damages, which are followed by the court.
5. Define the term 'Quantum Merit'. When this right can be claimed by aggrieved party. What are its limitations?
6. What is specific performance? In which situations the court grants order of specific performance. Explain when this order is not done?
7. Explain various rules regarding damages, which were laid down in Hadley Vs. Baxendale case. To what extent these rules are applicable in India?
8. Distinguish between Liquidated damages and Penalty. Explain it in the context of English and Business law

9. Write notes on the following:
   (a) Anticipatory Breach
   (b) Liquidated Damages.
   (c) Order of specific performance
   (d) Quantum Merit.
10. Comment on the following:
    (a) Liquidated damage and Penalty are one and same.
    (b) Anticipatory Breach does not discharge contract automatically.
    (c) Nominal damage is granted only for recognizing decree for damage.
    (d) Specific performance can be claimed when compensation is not a adequate remedy.
    (e) Stipulation regarding increased rate of interest after default is also a penalty.
    (f) Damages are not to be in the nature of punishment.
    (g) Injunction is a preventive relief.
    (h) Exemplary damage is awarded by the court for compensating loss of reputation and mental pain etc.

PRACTICAL PROBLEMS

1. Ram agrees to supply 200 bags of rice to Shyam on 5th September at a particular price. Shyam was to make payment on 10th September. On the due date of performance Ram refuses to deliver rice. Examine nature of Shyam's Obligations in this contract and how can he be released from it?
2. A was in agreement for supplying furniture to B on 1st January. On 15th December A informs to B that he will not make supply of furniture to him. What is legal remedy available to B? When can he use it against A?
3. A enters into an agreement to marry B on 15th September. But before 15th September A married with C. Examine legal validity of the contract between A and B.
4. Mohan was to supply 500 bags of sugar to Sohan. On the 18th January and Sohan subsequently was to pay for that. On the due date Mohan refused to supply sugar to Sohan. But Sohan did not accept Mohan's refusal and continuously demanded performance. On 5th December the Government makes a law debarring the individual from buying or selling more than 10 bags of sugar at a time. Is contract discharged? Suggest legal remedies to Sohan if any?
5. X was in contact to pay Rs. 10,000 to Y on a particular date. X does not pay that money on the due date. As a consequence of it can Y claim for any compensation for being ruined?

6. A, who is a tailor, delivered a sewing machine and some cloth to Railway Coy, to be delivered at a place, where festival was to be held. He was expecting to earn more profit at the festival, but did not bring this fact to the notice of Railway authorities. The goods were delivered by Railway Coy after the festival. Can A claim, the loss of profit which he would have earned during festival by selling those goods?

   (No, he has not informed Railway Coy of the special circumstance of festival)

7. Banker agreed to advance loan to A on a particular day by crediting amount of A. After that date A draws two cheques, which were dishonoured, because the banker had not credited amount of loan sanctioned to the account of A. can A claim for Exemplary damages? Explain with reason?

8. A made an agreement for hiring B's shop on rent and paid one months rent in advance. B could not give possession of that shop to A. As a result of it, A could not do any business for 6 months and filed suit for damages as to compensate his loss. Will he succeed in getting it?

   (No, he will not get more than refund of his advance, because it was his duty to mitigate loss, which he did not do)

9. A agrees to lend sum of Rs. 10,000 to B @ 10 per cent per annum for one year on a condition that if B does not refund money on the due date, he will have to pay interest @ 30 per cent per annum from the date of default. B defaults in repaying money. Is A, entitled to recover increased rate of interest?

10. A agrees to deliver 50 Maunds of salt petre to B on 1st January at a certain price. Before 1st January B makes an agreement with C to sell salt petre at the price, which is higher than market price of January. A does not deliver salt petre to B. Can B recover loss for that price from A which is higher than contract price? (No) only the difference between market price on 1st January can be recovered as compensation.

11. A agreed to sell 500 cotton bales to B. on 5th September at a particular price. A knows nothing about the business of B. A fails to deliver cotton balls. Having no cotton bales B was forced to close the mill. Is A responsible for the loss caused to B on account of closure of the will?

12. A, a builder agrees to construct two floors on condition that B will make payment in two instalments, e.g. first on the completion of 1st floor of building and second on the completion of second floor. A constructed 1st floor and B refused to pay. Suggest suitable legal remedies to A which he can use against B.

■■■

Chapter 12

Contract of Indemnity and Guarantee

Learning Objectives

- Understand the meaning and concept of Indemnity and Guarantee.
- Compare these two contracts in terms of their basic features.
- Examine limit and nature of surety's liability.
- Enumerate various types of losses for which the contract of Indemnity can be made
- Analyse the surety's legal position in terms of his rights and liabilities.

INTRODUCTION

Contracts of indemnity and guarantee are very much a part of general contract, but with some special features. It is therefore special provisions from sections 124 to 147 have been provided in Indian contract Act to deal with these special contracts.

MEANING AND DEFINITION OF CONTRACT OF INDEMNITY

A contract of indemnity is entered into for compensating losses or other party. These losses may or may not occur in future. Thus a contract of indemnity in a part of contingent contract. The performance of it depends on happening or non-happening of certain event in future which may cause the losses to another party.

Thus, a contract of indemnity is a contract in which one party promises to compensate or protect other party from the losses arising in future.

According to section 124 of Indian contract Act, "a contract of indemnity is a, contract by which one party promises to save the other from loss caused to him either by the conduct of the promisor himself or by the conduct of any third party."

The definitions of contract of indemnity given under this section seems to be very narrow. This is so because according to this definition a contract of indemnity is made only for compensating:

(i) losses arising out of a conduct of the promisor.
(ii) losses arising out of conduct of third party
(iii) losses which are express in nature.

Example: A has filed a suit against B in the court of law. C makes a promise to A that whatever the losses A will suffer on that suit he will compensate him for the same. A contract between A and C is a contract of indemnity.

However, the definition of a contract of indemnity given in English Mercantile Law is an exhaustive one. According to this definitions a contract of indemnity also includes losses caused to the party by an event or accident.

According to English Law a contract of indemnity has been defined as, "a promise to save another harmless, from loss caused as a result of a transaction entered in to at the instance of the promisor."

It is therefore, in our country broader interpretation of a contract of indemnity is followed by the courts. And a contract of indemnity can be made for compensating the following losses.

(i) loss arising out of a conduct of parties.
(ii) loss arising out of an event or accident.
(iii) Express losses.
(iv) Implied losses.

In this context, in a case **Regional Manager Oriental Fire and General Insurance Coy. VS. Saving Solvent oil Extractions, Ltd, (1997)6, Andh, L.D 1, DB, A.P,** the court observed that, the English definition of indemnity is wide enough to include a promise of indemnity against loss arising from any cause whatsoever, e.g. loss caused by fire or by some other accident. Indeed every contract of insurance, other than life insurance is a contract of indemnity.

Similarly in **GAJANAN MORESHWAR VS. MORESHWAR MADAN (1942)** A.I.R Bom. 302, 304,) case, the court has made it clear that "Section 124 and 125 of Indian Contract Act are not exhaustive of the law of indemnity and the court here would apply same equitable principles that the courts in England do".

Characteristics of Indemnity

(i) A contract of indemnity is entered into between two parties namely indemnifier who makes a promise to indemnify loss and indemnity holder whose losses are made good by the indemnifier.
(ii) A contract of indemnity is a special contract, thus it must satisfy all essential conditions of a valid contract. such as contractual capacity, lawful object, consideration and free consent etc.
(iii) According to judicial interpretations, contract of indemnity includes losses arising out of a conduct of the party and happening of an event or accident. It also includes not only express promise but also a implied promise for compensating losses.

Example: A hires a taxi for the purpose of going to Bombay. On the way he meets with an accident and the taxi is badly damaged. The owner has a right to get compensation for this loss from A., because there was an implied promise of indemnity on the part of A.

(iv) A contract of indemnity is made primarily for compensating losses of another party which may be caused to him either by the conduct of party or by any event or accident. Thus all insurance contracts except life insurance contracts are considered as a contract of indemnity.

Rights of Indemnity Holder (Section 125)

In a contract of indemnity, the indemnity holder who is to be compensated for the loss has the following rights

(i) **Damages**: An indemnity holder is entitled to recover the amount of damage which he has been compelled to pay to another party in a suit to which contract of indemnity is applicable.

(ii) **Costs**: An indemnity holder is also entitled to claim all costs which he has incurred for defending himself in a suit to which the promise of indemnity is applicable. Such costs may include all incidental charges and legal expenses paid in that suit.

(iii) **Other payments**: In a contract of indemnity if the indemnity holder has made any payment to another party on the compromise of that suit to which contract of indemnity is applicable, he is entitled to recover such payment from the indemnifier provided he has acted as a person of reasonable prudence or such compromise has been allowed by the indemnifier.

When Does Liability of Indemnifier Arise?

A contract of indemnity is made for the purpose of indemnifying losses. In this contract indemnity holder has got some rights against indemnifier such as to claim damage, costs and other payments. Now the question arises that at what point of time the liability of indemnifier commences? Is it after having made payments by the indemnity holder or just when the liability of payment arises on his part.

Indian contract Act does not contain any provision regarding commencement of indemnifier's liability. And the courts are divided on this issue. Judicial interpretations given by various high courts can be summarised as under.

(i) High courts of Bombay and Nagpur have held that the indemnifier is not liable until and unless the indemnity holder has suffered actual loss or has discharged the liability. It means the liability of indemnifier commences after the indemnity holder suffers actual loss or he has made payments which he is entitled to recover from the indemnifier.

(ii) But, the high courts of Calcutta, Allahabad, Patna and Madras have held that the indemnity holder can compel indemnifier to compensate his losses even before he has actually discharged the liability or has made the payment. It means it is enough for making the indemnifier liable that the liability of indemnity holder has arisen in a suit to which contract of indemnity is applicable.

(iii) On the review of whole subject, the Bombay high court held that as soon as the liability of indemnity holder arises and becomes absolute, he may call upon the indemnifier to protect him from losses. This point of view is considered to be more equitable and acceptable.

Case: **OSMAN JAMAL & SONS VS. GOPAL (1919), 56, C.1, 262.**

In this case it was held that, the official liquidator of the company was entitled to recover the amount, even though the company had not actually paid the supplier. The court observed that, indemnity is not necessarily given by repayment after payment. Indemnity requires that the party to be indemnified shall never be called upon to pay. Thus liability on the part of indemnity holder must be absolute to call indemnifier to pay off.

DEFINITION AND MEANING OF CONTRACT OF GUARANTEE

According to section 126 of this Act, "A contract of guarantee is a contract to perform the promise or discharge the liability of third person in case of his default".

Thus the contract of guarantee is made to ensure performance of a contract or discharge of obligation by the promisor. In case if he fails to do so, the person giving assurance or guarantee becomes liable for such performance or discharge.

In a contract of guarantee there are three parties namely *the principal debtor*– who is primarily liable to pay debt or discharge obligation, the creditor – to whom *the principal debtor* is liable to pay and surety gives guarantee to him *the surety* – who takes responsibility that if the principal debtor fails he will discharge the obligation.

Example: A borrows a sum of Rs. 10,000 from the bank. B gives guarantee to the bank that in case A defaults in repayment, he will repay to the bank. This is a contract of guarantee. A is a principal debtor, the bank is creditor and B is surety.

Characteristics of Contract of Guarantee

(i) Essentials of a valid contract – The contract of guarantee is a special contract. It must possess all essentials of a valid contract like contractual capacity, free consent, lawful consideration and lawful object etc.

(ii) Concurrence of the party – In a contract of guarantee, there are three parties, principal debtor, creditor and surety. To be legally valid there must be concurrence of all parties to a contract of guarantee and to its terms and conditions. In case, if some one becomes surety to the creditor without the consent of principal debtor, the contract is not enforceable.

(iii) **Consideration –** Like all other contracts, the contract of guarantee must be supported by lawful consideration. But there is little difference regarding consideration for the promise of surety. It is not necessary that the surety must get some consideration directly from the creditor. Rather, the benefit enjoyed by the principal debtor is considered sufficient consideration to support the promise of the surety.

Example: A agrees to sell goods worth Rs. 5000 to B on credit provided C becomes surety for the payment. C agrees with the consent of B to give guarantee to A. In this contract A who is a principal debtor gets benefit of credit sale. And it is sufficient consideration to support the promise of C to A. There is no need that C should get separate consideration for his promise.

(iv) **Primary liability –** In a contract of guarantee there is a primary liability on the principal debtor to repay or to discharge obligation. It is only at his default, the surety may be called upon to repay. Thus the liability of surety is secondary in nature and will arise only in case the principal debtor fails to repay. The surety gives a guarantee for the debt which exist on the pat of principal debtor.

(v) **Implied indemnity –** In a every contract of guarantee, there is an implied indemnity. The surety gets benefit of it. In case if the surety is called upon to discharge the obligation of the principal debtor, the surety after having done so is entitled to claim compensation for the losses sufferred by him, from the principal debtor.

(vi) **Disclosure of facts –** Though, the contract of guarantee is not a 'contract of utmost good faith'. But it is a duty of the creditor that, he must disclose to the surety, all those facts likely to affect the degree of his responsibility. Section 142 and 143 of this Act state very clearly that the guarantee obtained by means of misrepresentation or concealment of material facts by the creditor is invalid. Thus validity of contract of guarantee depends upon mutual trust and good faith on the part of creditor.

(vii) **Form of a contract –** According to section 126 of this Act the contract of guarantee may be made in writing or by the words of mouth. Similarly it may be implied contract directly understood from the conduct of the parties.

DIFFERENCE BETWEEN CONTRACT OF INDEMNITY AND A CONTRACT OF GUARANTEE

Though these two contracts are species of a general contract, but are distinct from each other on the following grounds:

Basis	Contract of indemnity	Contract of guarantee
1. Meaning	It is a contract made for compensating losses of another party caused to him either by the conduct of the parties or from an event or accident.	It is a contract, to perform the promise or discharge liability of third party in case of his default.
2. Number of Parties	There are two parties in a contract of indemnity namely indemnity holder and indemnifier.	In a contract of guarantee, there are three parties, the principal debtor, creditor and the surety.
3. Number of contracts	In indemnity there is only one contract that is between indemnity holder and indemnifier.	There are three contracts in guarantee. One between principal debtor and creditor, another between surely and creditor and third one between principal debtor and surety.
4. Nature of liability	In a contract of indemnity, the liability of indemnifier who makes promise to compensate the loss, is primary in nature	In a contract of guarantee, the the liability of the surety is secondary in nature This is so because his liability will arise only if the principal debtor defaults.
5. Object of contract	The main purpose of a contract of indemnity is to protect the indemnifier form losses	The contract of guarantee is made with an object of providing security or ensuring discharge of liability.
6. Existence of liability	In a contract of indemnity the liability or loss to the indemnity holder is contingent, which may or may not arise.	But in a contract of guarantee, the liability or debt being guarantee is already in existence.
7. Interest	A person who promises to indemnify loss may have some interest in the contract or in that transaction. guarantee given by him.	But in a contract of guarantee the surely should have no other interest apart from
8. Right of the Party	In a contract of indemnity, even after having compensated losses; the indemnifier can not sue third party in his own name, because, there is no privity of contract.	In a contract of guarantee, after having discharged, a liability of principal debtor, the surety can sue principal debtor in his own name.

Kinds of Guarantee

A contract of guarantee may be made for the various purposes as to enable a person to get loan, employment or goods on credit etc. More commonly a guarantee may be given for:

(i) Securing loan (ii) Getting goods on credit (iii) procuring employment.

A contract of guarantee may be of the following kinds.

(i) Prospective and Retrospective
(ii) Specific and continuing

In case, a contract of guarantee is made for existing debt, it is known as 'prospective guarantee.' As against it, if a guarantee is given for a future debt or future transaction it is known as 'retrospective guarantee'.

Similarly, contract of guarantee is made for a particular transaction is known as 'specific or simple and it covers only that single transaction.

Example: A borrows a sum of Rs. 5000 from the bank. B gives guarantee for repayment by A. This is an example of specific or simple guarantee. As A repays that debt, B ceases to be liable.

But, if a contract of guarantee is made for a particular transaction having many series or parts thereof it is known as continuing guarantee. In such case, the liability of the surety extends to all those series which are involved in that transaction. However, after having completed a few series, the surety may withdraw himself from a contract of guarantee.

Example: A employs B as his employee for recovering rent of As premises on monthly basis. C gives guarantee to A for the collection and payment of monthly rent by B. for the period of one year. In this contract collection of rent is a particular transaction having twelve series, thus it is a continuing guarantee.

Revocation of Continuing Guarantee

Continuing guarantee may be revoked in any one of the following manners:

(i) By notice – After having completed some series of transaction for which guarantee has been given, the surety by giving notice of revocation to the creditor may revoke a contract of guarantee. In such case, the surety will be liable for all those series which have been completed till that notice.

(ii) By death of surety – A continuing guarantee may also be revoked in case of death of the surety. However for the series completed prior to the death of surety, the estate of surety will be liable even without giving a notice of death to the creditor.

(iii) By other modes – In addition to notice by the surety or his death, a contract of continuing guarantee will be revoked under all circumstances in which the surety is discharged from his liability. These circumstances are being discussed ahead.

NATURE AND EXTENT OF SURETY'S LIABILITY

In the eyes of law the surety is considered as a 'Favoured Debtor'. His liability arises only when the principal debtor defaults. The following provisions of law are related with the extent and nature of his liability.

(i) **Liability of the surety is secondary:** In a contract of guarantee, the principal debtor is primarily liable to pay or discharge liability. It is only at his default, the liability of the surety arises and he may be called upon to discharge it. And the creditor is not required to give any notice to this effect to the surety.

(ii) **Liability of the surety is contingent:** In a contract of guarantee liability of the surety is contingent or conditional in nature. It may or may not arise It will arises only when the principal debtor commits default. And it is not certain that he will default. In practice, generally he discharges his liability to the satisfaction of the creditor.

(iii) **The liability of the surety is immediate in nature:** Once the principal debtor commits default, immediately the creditor may proceed against the surety. In is not necessary that he should first exhaust his remedies against the principal debtor. Thus, on default by the principal debtor, the creditor instead of to sue the principal debtor, can file suit against the surety.

(iv) **The liability of surety is 'co-extensive':** In a contract of guarantee, the liability of the surety is co-extensive with that of the principal debtor. He is liable for those sums that the principal debtor is liable for. His liability cannot be more than that of principal debtor. In case, the liability of the principal debtor is scaled down or extinguished by the creditor or by operation of law, either in whole or in part, the liability of the surety would also be reduced or extinguished to the same extent.

(v) **Surety may limit his liability:** Although the liability of the surety is co-extensive with that of principal debtor. But he has a right to limit his liability. He can do it by declaring it expressly at the time of making a contract of guarantee. In such a case, irrespective of all other factors, the liability of the surety will not go beyond that limit as declared by him.

(vi) **Liability in continuing guarantee:** In case of continuing guarantee, the liability of the surety extends to a series of transaction over a period of time, not to a specific number of series but to any number of them. It makes the surety liable for unpaid balance.

(vii) **Liability of the surety where original contract between the principal debtor and the creditor is void or voidable:** In a contract of guarantee, there are two independent contracts, one between principal debtor and creditor and another between the creditor and the surety. And law does not treat, principal debtor and surety as one person. Thus if a contract between the principal debtor and the creditor is void, the surety will be liable as if he is principal debtor.

Example: A, who is a minor, borrows a sum of Rs. 20,000 from the bank. B gives guarantee to the bank. The contract between A and the bank is void, because

A has no contractual capacity. The bank cannot sue the minor A. But B will be liable to discharge A's liability towards the bank.

Similarly if the creditor does not sue principal debtor with in a period of limitation or, the principal debtor is discharged from his liability by operation of law or death, the surety will remain liable.

Rights of Surety

In a contract of guarantee, the surety is considered as 'favoured debtor' with the following rights.

(i) against the principal debtor
(ii) against the creditor, and
(iii) against the co-sureties (if any).

A. Rights against principal debtor:

The surety has got the following rights against the principal debtor.

(i) Right of subrogation: The surety will get right of subrogation when he fulfils the obligation of the principal debtor fully. In other words, if the principal debtor commits default, and the surety pays the debt to the creditor, the surety steps in to the shoes of creditor. The surety will be invested with all the rights which the creditor has against the principal debtor. It has been held by the courts that, the surety is entitled to every remedy which the creditor has against the principal debtor including securities held by the creditor and all means of payment by the principal debtor.

Example: A has borrowed Rs. one lac from the bank. B stands surety to the bank for the repayment. On due date A defaults and the banks calls upon B to repay. B makes repayment to the bank. The bank was also holding assets worth Rs. 20,000 as a security for this loan. On repayment B is entitled to recover assets held by the bank as security and will further proceed against A for the balance.

(ii) Right of indemnity: In a every contract of guarantee, there is an implied promise by the principal debtor that any loss caused to him will be indemnified by the principal debtor. Thus the surety is entitled to recover from the principal debtor whatever sum he has rightfully paid under the contract of guarantee.

In other words indemnity is applicable only on those payments made by the surety in connection with guarantee, which are just and equitable. It covers, principal amount, interest thereon, legal expenses if any and the cost of the suit.

Example: Ram was indebted to Shyam for Rs. 20,000 and Mohan stood as surety for the repayment. Ram defaulted repayment and Shyam filed suit against Mohan. Finally Mohan was asked to pay the amount along with interest and cost of suit which was around Rs. 5000. After making payment, Mohan is entitled to recover Rs. 20,000 + 5000 from Shyam.

B. Rights of surety against the creditor:

The surety has the following rights against the creditor.

(i) **Right to claim securities:** Where the principal debtor has given securities in addition of guarantee, of the debt. In case he fails to repay and the surety becomes liable to pay. The surety is entitled to those securities which are held by the creditor. If the creditor loses or without the consent of surety, parts with, any security, the surety is discharged from his liability to that extent.

Example: A borrows sum of Rs. 10,000 from B for three month. C stands surety, in addition to securities worth Rs. 5000. Without the consent of C, B returns security worth Rs. 2000 to A. In case A defaults and C makes repayment. He is entitled to get back security of Rs. 5000 from B.

(ii) **Right of set off:** In a contract of guarantee, if the principal debtor has got any cross claim against the creditor, the surety becomes entitled to that claim against the creditor. And the surety may have a benefit of set off while determing the extent of his liability.

Example: A has borrowed sum of Rs. 30,000 from B. C stands as surety in the transaction. B has purchased goods worth Rs. 5000 from A on credit. A defaults in repayment and C was called upon to pay. C is entitled to a right of set off and his liability will be limited to Rs. 25000 only.

(iii) **Right to share reduction:** In a contract of guarantee, if there has been some reduction in the amount of debt being guarantee by the surety. The surety is entitled to such reduction and his liability will also be reduced to that extent.

Example: A who is a farmer borrows sum of Rs. 20,000 for buying tractor from the Agriculture Deptt. B becomes surety for that loan. Later on, the State Government declares 25% subsidy on that loan. B is entitled to share the reduction in the amount of debt.

(iv) **Right to demand termination of employee:** In a contract of fidelity guarantee regarding honest behaviour on the employment, the surety has a right to demand dismissal of the employee if he defaults in his behaviour.

C. Rights against co-sureties:

Where the debt is guaranteed by two or more persons, they are known as co-sureties. The surety has following rights against other co-sureties.

(i) **Right of contribution -** Where two or more persons stand sureties for the same debt either jointly or severally, the co-sureties are liable themselve to pay equal share of the whole debt. In case if any one of them has been compelled to pay the whole debt, he is entitled to get contribution in equal ratio from other co-sureties.

Example: A, B and C have guaranteed a loan of Rs. 45000 taken by D from E. D defaults in repayment. A, B and C are liable to the extent of Rs. 15000 each.

(ii) Co-sureties giving guarantee for different amount: Where the same debt is guaranteed by two or more co-sureties, offering guarantee for different amount, they will be liable in equal ratio subject to the maximum of the amount of guarantee given by them.

Example: A, B and C stand sureties to the extent of Rs. 10,000, 20,000 and 40,000 respectively to D. In case he makes default of Rs. 50,000, the liability of A, B & C will be 10,000, 20,000 and 20,000 respectively.

DISCHARGE OF SURETY

In a contract of guarantee, the surety has a liability parallel to that of principal debtor, which arises in case of default of principal debtor. The surety is said to be discharged from his liability when his liability comes to an end - he is no more liable to the creditor. The liability of the surety comes to an end in the following manners

A. By Revocation.
B. By the conduct of creditor
C. By invalidation of contract of guarantee.

This can be well understood with the help of following chart.

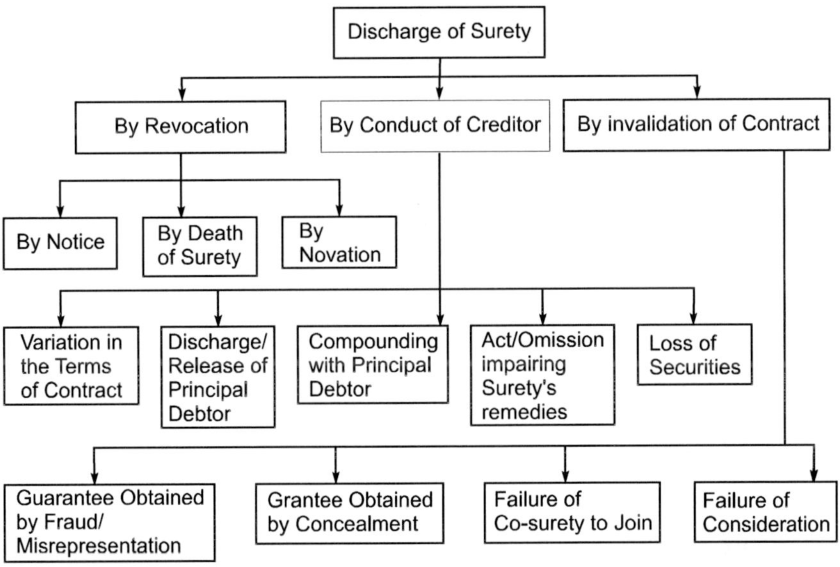

A. By Revocation:

The surety gets released from his liability in a contract of guarantee by revocation under the following situation.

(i) **By Notice of revocation:** In a contract of continuing guarantee the liability of surety extends to various series of a transaction. In such case, the surety by giving notice to the creditor may revoke the contract for remaining series. But he will be liable for the series which have been completed before such notice.

(ii) **By death of surety:** A contract of continuing guarantee is also revoked at the death of the surety for the remaining series of that transaction. The legal representative of the surety will be liable for the series which have been completed by the time of death of surety.

(iii) **By novation:** By mutual consent of all parties, original contract of guarantee may be replaced by new contract. In such case the surely will be discharged from his liability in the original contract.

B. By conduct of creditor:

The surety will be discharged from his liability in a contract of guarantee by the conduct of creditor under the following circumstances.

(i) **By variation in the terms of contract:** Any material variation or change regarding terms of a contract of guarantee by the creditor and principal debtor without consent of the surety will discharge him from his liability as to transaction subsequent to such change. Material variations means the variations which effect interest of the surety in a significant way.

Example: A is appointed as salesman by B. C gives guarantee for his honest behaviour during employment. Later on A and B agree that A would also be liable for realising debtors and B will pay him higher salary. C is no more liable as a surety in a contract.

(ii) **By release or discharge of principal debtor:** The liability of the surety is secondary in nature. Thus, if the principal debtor is released or discharged from his liability by any act or omission of the creditor, the liability of the surety will also come to an end.

Example: A who is a farmer has borrowed sum of Rs. 20,000 for buying some agriculture tools on the guarantee given by B. Later on, as a part of the State Government policy towards agriculture, A has been exempted from repaying that loan. B would get discharged from his liability as a surety.

However in case of death or insolvency of the principal debtor or failure of the creditor to sue with in period of limitation would not lead to discharge of liability of the surety.

(iii) **By compounding with principal debtor:** A contract between the creditor and principal debtor whereby the creditor extends time of payment or makes promise not to sue the principal debtor in case of his default. The surety will be discharged from his liability in that contract of guarantee.

Example: X has borrowed Rs. 5000 from the bank on the guarantee provided by Y. On the date of repayment X becomes unable to repay and enters into an agreement with the bank for extending period of repayment. The bank agrees to it. Y will get discharged from his liability as surety.

(iv) **By impairing surety's remedy:** Any act or omission of the creditor which damages the rights of surety would lead to his discharge from liability.

Thus if the creditor does any act which is inconsistent with the rights of surety or omits to do any act which is his duty to do and the eventual remedy of the surety against the principal debtor is impaired, the surety is discharged.

Example: A was appointed as a cashier in the bank on the guarantee given by B for the recovery of loans. It was also agreed that, the bank would provide performance report of A to B on monthly basis. But the bank does not do so, B will be discharged from his liability.

(v) **By loss of security:** While making a contract of guarantee, in addition to guarantee, some security has also been given to the creditor. In case the creditor loses that security or part with it without consent of the surety, the surety will be discharged from his liability to that extend.

Example: X borrows Rs 20,000 from bank on a guarantee given by Y. X has also pledged assets worth Rs. 5000 as security. Due to fire in the premises of the bank that asset was also destroyed. Y will be released from his liability to the extent of Rs 5000

C. By invalidation of contract of guarantee:

The surety will be discharged from his liability in the following cases on account of a contract being invalid.

(i) **Guarantee obtained by misrepresentation:** Where the guarantee has been obtained by creditor by using misrepresentation or fraud, a contract of guarantee will be invalid and the surety will be discharged.

(ii) **Guarantee obtained by concealment:** Where the creditor obtains guarantee by means of keeping silent or concealing material facts, a contract of guarantee is invalid and provides sufficient ground for the surety to get discharged.

(iii) **Failure of consideration:** Lawful consideration is required in a contract of guarantee. In case of failure of such consideration, a contract becomes invalid and leads of discharge of surety from his liability.

(iv) **Failure of co-surety to join:** Where a person agrees to be surety in contract on a condition that the creditor shall not act upon unless co-surety joins. In case such person does not join as co-surety, the surety will be discharged from his liability.

Review Questions

1. Define a contract of indemnity. Discuss its characteristics.
2. Explain various rights of indemnity holder.
3. Define a contract of guarantee. Discuss various features of it.
4. Distinguish between contract of indemnity and contract of guarantee.
5. Explain various kinds of guarantee and discuss those situations when the continuing guarantee is revoked.
6. Who is surety. Discuss his right, as against principal debtor, creditor and co-sureties.
7. Explain various situations in which the surety will be discharged from his liability in a contract of guarantee.
8. Discuss the nature and extent of surety's liability in a contract of guarantee.
9. 'Liability of surety is coextensive with that of principal debtor' comment.
10. Surety is a 'favoured debtor' in a contract of guarantee' comment.

Practical Problems

1. A hired car from B for going to Calcutta. While on the route the car collided and it was badly damaged. Is A responsible for loss to B.

   (Yes, implied indemnity).
2. A forged a signature of B and presented forged transfer of shares for registration to a company. The company registered the transfer. Is company entitled to recover loss arising from the act of A?

   (Yes implied indemnity)
3. X makes an agreement with Y for killing Z in consideration of Rs. 50,000 and Y promising to indemnify X for his act. As a consequence of this act X was fined Rs one lack. Can he recover it from?

   (No, object of an agreement is unlawful.)
4. Ram borrows sum of Rs. 20,000 from the bank and Shyam stands surety to the bank for repayment. But Ram does not know about guarantee given by Shyam. On due date Ram refuses to pay. Can a bank recover this amount from Shyam as surety.?

   (No) there is no concurrence for the agreement of guarantee among Ram, bank and Shyam.

5. A borrowed sum of Rs. 20,000 from the bank and pledged assets worth Rs. 10,000 along with guarantee given by B. On due date A fails to repay. Can the bank sue B without returning assets to him? (Yes).
6. P got house from M on rent. N provided guarantee to M for the payment of rent by P on the condition that, the rent was paid initially for three months and thereafter from week to week. After 4 months N gave notice to M revoking his guarantee. Examine the extent of N's liability as a surety.
7. A was in agreement with B for building a ship for a stipulated amount paid by B when the work reaches to certain stages. C provides guarantee for A's due performance. B without the knowledge of C makes advance payment of two instalments to A. Is C discharged from his liability (Yes),
8. A borrows sum of Rs. 80,000 from the bank. B, C and D stood as co-sureties for the payment to the extent of A-20,000, B-30,000, C-30,000. A makes default of Rs. 50,000. How it would be shared by B, C and D.
9. X borrowed Rs. 20,000 from Y for three months on the guarantee furnished by Y. On due date X failed in repayment and Y extended date of payment for next two months without consent of Z. Is Z liable as surety. (No)

■■■

Chapter 13

Contract of Agency

Learning Objectives

- Develop an understanding about basic nature of agency.
- Understand an implication and difference between a contract of agency and a general contract.
- Remember various modes of creating agency specially agency by ratification.
- Learn duties and right of both agent and principal.
- Understand the basic concept of agent's liability.
- Analyse the position of principal in relation with third party.

INTRODUCTION

In business no one can do every thing at his own. He needs to delegate part of his authority to others to get things done. He may do so either by appointing some one as his employee or as his agent. Where some one is appointed an agent, he acts on behalf of the person appointing him. Legal status of an agent is quite different from employee. An agent acts as an employee, but on behalf of that other person making him liable by his acts.

MEANING AND DEFINITION

The person who is appointed to work for another person on his behalf is technically known as agent. According to section 182 of this Act, "an agent is a person employed to do any act for another or to represent another in dealing with third person". The person who does act or represent other is known as agent and the person who is so represented is called the 'principal'. And the contract through which relationship of agency is created between the agent and the principal is known as contract of agency. The contract of agency is also a species of a general contract with some distinct features.

Thus a contract of agency is made for creating relationship of agency between principal and agent.

The relationship of agency is based on the following rules.

(i) "Qui facit per alium facit per se" i.e. one who does through another does by himself. It means that acts done by an agent are binding on the 'principal' who appoints him. And these acts will have same legal consequences as would have been done by the principal himself.

(ii) The person may appoint some one as his agent for doing those act which he is expected or authorised to do. But this rule has many exceptions in practice such as in a contract of personal nature involving personal services, skill and qualification an agent can not be appointed for performing the promise.

(iii) An agent is basically a representative of his principal. It is a representative character of his functioning which distinguishes him from other employees. In fact an agent represents his principal in dealing with third party.

(iv) The main job or role of an agent is to bring third party into contractual relationship with his prncipal. As soon as this relationship is established he is no more in picture.

Essentials of Contract of Agency

The Contract of agency has the following distinct essential features.

(i) ***Agreement:*** To form a contract of agency, there must be an agreement between principal and agent. which leads to creations of relationship of agency. Thus the contract of agency is based on true nature of relationship. Such agreement may be express or implied by circumstances, by operation of law and intention of the parties.

(ii) ***Contractual capacity:*** In a contract of agency there are two parties namely the principal and agent. The principal must have contractual capacity. According to section 183 of this Act, "any person who is of age of majority according to law to which he is subject, and who is of a sound mid may employ an agent."

However, agent need not to have contractual capacity. According to section 184 of this Act. "as between principal and third person, any person may become an agent," This is so because an agent does not make contracts on his own. In case an agent has no contractual capacity, such as minor agent, the interest of third party is not going to be affected. Rather such agent will not be responsible to his principal, but third party will be bound by that act to the principal.

Thus the principal must have contractual capacity, but it is not necessary to have such capacity for the agent.

(iii) ***Consideration:*** Although the relationship of agency is created by agreement, but it is not necessary that such agreement must be supported by a lawful consideration. According to section 185 of this Act no consideration is required to create an agency.

(iv) ***Privity of contract between principal and third party:*** An agent acts on behalf of his principal. He establishes privity of contract between principal and third party. Whatever he does on behalf of his principal, with in the scope of authority given to him, all such acts will be binding on the principal in relation with third party.

Example: A has been appointed agent of B. A buys raw material for B on credit from C. In case B refuses to pay, C can sue him for the recovery of payment. It is because there is a privity of contract between B and C.

CREATION OF AGENCY

Relationship of agency is created in the following manners:

A. Agency by express agreement.

B. Agency by implied aground or implied.

agency

A. Agency by Express Agreement

This is very popular and usual mode of creating relationship of agency between two person. Any one, who has a contractual capacity can appoint another as his agent either by the words of mouth or by making written agreement. Such agency is known as agency by express agreement. Agreement for appointing an agent is made by executing deed of 'power of attorney'. It authorises an agent to act on behalf of his principal with in the scope of authority mentioned in the agreement. Where an agent is appointed for doing some specific job or dealing with third party on that job, a special power of attorney is executed. But, to give an authority to an agent for doing all acts on behalf of the principal or to represent him in all dealings, a general power of attorney in executed in his favour.

B. Agency by Implied Agreement.

A relationship of agency is also created by conduct of parties, and circumstances. Such agency is known as implied agency. Implied agency arises when a person is placed in such situation, that he is bound to act as an agent of other without making formal agreement with him.

Agency may be implied from the circumstances, conduct of the parties, ordinary course of dealings and business traditions and customs. It mainly includes the following.

(i) ***Agency by estoppel:*** Where the person, either by the words of mouth or in writing or by his conduct induces another person to believe that someone is working as his agent, in reality he is not his agent. Any person who is so induced if makes any transaction with so called agent, such transaction will be binding on the person inducing so and he will be liable as principal. Such agency is known as agency by estoppel.

Example: Y, in the presence of X tells to Z that Y is working as X's agent. But really he is not an agent and at the same he is not contradicting the statement of Y. Z makes contract with Y believing that he is an agent of X. This contract is binding on X; because there exists agency by estoppel between X and Y.

According to section 234 of this Act "when an agent has, without authority, done acts or incurred obligation to third parties on behalf of his principal, the principal is bound by such acts or obligations if he has by his words or conduct induced such third parties to believe that such acts and obligations were with in the scope of agent's authority."

However it is to be noted that in case of agency by estoppel the principal remains passive giving an impression to third party that he is the principal.

Example: A consigns some goods to B for sale and gives an instructions to him not to sell them below a fixed price. C who is unaware of these instructions, makes contract with B to buy the goods at a price lower than a fixed one. This contract will be binding on A.

Thus agency by estoppel is created under the following situations.

(a) a person who is not really an agent, but is being considered as an agent
(b) a person is being considered as an agent, though he ceases to be an agent.
(c) a person is being considered as an agent, for having more authority than actually he has.

(ii) *Agency by holding out:* In fact agency by holding out is a branch of agency by estoppel with a little difference that in case of holding out, the relationship of agency is created by some positive or affirmative act on the part of the principal. In this case, the principal himself holds out that someone is his agent. Here, there is some active assertion or representation by the principal to induce another person for believing that someone is his agent or has been given more authority than actually he has.

Example: A allows his servant B to buy the goods on credit form C and pays for them. On one occasion. A has asked his servant to buy the goods for cash. But he bought the goods on credit and misappropriated cash given to him. The principal is bound by this transaction as he has held out his servant to buy the goods on credit in the past, giving impression that the servant is his agent having authority to buy goods on credit for the principal.

(iii) *Agency by Necessity:* Under certain situations, it becomes necessary for the person to act as an agent of another person without his authority. Such agency is known as 'Agency by necessity".

In other words, an agency by necessity is conferred by law in certain cases, where a person is faced with an emergency in which the property or interest of another person may be in danger, and it becomes necessary to act in order to preserve the property or interest, before the instructions of the owner can be obtained. In such case, law assumes, the consent of the owner to the creation of the relationship of principal and agent, which is known as agency by necessity. For creating relationship of agency by necessity the following conditions must be satisfied

(i) there must be a emergency situation, which makes it necessary for the person to act as an agent.

(ii) it should be impossible for the person who is acting as an agent to communicate with another person for whom he is acting.

(iii) the person must have acted as an agent on behalf of another person, bonafide in the interest of that another person.

(iv) the person, acting as an agent must have acted with reasonable prudence taking in to account, danger, expense and time factor.

Example: A sends a consignment of oranges to B in Bombay asking him to send to C at Calcutta. When the consignment reached in Bombay B found that the oranges are getting perished and may perish totally by the time consignment reaches Calcutta. It is therefore B sells oranges for the best obtainable prices without an authority of A. The transaction of sale will be binding on A, because B has acted as an agent by necessity for A.

Agency by necessity may be established under the following situations.

(a) ***Emergency situations:*** In an emergency situation the agent is entitled to do all such acts for saving principal from losses as a person of reasonable prudence would have done to save himself under such situations. All those acts will be binding on the principal, because agency by necessity has been created.

(b) ***Husband and wife:*** In case, the husband fails to provide for basic necessities of life of his wife, the wife may act as an agent of husband, in necessity and can pledge his credit and the husband will be bound such acts.

(c) ***Protection of property:*** Where, the person is entrusted with the property of another person, which he has to protect or preserve. The person so entrusted is entitled to do all necessary acts for protecting the property of the owner and such owner will be bound by those acts under the relationship of agency by necessity.

Case: GREAT NOTHERN RAIL COY. VS. SWAFFIELD

(1874, L.R-9, Ex-132) In this case, a horse was sent through railway company. On reaching to its destination, no one could receive it. Due to lack of proper accomomdation for it, the railway company put it in stable for horses on rent. In was held that the railway company has acted as an agent in necessity on behalf of the owner of a horse, therefore rent for putting horse in stable will be paid by the owner.

(iv) ***Agency by ratification:*** Ratification implies an approval of the acts which have been done without an authority of the person approving them. In other words, where the person has done some act for another person without his prior authority or consent. Later on the person for whom such acts have been done can either reject them altogether or may accept those acts. In case he accepts, he becomes bound by such acts as these acts would have been done by his authority or consent. The relationship of agency arising out of such approval or acceptance is known as agency by ratification.

According to section 196 of this Act, "where acts are done by one person on behalf of another, but without his knowledge or authority, he may elect to ratify or to disown such acts. If he ratifies them the same effect will follow as if, they have been performed by his authority".

Section 197 of this Act states that "ratification may be express or may be implied by the conduct of the person on whose behalf the acts are done".

Example: Ram buys some raw material for Shyam, but without his authority. Later on Shyam makes use of that raw material, which have been purchased without his authority, in the production process. Thus it is implied by his conduct that he has accepted or ratified the act of Ram. And as a result of it relation of agency will be created by implied ratification

Requirements of valid ratification: A ratification to be valid and effective must fulfil the following conditions.

(a) ***Acts done on behalf of principal:*** An act to be ratified must have been done on behalf of the person ratifying it. Thus, if the act is done not in the name of the principal, but in the name of agent himself, such act cannot be ratified.

Example: A authorised B to purchase wheat for him at specified price. But B purchased wheat at a higher price that too in his own name. A can not ratify this transaction, bccausc if has been done in the name of B who is acting as an agent.

(b) ***Existence of the principal:*** The principal must be in existence at the time when the act was done on his behalf by an agent. Thus if an agent does some act on behalf of the principal, but the principal was a non-existing at that time. Later on, he cannot ratify those acts.

Case: KELNER VS. BAXTER (1866, LR-2, CP-174). In this case, the promotors of the company to be formed for managing a hotel, made an agreement on behalf of the proposed company, for buying wine from a plaintiff. On the formation of a company, the company intended to ratify that agreement. It was held that the promotors of the company were personally liable for that agreement, because the company was not in existence at that time and thus could not be made liable for the agreement made by the promotors.

However, under section 15 of Specific Relief Act 1963, if a pre-incorporation contract is with in the object of the company, the company can ratify it and it becomes binding on the company and third party.

(c) ***Contractual capacity:*** The person on whose behalf the act is being done, at that time he must have contractual capacity. Thus an act done on behalf of the minor can not be ratified by him on attaining age of majority. Because at the time when act was done he was not competent to contract.

(d) ***Full knowledge of principal:*** The principal who is to ratify an act must have full knowledge about that act. Section 198 of this Act clearly states that "no valid ratification can be made by a person whose knowledge of the fact is materially defective."

(e) ***Whole transaction:*** The ratification to be legally valid must relate to whole transaction or act. Partial ratification is not valid. Section 199 of this Act states that "a person ratifying an unauthorised act done on his behalf ratifies the whole of the transaction of which such act formed a part"

(f) ***Lawful act:*** The principal can ratify only lawful acts which have been done by an agent without his authority. An act which is void or unlawful can not be ratified.

(g) ***Reasonable time:*** To be valid, the ratification of an act must have been done with in reasonable time. After the expiry of reasonable time, an act cannot be ratified.

(h) ***Damage or loss to third party:*** Where the ratification of an act results in any injury or damage or loss to third party, such ratification is not valid. According to section. 200 of this Act, "ratification which has the effect of subjecting a third person to damage or terminating any right or interest of a third person, cannot be made".

Example: A has hired a car from B for one month. C on behalf of B takes back that car from A after fifteen days. A suffers a loss due to imature return of a car B can not ratify the act of C, because it results in loss to A.

(t) ***Communication:*** A ratification to be valid must have been communicated to third party involved in that transaction as to make transaction binding upon him.

A. DUTIES OF AGENT

Duties and rights of an agent are largely determined by the mutual agreement between agent and the principal. The main duties of an agent are as under.

(i) ***Duty to perform the work:*** An agent is appointed to do work or to act for the principal. Therefore, he must perform that act in satisfactory manner. If he fails to do so, he will be liable to the principal for any loss or damage arising out of it.

(ii) ***To exercise reasonable skill, care and diligence:*** An agent must perform the acts related to the business of agency with a reasonable care, and diligence. He must exercise reasonable degree of skill which the person of average skill would have done in his own case. In case, loss or damage caused to the principal due to his negligence, want of skill and misconduct, will be compensated by him.

Example: A was appointed an insurance agent by B to effect an insurance on a ship. He omits to see that the usual clauses of marine insurance are inserted in the policy. Later on, the ship was lost. Due to omission of clauses nothing can be recovered from the underwriting firm A is bound to compensate the loss caused to B due to his negligence and carelessness.

(iii) ***To render proper accounts:*** An agent is bound to render proper accounts to his principal on demand. He must explain those accounts to the principal and produce the vouchers in support of the entries made therein. Once necessary accounts have been rendered and accepted by the principal, and the same cannot be reopened by the principal

(iv) ***To follow directions of the principal:*** An agent is bound to conduct the business of his principal according to his directions. In the absence of necessary directions or instructions, an agent must follow usual practice of the trade which prevails in similar type of business. If he does not do so, he will be liable to compensate the principal for the losses.

(v) ***To communicate with principal:*** It is the duty of an agent to use all reasonable diligence in communicating with his principal and in seeking his instructions, in case of difficulty. But in case of emergency when he cannot communicate with the principal he should take all reasonable steps to protect interest of his principal.

(vi) ***Not to act on his own:*** An agent is appointed to act on behalf of the principal. He must not act at his own, while dealing with third party. But if an agent is personally interested in the transaction so his duty towards the principal and his personal interest may come in conflict with each other. In consequence of such situation if he gets unfair benefit the principal is entitled to (i) rescind the transaction (ii) recover compensation from the agent.

(vii) ***Not to make secret profits:*** An agent is expected to work for the principal. Thus it is his prime duty not to earn any secret profit in any transaction made by him with third party. According to section 216 of this Act, if the agent deals in the business of agency on his own account without the knowledge of the principal, the principal is entitled to claim from the agent any benefit which may have resulted to him from the transaction.

(viii) ***To pay sums received for the principal:*** The agent is bound to pay to his principal, all sums received on his account. He may deduct therefrom all money due to himself in respect of advances made or expenses-incurred by him in conducting such business and also such remuneration as may be payable to him for acting as agent.

(ix) ***Not to delegate authority:*** As a matter of rule the agent cannot delegate authority to a third person without the consent of the principal except in case where the nature of business requires such delegation.

(x) ***Not to set up adverse title:*** The agent should not set up an adverse title to the property in his hands against the principal. It means he must not set up his own title or the title of the third party to the goods or property received by him from his principal in the capacity of a agent.

(xi) ***To protect interest of principal on his death or insanity:*** In case, an agency is terminated on the principal becoming insolvent or dying, the agent is bound to take all reasonable steps on behalf of the representative for the protection and preservation of the interest of deceased principal.

(xii) ***Not to use information against the principal:*** In the course of business of agency the agent may get information regarding various transaction. It is his duty not to use that information against the interest of principal. In case he does so, he will be liable to compensate the losses suffered by the principal.

B. RIGHTS OF AGENT

The agent has the following rights against the principal.

(i) ***Right to receive remuneration:*** An agent has a right to receive agreed remuneration on the completion of his work. And in absence of an agreement reasonable remuneration will be paid to him. According to section 219 of this Act, "in the absence of any special contract, payment for the performance of any act is not due to the agent until the completion of such act". Though the completion of the work depends on the terms of contract and nature of work, but an act is deemed to be complete when the agent has done whatever was necessary on his part.

Example: A was appointed as an agent for buying 100 tones of raw material for B at specified price. A made an agreement for buying that raw material from C. On making an agreement he becomes entitled to get his remuneration regardless of the fact that when that raw material is actually supplied by C.

However, the agent who is guilty of misconduct in the business of agency is not entitled to any remuneration in respect of the business which he has misconducted.

(ii) ***Right to retain money:*** An agent works on behalf of the principal. In the business of agency he may receive any sums on account of the principal. He has a right to retain which he has spent and which he has advanced in the operation of business of agency.

According to section 17 of this Act, "an agent may retain, out of any sums received on account of the principal in the business of agency, all moneys due to himself in respect of advances made or expenses properly incurred by him in conducting such business, and also such remuneration as may be payable to him for acting as an agent.

However, it may be noted that an agent can not retain sums received by him in one business for his remuneration or commission in other business. And this right can be exercised only on sums received on account of the principal, in the business of agency.

(iii) ***Right of lien:*** It is a right to retain the property of other unless certain claims or debts are satisfied. According to section 221 of this Act, "in the absence of any contract contrary to it, an agent is entitled to retain goods, paper and other property, whether movable or immovable of the principal received by him until the amount due to him for commission, disbursement and services in respect of the same has been paid or accounted for to him."

Section 171 of this Act states that in the absence of contract contrary to it factors, bankers and Attorneys of high court have the right of general lien. Thus besides these, all other agents have right of particular lien. Under this right an agent can retain only those goods in respect of which charges or claims are due. The right of lien can also be claimed by the sub-agent appointed properly.

(iv) ***Right of indemnity:*** An agent has a right to get compensation for all losses caused to him in discharging his duty as an agent. According to section 222 of this Act, "an agent has a right to indemnify against the consequences of all lawful act done by him in exercise of authority conferred upon him."

According to section 223 of this Act, "where one person employs another to do an act and the agent does the act in good faith, the agent has a right to be indemnified against the consequences of the act, even though if causes injury to the right of third person.

Example: X who possesses some goods belonging to Y requests Z to sell these goods. Z is not aware of ownership of goods sells those goods to A and hands over proceed of sale to X. Later on, Y who is a real owner of the goods sues upon A and recovers value of the goods sold. X is liable to indemnity Z for these losses.

However the right of indemnity does not extend to those acts which are known to the agent to be unlawful.

(v) ***Right of compensation:*** The right of compensation is available to the agent for the injuries caused to him by the neglect and want of skill on the part of the principal. But if such injuries are caused to him by his own neglect and want of skill he can not claim compensation form the principal.

Similarly an agent is also entitled to compensation for the losses caused to him due to pre-mature revocation of agency.

According to section 205 of this Act, "where there is an express or implied contract that the agency should be continued for any period of time, the principal must make compensation to the agent for any pre-mature revocation of the agency without sufficient cause".

(vi) ***Right to appoint sub-agent:*** An agent has a right to appoint sub-agent under the situation when it is necessary by the nature of business of agency or when he has got implied or express authority to do so.

A. Duties of Principal

The principal has the following duties towards an agent.

(i) The principal has a duty to pay the agent his commission and remuneration as per the terms of agency on the completion of the work.

(ii) The principal is under duty to indemnify the agent against the consequences of all lawful acts done by the agent in the business of agency.

(iii) The principal is under obligation to compensate an agent for all losses caused to him due to neglect and want of skill on the part of the principal.

(iv) The principal is also under duty to indemnify an agent against the consequences of acts done by the agent in good faith even it causes an injury to third party.

B. Right of Principal

The principal has a right to enforce duties of an agent against him which are briefly as under.

(i) The principal has a right to ensure that the agent follows his instructions while conducting business of agency. In case the agent deviates from given instructions and the principal suffers lose, he has a right to claim compensation for it.

(ii) In case, an agent misconducts or neglects or due to want of skill on his part, the principal suffers a loss, he can claim compensation for it.

(iii) The principal has a right to demand books of account and seek necessary explanation regarding entries made therein.

(iv) In case the agent deals on his own in the business of agency and makes personal gain out of it. The principal has a right to claim such benefit from the agent.

(v) Where the agent, without the knowledge and permission of the principal makes any secret profit out of business transactions of agency. The principal is entitled to recover such profits from the agent.

(vi) In case the agent makes breach of contract or breach of duty, the principal can refuse to admit the rights of an agent and if the principal suffers any loss, he can claim compensation from the agent.

AUTHORITY OF AGENT

An agent acts on behalf of the principal. What ever he does within the scope the of authority given to him, such acts will be binding on the principal. The right of an agent to bind the principal by his act is known as an authority of agent.

According to section 226 of this Act, "contracts entered in to through an agent and obligation arising form the acts done by an agent, may be enforced in the same manner and will have same legal consequences, as if the contracts had been entered in to and the acts done by the principal in person".

The contents of the above section make it clear that the acts done by the agent on behalf of the principal will have same legal consequence as would have been done by the principal himself provided such acts had been done with in the scope of authority given to him.

The scope of authority of an agent can be determined by taking in to account the following types of authority of agent.

(i) Actual authority

(ii) Apparent or ostensible authority.

(iii) Emergency authority.

Actual Authority

Actual authority of an agent means an authority which has been conferred upon him by the principal. It may be either express or implied authority. An authority is said to be express if it is given to him in writing or by the words of mouth. On the other hand, implied authority means a authority which is inferred either from circumstances of from conduct of parties, bussiness usage and intention of the parties.

Example: A in Delhi manges shop of B who lives in Mumbai. A habitually buys goods for the shop on credit on behalf of B. And B occasionally comes to Delhi and pays for it. Thus it is impled from the conduct of both A ad B that A had an authority to buy the goods on credit.

Apparent Authority

An agent is appointed for doing some act or all acts in the business of agency. And actual authority is given to him for doing those acts. In addition to those acts for which authority has been given, the agent has to perform many other necessary acts which may be incidental to the main acts. Authority to bind the principal by such acts is known as apparent authority. Apparent authority is an authority which appears to others and may coincide with actual authority. Sometimes, it may be in excess of actual authority.

According to section 188 of this Act "an agent having an authority to do an act or to carry on business has authority to do every lawful things which is necessary in order to do such act or which is usually done in the course of conducting such business".

The contents of the above section reveals that an apparent authority is used by the agent for doing all necessary lawful acts for conducting business of agency. And the principal will be bound by those acts.

Case: RAYN VS. PILKINGTON (1959, 1WL.R, 403). In this case, estate agent was appointed and instructed by the owner to find buyer for a property. Accordingly an agent did so and accepted from a prospective purchaser a deposite as an agent. It was held that estate agent was not given authority to accept deposites, but he had acted with in the scope of his apparent authority.

Emergency Authority

While conducting the business of agency an agent may meet some emergency situations. In those situations it is his duty to do needful for protecting the principal from a loss. Authority to do such needful acts is known as 'emergency authority.

According to section 189 of this Act, "agent has also authority in an emergency, to do all such acts for the purpose of protecting his principal from loss as would be done by a person of reasonable prudence in his own case, under similar circumstances."

To bind the principal, by the act of agent done under emergency authority, the following conditions should be satisfied.

(i) There should have been an emergency.
(ii) The principal must have been suffering from loss.
(iii) An agent must have acted with reasonable prudence.

(iv) He must have done all needful things to protect the principal from loss, which a person of reasonable prudence would have done in his own case under similar circumstances.

Example: A sent consignment of fruits of B, his agent at Calcutta to forward it to Bombay. When the consignment reached to Calcutta B finds that fruits are getting spoiled fastly and by the time the consignment reaches to Bombay, the entire lot may be spoiled. Thus B sells the consignment for best obtainable prices without an authority from A, but under emergency authority.

DELEGATION OF AUTHORITY BY AGENT:

As a matter of rule "a delegate cannot further delegate". Thus an agent to whom authority has been delegated by the principal cannot delegate it further to another person.

According to section 190 of this Act, "an agent cannot lawfully employ another to perform acts, which he has expressly or impliedly undertaken to perform personally unless by the ordinary custom of trade a sub agent may, or from the nature of agency, a sub-agent must be employed."

The above section makes it clear that generally a agent cannot appoint another person as his agent and delegate authority to him. But under certain circumstances, he may delegate part of his authority to another person. These circumstances are as under

(i) Where ordinary custom of trade permits the appointment of sub-agent.

(ii) Where the nature of business of agency is such that it cannot be carried out without appointing sub-agent.

(iii) Where the acts to be done are purely ministerial in nature can be delegated.

(iv) Where, there would have been some unforseen emergency which requires the appointment of sub-agent to cope with the situation.

(v) Where the principal agrees to the appointment of sub-agent.

Sub-Agent

According to section 191 of this Act, "sub-agent is a person employed by and acting under the control of the original agent in a business of agency."

Thus sub agent is appointed by the agent. And by appointing sub agent, the original agent delegates part of his authority to him. Sub-agent acts under the control of original agent and there exists a relation of principal and agent between original agent and sub-agent.

Where the appointment of sub-agent is proper with in above mentioned situations, he beares the following relations with the principal ad original agent.

(i) In all transactions and agreements made by sub-agent with third party, the principal will be represented. Though there is no privity of contract between the principal and sub-agent, but the principal would be liable for the acts of sub-agent as if those would have been done by the original agent appointed by him.

(ii) The original agent will be liable to the principal for the acts of sub-agent. It is because for the work delegated to sub-agent, the original agent will have ultimate liability.

(iii) The sub-agent will not directly be liable to the principal. He is appointed by and works under the control of original agent, thus will be liable to him only. In brief sub-agent will be liable to original agent and the original agent will be liable for the acts of sub-agent to the principal.

However where an agent, without having authority to do so, has appointed a person as sub agent. (i) The principal will not be represented by the acts of sub-agent. (ii) The original agent will be liable for the acts of sub agent both to the principal and to third person.

Substituted Agent:

A substituted agent is a person who is named by the agent and holds express or impled authority from the principal to act for the principal. There is a direct privity of a contract between the principal and substituted agent for such part of business of agency which is entrusted to him. Although a substituted agent is an agent of the principal but he is named by the original agent at the request of principal.

While naming substituted agent for the principal, an agent is bound to exercise same amount of discretion as a man of a ordinary prudence would exercise in his own case. If the agent does so, he is not responsible to the principal for the acts or negligence of the substituted agent.

Example: A appoints B as his agent for selling his property in auction and request B to name some reliable solicitor for that purpose. B has named C as a solicitor. There is a direct privity of contract between A and C thus C is a substituted agent.

Difference between sub-agent and substituted agent

	Sub-agent	*Substituted agent*
1. Appointment	Sub-agent is appointed by the original agent	Substituted agent is named by the original agent and appointed by the principal.
2. Privity of contract	There is no privity of contract between sub-agent and the principal	There is a direct privity of contract between the principal and substituted agent.
3. Liability	A original agent is liable for the acts of sub-agent towards the principal.	A original agent is not liable to the principal for the acts of substituted agent.

4.Direction and control	Sub-agent works under the control and direction of a original agent.	Substituted agent works under the direction and control of the principal
5. Relationship	Sub-agent is an agent of a original agent	Substituted agent is an agent of the principal, thus is also known as co-agent.

POSITION OF PRINCIPAL IN RELATION TO THIRD PARTY

All acts done by an agent on behalf of the principal with in a scope of his authority are binding on the principal. In fact the principal is being represented by his agent to deal with third party. The legal position of the principal in relation to third party may be understood with the help of following situation.

A. Agent acts for named principal.
B. Agent acts for unnamed principal.
C. Agent acts for undisclosed principal.

A. Where an Agent Acts for Named Principal:

The legal position of the principal whose name and existence are disclosed by the agent, is as under

(i) ***Liability of the principal for the acts with in an authority of agent:*** The principal will be responsible for the acts and contracts of agent with third party provided such acts or contracts are with in the scope of his authority and in the course of his employment as an agent.

According to section 226 of this act, "agent's acts and contracts will have the same legal effect as if the contract had been entered into and the acts done by the principal in person".

Example: A is appointed as an agent to buy raw material for B. A buys raw material from C on credit on behalf of B. This transaction is binding on B as well as on C.

(ii) ***Liability of the principal when agent exceeds authority:*** Where an agent does acts, some of them fall with in the scope of authority and others are beyond the scope.

- if the acts with in and beyond the scope of authority can be separated, the principal will be bound by those acts which are within the scope of authority of the agent.

- if the acts cannot be separated, the principal will not be bound by such acts and he is entitled to repudiate all acts done with in or beyond the scope of agent's authority.

Example: X was appointed as an agent for buying a horse for Y: But X buys a horse and carriage for Rs. 10000/-. The acts of this transaction cannot be separated, thus Y will not be liable for this transaction.

(iii) ***Liability of the principal for the notice given to agent:*** Any notice given to the agent in the course of business of agency transacted by him with third party and any information obtained by the agent shall have same legal consequences as if, it had been given or obtained by the principal. Thus, notice to the agent is the notice to the principal and the principal will be liable to third party for such notice or information.

(iv) ***Liability of the principal for misrepresentation or fraud by agent:*** The principal is liable for the misrepresentation made or fraud committed by the agent in the course of the business. Such misrepresentation or fraud will have same effect on agreement made by agent as if, these had been made or committed by the principal.

Example: A is working as an agent of B for selling goods. For inducing customers. A makes misrepresentation about the quality of goods and sells goods to C. B will be liable to C for misrepresentation made by A.

(v) ***Liability of the principal for agents unauthorised acts:*** Where the principal by his words or conduct induces third person to believe that the unauthorised acts of an agent are with in the scope of agents's authority, the principal shall be bound by such acts.

Example: X is appointed as an agent by Y for buying goods for him. On one occasion X buys goods on credit and Y pays for it though X had no authority to buy goods on credit. Again X buys goods on credit from Z. Y is responsible to Z for the payment.

B. Agent Acts for Unnamed Principal

It is a rule of law that once an agent discloses that he is acting as an agent the contract made by an agent binds the principal, though the principal has not been named by agent. On being discovered the legal position of unnamed principal is the same as where the principal is named. However, if the agent declines to disclose the identity of the principal, he becomes personally liable on that contract to third party.

Example: A is working as an agent of B for selling his goods. For making a contract of sale with C, A writes 'for the principal' without mentioning name of the principal. B is liable for this contract, though his name has not been mentioned.

C. Agent Acts for Undisclosed Principal:

An agent acts on behalf of the principal. His role is to bring third party in to contract with the principal. He simply represents the principal in dealing with third party.

However, if the agent does not disclose the existence of his principal, he is personally liable on that contract. Third party can sue upon him and he can also sue upon third party. But agent's right of action comes to an end with the intervention of undisclosed principal.

The undisclosed principal can intervene and may ask third party to perform contract. The rights of undisclose principal are protected by section 231 of this Act.

This Section provides that, "if an agent makes a contract with a person, who neither knows nor has reason to suspect that he is an agent, his principal may require performances of the contract; but other contracting party has, as against the principal, the same rights as he would have against the agent if the agent had been the principal".

The contents of the above section make it clear that

(i) Undisclosed principal may require third party to perform the contract.
(ii) third party has a right to sue upon agent in that contract.
(iii) third party has a right to claim performances of a contract as against the undisclosed principal.

However the right of undisclosed principal to intervene and sue third party is subject to the following condition

(i) An undisclosed principal may require the performances of a contract, subject to rights and obligations between the agent and third party of a contract.
(ii) If the principal discloses himself before the contract is completed, the other contracting party may repudiate the contract, if he can show that, if he had known, who the principal was or had he known that the agent was not a principal, he would not have entered into the contract.
(iii) An undisclosed, principal has no right to intervene if he has been excluded from the contract by express or implied terms of the contract made by the agent.

PERSONAL LIABILITY OF AGENT TO THIRD PARTY

An agent is appointed to represent the principal in dealing with third party. As soon as third party comes in to contractual relation with the principal, the role of agent is over. Neither he can enforce that agreement against third party nor he is personally liable in that agreement to third party.

Thus, in ordinary course of business of agency, an agent does not become personally liable. It is the principal on whose behalf the agent acts can enforce that agreement against third party.

But, under certain situations an agent who has a representative role incurs personal liability in the agreements made by him on behalf of the principal. These situations are as under.

(i) ***Foreign principal:*** An agent who acts for the principal or buys and sells the goods on behalf of the principal residing abroad, will be held personally liable for all transactions made by him.

(ii) ***Undisclosed principal:*** When an agent acts for the undisclosed principal, the agent incurs personal liability. An undisclosed principal means the name and identity of the principal is not being disclosed by the agent while dealing with third party.

(iii) ***Non-existing principal:*** When the agent acts for non-existing or fictitious principal, the agent will be personally liable for that act, because it would be presumed that he has acted personally.

(iv) ***Express agreement:*** When an agent, while contracting with third party expressly agrees to be personally liable on the contract, he can be held personally liable in that contract.

(v) ***Where principal cannot be sued:*** When the agent acts on behalf of the principal, though name and identity has been disclosed, but can not be sued, the agent will be personally liable in such a case. But if it is in the knowledge of third party that the principal can not be sued, the agent will have no personal liability.

(vi) ***Agent exceeds his authority:*** At the time of appointing an agent, Generally, authority is given to him. And he is expected to act with in the scope of his authority. Thus, if an agent exceeds his authority while dealing with third party, the agent will be personally liable for those acts

(vii) ***Agency coupled with interest:*** The business of agency may have subject matter. When an agent has some personal interest in that subject matter, the agency is said to be coupled with interest. In case of agency coupled with interest, the agent will be personally liable to third party to the extent of his interest.

Example: A owes sum of Rs. 20,000 to B. A appoints B as his agent for selling his property in auction and recover a sum due to him. In this case B has got personal interest for selling property of A in auction. Thus agency is said to be coupled with interest and to the extent of Rs. 20,000 B will be personally liable.

(viii) ***Trade usage and customs:*** Sometime, it may be customary in the business of agency that what ever an agent does for his principal, the agent is held personally liable for those acts to third party. In all such case the agent incurs personal liability.

(ix) ***Agent acts on his own:*** An agent is expected to act for the principal on his behalf. When an agent does some acts or makes contract in his own name, may be for the principal, the agent will be personally liable for such acts or contracts.

TERMINATION OF AGENCY

Agency is said to be terminated, if the relationship between agent and principal comes to an end. Agency may be terminated in any of the following manners.

A. Termination of Agency by the act of parties.
B. Termination of Agency by operation of law.

A. Termination of Agency by Act of Parties

The relationship of agency may be terminated by the acts of the parties under following situations

(i) ***By agreement between principal and agent:*** The relationship of agency is generally created by mutual agreement between the principal and agent. They are free to terminate relationship of agency by mutual agreement at any time.

(ii) ***Revocation by the principal:*** The principal can revoke authority of an agent at any time, before the authority has been exercised so as to bind the principal. Such revocation may be either express or implied by the conduct of the parties.

The principal shall have to pay compensation to the agent in case he revokes agent's authority without assigning sufficient cause, before the period for which it was delegated to him.

However, the principal cannot revoke agent's authority under the following situation and such agency is known as '**Irrevocable Agency**'.

(i) ***Agency coupled with interest:*** According to section 202 of this Act, "where the agent has himself an interest in the property which forms the subject matter of agency, the agency cannot, in the absence of an express contract, be terminated to the prejudice of such interest.

(ii) ***Where agent has incurred personal liability:*** While exercising an authority in the business of agency, if the agent has incurred personal liability, the principal cannot revoke authority of the agent.

(iii) ***Partial exercise of authority by agent:*** According to section 204 of this Act, "where the agent has partly exercised his authority, it becomes irrevocable, so far as regards such acts and obligations as arise from the acts already done in the agency.

It is to be noted that an agent after giving reasonable notice to the principal may also renounce the business of agency.

B. Termination of Agency by Operation of Law:

The relationship of agency, between the principal and agent may be terminated by operation of law in the following situations.

(i) ***Completion of business:*** Where the relationships of agency has been created for doing particular business. As soon as the business is completed, agency will be terminated automatically.

(ii) ***Expiry of time:*** Where the agent has been appointed for a particular period of time, at the expiry of that period, he ceases to be an agent.

(iii) ***Destruction of subject matter:*** An agency which has been created to deal with particular subject matter will be terminated on the destruction of that subject matter.

Example: A was appointed as an agent for selling a house of B in auction. Before auction, the house gets fire and destroyed. Agency will get terminated.

(iv) *Insolvency of the principal:* In the business of agency, if the principal is declared as an insolvent, as soon as the fact of insolvency comes to the knowledge of an agent, the relationships of agency will be terminated.

(v) *Death of the principal or agent:* An agency will get terminated on the death of the principal or an agent. In case, the principal dies, the agent is bound to take all reasonable steps for the protection and preservation of principal's interest on behalf to his representative.

(vi) *Insanity of the principal or agent:* Where, the principal or his agent becomes of unsound mind, the relationship of agency will be terminated. In case, the principal becomes of a unsound mind, the agent is bound to take reasonable steps for protecting and preserving the interest of the principal.

(vii) *Dissolution of a company:* Where the principal or agent is a body corporate or incorporated company, on the dissolution of such company, an agency will get terminated.

(viii) *Termination of sub-agents authority:* In case, the principal revokes, the authority of his agent, it will lead to automatic termination of sub-agent's authority appointed by original agent.

Effect of termination of agency

According to section 208 of this Act, as between the principal and the agent, termination of agency is effective only when it becomes known to the agent. But so far as third parties are concerned termination of agency takes effect when it is known to them. It is therefore relationship of agency between the principal and the agent ceases to exist when notice of such termination comes to the knowledge of the agent. To make termination of agency effective as against third parties the principal must give a public notice regarding termination of agency.

Even in case of death or insanity of the principal, termination of agency becomes effective when the fact of death or insanity comes to the knowledge of the agent.

Review Questions

1. Define the term agent. Discuss the nature of his role.
2. Explain various modes of creating relationship of agency in brief.
3. How the agency is created by ratification. Discuss various requirements of a valid ratification.
4. 'One who does through another, does by himself'. Comment.
5. Explain the various duties of an agent against the principal.
6. 'Rights of agent are duties of the principal' Explain it.
7. Explain nature and scope of authority of an agent.

8. "Delegate of authority cannot further delegate it" comment.
9. Define sub-agent. Discuss his role with regard to principal and original agent.
10. Define sub-agent and substituted agent. Distinguish between these two.
11. Discuss the legal position of the principal in relation with third party.
12. Explain the circumstances under which an agent is personally liable for the acts done by him on behalf of the principal.
13. Write notes
    (i) Agency by Holding out (ii) Agency by necessity.
    (iii) Irrevocable agency (iv) Sub-agent.
    (v) Undisclosed principal (vi) Authority of agent.
14. What is termination of agency? When the agency is terminated by operation of law.

PRACTICAL PROBLEMS

1. A, who is a minor has been appointed as an agent by B to buy raw material for him. A buys 10 tons of raw material on behalf of B on credit from C. Later on C refused to pay because A who has made transaction is minor. Can C claim the price from B (Yes, agent may be a minor).
2. Ram appoints Hari as his agent on specific commission for selling some goods. Hari agrees to it. There is no consideration in this agreement between Ram and Hari. Is this agreement is enforceable? (Yes, agency does not require consideration).
3. A tells to B in the presence of C that A is B's agent, in fact he is not an agent. B does not refuse it. Later an C makes a contract for buying goods with A, believing that he is B's agent. Is B bound by this contract? (Yes, there is an agency by estoppel).
4. X has been working as an agent of Y for the last one year. Now his services have been terminated by Y, but no notice was given to this effect by Y. X subsequently purchased some goods on credit in the name of Y from Z. Is Y liable to pay the price? (Yes).
5. A allows his servant to purchase goods for him in the past on credit from B. On one occasion he pays cash to his servant for buying the goods. But the servant misappropriated that money and bought the goods on credit form B. Is A liable to pay for the goods? (Yes, there is an agency by holding out).
6. A railway company has carried a horse from Bombay to Delhi, appointed destination. On the arrival at Delhi no one comes forward for getting delivery of the horse. The railway company has handed over the horse to stable keeper on rent. On tracing real owner of the horse, the railway company claimed for the rent. Is this claim valid? (Yes, there is an agency by necessity).

7. A got married with B. After some time A fails in providing basic necessaries of the life to his wife. His wife for the fulfillment of basic necessities pledges the property of her husband. Is an agreement of pledge valid? (Yes, there is an agency by necessity).
8. A purchased one hundred tons of wheat in his name for B without B's authority. Later on B ratifies the transaction. Is ratification valid (No, A has acted at his own).
9. A is a managing director in a particular company. He accepts the offer made by B for buying goods purporting to act as an agent on behalf of the company. Later on B withdrew his offer and ratifies the act of managing director. Examine legal position of the offer and acceptance.
10. A has rented his car to B for one month to be used for carriage purpose. C gets the car back from B without A's permission after fifteen days. As a result of it B suffers a loss. A ratifies C's act. Does it amount to a valid ratification? (No it implies loss to B).
11. R has been appointed as an agent to sell one house of B. R finds out buyer of the house and gets an advance of Rs. 20,000 form him. Later on he misappropriates this amount. Can buyer of the house claim this amount from B.? (Yes, the act of R was with in his scope of authority).
12. A made an agreement with a stock broker for buying 500 equity shares of a particular company named as Blue and Green Coy Ltd. The broker did not buy these share in an open market, rather sold 500 equity share of that company which he owned, to A. Is A bound by this agreement? (No, the broker has worked in contradiction to his duty).
13. A appoints B as his agent to recover Rs. 20000 from C and invest it on good securities. B recovered the amount and 50% of it was invested on the good securities and remaining balance was invested on the securities which B knew to be bad securities. A suffers a loss of Rs. 1000 from bad securities. Is B entitled to a remuneration on Rs.20,000 ? Who shall be liable for a loss of Rs. 1000 on bad securities.
14. A at the request of B sells goods being possessed by B without having right to sell the goods. A, not knowing this, sells the goods and hands over the proceeds to B. Later on, C who is a real owner of the goods sues A and recovers value of goods as well as legal cost. Is B liable to A to reimburse payments? (Yes).
15. Ram was appointed as an agent by Shyam for selling Shyam's property in auction and made out sum of Rs. 20,000 out of the proceeds which Shyam owes to Ram. Can Shyam revoke authority which he has given to Ram? (No, agency is coupled with interest of Ram).

■■■

Chapter 14

Contract of Bailment and Pledge

Learning Objectives

- Get familiar with the concept of bailment of goods and types of bailment.
- Analyse rights and duties of bailor and bailee.
- Remember the rights and duties of finder of goods.
- Compare bailment of goods and pledge of goods
- Get an idea about when non owners can create valid pledge of the goods.

INTRODUCTION

Sometimes, the owner transfers physical possession of goods to another person without affecting the right of ownership. Such transfer of physical possession or delivery of goods may be made for various purposes, i.e. for safe custody, as a security and in some cases for the use of that another person etc. But in all these case, that person to whom the goods are delivered will have very limited right that too only for a short period of time. Such types of transaction are made in the form of a contract of 'bailment'.

DEFINITION

According to section 148 of the Indian Contract Act bailment is, the delivery of goods by one person to anther of same purpose, upon a contract that, they shall, when the purpose is accomplished, be returned or otherwise disposed of according to the directions of the person delivering them.

Thus bailment is a contract where upon the physical possession of goods is transferred by one person to another for some purpose which may vary from situation to situation. The person who transfers possession of the goods is known as 'bailor' and to whom it is transferred to is known as 'bailee', and the contract between them is known as 'bailment'.

Essential Features of Bailment

The contract of bailment has the following important features.

(i) ***Delivery of goods :*** The contract of bailment implies delivery of goods by one person to another. Delivery of goods involves transfer of physical possession. According to section 149 of this Act delivery of goods may be either 'actual' or constructure. When the bailor hands over the goods physically to the bailee it is known as actual delivery and on the other hand, if the bailor does some act which has an effect of putting goods in the possession of another person, it is known as constructure delivery. As a result of such act another person gets authorisation or control over the goods without removing the goods physically.

(ii) ***Agreement:*** In case of bailment there is an agreement between bailor and bailee. It is under such agreement goods are delivered by the bailor to the bailee. Such agreement may be either express or implied from the circumstances.

(iii) ***Purpose:*** In a contract of bailment the bailor delivers the goods to the bailee for some purpose. The purpose may vary situation to situation depending upon the need of the person and circumstances. Delivery of the goods may be given for the purpose safe custody, forth security of loan or may be for the use of the bailee. The goods delivered by one person to another either by mistake or without purpose will not be included in the contract of bailment.

(iv) ***Return of goods:*** The contract of bailment implies that when the said purpose for which the goods have been delivered is accomplished, the goods will be returned back to the bailor or will be disposed of according to the directions of the bailor. It is however to be noted that goods may be returned either in original form or in an altered form.

***Example*:** A has given a piece of cloth to the tailor for making a shirt out of it. The tailor stitched it for making a shirt and when it is completed, he becomes bailee and he will return in an altered form.

Besides the above features, it is also to be noted in bailment that the ownership of the goods is not transferred to the bailee.

KINDS OF BAILMENT

The contract of bailment may be entered into for various purposes. Sometimes is may be for the benefit of bailor or bailee and sometimes it may be made for the mutual benefits of both the partes. Broadly the bailment can be classified an under:

(i) ***For the benefit of the bailor:*** Delivery of the goods exclusively for the benefit of the bailor will be included in this category. For example bailment for safe custody without any charge or hire.

(ii) ***For the benefit of the bailee:*** Sometimes, the goods may be bailed only for the benefit of bailee such as bailment for use of bailee without any hire or rent.

(iii) ***For the mutual benefits:*** In majority of the cases, the contract of bailment is made for the mutual benefit of both bailor and bailee. For example bailment of the goods as security for processing loan, or bailment of the goods to which some value is added for reward such as cloth is altered into specific garment for charges.

(iv) ***Bailment for reward:*** Where the transaction of bailment involves, payment of remuneration either to the bailor or to the bailee, it is known as bailment for reward.

Example: A lends his car to B for carriage on rent. A will get remuneration. Similarly A deposits his valuables in the bank for safe custody and the bank takes charges for it. In this case the bailee is entitled to a remuneration.

(v) ***Gratuitous bailment:*** Where in a transaction of bailment neither the bailor or the bailee is entitled to any remuneration, it is known as gratuitous bailment such as lending a car to a friend without any rent or delivery of goods to a friend for safe custody without any charge, etc. In such transactions of bailment, the detriment suffered either by bailor or by bailee as the case may be is enough consideration for supporting validity of a transaction.

RIGHT AND DUTIES OF BAILOR AND BAILEE

In a contract of bailment, the bailor and the bailee have got certain rights and duties against each other which are as under:

A. Right of Bailor

The bailor has got the following rights in a contract of bailment against the bailee.

(i) ***Right to terminate bailment:*** The bailor has right to terminate the transaction of bailment if the bailee makes unauthorised or wrongful use of the goods bailed to him. An unauthorised use of goods means the bailee is using that goods without having the right to do so or he has a right to use goods for specific purposes but he is using it for the purpose other than specific one.

(ii) ***Right to seek return of goods:*** In a transaction of gratuitous bailment, the bailor has a right to demand return of goods even before the expiry of specific period or accomplishment of specific objective for which the goods have been bailed. But in case of such immature return, if the loss suffered by the bailee is greater than the benefit derived from the use of goods, the bailor has to compensate him for the excess of loss.

(iii) ***Right to demand any natural increase in goods bailed:*** In a contract of bailment, if there is an increase in the goods bailed to the bailee, the bailor is entitled to demand return of such increased portion along with goods originally given on bailment. Such as if a pregnant cow is given on bailment and she gives a birth to a baby cow, the bailor has an equal right of return against that calf along with a cow.

(iv) *Right to enforce duties of bailee:* In fact, the duties of the bailee are the rights of the bailor. And the bailor can enforce those duties of bailee even by filing a suit against him.

B. Duties of Bailor

In a contract of bailment the bailor has got the following duties regarding the goods bailed towards the bailee.

(i) *Duty to disclose faults in the goods:* The bailor is under legal obligation to disclose all defects or faults lying in the goods bailed to the bailee. But in case of gratuitous bailment, the bailor's duty is limited only for disclosing known defects. In a bailment for reward he is liable for both known as well as unknown faults in the goods. Thus if the bailee suffers any loss due to these faults the bailor will be liable to compensate him.

(ii) *Duty to bear expenses incurred by the bailee*: In case of a gratuitous bailment if the bailee has carried out some work on the goods bailed as per the terms of bailment or has spend some money for the reasonable maintenance of the goods, such expenses will ultimately be borne by the bailor. And in case of bailment for reward, the bailor will be liable only for extraordinary expenses.

(iii) *Duty to indemnity losses of bailee:* In case of gratuitous bailment, due to immature return of goods if the bailee has suffered losses which are more than the benefit derived, it is the duty of the bailor to indemnify those losses suffered by the bailee.

(iv) *Duty to compensate loss of the bailee due to defective title:* Where the bailor has no right to bail the goods or his title of those goods is defective, and the bailee suffers any loss due to such defective title. The bailor is under legal obligation to compensate those losses of the bailee.

Example: A has stolen car from B. A gives it to C on rent. In the meantime B comes to know about it and gets the car recovered from C. In this process C suffers a loss, he is entitled to get compensation from A who is the bailor of that car.

(v) *Duty to take goods from the bailee:* Bailment is made for a specific purpose. On the completion of that purpose, the goods bailed should be returned to the bailor. If the bailor refuses to take those goods and the bailee suffers an loss, he is entitled to get compensation from the bailor. Thus the bailor must accept the return of goods from the bailee on time.

C. Rights of Bailee

The bailee has got the following rights against the bailor:

(i) *Right to enforce bailor's duty:* The duties of the bailor are the rights of the bailee. Therefore, the bailee is entitled to sue upon the bailor for enforcing the bailor's duties.

(ii) ***Right to be indemnified:*** In a contract of bailment, if the bailee suffers any loss due to defective title of the goods on the part of the bailor, he is entitled to get indemnified. These losses many arise, because the bailor was not entitled to make bailment or to receive back the goods or to seek the disposal of goods, etc.

(iii) ***Right to claim compensation:*** Where the bailee suffers a loss due to the faults lying in the goods bailed, he has a right to claim compensation. In case of gratuitous bailment his liability is confined only upto those faults which were known to him, but in a bailment for reward he will be liable for both known or unknown faults.

(iv) ***Right to sue the wrongdoer:*** As long as the goods are in the possession and use of the bailee as per the terms of bailment, he has all rights against any wrongdoer which are enjoyed by the owner of the goods. It means if the bailee has been deprived of the use of goods or an injury has been caused to him by a third party he is entitled to sue him.

(v) ***Right to return goods to any one of the joint bailors:*** In a contract of bailment in which two or more bailors jointly make a bailment. On the accomplishment of the purpose of the bailment, the bailee can return the goods to any one of the joint bailors. And it is necessary for him to inform another joint bailor.

(vi) ***Right to recover expenses:*** The bailee is entitled to recover general expenses or charges for his services which he has rendered as per the conditions of bailment or under any logical obligation, he can recover these from the bailor. But in case of bailment for reward he is entitled to recover only extraordinary expenses incurred by him.

(vii) ***Right against third party or owner:*** In case, the purpose of the bailment is accomplished and the bailee returns the goods to the bailor in good faith. The bailee has a right against third party who has a claim against goods to protect himself. Thus the bailee will not be liable to such third party.

(viii) ***Right of lien:*** It is a right to retain possession of the property of another person until some debt or claim against that person is paid. This right is known as possessory lien and therefore as soon as possession of the property is lost, this right will also be lost. The right of lien may be of two types – particular lien and general lien.

In a particular lien, the person exercising this right can retain the possession of that property in respect of which debt or claim is due. But in general lien any property may be retained unless and until any of the debts or claim against that another person is satisfied. This right is available only to special type of bailees such as banker, factor, warmfinger, attorneys of high courts, etc., and policy brokers. And all other bailees enjoy right of particular lien. According to section 170 of this Act, the right of particular lien has been conferred upon the bailee. This section further provides that, "where the bailee has in accordance with the purpose of the bailment rendered any service involving the exercise of labour or skill in respect of the goods bailed, he has, in the absence of a contract to the contrary, a right to retain such goods, until he receives due remuneration for the services he has rendered in respect of them".

Thus the right of particular lien is available to the bailee subject to the fulfillment of the following conditions.

(i) The bailee must have rendered some services on the goods bailed.
(ii) Such services must involve use of labour and skill of the bailee.
(iii) Such services have been rendered by the bailee according to terms and condition of the contract of bailment.
(iv) There must not be any contract contrary to the above conditions such as condition to pay service charges at future data, etc.
(v) The bailee can exercise this right only for the payment of due remuneration for the services rendered by him.
(vi) Services rendered by the bailee must be complete.

Example: A has delivered a car to B for making necessary repair on it. B did it as per the term and condition or the bailment. In this case B is entitled to retain the possession of the car until A makes payment of service charges to B provided B has repaired the car. But, as per the term of a contract if the payment of charges is to be made after two months, B is not entitled to the right of lien.

It is however to be noted that the right of lien comes to an end under the following circumstances.

(i) The person who in entitled to this right has lost the possession of goods.
(ii) There is a term in a contract which is contrary to this right.
(iii) Right of lien is terminated as soon as the payment of debt or claim is made or tendered.
(iv) Right of lien available to the bailee may be waived by him voluntarily.

D. Duties of Bailee

In a contract of bailment, the bailee is subject to following duties.

(i) ***Duty to take reasonable care:*** In all cases of bailment, most important duty of the bailee is to take reasonable care of the goods bailed to him. Reasonable care of goods means that much care as person of reasonable prudence would have taken in case of his own goods and under similar circumstances.

According to section 151 of this Act, "in all cases of bailment, the bailee is bound to take as much care of the goods bailed to him, as a man of ordinary prudence would, under similar circumstances take of his own goods of the same bulk, quality and value as the goods bailed".

In case the goods are damaged or destroyed due to lack of reasonable care, the bailee will be liable for the loss. But in spite of taking reasonable care if the goods are damaged, the bailee will not be liable for such losses.

Martin vs. London Country Council (1947, K.B., 628) In this case, plaintiff was brought as a patient to a paid hospital. On entry she handed over two pieces of jewellery and a cigarette case to the hospital authorities. These were stolen by a thief. The hospital authorities were held liable as a bailee, because they had failed in taking as much care as the nature of articles demanded.

(ii) ***Duty not to make unauthorized use of the goods bailed:*** The transaction of bailment may be made for the use of goods by the bailee. The bailee is under obligation to use the goods in the manner as prescribed and for the purpose as mentioned in the contract. And he must not use the goods in a manner which is inconsistent with the terms of a contract. In case he makes an unauthorised or inconsistent use of the goods and the goods are damaged he shall be liable to pay compensation to the bailor.

Example: A hired his horse to B, who shall use it for the purpose of riding. But B used for carriage purpose and the horse got injured. B will be liable for the loss. Similarly A rented his car to B for going to Mumbai. But B goes to Lucknow and on the way meets with an accident and car was damaged. B shall be liable for unauthorised use of the goods.

(iii) ***Duty not to mix the goods with his own goods:*** There is a duty on the part of the bailees that he must not mix the goods bailed with his own goods. In case he mixes, them with his own with the consent of the bailor, both of them will have same interest as they had before mixing the goods. But, if the goods are mixed without consent of the bailor and goods can be separated out, all expenses and damage arising out of it shall be borne by the bailee.

In case the goods are not separable, the bailee shall be liable to compensate the bailee for a loss.

(iv) ***Duty to return the goods:*** The transaction of bailment is always made for some specific purpose. And as soon as the purpose is accomplished it is a duty of the bailee to return the good to the bailor. In case, delay occurs in returning the goods and in the meantime, the goods are destroyed, the bailee will be liable for the loss to the bailor.

In case of gratuitous bailment the bailor has a right to demand immature return even before the specific period for which the goods are bailed. If, the loss suffered by the bailee on account of immature return is more than the benefit derived by him, the bailor will compensate the loss.

(v) ***Duty to return any natural accretion to the goods:*** In case there has been a natural accretion to the goods bailed. It is his duty to return it along with the goods to the bailor

Example: A leaves a pregnant cow with B to be taken care of. Later on the cow gives a birth to a calf. B is under duty to return both the cow as well as calf to A.

(vi) ***Duty not to set up adverse title:*** Section 117 of the India Evidence Act provides that, "no bailee shall be permitted to deny that his bailor had, at the time of bailment authority to make such bailment". In other words, the bailee can not deny the title and right of the bailor. Thus if the bailee return the goods to the bailor in good faith he shall have no liability towards third party who may be real owner of the goods.

Right of Bailor and Bailee against Wrongdoer

(i) In case, the bailee is deprived of the use or possession of the goods bailed or does any injury, the bailee is entitled to use such remedies as the owner might have used in the like case, if bailment had not been made.

(ii) Either the bailor or the bailee may bring a suit against the wrongdoer for such deprivation or injury (section 180).

(iii) Whatever is obtained by way of relief or compensation in any such suit insto be apportioned as between the bailor and the bailee according to their respective interest (section 181).

TERMINATION OF BAILMENT

A contract of bailment stands terminated under the following situations.

(i) ***Expiry of specified period:*** In case the contract of bailment is made for a specific period of time. As soon as that period expires, a contract of bailment gets terminated.

(ii) ***Specific purpose:*** The goods are generally bailed to the bailee for a specific purpose. On the accomplishment of such purpose, the contract of bailment will automatically be terminated.

(iii) ***Termination of gratuitous bailment:*** In a contract of gratuitous bailment, the bailor has got right to demand return of the goods even before the accomplishment of purpose or expiry of specific period of time. On the return of the goods, the bailment will come to an end.

(iv) ***Inconsistent use of the goods:*** In case the bailee makes unauthorised or inconsistent use of the goods bailed, the bailor may demand return of the goods and can seek termination of the bailment.

(v) ***Death of bailor or bailee:*** A contract of the gratuitous bailment will come to an end in the event of death of bailor or the bailee.

FINDER OF THE GOODS

Where the person who finds the goods lost by another person, and takes custody of those goods. He gets same legal position in the eyes of low as a bailee in a gratuitous bailment. Thus he is subject to some rights and obligations.

According to section 71, "a person who finds goods belonging to another and takes them into this custody is subject to same responsibility as a bailee".

A. Rights of Finder of Goods

The finder of the goods who takes custody of those has the following rights against the owner of the goods.

(i) ***Right to possess the goods:*** The finder of the goods is entitled to possess those goods until he traces the real owner, against everyone except the true owner.

(ii) ***Right to claim for reward:*** Generally the real owner of the lost goods declares some reward for the finder of the goods. The finder of goods may sue the real owner for such reward.

(iii) ***Right of lien:*** According to section 168 of this Act, a finder has a right to retain possession of the goods until he receives reasonable compensation for expenses, incurred in connection with preservation of goods and finding out of the owner.

(iv) ***Right of sale of goods:*** In spite of making reasonable efforts if the bailee does not succeed in tracing real owner of the goods, he has a right to sell off those goods, but under the following situations

(a) When the thing is in danger of perishing or losing greater part of its value or,

(b) When the lawful charges of the finder in respect of things found, amount to two third of its value.

B. Duties of Finder of Goods

Finder of goods is subject to the following duties for preserving the goods and protecting an interest of true owner.

(i) A finder of goods must take reasonable care of those goods. Due to lack of reasonable care, if the goods are destroyed he shall be liable to the real owner for the loss.

(ii) A finder of goods must make all reasonable efforts to trace the real owner of the goods.

(iii) On tracing the real owner he must return the goods to him.

(iv) A finder of goods is also under obligation for returning natural accretion to the good like the bailee.

PLEDGE

The contract of bailment is made for various purposes. A pledge is a special kind of bailment which is made for providing security to the lender against the loan given by him.

According to section 172 of this Act, "pledge is the bailment of the goods as security for payment of a debt or for performance of promise. The person who delivers the goods is known as 'pawnor' and to whom the goods are bailed known as 'pawnee'."

Thus pledge is bailment of goods as a security for procuring loan or for performance of promise.

Characteristics of Pledge

Pledge is a special kind of bailment. It has the following characteristics.

(i) ***Delivery of goods:*** As a kind of bailment, the transaction of pledge involves transfer of physical possession of goods to the 'pawnee'. Such transfer may be in the form of 'actual delivery' or in the form of constructure delivery.

(ii) ***Purpose of delivery:*** In a pledge, the goods are delivered to the pawnee for a specific purpose, i.e. as a security for payment of debt. Thus so long as debt is not paid, goods will be in the possession of the pawnee.

(iii) ***Return of goods:*** In a transaction of pledge, as soon as the debt or loan procured by the pawnor is paid, the goods will be returned by the pawnee to him.

(iv) ***Transfer of special interest:*** While pledging the goods the pawnor transfers special interest with regard to those goods to the pawnee. But general interest remains with the pawnor.

DIFFERENCE BETWEEN BAILMENT AND PLEDGE

Through the pledge is a special kind of bailment, but it differs on the following points

(i) ***Purpose:*** The pledge is a bailment of the goods as a security for paying debt or performing performance. But the bailment can be made for varities of purposes other than those two, such as safe custody, for the use of bailor or for creating additional value in the goods, etc.

(ii) ***Use of good:*** In pledge, the pawnee is not entitled to use the goods bailed to him. Rather he has a special interest on the goods of retaining possession so long as debt is not paid. But in many other transaction of bailment the bailee may enjoy not only the possession but also the use of goods.

(iii) ***Sale of goods:*** In case of pledge, if the pawnor fails in repaying debt or performing promise, the 'pawnee', by giving reasonable notice to the pawnor can sell those goods. But in bailment, the bailee has no right to sell the goods bailed to him.

(iv) ***Scope:*** All transaction of pledge are bailment, but all transaction of bailment are not pledge.

RIGHTS AND DUTIES OF PAWNOR AND PAWNEE

A. Rights of Pawnor

The pawnor has the following rights:

(i) ***Right to redeem goods:*** As stated earlier that in case, the pawnor fails to pay debt, the pawnee has a right to sell the goods. But before the actual sale of goods by the pawnee, the pawnor has a right to redeem the goods.

(ii) ***Right to receive accretion:*** In case some increase or accretion takes place to bailed goods, the pawnor has a right to receive back that increase or accretion.

Example: A company has borrowed sum of Rs. 10 lac from the bank and as a security for the loan the company pledged equity shares of another company with the bank. Meanwhile, some bonus shares accrued on account of pledged shares. Thus on repayment of that loan the company has a right to get shares original shares along with bonus shares.

(iii) ***Right to enforce of duty of the pawnee:*** The pawnor, as a bailor has a right to get all duties of pawnee enforced by filing a suit against him.

B. Duties of Pawnor

The pawnor has the following duties:

(i) ***Duty to meet obligation on time:*** The pawnor is under duty to pay debt on time according to terms of a pledge and comply with other conditions of the pledge.

(ii) ***Duty to bear extraordinary expenses:*** In case the pawnee, incurs some extraordinary expenses with respect to goods pledge, it is the duty of pawnor to compensate the pawnee for those expenses.

(iii) ***Duty to compensate pawnee for defective title:*** Where the pawnee suffers any loss due to some defects in the title of pawnor, it is the duty of pawnor to compensate the pawnee for those losses.

C. Rights of Pawnee

The pawnee has following rights as against the goods pledged and the pawnor.

(i) ***Right of retainer:*** The pawnee has a right to retain the goods pledged with him until his debt or dues are cleared or paid. He can exercise this right not only for the debt, but also for an interest due on the debt and all other necessary expenses incurred by him. This right may be known as 'pledger's right of particular lien.

(ii) ***Right of retainer for subsequent advances:*** When the pawnee lends money to the pawnor after the date of pledge without taking any further security, it shall be presumed that, right of retainer over the pledged goods extends to subsequent advance made.

(iii) *Right to recover extraordinary expenses:* Where the pawnee incures some extraordinary expenses for preserving the goods pledged, he is entitled to recover these expenses from the pawnor. But the pawnee can not exercise right of retainer for the recovery of such expenses.

(iv) *Right to sue the pawnor or sell the goods at his default:* In case the pawnor fails to pay debt or perform promise the pawnee can exercise any of the following rights.

(a) he may retain goods as collateral security and file a suit against the pawnor for the recovery of amount.

(b) after giving reasonable notice to the pawnor, he can sell the goods pledged.

D. Duties of Pawnee

The pawnee is subject to the following duties and obligations in a contract of pledge.

(i) *To take reasonable care:* The pawnee is under legal obligation to take reasonable care of the goods pledged to him.

(ii) *Not to use goods:* The pawnee generally is not entitled to use the goods pledged to him. In case the pawnor allows him, he must make authorised use of the goods.

(iii) *Not to mix the goods:* The pawnee is under duty to keep goods pledged separately and not to mix them with his own goods.

(iv) *To return goods:* On the payment of debt of performance of a promise, the pawnee must return the goods to the pawnor. Any under delay which causes damage or loss to goods will be the liability of the pawnee.

(v) *To return increase in goods:* In case there has been any natural increase in the goods pledged, it is a duty of the pawnee to return such increase to the pawnor.

(vi) *Not to set up an adeverse title:* It is also a duty of the pawnee that he must not deny the title and right of pawnor. And he must not set up his own title or title of third party on the goods pledges.

PLEDGE BY NON-OWNERS

As a rule of law it is the real owner of the goods or the person duty authorised by him can create a valid pledge of those goods. But in practice, there are many situations under which even a non-owner or the person who is not authorized to pledge can create a valid pledge. These exceptions are as under.

(i) *Pledge by mercantile agent:* The mercantile agent, who has got the possession of goods or documents of title with the consent of owner pledges those goods without any authority, even then such pledge will be valid provided the following conditions are fulfilled.

(a) The goods or document of title of goods are in the possession of a mercantile agent with the consent of owner.
(b) He pledges the goods in an ordinary course of business of agency.
(c) The pawnee has acted in good faith believing that the mercantile agent has a right to pledge the goods.

(ii) *Pledge of goods obtained in voidable contract:* In case the person obtains possession of the goods in a voidable contract in which the consent of another party has not been free. If these goods are pledged before the contract is declared as void by an aggrieved party, such pledge is also legally valid provided the pawnee has acted in good faith.

(iii) *Pledge by the person having limited interest on the goods*: When the person has limited interest on the goods and he pledges those goods, such transaction of pledge will be valid up to the extent of his interest.

Example: A has pledged the goods as a security for the payment of loan of Rs. 10,000 which he has taken from B. B further pledges these goods to C for the payment of loan to Rs. 15,000. The pledge of goods by B to C is valid to the extent of Rs. 10,000.

(iv) *Pledge by one of the joint owners:* In case the goods are owned jointly by two or more persons. And one of the joint owners pledges those goods, such pledge is valid provided.

(a) he has got possession of goods with the consent of other joint owners.
(b) the pawnee must have acted in good faith believing that the joint owner is authorised to pledge the goods.

(v) *Pledge by the seller having possession of goods after sale:* When the seller has sold the goods, but he is still possessing those goods. In case he pledges those goods, the pledge is valid provided the pawnee has acted in good faith and had no notice of earlier sale.

(vi) *Pledge by the buyer in possession of goods in agreement to sell:* Where the buyer buys the goods under agreement to sell. Before he gets ownership he pledges those goods. Such pledge is valid provided the pawnee has acted in good faith.

Example: A buys a machine worth Rs. 2000 on hire purchase basis. The payment is to be made in twenty equal installments. After having paid a few installments he pledges that machine with B, the pledge is valid provided B has acted in good faith having no notice of hire-purchase.

Review Questions

1. What is bailment? Discuss its essential features.
2. Explain the various types of bailment?

3. What is lien? Explain the various types of lien and discuss, bailees particular lien.
4. Distinguish between bailment and pledge.
5. Explain various rights and duties of the bailor.
6. Discuss the rights and duties of the bailee.
7. Explain rights and duties of the finder of the goods.
8. Can a non-owner create a valid pledge? Explain the exceptions.

Practical Problems

1. A went to see an exhibition. A parked his car in a field belonging to a farmer who has permitted the parking of vehicles in his field. After sometime A returned to the field and found that the car has been stolen. Is the farmer liable for the loss of car to A? (Not he is not a bailee).
2. M is going out of station and leaves his car with N for safe custody N. does not charge anything from M. Is it a contract of bailment? (Yes)
3. A customer visited a restaurant for having dinner. As soon as he entered the restaurant, a waiter took his coat without being asked to do so and hung it on a hook behind him. When the customer after finishing diner was to leave the customer found that the coat is missing. Is the owner of that restaurant liable for a loss of a coat? (Yes he has acted in the position of the bailee)
4. A has borrowed a sum of Rs. 50,000 from a bank and pledged some shares of joint stock company. Later on the company issued bonus share on those pledged shares. Is A entitled to receive those bonus shares. (Yes)
5. M found a car. He took it in his custody. He has only one car garage in which he used to park his car. Thus he parked the found car outside the garage. That car has been stolen. N who is a owner of that car claimed compensation from M. Is he entitled to it. (Yes)
6. A has taken a horse from B on hire for riding purpose. But A used it for carriage purpose. The horse got injury while doing the job of carriage. Is A liable for this loss to B. (Yes A has made unauthorised use of that horse).
7. Ram has given a piece of cloth to a tailor for making a suit out of it. The suit was half stitched. Ram refused to pay tailoring charges. Can a tailor exercise right of lien over the half stiched suit. (No)
8. A has pledge some goods with B and secured loan of Rs. 10,000 against it. B further pledged these good with C as a security for paying a loan of Rs. 15000. Can A take his goods from C without making any payment to him. (Yes by making payment of Rs. 10,000)

■■■

Part 2

Sale of Goods Act 1930

Chapter 15

Law of Sale of Goods

Learning Objectives

- Understand the meaning of contract of sale and compare it with hire-purchase agreement and bailment.
- Develop conceptual clarity regarding subject matter of contract of sale.
- Get familiar with various types of goods and find out their suitability for sale and agreement to sell.
- Examine legal consequence of getting goods destroyed.

INTRODUCTION

Sale and purchase of goods is a common transaction in business. *Sale of goods* in business *fetches revenue* which is further used in the process of business. Sale and purchase of goods cannot be separated from each other because same transaction is a sale for one party and purchase for another. Transactions in the nature of sale of goods form the subject matter of the sale of goods Act, 1930 (applicable to whole of India except Jammu & Kashmir).

The Act covers topics such as the concept of sale of goods, warranties and conditions arising out of sale, delivery of goods and passing of property and other obligations of the buyer and the seller, the documents of title to goods and the transfer of ownership on the basis of such documents. The Act came into force on 1st July, 1930. It extends to the whole of India, except the state of Jammu and Kashmir.

Certain minor amendments were made in this Act in 1963. This Act closely follows the provisions of English law on the contract of sale. Since contract of sale is a specific contract, thus general provisions of Indian Contract Act are also applicable on it, provided they are not inconsistent with the express provisions of sale of Goods Act.

This Act contains rules and regulations relating to various types of contracts of sale of goods. It provides definition of various terms and covers detailed rules to the effect of destruction of goods, conditions and warranties applicable on this contract, transfer of ownership and delivery of goods and position and remedial measures available to an unpaid seller.

DEFINITION AND ESSENTIALS OF A CONTRACT OF SALE

Section 4 (1) of this Act defines a contract of sale "as a contract, whereby the seller transfers or agrees to transfer the property in goods to the buyer for a price."

From the definition the following essentials of a contract emerge:

(i) *There must be at least two parties:* Contract of sale is a specific contract. It is formed by offer and acceptance. To form it, either the buyer will give an offer to buy goods to the seller or the seller gives an offer to buyer. On acceptance of such offer the contract of sale is formed. The buyer is a person who will make payment of price to the seller and will get ownership as well as possession of goods. And the seller transfers or promises to transfer ownership and handsover the possession to the buyer in consideration of money.

However, it is to be noted that a person can not buy his own goods or cannot sell his goods to himself.

C.M. Transport Company Vs. ITO. (1966). In this case a company resolved to transfer some buses to a partnership firm consisting of certain persons who were also the members of the company. Income Tax officer considered such transfer as a sale, because the company has a legal entity and can be a seller. This decision was upheld by the supreme court.

Bell Vs. Lever Brothers Ltd. In this case X is the owner of certain good, but he is not aware of this fact. Y pretends to be the owner of goods makes contract to sell them to X who is already owner of those goods. There is no contract between X & Y. However, a part, owner of goods can sell those goods to other part owner as to make him sole owner. (Section 4).

Thus two parties having genuine legal entity are needed for making a contract of sale.

(ii) *Subject matter of contract of sale:* The subject matter of a contract of sale is goods. It includes all types of movable properties such as stock, shares and growing crops etc. Sale and purchase of immovable property is not covered by this Act. But it is regulated by the provision of Transfer of Property Act. Similarly contracts relating to services are not treated as contract of sale.

(iii) *Transfer of property:* Transfer of property or ownership of goods is an essential feature of the contract of sale. The ownership of goods is transferred from seller to buyer. According to section 2 (II) of this Act, property or ownership means general property in goods and not a merely special property. Which means special interest in goods.

Example: A borrows a sum of Rs. 10,000 from B and pledges his property against this loan to B. In this case A transfers special property to B, by handing over possession, but retaining its ownership. Thus it is not a contract of sale.

However for transfering ownership of goods physical delivery of goods is not necessary.

(iv) *Price consideration:* In a contract of sale payment of price is made by the buyer to the seller. It constitutes consideration for the promise of the seller. The consideration in a contract of sale must be in money. However it may be partly in money and partly in goods.

ALDRIDGE VS. JOHNSON (1857, 7, E & B. 885). In this case, A agrees to exchange with B 100 quarters of barle at $2 p.q. and, for 52 bullocks valued at $6 p.d. and pay the difference in cash. The contract was held a fit contract for sale.

(v) *Essentials of valid contract:* The contract of sale must possess all essential elements of a valid contract such as lawful consideration, contractual capacity and free consent etc. This is so because, the contract of sale is a species of a general contract.

SALE AND AGREEMENT TO SELL

Every contract of sale involves transfer of ownership of goods of course it is transferred from seller to buyer. Where the ownership is transferred just at the time of making a contract it is known as 'sale.' And if the seller promises to transfer it at some future date, it is known as 'agreement to sell'. Distinction between these two is of a prime importance. The points of distinction between these two are as under:

(i) *Nature of contract:* Sale is an executed contract, because ownership has been transferred. While as agreement to sell is an executory contract, because it is yet to be performed.

(ii) *Transfer of property:* In a 'sale' the property in goods passes to the buyer immediately at the time of making the contract. But in a 'agreement to sell', transfer of property in goods takes place at some future date, may be subject to fulfilment of certain conditions. Till that date seller continues to be the owner of those goods.

(iii) *Nature of rights:* In a 'sale' general property in goods is transferred to the buyer. And the buyer can exercise all ownership rights in respect of those goods. He gets rights on those goods, which is known as 'Jus-in rem'. The net legal effect of this right is that if something goes wrong with those goods, it is only the owner who has got all sort of rights to deal with those goods such as if the seller would resell those goods, the buyer can recover those from the second buyer. While as, is an agreement to sell, the buyer gets very specific rights which is known as 'Jus-in personam.' e.g. right against particular individual. In nutshell, the buyer has rights regarding those goods only against the seller and nonelse.

(iv) *Risk of loss:* The golden rule of law is that risk follows ownership. It implies that who so ever is a real owner of goods will bear the risk of getting goods destroyed. Therefore, in a 'sale' when the goods are destroyed even in the possession of seller without his fault, the buyer of those goods will bear the loss. On the other, in an agreement to sell, in case the goods are destroyed, in transit, or in the possession of buyer without his fault, the loss of goods falls on the seller.

(v) *Breach of contract by buyer:* In a 'sale' if the buyer wrongfully refuses to accept the goods and pay the price. The seller can file a suit against the buyer for the price even if the goods are in his possession. The seller can also exercise right of lien, stoppage in transit and resale. But in an agreement to sell, only remedy available to seller is that he can claim for damage if the buyer fails to accept delivery and pay for goods.

Example: A sells 100 bags of rice to B for Rs. 5000/-. B refuses to accept delivery of rice bags. A can file suit against B for price, even the goods are in the possession of A. But instead if it was an agreement to sell, A is entitled only to claim for compensation on the breach of contract by the buyer.

(vi) *Breach of contract by the seller:* In a 'sale', if seller makes breach of contract, the buyer gets two rights. The buyer can file suit against seller for damages and can also use the rights to follow property in the hands of subsequent buyer. While as, in an agreement to sell, the buyer can only claim for damages.

Example: Ram agreed to sell a particular horse to Shyam for Rs. 10,000. Subsequently Ram sells same horse to Mohan for Rs. 12,000. In this case, there is an agreement to sell, Shyam can only claim for damages. But had there been a 'sale' Shyam would have recovered horse from Mohan along with a claim for damage.

(vii) *Insolvency of a seller:* In, a 'sale', seller becomes insolvent, while the goods are lying in this possession. The buyer is entitled to claim goods from official receiver, because ownership of those goods is with the buyer. But in case of agreement to sell, the buyer can not claim goods even if he has paid the price. Buyer's only remedy in this case is to claim rateable dividend for the price paid to seller.

(viii) *Insolvency of the buyer:* In case of 'sale' if the buyer becomes insolvent, price has not been paid, and the goods are in the possession of seller. The official receiver of the buyer will recover those goods from the seller and for the unpaid price, the name of seller will be included in the list of creditors of the buyer. But in an agreement to sell, if buyer becomes insolvent, before paying price, the seller may refuse to hand over the good to the official receiver. This is so because the ownership has not been transferred to the buyer.

SALE AND HIRE-PURCHASE AGREEMENT

Hire-purchase agreement resembles with contract of sale in many respects, but it is distinct from it. A hire-purchase agreement is an agreement for hire, with an option to purchase. Here, buyer agrees to make payment of price in fixed number of instalments. Till the payment of last instalment, ownership of those goods remains with the seller. And the payment made by the buyer till that date is considered as hire-charges for the goods. In case the hire-purchaser makes default in paying any instalment, the seller can recover the goods from buyer and payment of instalment till that will be treated as hire-charge, which cannot be recovered by the buyer.

Thus the hire-purchase agreement, is more likely to be an agreement to sell. It becomes sale after the fulfilment of certain conditions such as payment of last instalment etc.

Example: A buys a machine worth Rs. 50,000 on hire-purchase basis from payment is to be made in 10 monthly instalments of Rs. 5000 each. This is an agreement of hire-purchase. A will become owner of that machine on the payment of the 10th instalment. In case A makes any default regarding payment of any instalment, B has the right to recover the machine from A and treat the payment of instalment as hire-charge.

Hire-purchase agreement is also distinct from sale by instalment payment. In sale by instalment payment, ownership is transferred from seller to buyer on the payment of the first instalment. As the buyer pays instalment it is reduced from the price of goods. Sale by instalment payment is more likely to be a 'sale' for all practical purposes.

Distinction between sale and Hire purchase is as under:

Basis	*Sale*	*Hire-purchase*
1. *Transfer of ownership*	In a 'sale' ownership is transferred at the time of making a contract.	In hire purchase agreement ownership is transferred at some future date, e.g. payment of last instalment.
2. *Nature*	Sale is an executed contract.	Hire-purchase is an executory contract.
3. *Contents*	Sale includes sale and an agreement to sell.	Hire-purchase includes agreement to sell and bailment.
4. *Termination of contract*	In case of a sale the buyer cannot terminate a contract by returning goods to the seller	In hire-purchase the hirer can terminate a contract by returning the goods to the owner.
5. *Transfer of possession*	In sale it is not necessary to transfer the possession of good immediately with ownership.	In hire-purchase physical possession of goods is transferred immediately.
6. *Sales Tax*	In a sale, tax is levied at the time of making a contract.	But in hire-purchase sales tax can not be levied unless it becomes a sale.

7. *Resale*	In a sale, the buyer can resell the goods, because he is the owner.	But in hire-purchase the hirer can not resell those goods unless last instalment is paid.
8. *Right*	In a sale, the buyer gets the ownership right from the point of time of making a contract	Hire-purchaser gets rights of ownership only after the payment the final instalment.
9. *Application of Act.*	In a sale, all provisions of Indian Sale of Goods Act are applicable.	Hire-purchase agreements are governed and regulated by the provisions of the Hire Purchase Act 1972.

SALE AND BAILMENT

Bailment is a contract to deliver goods by one person to another for some purpose on the condition that when the purpose is over, the goods will be returned to the person delivering them. The bailment contract differs with 'sale' on the following grounds.

(i) *Transfer of property:* In a sale, the general property in goods is transferred to buyer at the time of making a contract. But in bailment specific property in goods passes to bailee, and that too for a temporary period of time such as right to use goods right to possess them and to deal with them according to the instructions of the bailor.

(ii) *Transfer of possession:* In a sale, possession of goods many or may not be transferred immediately at the time of making a contract. While in bailment goods are immediately handed over to the bailee.

(iii) *Return of goods:* In a sale goods are not returned to the seller. But in bailment, when the purpose is over, the goods are returned to the bailor or disposed off according to his instructions.

(iv) *Consideration:* In a sale, consideration is given to the seller in the form of money e.g. payment of price. But in bailment, consideration may or may not be present in the form of money such as in gratuitous bailment (without charge) money is not a consideration.

(v) *Use of goods:* In a sale, the buyer is entitled to possess and use the goods at his own. But in bailment goods will be used according to instructions and terms and conditions of bailment.

SALE AND CONTRACT FOR WORK AND LABOUR

In a contract of sale, physical possession and ownership of goods are transferred from seller to buyer. This differs from contract of 'work and labour', wherein one party supplies some raw material to another, who applies his skill and labour on that raw material. Here, the substance of the contract is the exercise of skill labour and the delivery of the goods is only a subsidiary component. The major element or an essence of a contract for work is the application of skill and labour. In any case the contract for 'work and labour' does not amount to a contract for sale of goods.

Distinction between these two can be understood with the help of following cases.

Robinson Vs. Graves. In this case, A is engaged as an artist for painting a portrait. B has supplied the necessary materials such as canvas, paint etc. to the painter. A will apply his skill & labour to paint that portrait. Since production of that portrait was considered as a substance of the contract. It was held that it is a contract for work & labour and not a contract of sale.

Lee Vs. Griffin (1861, 30 L.J.B. 252). In this case a dentist agreed to supply a set of artificial teeth to fit the mouth of a patient. The necessary material was wholly supplied by the dentist. It was held to be a contract of sale.

Example: A supplied a piece of a woolen cloth to B who is tailor for stitching it and making a coat. B used all other necessary materials for stitching that coat. It is a contract of work and labour, because material had been supplied by A and B provided his services. In case, A without supplying that piece of woolen cloth, asked B to make a coat for him, it would have been a contract of sale.

SUBJECT MATTER OF CONTRACT OF SALE

Like other contracts, the Contract of Sale has a subject matter which is 'goods'. The term 'goods' includes all kinds of movable properties including things which can be detached from the earth such as crop of cereals and fruits and grass etc.

According to section 2 (7) of the Sale of Goods Act the goods includes 'every kind of movable property other than actionable claims and legal tender money, and also includes stock and shares, growing crops, grass and things attached to or forming part of land, which are agreed to be severed before sale or under the contract of sale'.

Thus, the following points should be remembered regarding subject matter of contract of sale.

(a) Subject matter of contract of is 'goods'.
(b) The terms 'goods' includes all kinds of movable properties, except legal tender money and actionable claims. Actionable claims implies–claims which can be enforced through the court of law such as claim to recover debt etc.
(c) Rare, old and antique coins may form subject matter of contract of sale.
(d) Immovable properties are not covered under this Act.
(e) Things which are attached to land and can be severed from it may also become subject matter of contract of sale, such as growing grass, trees, crops etc.
(f) Stock and shares have expressly been included in 'goods'.

(g) Similarly things like goodwill, copyright, trademark, patents, water, gas and electricity are all goods and may be the subject matter of contract of sale.

TYPES OF GOODS

The goods which form the subject matter of a contract of sale may be classified as under.

(i) *Existing goods:* Goods, which are in existence at the time of making a contract of sale are known as existing goods. Such goods are in the ownership and physical possession of the seller when he makes contract of sale. However, in case of sale by an agent or pledgee, goods are possessed by an immediate seller but not owned by him. Rather, the seller may have the authority to sell the goods. Some times, bailee or an agent may hold goods on behalf of the owner. Existing goods may be specific, unascertained or ascertained goods.

(a) *Specific goods:* According to section 2 (4) of this Act, 'specific goods means goods identified and agreed upon at the time, when contract of sale in made'. In other words specific goods must have been separated out from the lot of goods. However, the goods will not become specific, merely because, the source of supply has been identified.

Example: A has two horses, one black and another one white. He agrees to sell white horse to B. In this case, the subject matter is specific. But if A has two white horses, unless that particular horse is identified and individualised from the remaining horses it will not become a specific one.

(b) *Ascertained goods:* The goods which are ascertained and identified after the formation of contract, are known as ascertained goods. However, in practice specific and ascertained goods are used interchangeably. The only point of difference is that specific goods are ascertained before or at the time of making a contract, but ascertained goods are identified and individualised after the formation of a contract of sale.

Lord Atkia has rightly observed that, ascertained goods probably means, 'identified in accordance with agreement after the time a contract of sale in made'.

Thus, when the quantity contracted for is set aside for a given contract, out of whole stock, the goods are said to be ascertained.

(c) *Unascertained goods:* The goods which are not, identified separately at the time of making a contract of sale are known as unascertained goods. In fact, at the time of making contract, those goods have been identified only by description. Such goods are also known as, 'generic goods' because, unless these are physically and individually separated from the lot, they are part of it.

Example: College has booking counter for HMT. watches. Ram makes an agreement for buying a particular wrist watch. He identifies it by description. Next day he visits the showroom of these watches and individualises particular wrist watch. Thus before separating the watch from the lot it remains unascertained goods and on being separated out from the stock it becomes ascertained goods.

(ii) ***Future goods:*** Future goods are goods, which will be owned and possessed by the seller at some future date. Though, necessary arrangement must have been made to procure them but, these are yet to be owned and possessed by the seller.

According to section 2 (6) of this Act, 'Goods to be manufactured, produced or acquired by the seller after making contract of sale' are future goods. These may be the goods which are not existing or are to be procured by the seller. Since, these goods are not in the ownership and possession of the seller, he cannot make sale for these goods. Rather agreement to sell may be made for such goods.

Example: A agrees to sell entire crop of wheat grown by him next year to B at a particular price. It is an agreement to sell for future goods.

(iii) ***Contingent goods:*** Contingent goods are type of future goods the acquisition of which depends on the happening or non-happening of future contingency. According to section 6 (2) of this Act, there may a contract for the sale of goods, the acquisition of which by the seller depends upon contingency, which may or may not happen. Such goods may be subject matter of 'agreement to sell.'

The contract of sale for contingent goods can be enforced only on the happening of that contingency upon which acquisition of goods by the seller depends. In case contingency does not happen, the seller will not get possession and ownership of those goods and contract will become void.

Example: A agrees to sell the cargo of ship to B which is being brought from London to Mumbai. The ship may or may not arrive. Acquisition of goods on the part of A depends upon the arrival of the ship. In case that ship sinks in the ocean, contract between A and B becomes void.

EFFECTS OF DESTRUCTION OF GOODS

In a contract of sale, the 'goods' constitute the subject matter of contract. In case the subject matter gets destroyed the contract of sale will become void. In a contract of sale, the goods may perish or be destructed before the sale is complete. Effect of destruction of subject matter of a contract of sale may be studied under the following two heads.

(i) Goods Perishing before Making a Contract (Section 7)

Where the contract of sale in made for specific goods, the contract is void, if at the time, when the contract was made, the goods have without the knowledge of the seller, perished to become so damaged as no longer answer to their description in the contract.

To make the contract void, under this section, the following conditions must be fulfilled:

(a) The contract of sale must have been made for specific goods.
(b) The goods must have been damaged or perished before entering in to a contract of sale.
(c) It was not in the knowledge of the seller that goods have been perished or destructed.
(d) The goods must have been damaged as no longer they are answer to the description.
(e) Perishing of goods includes loss of goods by theft and loss of their commercial value.

Asfar Coy Ltd Vs. Blundell (1896, 1.Q.B., 123). In this case contract was made for selling a cargo of dates. The dates were contaminated with sewage, so as to be unsaleable as dates. It was held that contract was void, because the dates have lost their commercial utility.

Borrowlane Etc. Vs. Phillips (1929, 1.K.B. 574). In this case, it was agreed to sell 700 bags of grownd nuts lying in a particular warehouse. But it was found that 109 bags had been stolen before contract was made but both the parties were not aware of it. It was held that contract was void.

(ii) Goods Perishing After Agreement to Sell, But Before Sale (Section 8)

In an agreement to sell specific goods, the goods without any fault on the part of buyer and seller perish, before the risk passes to buyer, the contract of sales becomes void and both parties are excused from performance of a contract.

The contract of sale can be avoided on the above basis, provided the following condition are fulfilled:

(a) The contract of sale must have been made as an 'agreement to sell' and not a 'sale'.
(b) The subject matter of an agreement to sell must be specific goods.
(c) The goods must have been damaged or perished before the risk passes to buyer.
(d) The goods have been perished or destructed without any fault on the part of buyer and seller.

Example: A has 300 cotton bales in his godown. He makes an agreement to sell 50 cotton bales to B at a particular price. At the time of making contract, the godown gets a fire and the whole stock was destructed by fire. The contract of sale is not void, because 50 cotton bales which constitute subject matter of a contract, have not been identified and separated from the stock, and are not specific goods.

Section 7 and 8 of this Act are applicable only in case of loss of specific goods, and that too without any fault of buyer and seller.

PRICE FIXATION

In a contract of sale, fixation and payment of price is also an important feature. No sale can take place without a price. The term 'price' has been defined under section 2 (10) of this Act, 'the money consideration for a sale of goods'. However, where goods are sold for a fixed amount, and that amount is paid partly in terms of cash and partly in terms of valued goods.

In a contract of sale, the payment of price is made by the buyer. It may be paid either at the time of making contract or at some future date.

Modes of fixing price: With regard to price-fixation section 9 and 10 of this Act are applicable. According to these provisions, there are five methods of fixing price, which are as under.

(a) *Expressly mentioned in the contract:* It is a usual way of fixing the price in a contract of sale. Both parties by mutual agreement may determine the price of goods. But the price fixed by the parties must be a definite sum.

(b) *In a manner provided by contract:* The manner, in which price of the goods will be fixed may be mentioned in a contract it self such as 'market price', 'cost plus' and 'how much other customers pay' etc.

(c) *By usage:* Where the price is not mentioned in the contract or the manner to fix the price has not been laid down in a contract, it will be fixed by prevailing business usage. These usage may be well established practice for fixing the price in that kind of business such as 'price advertised', 'price marked on goods' and 'discount on sale price' etc.

(d) *By third party:* The price to be paid by buyer may be fixed by third party provided third party accepts it. In case he fails to fix price, agreement will become void. Where, the third party has been prevented from fixing price either by the seller or buyer, party at default will be liable to pay compensation to other party.

(e) *Reasonable price:* Where the price is not fixed by any one of the foregoing methods the buyer is liable to pay reasonable price which depends on the circumstance of each case.

However, after making a contract sale, if there is any increase in custom, excise duty or any tax on sale or purchase it will be added to the price. Similarly any decrease in these will be deducted from the price to be paid by the buyer.

As far as mode of payment is concerned, the seller is not bound to accept any kind of payment except in legal tender money. He is not bound to accept payment by cheque.

EARNEST MONEY OR SECURITY DEPOSIT

Sometimes, the buyer may make part of payment in advance to the seller. Such payment may be earnest money or security deposit. When such payment is made as a part of price in advance, in case contract was not performed either by buyer or seller, it is to be refunded to the buyer. In case the contract is performed it will be deducted from the total price of the goods purchased. But it is paid as a guarantee for the performance of a contract by the buyer on his failure to perform, the seller has a right to forfeit that advance.

S.H. Cotton Mills Vs. Tata Aircraft Ltd (1970, 2,S.C. 482). In this case, the purchaser deposited Rs. 2.5 lacs as earnest money being 25 per cent of the value of goods. A term of contract provided that full value of the goods will be paid before taking delivery of the goods. The purchaser failed to pay the value of goods by the stipulated time. It was held that seller was entitled to forfeit the earnest money, because the buyer makes a breach of contract.

Review Questions

1. Define the term 'contract of sale'. Discuss essential features of a valid contract of sale.
2. Distinguish between 'sale' and 'agreement to sell'.
3. Make distinction between;
   (a) Sale and Hire purchase agreement.
   (b) Sale and Contract of Bailment.
   (c) Sale and Contract for work and labour.
4. How is a contract of sale performed. Explain the various modes in which a contract of sale can be made.
5. What is the subject matter of a Contract of Sale? Discuss the various types of goods which the constitute subject matter of a Contract of Sale.
6. Explain section 788 in connection with destruction of subject matter of a contract.
7. Explain various mode of fixing price of goods in a contract of sale.
8. Write notes
   (a) Existing goods.
   (b) Earnest money or security deposite.
   (c) Future goods.
   (d) Goods

9. Comment on the following:
   (a) Risk follows ownership.
   (b) Contract of sale is a specific contract.
   (c) Payment of price as consideration in a contract of sale.
   (d) Transfer of property in goods is an essence of contract of sale.
   (e) Earnest money may be paid either as a part of price or security for performance.
   (f) 'Sale' is made only for existing goods.

PRACTICAL PROBLEMS

1. A agrees to sell a Maruti car to B for Rs. 1.5 lacs. Before making agreement the car was stolen and it was not in the knowledge of the parties. Is A bound to deliver Maruti car to B? (No)
2. Ritesh makes contract of sale for selling heavy machine costing Rs. 2 lacs to Hitesh on a condition that Hitesh will pay Rs. one lac in cash and will deliver a second hand car valued at Rs. one lac. Is contract of sale valid? (Yes, payment of price is made partly in cash and partly in goods.
3. Ram enters in to a contract of sale with Shyam for selling photostate machine to him for Rs. 30,000. Invoice of the machine has been made in favour of Shyam, payment has not been made. The machine is lying in the godown of the seller. Meanwhile, his godown sets on fire and the machine is destroyed. Can Shyam claim loss of machine from Ram? (No, ownership of machine has been transferred to Shyam and machine gets destroyed without any fault of Ram).
4. A transport company has resolved and transferred 10 buses to a partnership firm, which consists of certain people who are owners of the company. Transfer was made at a particular price. Is it a contract of sale? Examine the validity of this contract. (No person can sell his goods to himself).
5. A is an agent of foreign currency. B, makes an agreement with him for purchasing 100 pounds for Rs. 7500. Is contract of sale is valid (No currency can not be sold or purchased).
6. Mohan and Sohan agree that Mohan will sell his second hand car to Sohan at a price which will be determined by a particular car mechanic. But the car mechanic refused to do the job of price fixation. On such refusal can Sohan compel Mohan to sell that car for any other price? (No)
7. A purchased a machine for Rs. 50,000 from B on instalment payment basis. The payment is to be made in five equal monthly instalments. A defaults in making the 3rd instalment. Is B entitled to get back the machine from A? (No). What is the legal remedy available to him?

8. X agrees to sell a horse to B on a condition that, B will keep it for six days on trial basis and have the option to return on the expiry of 6 days period, if he does not find it suitable. Three days after, the horse dies due to some illness without the fault of A or B. Can this agreement be avoided. (Yes)
9. A agrees to sell the entire crop of wheat to be grown in his farm to B at a particular price. Before the crop was ready for harvesting it is totally destroyed due to natural calamities. Is A bound to deliver wheat to B? (No).
10. A sold a piano to B for Rs. 2000 on hire-purchase basis to be paid in 10 equal instalments. After paying the 5th instalment B refused to pay remaining instalments. Can A recover the piano from B. (Yes).

■■■

Chapter **16**

Conditions and Warranties

Learning Objectives

- Understand the meaning and application of conditions and warranties in a contract of sale.
- Apply these two concepts in practice when you buy the goods.
- Compare conditions with warranties.
- Learn implied conditions and warranties applicable on the seller.
- Apply the rule of 'Caveat Emptor' and remember the consequences of not following this rule in practice.

INTRODUCTION

We are all consumers in one way or the other. We buy goods for satisfying our needs or for producing other goods. While making a decision to buy we take into account the various claims made by the seller regarding those goods. In a contract of sale, parties make certain stipulations or statement, i.e. agree to certain terms. All stipulations or statements cannot be treated on the same footing. Some may be intended by the parties to be of a fundamental nature, e.g. quality of goods to be supplied, the breach of which, therefore, will be regarded as a breach of the contract. Some may be intended by the parties to be binding, but of a subsidiary or inferior character, e.g. time of payment, so that a breach of these terms will not put an end to the contract but will make the party comitting the breach liable to damages. The former stipulations are called 'conditions' and the latter 'warranties'.

CONDITION AND WARRANTY

Condition: Condition is that stipulation which goes into the root of contract of sale and forms the basis of such contract.

It is so important for the contract that, without fulfilling such stipulation, the contract of sale can not be performed. It is essential and fundamental to the main purpose of a contract. Thus, non-fulfillment of such stipulation may result in breach of contract.

According to section 12 (2) of sale of Goods Act, 'a condition is a stipulation, essential to the main purpose of a contract, the breach of which gives rise to a right to treat the contract as repudiated.'

Baldry Vs. Marshall. In this case, B consulted M a motor car dealer, for a car which is suitable for touring purpose. M suggested 'Buqatti' car and B accordingly purchased it. The car turns out to be unfit for touring purpose. It was held that suitability of a car for touring purpose is a condition. It was so vital that, if it is not fulfilled, it would defeat the very purpose of contract for which B bought the car. He was, therefore, entitled to reject car and get his money back from the dealer.

Warranty: According to section 12 (3) of this Act 'a warranty is a stipulation, collateral to the main purpose of a contract, the breach of which gives a rise to a claim for damages, but not to a right to reject the goods and treat the contract as repudiated.'

It becomes clear from the definition that, the warranty is also a stipulation, but supportive or subsidiary for the main purpose of the contract of sale. It is therefore, if the party makes breach of such stipulation, another party has a right only to claim for compensation. He cannot avoid the contract.

The basic concept of **condition** and **waranty** can be understood with the help of following example.

Example: A is willing to buy a car. He visits to nearby dealer of a car and tells him that he needs a car which runs 20 km. on one lt of petrol. The car dealer supplies a car to him on a contract of a sale. Later on, it appears that the car can hardly run 10 km. with one lt. of petrol. A can avoid this contract, because stipulation made by him regarding fuel consumption was a condition, essential for the purpose of contract. But if A visits dealer to buy a car. The dealer suggests that he has a car which runs 20 km/1lt. A makes an agreement to buy that car. Later on it turns out that car can run 10 km/1 lt petrol. It amounts to breach of warranty, because stipulation made by the dealer in supportive one. Thus can only claim for compensation. He is not entitled to avoid contract.

DISTINCTION BETWEEN CONDITION AND WARRANTY

The use of the term condition or warranty in a contract of sale is immaterial, unless and untill parties are intended to make it or not to make it basis of a contract. Distinction between these two can be made on the basis of following points.

(a) ***Nature of stipulation:*** Condition is a stipulation which is essential and fundamental in nature. It is so significant for the main purpose of contract that non-fulfillment of it leads to breach of contract. While as, warranty is a stipulation which is supportive and collateral in nature. Though it is also related to the main purpose of contract, but to a small extent. It is therefore the contract of sale can be performed, even without fulfilling it.

(b) *Consequences of breach:* In a contract of sale, if the party makes breach of condition, the other becomes entitled to avoid the contract. It is because condition is essential for the major purpose of a contract. But in case of breach of warranty, another party can only claim for compensation, if he has suffered any loss.

(c) *Treatment of stipulation:* Breach of a condition has much wider implications on the contract as compared to breach of warranty. Thus breach of condition can be treated as a breach of warranty; but breach of warranty can not be treated as breach of condition.

Difference between condition warrantee

	Condition	*Warranty*
1. Nature	It is fundamental in nature and essential for main purpose of contract.	It is supportive and collateral for the contract.
2. Breach	Due to breach of condition the contract may be avoided.	It's breach may give a rise to a right to claim for compensation.
3. Treatment	Breach of condition can be treated as breach of warranty.	Breach of warranty can not be treated as breach of condition.

When a breach of condition is to be treated as breach of warranty. Section 13 of this Act provides for certain circumstances where a breach of a condition may be reduced to the status of warranty. And consequently, the buyer loses his right to reject the goods and avoid the contract. In such case, his only remedy is to claim for compensation. Breach of condition can be treated as a breach of warranty under the following circumstances.

(a) *Voluntary waiver by the buyer:* Where a contract of sale is subject to certain conditions to be fulfilled by the seller, the buyer may, (i) waive the condition (ii) elect to treat breach of condition as a breach of warranty. The conditions in a contract of sale for the seller are for the benefit of the buyer, therefore this option of waiver has been given to the buyer. In case when he waives the condition, later on he can not compel the seller to fulfil it.

Example: A agrees to supply 100 bags of wheat of a particular quality to B at the rate of Rs. 1500 p.q. But he supplies wheat of some what inferior quality, the price of which is Rs. 1200 p.q. There is a breach of condition on the part of seller. B has a option to treat it as a breach of warranty and instead of avoiding contract, he can claim for compensation of Rs. 300 p.q. of wheat.

(b) *Compulsory treatment by buyer:* when the contract of sale is not severable and the buyer has accepted the goods or part there of, the breach of any condition by the seller can only be treated as a breach of warranty.

According to section 42 of this Act, a buyer is deemed to have accepted the goods;

(i) When he intimates to the seller that he has accepted goods.

(ii) When the good have been delivered to him he does any act in relation to them which is inconsistent with ownership of the seller such as he has pledged the goods. or, when after the lapse of reasonable period of time he retains the goods without intimating to the seller that he has rejected them.

However if the contract is severable, the buyer has accepted part of the goods, he can still exercise his right to reject the remaining goods.

Hardy & Coy Vs. Hillerps & Flower (1923, 2.K.B. 490). In this case, a buyer took delivery of consignment of wheat, and resold and despatched a part of it to a sub buyer. Later on, it was discovered that wheat supplied was not of a contracted quality and he gave the seller notice of rejecting remaining quantity of wheat. But it was held that transferring possession to sub-buyer, was an act inconsistent with the ownership of seller, and, therefore, the buyer was deemed to have accepted the goods.

EXPRESS AND IMPLIED CONDITIONS AND WARRANTIES

The contract of sale may be based on many conditions and warranties. These condition and warranties may be either express or implied. Both the parties of a contract of sale, are free to include any condition or warranty in that contract. They may attach any degree of significance to these terms and conditions. When the conditions and warranties, provided in a contract of sale, have been made in writing or have been explained to each other by the words of mouth, such conditions and warranties are known as express conditions and warranties. Thus, where, the buyer desires to buy white Maruti car, the colour of the car becomes express condition.

Similarly, buyer and seller by mutual agreement may provide for any condition and warranty.

In addition to express conditions, there are certain conditions and warranties, which are applicable in a contract of sale, by operation of law. These are known as implied conditions. Unless, there is a contrary intention which appears from contract, these conditions would be applicable automatically.

However, such implied conditions can be altered or negated by an express agreement or by a custom or traditions prevailing in that business. In this regard following two guide lines seem to be very important.

(a) Expressum Facit ceassare Tacitum, i.e. what is expressed makes what is facit or implied to cease.

(b) Modes. et. conventio vincent legem, i.e. custom and agreement over rule law, i.e. implied conditions and wrranties.

Thus implied conditions and warranties are applicable provided there is no contrary intention of the parties to it.

Sale of Goods Act provides the following implied conditions and warranties. These are applicable for the seller.

IMPLIED CONDITIONS

Following implied conditions are laid down by law for a contract of sale.

1. ***Condition as to title:*** The contract of sale involves transfer of title or ownership. Therefore in a every contract of sale, there is a implied condtion for the seller that, in case of a sale he has ownership and right to sell. And in a agreement to sell, he will get this right in future at the time of transfering ownership to the buyer.

This condition clearly states that no one can sell what is not being owned by him or on which he has no right to sell. In this regard the rule of law is 'one can not give, what one does not have'. Thus if the seller has no valid title of the goods he can not sell them to buyer. The condition of title is very essential for protecting the interest of innocent buyer.

When the seller, sells the goods without ownership and right to sell, it will amount to breach of condition on his part. The buyer is entitled to return goods and get the money back from the seller.

Rawland, Vs. Divall (1923, 2,K.B. 500). In this case, A purchased second hand motor car from B and used it for some time. Later on it was discovered that the car had been stolen by B. consequently. A had surrendered the car to real owner. It was held that A could recover, in full, the price of the car from B.

With regard to, condition as to title it is to be noted that, to sell the goods it is not enough to have ownership. Rather the owner of the goods must have a right to sell those goods. Sale of goods without right will also amount to breach of condition;

Niblett Ltd Vs. Confectioners Material Coy. In this case, certain tins of condensed milk bearing the label "NISSLY BRAND" were sold by A to B. Another manufactures of condensed milk under the brand name of 'Nestle' claimed that it was an infringement of their trade mark. In order to save themselves from any liability under trade mark law B had to remove the labels and sold the naked tins at loss. A was held liable for breach of implied condition that they had a right to sell.

2. ***Condition in a sale by description:*** Sometimes the contract of sale of goods is made by description. Such description may be related to various physical as well as chemical characteristics of the goods. In such a contract, there is a implied condition for the seller that he must deliver the goods which are corresponding to given description. In other words, goods supplied must be same as were described by the party. If it is found that the goods are not corresponding to given description, the buyer has a right to reject the goods.

In this regard, Lord Blackburn has rightly observed that 'if you contract to sell peas, you can not oblige a party to take beans. If the description of an article tendered, is different in any respect, it is not the article bargained for, and the other is not bound to take it.'

The term 'sale of goods' by description is wide and includes the following situations.

(a) It includes a case, where the buyer has never seen the goods and buys them only on the basis of description given by the seller.

Example: A makes contract of sale for selling a reaping machine by describing it to be only one year old and had been used only to cut 50 to 60 acres. On the delivery of machine, the buyer found that the machine was extremely old. It is breach of condition, and the buyer is entitled to reject the machine, because it does not correspond with given description.

Similarly, if the buyer agrees to buy a 'Phillip-Juicer-made in Japan,' and the seller supplies him Phillip-Juicer- made in Hong Kong. It does not correspond with given description.

(b) Buyer has already seen the goods, but he purchases them on the basis of description of those goods given by the seller.

Example: In an auction sale, the buyer purchased a set of liner napkins and table cloths, which were described by the seller as 'dating from seventeenth century.' The buyer ws a dealer in antiques, he purchased these after seeing them. But, later, that set appeared to be an 'eighteenth century set.' Since the buyer has relied on the description, even after seeing the goods. It is breach of condition and he can return goods.

(c) The method of packing goods may also form part of description.

Example: A agrees to buy 500 tins of canned fruit to be packed in cases. Each case contains 50 tins. On the supply of cases containing more or less than 50 tins, the buyer is entitled to reject the goods. In this case, sale was made by describing goods in terms of quantity in packed form. Therefore packing of goods must be according to given description.

3. *Condition in a sale by sample:* When the contract of sale is made by showing sample of goods to the buyer, there is a implied condition for the seller that;

(a) Bulk of goods supplied to the buyer shall correspond with the sample in quality.
(b) Buyer shall be given reasonable opportunity of comparing bulk with the sample.
(c) The goods shall be free from any defects which may render them unmerchantable (to be sold under that sample). Such defects may be either 'latent' or 'patent'. The latent defects are those, which can not be discovered by making reasonable examination of sample and implied condition applies only to these defects. On the other, patent defects can be discovered by the buyer by making reasonable examination of the sample, and the condition does not apply to such defects.

Example: A sold to B certain quantity of worsted coating equal to sample. The coating supplied by A was equal to sample, but had a latent defect. As a result of which, the cloth was found to be unfit for making coats. B has a right to reject the goods. Reason, being that the defect was latent which could not be discovered by making reasonable examination.

4. *Sale by sample as well as by description:* When goods are sold by showing sample and giving description, there is a implied condition for the seller that the bulk of goods supplied to the buyer shall correspond both with sample and the description. When the goods supplied do correspond only with sample and not with description, the buyer is entitled to reject the goods.

Example: A agreed to sell B some oil described as 'Foreign Refined rapeseed oil,' equal to sample.

A supplied the oil though, corresponded with the sample, but was adulterated with palm oil. Thus it amounts to breach of condition, because the oil supplied is not according to description given at the time of making a contract.

WALLIS VS. PRATT (1911, A.C. 394). In this case, seeds were sold by sample as 'English sainfoin seeds' and described as 'common English Sainfoin'. The seeds supplied were found to be 'Gaint sainfoin'. It was held that there was a breach of condition as to description and therefore the buyer could recover damages.

5. *Condition as to quality and fitness for purpose:* The general rule with regard to contract of sale is that, a buyer is supposed to satisfy himself about the quality and suitability of goods for his purpose. Thus, later on, if the goods purchased are found unsuitable or unfit for the purpose of the buyer, he will have no legal remedy against thc sellcr.

However, there are certain exceptions to this rule. Under these exceptional circumstances, implied condition as to fitness for the purpose is applicable on the seller. And the seller is bound to supply the goods which are suitable for the purpose of the buyer provided;

(a) At the time of buying the goods, a buyer must have disclosed his purpose to the seller, expressly or in a implied manner.

(b) The buyer must have relied upon the skill and judgement of the seller for supplying goods fit for the purpose of the buyer.

(c) The goods sold must be of description which the seller deals in the ordinary course of his business.

It means the seller is not a casual seller, rather it is his business to sell those goods.

Example: A draper wanted to buy hot water bottle. He visited chemist shop and asked him to supply hot water bottle and made it clear that for what purpose he is buying that bottle. The chemist supplied hot water bottle and told him to use it only for hot water, because it may not stand boiled water. While using the bottle, it got brust and A was injured. A is entitled to claim damage for breach of implied condition, because the bottle was unfit for the purpose of the buyer.

However, it is to be noted that, when the goods can be used only for one particular purpose, the buyer need not tell his purpose to the seller.

Example: A purchased refrigerator from B. Later on it was discovered that it failed in to make ice. Thus B is entitled to avoid the contract on the ground of breach of condition.

The condition as to fitness shall not be applicable in the following cases:

(a) The buyer suffers from some abnormality with respect of use of goods but does not disclose it to the seller at the time of making a contract of sale.

Example: A's skin is allergitic to some cosmetic. She buys that cosmetic without disclosing this fact to the seller. On the use of cosmetic she gets her skin damaged due to allergy. The seller is not liable for damages.

(b) When the buyer buys the goods, under some patent or trade mark, the condition as to fitness will not be applicable.

Example: A buys 'Bournvita' from a chemist as a health drink. He uses it, but does not get any improvement in his health. He has no claim for damage against the chemist.

6. *Condition as to merchantable quality:* Merchantable quality implies that, goods should be resaleable in the market under the particular description by which they are known.

According to section 16 (2) of this Act, "where goods are bought by description from a seller, who deals in the goods of that description (Whether he is manufactures or not) there is an implied condition that the goods shall be of merchantable quality."

Example: A made an agreement to sell 50 tyres to B at a particular price. On the supply of tyres, it was discovered that all tyres are carrying small wholes in the tube inside tyre. B has a right to reject the goods due to unmerchantable quality of the tyrers.

JACKSON VS. ROTEX MOTORS & CYCLE COY LTD, (1910, 2,K.B. 937). In this case R placed an order for 600 motor horns of varying description. Some of the horns were dented and badly polished. R, rejected entire consignment. It was held that the defects in the horns had rendered them unmerchantable, thus R is entitled to reject them.

7. *Condition to wholesomeness:* In a contract of sale of eatables and provisions, there is an implied condition on the part of the seller that the goods shall be wholesome. It means, the goods supplied by the seller must not be dangerously adulterated and must be fit for human consumption.

Example: A bought milk from a dairy owner. The milk was contaminated with germs of typhoid fever. By consuming that milk A's wife got infected and died. A is entitled to claim damages from the dairy owner.

Jackson Vs. Weston & Sons (1909, 9,R.B. 193, C.A). In this case, a grocer sold tinned salmon, which was poisonous. It resulted in to the death and illness of many persons. It was held that the grocer was liable for damages, because of breach of condition of wholesomeness.

IMPLIED WARRANTIES

Implied warranties are those stipulations, which are supportive or collateral to the purpose of contract. These warranties are applicable in a contract of sale by operation of law; provided there is nothing contrary to them. These warranties are related to the implied 'condition as to title'. These are as under.

1. *Warranty as to quite possession:* In a every contract of sale, unless contrary intention appears, there is an implied warranty that the buyer shall have and enjoy quite possession of the goods. The right of peaceful use and possession may be disturbed due to defective title or ownership.

This warranty may be considered as an extension of implied condition of title which is provided under section 14 (A) of this Act.

If the possession or use of goods by the buyer is disturbed by a person having superior rights than that of seller, the buyer may hold seller responsible for breach of warranty.

Example: A purchased second hand car from B. A, thereafter spent some money on its repair and used it for some time. The parties were not aware of the fact that the car was stolen one. Consequently A was forced to return the car to its real owner. He is entitled to recover cost of car and the amount spent on its repair from B. This is so because, B, is liable for breach of warranty.

2. *Warranty of freedom from encumbrances or economic charges:* After having purchased goods, the buyer is entitled to assume that the goods are free from any economic charge or encumbrance in favour of third person. If the goods are found subject to some charge in favour of third party, the seller will be liable to pay compensation for it to the buyer.

However, this warranty will not, be applicable where the buyer has been informed of such charge or has a notice of the same.

Example: A agrees to sell some goods to B which are already hypothecated to bank against a loan of Rs. 5000. B was not aware of this fact at the time of making a contract of sale. B had to pay Rs. 5000 to the bank to free them from charge in favour of the bank. B is entitled to claim this amount form A, because it is a breach of warranty.

3. *Warranty to disclose dangerous nature of good:* Sometimes, the goods sold by the seller may be dangerous in nature.

In such case there is an implied warranty for the seller that while selling such goods he must warn, the innocent buyer regarding probable dangers which may arise out of its use. If the seller fails to do so, and buyer suffers loss due to dangerous nature of goods the seller will be liable to compensate the buyer.

Clarke Vs. Army & Navy Cooperative Society Ltd. (1903, 1, K.B. 155, C). In this case, C purchased a tin of disinfectant powder from A. A knew that the tin was to be opened with special care, otherwise it may prove dangerous. He also knew that C was ignorant about it, but he did not warn C. While opening that tin the disinfectant powder flew in to her eyes and caused injury. It was held that A was liable to pay damage to C.

DOCTRINE OF CAVEAT EMPTOR

It is a fundamental principle of law relating to sale of goods. It implies that while buying the goods, the buyer must be cautious. The term caveat Emptor means 'Let the buyer beware.' This principle states that, at the time of buying goods, the buyer must make reasonable examination of the goods as to satisfy himself regarding suitability of goods for the purpose, he buys for and as to discover the defects.

After having purchased goods, if any defects appears on those, which could have been discovered through reasonable examination of goods, the seller shall not be liable for such defects.

It is very clear that, when seller displays goods in open market, it is up to the buyer to make proper selection. If goods turn out to be defective, the seller can not be held liable. When the buyer makes bad choice, nonelse, except him will be blamed and liable for.

Word Vs. Hobbs (1878, 4. A.C. 13). In this case, certain pigs were sold, "with all faults." The pigs were suffering from typhoid fever. They also infected other own pigs of the buyer. It was held that the seller was not bound to disclose that pigs were unhealthy. Caveat Emptor, being the rule, the buyer is not entitled to claim damage from the seller.

The doctrine of Caveat Emptor is, however, subject to the following exceptions:

(i) *Misrepresentation by seller:* Where the seller makes misrepresentation, the buyer relies on that and makes a contract of sale. The rule of caveat Emptor will not be applicable and the contract will be voidable at the option of the buyer.

(ii) *Concealment of defects:* Where the seller makes active concealment of defects in the goods or makes any false representation regarding goods amounting to fraud, the above rule will not be applicable. The contract of sale is voidable and the buyer can claim compensation from the seller for the loss.

(iii) *Condition as to fitness for the purpose:* While making a contract of sale, the buyer discloses his purpose to the seller. He relies on the skill and judgement of the seller for the supply of the goods. And the seller happens to be a persons who deals in those goods or whose business is to sell those goods. In this case, the seller is liable to supply goods fit for the purpose of buyer, and the rule of Caveat Emptor is not applicable.

(iv) *Sale by description:* In a contract of sale by description, where the goods are bought from the seller who deals in such goods, the goods supplied by the seller must be of merchantable quality. If the goods are not found to be merchantable, the seller can not take defence of doctrine of Caveat Emptor, because it does not apply in such case.

(v) *Usage of trade:* According to section 16 (3) of this Act implied condition of quality or fitness for a particular purpose may also be inferred from the trade custom and usage. Well established norms in a particular trade bind the seller to supply the goods which are suitable for the purpose of buyer, the rule of Caveat Emptor will not apply.

(vi) *Wholesomeness of the goods:* In a contract of sale of eatables and provisions the seller has to ensure that the goods supplied are free from any infection and dangerous adulteration which may make them unfit for human consumption. In such case the above rule is not applicable.

Review Questions

1. Define the terms 'condition' and 'warranty'. Distinguish between them and explain those situations when breach of condition can be treated as breach of warranty.
2. What is the Doctrine of Caveat Emptor? Discuss exception to this rule.
3. Explain two warranties in a contract of sale.
4. Explain the implied condition as to fitness for the purpose. Discuss the circumstances under which this condition is applied.
5. Define implied condition. Explain condition as to sale by sample and sale by description.
6. Discuss various implied conditions which are applicable for the seller in a contract of sale.
7. Comment on the following:
   (a) Condition can be reduced to warranty.
   (b) Seller is not bound to supply goods fit for the purpose of the buyer.
   (c) Condition is essential for the purpose of contract of sale.
   (d) Implied condition are equally important provided, the parties had no contrary intention to them.
   (e) Goods sold must be under the ownership and right of seller to sell.

PRACTICAL PROBLEMS

1. Railway company has purchased timber for making railway sleepers. The timber supplied by the merchant was found unfit for the purpose of Railway Coy. Give legal advice to Railway Company.
2. A wanted to buy a car. He visited car dealer and told him that he needs a car which runs 30 km/p.lt. petrol. The car dealer supplied a car to him. Later on, it appeared that the car hardly runs 15 km/p.lt. petrol. Is it a breach of condition or a warranty? (Breach of condition)
3. A purchased a ship from B, on the basis of representation that the capacity of the ship is 500 tons. But it appeared that capacity is only 400 tons. Can A avoid the contract? (No, it is breach of warranty).
4. Ram purchased a second hand machine form Shyam for Rs. 10,000. He spends sum of Rs. 5000 on its repair for making it usable. After sometime, it was discovered that the machine was stolen by Shyam. Consequently, Ram had to surrender the machine to the real owner. Suggest legal remedy available to A.
5. A agrees to buy 100 bags of 'Lal kila Basmati Rice' from B. @ Rs. 10,000p. bag. But B supplied 'Rajmahal Basmati Rice.' Can A rejects supply of Raj Mahal Basmati?
6. X purchased a piece of worsted coating by sample. Later on, it was found that there are some latent defects in cloth, which X could not discovered by making reasonable examination of that cloth piece. As a result of such defects it is not suitable for making coats. Is X entitled to reject the goods? (Yes)
7. N agreed to sell some oil to M, described as 'foreign refined rapeseed oil', equal to sample. N supplied that oil corresponding with sample, but adulterated with palm oil. Can M reject the supply of oil (Yes, though it is in accordance with sample but not according to description).
8. A lady purchased some cosmetic from a chemists shop in spite of knowing that her skin is sensitive to the use of such cosmetic. But she did not disclose it to the chemist. A used cosmetic and got some allergy. Can she claim damage from the chemist? (NO)
9. A is in the retail shop of B and wants to buy some bottles of cold drink. He is examining some of the bottles, but the bottle exposed. He got injury in his hand. Can he claim damage from B? (No, because there is no contract of sale between A & B).
10. Certain goods were sold by A to B equal to sample. B in turn sold them to C by sample. But Goods delivered to C were not according to the sample shown to him. Therefore C rejected the goods and gave a notice to B. Can B recover damage from A? (Yes).
11. A purchased a electric heater from B, under the impression that it is suitable for heating his room. But he finds that, the heater is not fit for his purpose. Can A avoid contract? (No).

■■■

Chapter 17

Transfer of Ownership and Delivery of Goods

Learning Objectives

- Understand the concept of transfer of ownership and relate it with sale and agreement to sell.
- Get familiar with an importance of transfer of ownership and apply it with regard to contract of sale and other civic rights.
- Examine various rules regarding transfer of ownership of goods in a contract of sale.
- Analyse those cases, when non-owner can pass valid title of goods to the buyer.
- Develop understanding about various types of delivery of goods.
- Remember rules regarding delivery of goods from seller to the buyer.

MEANING OF TRANSFER OF OWNERSHIP

The phrase 'property in goods' means ownership in goods. The 'ownership' of goods is different from 'possesion' of goods. The 'possesion' of goods refers to the custody of goods. Every contract of sale involves transfer of ownership. The ownership is transferred from the seller to buyer. On such transfer, the seller ceases to be a owner of those goods. Transfer of ownership is different from transfer of possession. These are two different aspects of a contract of sale. The ownership of the goods may pass on from the seller to buyer, but the goods may remain in the possession of the seller. Similarly a person may have possession of goods, but he may not be the owner of those goods. For example, an agent, servant, bailee or pledgee etc who may be in possession of goods of the owner.

Thus in a contract of sale, when the goods are sold to the buyer, the buyer becomes owner of those goods irrespective of the fact whether the buyer has taken delivery of goods or not. It is therefore transfer of ownership means transfer of general right of ownership to the buyer, On such transfer, the buyer can enjoy peaceful possession, can use and can further sell those goods.

SIGNIFICANCE OF TRANSFER OF OWNERSHIP

The, transfer of ownership of goods is primarily a concern of buyer and seller. It is up to them to provide, when, such transfer takes place. But rights and liabilities of the various other parties are related to such transfer. It is therefore very important to know the exact time of transfer of ownership. It is only on the basis of ownership, various disputes and claims regarding to those goods may be settled. The following rights and obligations of the parties are affected by such transfer;

(i) *Risk passes with the ownership:* According to section 26 of this Act, 'risk prima facie passes with property'. This rule states that, transfer of ownership of goods decides rights and liabilities of the seller and buyer. In case, the goods are destroyed, the real owner of those goods will bear the loss, regardless of the fact that who is having possession of those goods. Thus, when the ownership is transferred to the buyer, he becomes the owner of goods and if goods are damaged or lost, he will bear the loss.

According to section 26 of this Act, 'unless, otherwise agreed, the goods remain at the seller's risk untill the property therein, is transferred to the buyer, but when the property therein is transferred to the buyer the goods are at the buyer's risk, whether delivery has been made or not.'

However if the delivery of goods is delayed due to fault of the buyer or seller, the goods are at the risk of the party at fault.

Example: A purchased a car from the dealer. The ownership of the car has been transferred to A and he has made payment of price. But due to increased demand on account of festive season, the dealer could not supply the car with in reasonable time. Mean while, godown gets fire and that car is damaged. The loss of such damage will fall on the seller, though ownership of that car has been transferred to the buyer.

(ii) *Right to take action against third party:* When the goods are damaged due to some fault on the part of third party, it is the owner, who alone, can take action and not the person who was in possession of the goods at that time.

Example: A is a owner of a car. His brother B who is possessing that car drives it. Meanwhile he meets with an accident, in which the car is badly damaged due to fault of another party involved in that accident. It is only the A who can take action against that party.

(iii) *Right to file suit for price:* In a contract of sale, ownership of the goods is transferred to the buyer for the payment of the price. It is therefore, the seller becomes entitled to recover the price from the buyer only when the property in goods or ownership has passed on to the latter.

(iv) ***Insolvency of the seller or buyer:*** After having made a contract of sale, the seller or buyer may become insolvent. In such situations, the right of official Receiver or Assignee to take over goods depend on the fact that whether the party declared insolvent, is the owner of the goods or not. If the buyer has been declared insolvent, and ownership has been transferred to him, the goods are still in the possession of the seller. The official receiver of the buyer will claim the goods from the seller.

RULES REGARDING TRANSFER OF PROPERTY OR OWNERSHIP

In a contract of sale of specific or ascertained goods, the property or ownership passes to the buyer, at the time, when the parties are intended to do so. Thus the whole question of transfer of ownership is left to the intention of the parties. The parties are free to determine any time for transferring ownership from the seller to buyer.

But sometimes, the intention of the parties may not be clear from the contract itself. In such cases, conduct of the parties, and the circumstances of the case would be given due consideration for ascertaining intention of the parties.

For the purpose of knowing the time, of passing of ownership from the seller to the buyer, the goods may be classified in to three groups.

- Specific or ascertained goods.
- Generic or unascertained goods.
- Goods sent 'on approval' or 'sale or return basis'.

Unless, a contrary intention appears, the following rules, which are contained in section 18 to 24, are applicable for ascertaining intention of the parties.

1. Specific or Ascertained Goods

Specific goods means goods, which have been identified and agreed upon at the time of making a contract of sale. According to section 19 of this Act, 'where there is a contract for the sale of specific or ascertained goods the property in them is transferred to the buyer, at such time as the parties to a contract intend it to be transferred.' It further provides that, 'for the purpose of ascertaining the intention of the parties, regard shall be had to the term of a contract, conduct of the parties and the circumstance of the case.'

To know the intention of the parties, with respect to the time when the property in goods, is transferred to the buyer, the following rules are applicable.

(i) ***Specific goods in deliverable state:*** When the contract of sale is unconditional, is made for specific goods which are ready to be delivered, the ownership of goods passes to the buyer, when the contract is made. Delivery of goods and payment of price or both are posponed. (section 20).

By unconditional contract of sale, we mean that there is no condition regarding transfer of ownership of the goods.

Example: A sells some specific goods to B. The goods are at deliverable state. A puts a condition that the ownership will be transferred to B when he accepts the Bill of Exchange. The contract of sale is conditional and therefore ownership will pass to B when he fulfils the condition of accepting that bill of exchange.

Another essential point in this regard is that the goods must be in deliverable state. The goods are said to be in a deliverable state, when they are in such state that, the buyer would under the contract, be bound to take delivery of them. It means they are ready to be delivered then and there.

Example: A purchases personal computer from B. He makes payment promptly and asks B to send the computer to his house. The ownership of that computer is passed on to B immediately at the time of making contract. But if A agrees to buy the computer which will be assembled by the B. This case is different and ownership of goods is not going to be transferred immediately.

(ii) *Specific goods not in deliverable state:* At the time of making a contract, the goods may not be in a deliverable state. To make them ready for delivery, the seller has something to do to the goods such as packing sealing, polishing, extra fitting and filling them in containers etc. In such case, ownership will be transferred on the completion of such acts.

According to section 21 of this Act, 'where there is a contract of sale for specific goods and the seller is bound to do something to the goods for the purpose of putting them in to deliverable state, the property does not pass untill such thing is done and the buyer has notice thereof.'

Example: A agrees to buy golden ring from a jeweller. To put it in delivery state, the ring is got to be polished. While polishing the ring it is damaged. Since ownership of the ring is yet to be transferred to A thus he will not be liable to bear the loss.

RUGG VS. MINETT (1809, 11, EAST 203). In this case, A purchased certain quantity of oil from B. The oil was to be filled in tins to put it in deliverable state. B filled up some of tins and informed the buyer. In the meanwhile, godown gets fire and entire stock of oil was destroyed. It was held that A will bear the loss of oil which was filled in tins.

(iii) *Specific goods to be measured or weighted for determining price:* Sometimes, the contract of sale is made for specific goods, which are in a deliverable state. But to determine the price of the goods, they are to be measured, weighted or tested. The ownership of such goods will be transferred when the task of weighting, measuring or testing is complete.

According to section 22 of this Act, 'where there is a contract of sale for specific goods, in a deliverable state, but the seller is bound to weight, measure, test or do some other act with reference to goods for the purpose of ascertaining the price, the property does not pass, until such act or thing is done and the buyer has notice thereof.'

Example: A agrees to sell a heap of wheat at a particular rate, to B. A had to weigh the wheat for ascertaining the price of wheat sold to B. The ownership of the heap of wheat will be transferred to B when A completes the task of measuring wheat and informs B about it.

ZAGUARY VS. FURNELL (1809, 2, CAMP, 240). In this case, A sold to B 289 bales of goat skins. Each bale contained five dozens skins, and the price was for certain sum per dozen of skins. Before A could count goat skins in each bale, the bales were destroyed by fire. It was held that the property in goods had not passed to the buyer and therefore the loss caused by fire had to be borne by A.

2. Unascertained and Future goods

Where there is a contract of sale for unascertained goods, no property in goods is transferred to the buyer unless the goods are ascertained. (section 18).

Thus, no ownership is transferred to the buyer, until the goods are identified and become ascertained.

Example: A is a dealer of rice. He agrees to sell 100 quintals of rice to B at a particular price. Unless the 100 quintals are not separated from the godown, the ownership will not pass on to B.

In the process of ascertaining the goods two sub-processes are involved, i.e. process of ascertainment and process of appropriation. In the process of ascertainment, goods are identified and separated from the lot. And through the process of appropriation, the goods are selected with an exclusive intention of using them for performing the contract with mutual consent of both parties.

Appropriation can be done by putting goods in suitable receptacles, i.e. by putting goods in bags or boxes or putting oil in bottles or casks. Sometimes, the seller delivers the goods to the carrier or to the bailee for transmitting them to the buyer, without reserving right of disposal the property in goods, it also amounts to appropriation

The following points should be noted with regard to an appropriation:

(a) Appropriation is an act showing an intention to identify and determine specific goods.
(b) It is bilateral act which is done by mutual consent of the buyer and seller.
(c) The consent of the seller or buyer may be given before or after the appropriation is made.

(d) Appropriation of goods can be made either by the seller with the consent of the buyer or by the buyer with the consent of seller.

(e) The consent may be express or implied.

However it is to be noted that as soon as the goods are appropriated unconditionally either by the buyer with the consent of seller or vice-vessa, the property in goods passes to the buyer.

With regard to unascertained goods, agreement to sell can be made. It becomes sale when the goods are appropriated to the contract.

3. Goods are sent 'on Approval' or on 'Sale or Return Basis'

Sometimes, a contract of sale is also made 'on approval' or 'sale or return' basis. In this case, the buyer has the option to return the goods to the seller if he is not satisfied with the goods.

According to section 24 of this Act, 'When goods are delivered to the buyer on approval or sale or return basis or on other similar terms, the property therein passes to the buyer (a) when he signifies his approval or acceptance to the seller or (b) he does any other act adopting the transaction or (c) If the does not signify this approval or acceptance to the seller but, retains the goods without giving notice of rejection.'

(a) *When he signifies his approval or acceptance:* On the approval or acceptance of goods, when the buyer informs the seller, the property in goods passes to the buyer.

Example: A delivered scooter to B on approval basis. As soon as B approves it and gives notice of it to A, ownership of scooter will be transferred to him.

(b) *Adoption of transaction:* When the buyer does not send his express approval to the seller, but does some act regarding goods which shows that he has accepted goods, the property in goods will pass, on such adoption.

Example: A delivers some jewellery to B on sale or return basis. B pledges that jewellery to C. It means he has adopted the transaction and therefore ownership is transferred to him.

(c) *Failure to return the goods:* When the buyer does not intimate the seller of his approval or rejection and retains the goods, at the expiration of reasonable period of time the ownership passes to the buyer.

Example: A delivers a horse to B on approval basis for 10 days. On the expiration of 10 days period B does not inform the seller about approval or rejection but retains the horse, B is deemed to have become owner of that horse.

SALE BY NON-OWNERS

Every contract of sale involves transfer of ownership of goods. The ownership is transferred by the seller or by his agent to the buyer for the payment of the price.

The general rule of law, in this regard is that it is only the real owner of the goods or person authorised by him can sell the goods and thereby can transfer the title of those goods to another person.

Contrary to it, when the person is not a owner of the goods or he has no right to sell the goods, even if, he sells the goods, the buyer will not get any title. This is so because, 'no one can give what he himself has not got.' (Nemo dat quod non habet). Therefore, if the person deals with or sells the good without authority of the owner such transaction is not valid in the eyes of law.

Similarly, if the seller has no title or his title is defective, when it passes to buyer, all such defects will automatically be passed to the buyer. Hence the buyer either will not get any title or his title will also be defective.

Example: A has stolen a car from B and makes agreement to sell it to C. C buys the car in good faith, believing that A is a owner of that car. Later on, B recovers this car from C, because C had no title of that car.

According to section 27 of this Act, 'subject to the previsions of this Act, and of any other law for the time in force, where goods are sold by a person who is not the owner thereof and who does not sell them under the authority as, with the consent of owner the buyer acquires no better title what the seller had.'

An interpretation of the above section makes it clear that as per the law.

(a) Owner can sell goods and transfer title to the buyer.
(b) Any other person having authority and consent of the owner can sell the goods.
(c) In case, ownership is defective, such defects will also pass on to the buyer and his title or ownership will also be defective.

Exceptions to the Rule

The general rule regarding title of goods though protects the interest of real owner, but it is subject to the following exception.

1. *Title by stoppel:* (Section 27). When the real owner of the goods makes any statement by the words of mouth or in writing or induces the buyer to believe that the seller has the authority to sell. Later on if the owner denies it, he will, be stopped from doing so and the buyer will get good title of good purchased.

Example: A, who is a real owner of goods tells to B, who is a prospective buyer that C who is selling goods has been authorised by him to sell. B, will get good title of the good. In fact C is just a employee with A and has no authority to sell. But B, believing on the statement of A buys the good from C. B will get good title of the goods, though C had no authority to sell.

The following acts on the part of the real owner are fit to induce the buyer.

(a) The real owner is, standing by when the sale is affected.
(b) He is assisting in the process of sale.

(c) He is helping in putting goods in to the possession of another person.
(d) He has made representation to the prospective buyer regarding authority of the person selling goods.

O' Connor Vs. Clark (170, pa,st. 318). In this case, M who was owner of the wagon, allowed one of his employee K to get his name painted on it, M did it for the purpose of inducing the public to believe that wagon belonged to K. C purchased a wagon from K in good faith and C acquires good title, as M is stopped from denying K's authority to sell.

2. *Sale by mercantile agent:* (section 27). Where the mercantile agent, with the consent of the owner is in possession of the goods or of a document of title to the goods, any sale made by him in the ordinary course of business, the buyer will get good title provided he buys goods in good faith and for value.

Thus, the buyer will get good title of the goods though the mercantile agent had no authority to sell, provided the following conditions are satisfied.

(a) Mercantile agent is an agent, who has an authority in a customary course of business as for the purpose of sale, or to buy goods or to raise money on the security of goods.
(b) The goods, which are being sold must be in his possession with the consent of the owner, or he must have documents of title of those goods
(c) The agent has sold goods in ordinary course of business as an agent i.e. there should have been no emergency like situation.
(d) The buyer must have acted in good faith believing that the agent had authority to sell the goods.

Example: A was appointed as mercantile agent to buy raw material for B. But A has sold part of that raw material to C, who buys it in good faith believing that A who deals in that raw material will have authority to sell. C will get good title, though A was not authorised to sell the raw material.

Folk Vs. King (1923, 1, K.B. 282). In this case, F, the owner of a car delivered it to A, mercantile agent for sale on the condition that the car should not be sold at less than $ 575. A, however sold the car for $ 340 to K. Who bought it in good faith without notice of any fraud. A, misappropriated the amount. F sued K to recover the car. It was held that since A was in possession of a car with F's consent for the purpose of sale. Thus K obtained good title of that car.

3. *Sale by one joint owners:* According to section 28 of this Act, 'if one of the several joint owners of goods, has the sole possession of them by the permission of other joint owners and he sells them to a person, who buys them in good faith and has, at the time of contract of sale, no notice of fact that seller has no authority to sell, the buyer will get good title of goods.'

Example: A, B and C are joint owners, of some furniture. And with the consent of B and C the furniture was kept in the possession of A. A sells the furniture to

P who buys it in good faith and without notice that A had no authority to sell. P will get good title of the goods.

4. *Sale by person in possession under voidable contract:* According to section 29 of this Act, "where a seller is in possession of goods under a voidable contract and he sells the goods to a bonafide buyer, before the contract is rescinded, the buyer gets good title to goods."

For applying this rule, it is necessary that the following conditions must be satisfied.

(a) The seller must be in possession of good under a voidable contract in which the consent of one party is caused either by coercion, undue influence, misrepresentation and by fraud.

(b) Buyer must have bought the goods, without having notice of seller's defective title.

(c) The goods are sold before the aggrieved party avoids the contract.

Example: A buys B's car by seeking his consent at gun point. On obtaining possession and ownership of the car from B, A sells it to C. And C buys the car in good faith believing that A is a real owner of car and A has sold the car to C before B rescinds the contract. C gets good title of the car.

However, this exception is valid only in case of goods obtained under voidable contract. But in void contract an innocent buyer will not get good title of goods.

5. *Sale by seller in possession after sale:* According to section 30 (1) of this Act, 'where a person having sold the goods continues or is in possession of goods or of the document of title of the goods, if he resell the same goods to another buyer, the buyer shall get good title to the goods, provided he buys them in good faith and without notice of previous sale.'

For the application of this exception it is necessary that the seller must possess the good as a seller. If he holds the goods as bailee or hirer or in any other capacity the innocent buyer will not get good title of such goods.

Example: A buys some goods from B and leaves them with B for time being. Meantime, B resells same goods to C, who buys them in good faith and had no knowledge of previous sale. C will get good title of the goods, though A had no title to those goods.

Example 2: Shyam buys a refrigerator set from Ram and asks him to retain possession of that set as a bailee for 2 months period. In the meanwhile, Shyam who is holding that set as a bailee resells it to Mohan who buys the set in good faith having no notice of previous sale. Mohan will not get good title, because Shyam was holding refrigerator set as a bailee.

6. *Sale by the buyer in possession after sale:* According to section 30 (2) of this Act, "where the buyer has bought the goods in agreement to sell and has got possession of goods or document of title on those goods with the consent of the seller. Such buyer sells those goods to the second buyer, who buys these goods in good faith and has no knowledge of any right of original seller on those goods, he will get good title to the goods."

For applying this rule it is essential that the first buyer must have obtained possession of the goods or document of title with the consent of original seller.

Example: Ram buys a scooter from Shyam on instalment basis. In the contract, they agreed that Shyam will continue to be owner of that scooter till the payment of last instalment. Ram sold the scooter to Mohan, before the payment of last instalment. Mohan buys that scooter in good faith and has no knowledge about the arrangement between Ram and Shyam. Mohan will get good title, though Ram had no title of that scoter.

However, it is to be noted that if the person buys the option for purchasing goods and gets possession of those goods, with the consent of seller. If he sells those goods, the buyer, who buys in good faith having no information on that arrangement will not get good title.

7. *Sale by unpaid seller:* In a contract of sale, the unpaid seller has got a right to resell the goods. According to section 54 (3) of this Act, "where an unpaid seller, exercised his right of lien or stoppage in transit and gets back possession of the goods, if he resells such goods the subsequent buyer gets good title of the goods as against the original buyer". To apply this section it should be noted that a reasonable notice must have been given to the first buyer for paying the price or the goods must be of a perishable nature.

Example: A sold a car to B and A becomes unpaid seller on sale for Rs. 1.5 lacs. B did not pay the price. A resells that car to C. C will get good title as against B.

8. *Sale by finder of goods:* When the person finds the goods belonging to another and takes custody of those goods, spend some money on the maintenance. He can sell the goods under the following situations.

(a) If the goods are of perishable nature and losing their value day by day.
(b) The money spent by the finder of goods exceeds 2/3 of the total cost of the goods.
(c) On tracing the real owner of those goods, such owner refuses to pay lawful maintenance charges.

On selling the goods under any above situation the buyer will get good title to the goods, though the seller is not a bonafide owner of the goods.

Example: A lost his pet dog. B finds it and takes custody of the dog. He spent sum of Rs. 500 on the maintenance of that dog till the date he could trace its real owner. The real owner refuses to pay lawful maintenance charges. A sells the dog to D. D will get good title.

9. *Sale by pawnee or pledgee:* when the debtor makes default in repaying debt or performing the promise on due date, the pawnee or pledgee has a right to sell the goods which have been pledged against the debt after giving reasonable notice of this fact to the debtor. Though, the pawnee is not a owner, but if he sells goods the buyer will get good title.

Example: Ram borrows sum of Rs. 5000 from Shyam by pledging some goods to him. On due date Ram fails to repay the debt. Shyam gives reasonable notice to Ram for repaying debt, otherwise, the goods will be sold by him. Still Ram does not repay, Shyam sells the goods to Manohar, who will gets good title to such goods.

10. ***Sale by official receiver or assignee:*** In case, the person is declared insolvent by the court, his property is handed over to the official reciever or assignee. Though they are not owners of the property of insolvent but they can pass on good title to the buyer of that property.

DELIVERY OF GOODS

Delivery defined: In a contract of sale, not only ownership but as well as physical possession of the goods sold is handed over to the buyer. Though, it is not necessary to do it at the time of making a contract, but it is to be done for performing a contract. Thus, it is a duty of the seller to deliver the goods to the buyer or to his agent. The goods are said to have been delivered if they get in to the possession of another person.

According to section 2 (2) of this Act, delivery is a voluntary transfer of possession from one person to another. The person giving delivery must have parted with possession of the goods voluntarily.

Delivery of the goods sold, may be made by doing any thing which the parties agree or which has the effect of putting the goods in the possession of the buyer or any person authorised to hold them on his behalf.

Section 32 of this Act deals with basic rules regarding delivery of goods. This section provides that "delivery and payment are, by default, two concurrent conditions and must take place at the same time, provided the parties had no contrary intention to it".

Types of Delivery

Delivery of goods may be of following types;

(a) Actual delivery (b) Symbolic delivery (c) Constructive delivery.

(a) ***Actual delivery:*** In case of actual delivery the goods are physically handed over to the buyer or to his authorised agent. Thus it involves removal of goods from the possession of the seller and putting them in a possession of the buyer.

(b) ***Symbolic delivery:*** It is different from actual delivery. Such mode of delivery is used, where the goods are bulky and heavy. In such case, it is not possible to hand over them physically to the buyer. It is therefore some thing or some symbol which carries real possession with it, is given to the buyer. As a result of it, the goods are put under the control of the buyer.

Example: A agrees to sell 100 cotton bales to B which are lying in his godown. A, instead of physically handing over these to B, he hands over key of godown to B, so as to facilitate delivery of those bales. It amounts to symboliodelivery.

(c) *Constructive delivery:* It is different from actual and symbolic delivery. In such delivery, the person who is holding goods acknowledges that he is in possession of the goods on behalf of the buyer. It is known as constructive delivery.

Example: X sells 100 bags of wheat to Y the wheat is lying in the godown of Z. X gives an order to Z to delivery wheat to Y. Z agrees to hold the 100 bags on behalf of Y and makes necessary entry in his books. It amounts to constructive delivery of wheat.

RULES REGARDING DELIVERY OF GOODS

The following rules are applicable with regard to delivery of goods.

(i) *Types of delivery:* Goods may be delivered by the seller to the buyer by giving actual, symbolic or constructive delivery. The important thing in this regard is that buyer or his authorised agent should get possession of the goods.

(ii) *Delivery and payment are concurrent conditions:* Unless, otherwise agreed, the delivery of goods and payment of price are concurrent conditions. The seller should be ready and willing to handover possession of the goods to the buyer and the buyer should also be ready and willing to pay the price to the seller.

(iii) *Buyer to apply for delivery:* Unless, contrary intention appears, the seller is not bound to deliver the goods, until the buyer applies for it. In case of future or contingent goods, which are yet to be procured by the seller. It is the duty of the seller to inform that goods have been procured. Even in such case, the buyer has to apply for the delivery. In case he fails to apply, he has no remedy against the seller.

(iv) *Effect of part delivery:* Unless, contrary intention appears, when in the process of delivery, part of goods have been delivered. For the purpose of ascertaining time of passing property in goods, it will be assumed that whole lot has been delivered. But, when part delivery is made with an intention to separate it from remaining lot, it will not be considered as delivery of entire lot.

(v) *Place of delivery:* While marking contract of sale, the parties may decide about place of delivery and the goods must be delivered accordingly. But if a place has not been decided, the following rules will apply.

(a) The goods sold are to be delivered, at the place, at which they are at the time of sale.

(b) Goods agreed to be sold are to be delivered, at the place at which, they are at the time of agreement to sell.

(c) If the goods are not in existence at the time of agreement to sell, they are to the delivered at the place, at which they are being produced.

(vi) ***Time of delivery:*** In case, time is fixed for the delivery, the goods should be delivered accordingly. But if no time is fixed and the seller is to deliver goods. He must make delivery of goods within reasonable period of time. Reasonable period of time is a matter of fact, varies from situation to situation depending on facts and circumstance of the case.

(vii) ***Manner of delivery:*** When the goods are in the possession of third party, such goods can not be delivered, unless, third party acknowledges that he is holding the goods on behalf of the seller.

(viii) ***Expenses of delivery:*** Unless, otherwise agreed, expenses and incidental charges, which the seller incurs for putting the goods in to deliverable position, shall be borne by the seller.

(ix) ***Delivery of wrong quantity:*** When the goods are delivered in short quantity or in excess or mixed with other goods, the following rules will be applicable;

(a) When the goods delivered, are shorter than contracted quantity the buyer has a right to reject delivery. But if he accepts the goods, he will have to pay for that according to contract rate.

(b) When the seller delivers larger quantity more than contracted quantity, the buyer has the following options.

   i. he can reject delivery of goods.
   ii. he can accept contracted quantity and reject the excess.
   iii. he can accept whole quantity, he will have to pay for extra quantity according to contract rate.

(c) when the seller has mixed other goods with the goods for which contract is made and other goods are of different description. The buyer, either can reject whole lot, or can accept the goods according to contract and can reject remaining goods of different description.

(x) ***Instalment delivery:*** Unless, contrary intention appears, the buyer is not bound to accept delivery by instalments.

But, where, the contract of sale provides for instalment delivery which have to be separately paid for. In such case, if the seller fail to deliver instalment or the buyer fails to pay for that instalment. The question arises that whether such failure leads to repudiation of the whole contract or only that instalment should be repudiated in respect of which default is made. It depend on the fact of the case and the circumstances.

Maple Flock Coy Ltd. Vs. Universal Furniture Products (Wembley) (1943, 1, K. B. 14). In this case, A agreed to supply B, 10 tons of flock in twenty instalments. First, 15 instalments were satisfactory. But the sixteenth instalment was defective and subsequent deliveries were also satisfactory. The buyer wanted to repudiate the whole contract. It was held that the buyer could not do so, because the probability of default being made was negligible.

(xi) ***Delivery to carrier:*** The term 'carrier' means an agency to whom the goods are handed over for transmitting them to the buyer such as railway, shipping coy, transport agency and airways, etc.

In this regard, there is a general rule of law that delivery of goods to a carrier, whether named by the buyer or not, operates prima facie as delivery of goods to the buyer.

So far as transfer of property in good is concerned, it should be remembered that when the seller delivers the good to the carrier without reserving right of disposal, the property of goods passes to the buyer when the goods are handed over to the carrier. This is so because, the carrier is treated as an agent of the buyer.

Example: A of Delhi sells certain goods to B of Bombay. A sends the goods by railways and railway receipt was made in the name of B. In this case, as soon as goods are delivered to railways, the property in goods passes to B, because A has not reserved the right of disposal with him.

However it should be noted that the liability of the seller is not over just by delivering goods to the carrier. Section 30 (2) of this Act clearly provides that, "unless otherwise authorised by the buyer, the seller must make a reasonable contract with the carrier or wharfinger for the safe carriage of the goods".

In case the seller fails to make such arrangement for safe carriage and the goods are lost or damaged in transit, the buyer will hold seller responsible for such losses.

Sometimes, the goods are sent by sea transit, wherein it is quite usual to insure the goods. In such cases, the seller should give to the buyer such notice as shall enable him to insure the goods. If the seller fails to give such notice and goods are not insured the goods will be deemed to be at the risk of the seller.

The liability of the seller to inform the buyer will arise in F.O.B. contracts (Free on board) when the goods are delivered on board the ship. But in case of C.I.F. contracts (cost, insurance & freight) the seller is required to insure the goods.

Reservation of right of disposal: In a contract of sale, when the goods are delivered to the carrier for the purpose of taking them to the buyer, the property in goods passes to the buyer, provided the seller has not reserved the right of disposal. This is the right which is given to the seller by which he does not part with control over the goods, until certain condition are fulfilled. In other words, if the seller does some act which shows his intention that he will pass on the control over the goods to the buyer only when the buyer satisfies some conditions.

Example: Ram agrees to sell the goods to Shyam on the condition that goods will be delivered to him on the acceptance of 'Bill of Exchange'. The property in goods will pass on to Shyam only when he accepts the bill.

In the following two cases, the seller is deemed to have reserved the right of disposal with himself.

(a) Where the goods are delivered to railways or shipping company for carriage, but bill of lading or railway receipt as the case may be, is deliverable to the order of the seller or his agent and not to the buyer.

Example: A delivers goods to Railway company for the purpose of carriage to B. But instead of sending railway receipt to B, it is sent to C, the agent of A and asking him to hand over it to B on the payment of the price. A has reserved the right of disposal.

(b) Where the seller draws a bill of exchange on the buyer for the price of the goods and sends it along with railway receipt or bill of lading on a condition that those documents will be handed over to the buyer on the acceptance of that bill.

Acceptance of delivery: In a contract of sale, the goods are to be delivered by the seller to the buyer. Delivery of the goods becomes complete, when it is accepted by the buyer or by his authorised agent. Mere receipt of goods on the part of the buyer does not amount to acceptance. Rather acceptance of delivery is something more than this. In this regard, the following rules are applicable.

(i) When the goods are delivered to the buyer, which he has not previously examined. The buyer should be given reasonable opportunity of examining them as to ascertain that whether they are in conformity with the contract. He is deemed to have accepted delivery only on such examination.

(ii) The buyer is deemed to have accepted the goods.

  (a) When he intimates the seller that he has accepted the goods.

  (b) When the goods are delivered to the buyer, and he does any act in relation to them which shows that he has accepted them such as he resells the goods or pledges the goods.

  (d) When the buyer retains the goods, beyond reasonable time, without intimating the seller that he has rejected them.

(iii) Unless otherwise agreed, when goods are delivered to the buyers, and he refuses to accept them, he is not bound to return them to the seller. But the buyer must inform the seller that he refuses to accept the goods.

Liability of the buyer: When the seller is ready and willing to deliver the goods and requests the buyer to take delivery. But the buyer does not, with in reasonable period of time, after the request of the seller, take the delivery of the goods, he is liable to the seller for.

(a) Any loss caused to the seller by the neglect or refusal to take delivery of the goods.

(b) Reasonable charge for the care and custody of the goods.

According to section 44 of this Act, "where the neglect or refusal of the buyer to take delivery, amounts to a repudiation of a contract, the seller may sue the buyer for the price or for damage".

Review Questions

1. Define 'transfer of ownership'. Why it is important in a contract of sale?
2. Why it is important to know the exact time when the ownership passes to the buyer.
3. State briefly the rules regarding the transfer of ownership.
4. What is meant by reservation of right of disposal? When right of disposal is deemed to be reserved.
5. 'Delivery does not amount to acceptance of goods' comment.
6. What are the legal remedies available to the buyer? When goods of wrong quantity and quantity are delivered to him?
7. Explain briefly the rules relating to delivery of goods.
8. 'No seller can transfer better than the himself has'. Explain this rule and discuss various exception to this rule.
9. Write notes on the following:
   (a) Appropriation of goods.
   (b) Transfer of ownership of specific goods.
   (c) Modes of delivery of goods
   (d) Instalment delivery
   (e) Acceptance of delivery
10. Comment on the following:
   (a) Risk passes with ownership
   (b) Unconditional delivery to carrier is, prima facie, deemed to be delivery of good to the buyer.
   (c) Finder of goods can pass, goods title to the buyer.
   (d) Duty of the seller is not over, when the goods are delivered to the carrier.
   (e) Transfer of ownership is different from transfer of possession.

Practical Problems

1. A sold some furniture to B. B left the furniture in the shop of A. Meantime the shop sets on fire and that furniture is damaged along with other furniture. Who is to bear the loss of that furniture, which has been sold? (B will bear loss)
2. Ram sold a machine to Shyam on instalment payment basis with a condition that the ownership will be transferred to Shyam on the payment of final instalment. Before making payment of final instalment Shyam sells the machine to Manohar, who buys it in good faith. Will he get good title of that machine. (Yes)

3. A is a owner of a car. His brother drives it. While driving on the road he meets with an accident with B's car. In the accident A's car was badly damaged with the fault of B. Can A's brother has any legal remedy against B. (No, he is not a owner)
4. A delivered his scooter to B on approval basis. B kept that scooter with him for three months. He does not give any information regarding rejection of that scooter to A. In the meantime the scooter is damaged in the fire. Who is liable for loss? (B will be liable)
5. Y delivers some pieces of jewellery to X on sale or return basis. X pledges that jewellery with Z and does not give any information to Y regarding acceptance or rejection. Can Y recover that jwellery from Z? Give reasons. (No)
6. F is a owner of a car, instructed this agent A to sell the car at stipulated price, and not below that. But A sold the car to B at a price lower than the stipulated price and misappropriated that money. B bought the car in good faith, will B get good title of that car? (Yes)
7. A purchased B's car at gun point. Before B could rescind the contract A sells this car to C. Who buys the car in good faith. Can B recover this car from C? (No)
8. Ram sold a wrist watch to Shyam and same was delivered to him. Later on he delivered that watch back to Ram for repair. Ram resells that watch to Manohar. Is it valid sale? (No)
9. A sold raw material to B who is in Bombay, the raw material is to be delivered through Indian Railways. A handsover the raw material, to the Railways. And railway receipt is being sent to A's agent along with bill of exchange which is to be accepted by B. But in transit the raw material is damaged. Who will bear the loss? (A will be liable for loss)
10. Karim delivers a horse to John on trial for a week. Without negligence on his part, the horse dies on third day. Is John liable to pay the price? (No)

■■■

Chapter **18**

Unpaid Seller and His Rights

Learning Objectives

- Understand meaning and concept of unpaid seller in a contract of sale.
- Remember the various rights of unpaid seller and see that which one is used very often.
- Examine the nature and extent of right of lien and compare it with right of stoppage in transit.
- Analyse the rights of unpaid seller against the buyer of goods.
- Be clear about the concept of auction sale.

MEANING OF UNPAID SELLER

A contract is comprised of reciprocal promises. In a contract of sale, if seller is under an obligation to deliver goods the buyer has to pay for it. In case buyer fails or refuses to pay, the seller, as unpaid seller, shall have certain rights.

According to section 45 of this Act the seller of goods is deemed to be an unpaid seller:

(a) When whole of the price has not been paid or tendered.
(b) When bill of exchange or other negotiable instrument has been received as a conditional payment, and the condition on which it was received has not been fulfilled, by reason of the dishonour of the instrument or otherwise.

Thus to be considered as an unpaid seller, the following conditions must be satisfied.

(a) Whole of the price has not been paid. It implies that even if a major portion of the price has paid, but still the seller remains an unpaid seller.
(b) Goods have been sold and the price must be due.
(c) Bill of exchange, or cheque or other negotiable instrument was received as payment of the price, but the same has been dishonoured.

Thus the seller becomes an unpaid seller only on account of non-payment of the price. If some expenses incurred by the seller has not been paid, he can not be termed as unpaid seller. Similarly where the seller has sold the goods on credit again he can not be treated as unpaid seller, till the date of credit.

In case, where whole of the price has been tendered by the buyer and the seller has refused it, be can not be treated as unpaid seller.

Example: A sold goods worth Rs. 5000 to B on credit for three months. A will not be considered as unpaid seller during the period of three months. And he will become unpaid seller, when the price remains unpaid even after the expiry of credit period of three months.

RIGHTS OF UNPAID SELLER

The rights of unpaid seller can be put in two categories

- Rights against the goods • Rights against the buyer

(i) Rights against goods are as under:
   (a) Right of lien.
   (b) Right of stoppage in transit, and
   (c) Right of resale.

(ii) Rights against the buyer are as under:
   (a) Right to file suit for price.
   (b) Right to file suit for damages.
   (c) Right to file suit for interest.

The above mentioned rights of an unpaid seller do arise by operation of law, irrespective of the fact that whether they have made any agreement express or implied between them.

RIGHTS AGAINST THE GOODS

Where the ownership of goods has passed to the buyer:

I. *Right of lien:* Right of lien means right to retain possession of the goods, till certain debts or claims in respect of those goods are cleared. This right is related to physical possession of the goods. So any party who is entitled to it can use it only if he has got possession of the goods. So is the case with an unpaid seller, he can exercise this right if he has possession of the goods.

According to section 47 (i) of this Act, "the unpaid seller of goods who is in possession of them is entitled to retain possession of them until payment or tender of the price is made". He can exercise right of lien under the following cases:

(a) where the good have been sold on cash basis, without any stipulation as to credit.
(b) where the goods have been sold on credit, but the term of credit has expired.
(c) where the buyer becomes insolvent

To exercise rights of lien transfer of ownership is not significant, rather the seller needs to have possession of goods. Thus the right of lien will not be affected, even if the document of title such as bill of lading or railway receipt etc. have been handed over to the buyer.

Example: A sold 100 bags of cement to B on cash payment basis. The bags of cement have identified and separated out from the stock. But B fails in making payment. A is entitled to retain possession of these cement bags till the payment of price is made or offered.

Rules regarding right of lien:

(a) To exercise the right of lien the goods must be in actual possession of the seller. Due to any reason if he loses the possession, the right of lien will also be lost.

(b) The goods were sold on cash payment basis, but price has not been paid or tendered. It is sufficient ground for using this right.

(c) The goods were sold on credit, but the term of credit has been expired and full payment has not been made, the seller can use this right.

(d) When the buyer becomes insolvent, the seller can retain possession of the goods till the payment of price. According to section 2 (8) of sale of Goods Act insolvent means, "a person who has ceased to pay his debt, in the ordinary course of business, or can not pay his debts, as they become due, whether he has committed act of insolvency or not."

(e) The seller who is possessing the good in the capacity of bailee or agent or in any other capacity can exercise right of lien.

(f) In case documents of title have been handed over to the buyer but possession of the goods lies with the seller, he can exercise right of lien.

(g) The right of lien is available to the seller only for the price and not for any other charges such as godown charges and other maintenance charges etc.

(h) Right of lien is not divisible. Thus in case of part payment made by the buyer, the seller may refuse to deliver part of the goods to the extent of payment.

(i) In case, the seller has already delivered part of the goods to the buyer, he has a right of lien over the remaining goods, provided he has not waived right of lien in favour of the buyer.

Termination of right of lien:

(a) On giving possession of the goods to the carrier for the purpose of taking them to the buyer, with out reserving right of disposal, the right of lien will be terminated. This is so because, unconditional delivery to the carrier amounts delivery to the buyer him self.

(b) When the buyer or his authorised agent gets possession of the goods lawfully, the right of lien will come to an end.

(c) The seller has a option to waive his right of lien in favour of the buyer. He may do it expressly or it may be directly understood from his conduct and intention, such as extending term of credit may amount to implied waiver.

(d) When the buyer tenders the price, but the seller refuses to accept it, the right of lien will be lost.

(II) *Right of stoppage of goods in transit:* When the goods are on the move towards the buyer and the buyer becomes insolvent, the seller can exercise the right of the stoppage of goods in transit. By using this right, he can check the movement of the goods immediately and prevent the buyer from getting possession of the goods.

This right is considered as an extension of right of lien, because by using this right, the unpaid seller regains the possession of the goods.

This right of stoppage in transit arises, when the right of lien comes to an end, because the goods are no more in the possession of the seller. He has delivered them to the carrier. By using this right the unpaid seller may get those goods back from the carrier or may withhold delivery.

According to section 50 of this Act, "Subject to the provisions of this Act, when the buyer of goods becomes insolvent, the unpaid seller who has parted with the possession of the goods, has the right of stopping them in transit, that is to say, he may resume possession of the goods as long as they are in the course of transit and may retain them until payment or tender of the price."

When can this right be exercised: (section 50). An interpretation of the contents of above provision, makes it clear that the right of stoppage of goods in transit can be exercised by the unpaid seller, under the following situations.

(a) The seller must be an unpaid seller

(b) The ownership of the goods must have passed to the buyer.

(c) The goods must be in the course of transit i.e. neither in the possession of the seller nor in the possession of the buyer.

(d) The buyer of the goods has become insolvent.

(e) Goods may be stopped in transit only for the payment of the price.

Duration of transit section 51: The unpaid seller can exercise this right only when the goods are in the course of transit. The goods are deemed to be in transit when they are neither in the possession of the seller nor in the possession of the buyer. Rather, they are in the possession of a carrier, who is holding them in his own name for the purpose of taking them to the buyer.

According to section 51 (1) of this Act, "goods are deemed to be in the course of transit, from the time when they are delivered to a carrier or other bailee for the purpose of transmission to the buyer. Until the buyer or his agent takes delivery of them from such carrier or other bailee."

Some times, the buyer may apply for the delivery of the goods, at a different place other than the agreed one, the goods are in transit, until, they are received by the buyer or his agent at that place.

How the right of stoppage is exercised: (Section 52) The unpaid seller can exercise the right of stoppage of goods in transit in the following ways.

(a) by taking actual possession of the goods from a carrier.
(b) by giving notice of his claim to the carrier or other bailee in whose possession the goods are.

Such notice may be given either (a) to the person in actual possession of the goods or (b) to his principal. After receiving such notice, it is the duty of a carrier not to deliver the goods to the buyer, but to deliver them back according to the instruction of the unpaid seller. The expenses of redelivering the goods to him will be borne by the seller. If the carrier after receiving such notice, deliver the goods to the buyer or his agent, he shall be liable to the seller for conversion.

When the transit comes to an end: The unpaid seller can use this right, so long as the goods are in transit, As soon as the transit ends, the seller's right of stoppage will be lost. Transit comes to an end under the following situation.

(a) *Buyer taking delivery:* Once the goods reach in to the hands of the buyer or his agent, transit comes to an end. Even if the buyer or his agent takes delivery of the goods at some other place, before reaching to appointed destination, transit comes to an end.

(b) *Carriers's acknowledgment to the buyer:* As soon as, the goods reach to appointed destination, and a carrier acknowledges to the buyer or to his agent that he holds the goods on his behalf, the transit ends.

(c) *Wrongful refusal to the buyer:* After having arrived at a appointed destination, the carrier wrongfully refuses to deliver the goods to the buyer or to his agent, the transit is deemed to be at end.

Example: A sold some goods to B, to be delivered to him in Bombay. A handed over the goods to a carrier for the purpose of taking them to B. On the arrival at Bombay the carrier refuses to deliver the goods, unless some additional payment is made to him. On the arrival at Bombay the transit comes to an end.

(d) *Goods delivered to a ship:* In case, the goods have been delivered to a ship chartered by the buyer, if the buyer is a owner of that ship, transit ends as soon as goods are loaded on the ship. But if the buyer has deployed the ship as a carrier, the goods continue to be in transit.

(e) *Part delivery:* Where part delivery of the goods has been made to the buyer or his agent, the remainder of the goods may be stopped in transit. Unless such part delivery has been given in such circumstances as to show an agreement to give up possession of whole of the goods. section 51 (7).

However, to exercise the right of stoppage in transit it is not necessary that the buyer must have been declared as an insolvent by the court. His unsatisfactory or bad financial position provide sufficient ground for using this right.

Difference between Lien and Stoppage in transit

	Lien	*Stoppage in transit*
Possession of goods	To exercise right of lien the goods must be in the possession of the seller.	To exercise this right, the goods must be in possession of independent carrier or bailee
Insolvency the buyer	This right can be exercised for getting payment of the price. It is not necessary that the buyer must be insolvent. Even if he refuses to pay, the seller can use this right.	This right can be used only if buyer becomes insolvent. Or his financial position becomes unsatisfactory.
Termination	As soon as the seller parts with the goods, the right of lien will be terminated.	Right of stoppages will be terminated when the goods get in to the hand of the buyer or his agent.
Nature	The right of lien is a right to retain possession of the goods until payment of the price is made to the seller.	This right is used to regain the possession of the goods.
Exercise of the right	The right of lien is exercised by the seller himself.	The right of stoppage in transit can be exercised by the selller through the carrier or the bailee in whose possesion the goods are.

Effect of sub sale or pledge by buyer: As stated earlier that right of lien and right of stoppage in transit of unpaid seller will not be affected by sub-sale or pledge by the buyer. It is because the second buyer can not stand in a better position than his seller (first buyer). In the same way, where the sub-buyer produced delivery orders to the seller who indorsed them that he was willing to give delivery, but after delivery of part of goods, he refused to deliver the remaining on the ground that first buyer has not paid the price. The seller will be stopped from doing so. Thus the right of sub-buyer will get legal recognition provided sub sale must have been made with the consent of the seller.

Example: A sold 100 bags of wheat from his godown to B. B then sold 50 bags out of these to C. A told to C that the wheat bags would be delivered to him in due course. In the meantime B becomes insolvent. Thus A's right with regard to 50 bags which have been sold to C is lost, because he has recognised sub-sale made by B to C.

In the same way where the documents of title such as bill of lading or railway receipt etc. has been lawfully transferred to any person as a buyer and the buyer, in turn transfers these to second buyer, who buys them in good faith and for valuable consideration, the unpaid seller's right of lien or stoppage in transit would come to an end.

However, section 53 (2) of this Act states that "if such transfer of documents of title is by way of pledge, then the unpaid seller's rights are not completely defeated, but he can exercise these rights subject to the right of pledgee."

Example: A sold some goods to B and sent railway receipt to B. B, without paying for the goods pledged the railway receipt with C as a security for a loan of Rs. 10,000. B, becomes insolvent. A is entitled to get back railway receipt after paying Rs. 10,000 to C.

(III) *Right of Resale:* After regaining possession of the goods by exercising right of stoppage, the unpaid seller can exercise right of lien by retaining possession till the payment of the price. Still the contract of sale is in force and the buyer may get possession after making payment of price to the seller.

The most important right available to the unpaid seller is right of resale of those goods. Despite, using the above rights if the seller does not get the price he is entitled to resell the goods under the following situations.

(a) *Perishable goods:* Where the goods, being retained by the seller are of a perishable nature and losing the value and utility regularly, the unpaid seller can resell the goods for best obtainable prices. The goods are said to be of a perishable nature if they are getting physically and chemically deteriorated and becoming commercially unmerchantable.

(b) *Reasonable notice:* The unpaid seller, after having exercised right of stoppage and right of lien, giving reasonable notice to the buyer, the seller can resell the goods. By giving such notice the unpaid seller may express his intention that if price remains unpaid till the expiration of reasonable period of time, he will resell the goods.

Where the goods are resold under any above situations, and the unpaid seller fails to realise that much price, which he was expected to get from the original buyer. In this case he has right to claim any shortfall arising out of resale from the original buyer. But if he gets more than the original price he is not bound to return excess of the price to the original buyer.

However, if the goods are resold under any other situations except above mentioned, the unpaid seller will have no claim for short fall in price and if he gets more than original price he is bound to return the excess to the original buyer.

Notice of resale: Except in case of perishable goods, in all other case, the unpaid, seller is under legal obligation to give reasonable notice of this fact to the original buyer. The basic idea of giving such notice is that, on the one hand the buyer be given an opportunity for performing the contract by making payment of the price and getting delivery of the goods. On the other, the buyer, who is not in a position to pay the price may ensure that the goods are resold at reasonable price. This is so because, if any short fall arises, it is to be made good by him.

The second buyer of the goods will get good title as against the first buyer provided the goods were resold under any one of the situations mentioned earlier. But this rule is subject to the following exceptions.

• *Right to resell is reserved:* In a contract of sale, if the seller has expressly reserved the right of resale in case the buyer defaults in payment of price. He is not required to give any notice to the original buyer for resale of goods ownership has not been transferred to the buyer:

• *Right of withholding delivery of goods:* In a contract of sale, if ownership of the goods has not been transferred to the buyer, the unpaid seller has a right to withhold delivery. This right is similar to and co-extensive with his right of lien and stoppage in transit.

Rights of Unpaid Seller Against the Buyer

In addition, to the rights against the goods unpaid seller has certain rights against the buyer. These rights are known as right in personam, because these rights can be used against the buyer personally. These rights are as under

(i) *Suit for price:* In a contract of sale, the buyer is under legal obligation to pay the price of the goods. Where under a contract of sale, the property in goods has passed to the buyer, and the buyer wrongfully neglects or refuses to pay for goods, according to the term of a contract, the seller may sue him for the price of the goods. (section 55 (1).

Section 55 (2) of this Act provides, "if the contract of sale stipulates the payment of the price on a certain day irrespective of delivery and the buyer wrongfully neglects or refuses to pay such price, the seller may sue him for the price, although property in goods has not passed." Thus, the contents of this provision may be read as an extention of the contents given under section 55 (1).

Example: A sold some goods to B for Rs. 10,000\- and B agreed to pay the price after ten days of the contract. B refuses to pay the price on due date. A is entitled to file suit against B. Though property in goods has not been passed to the buyer, but the buyer was to make payment of the price on a certain day, which he refuses.

(ii) *Suit for damages:* In case the buyer wrongfully refuses or neglects to accept delivery of the goods and pay for it. The seller may sue upon him for damages.

According to section 44 of this Act, "where the property in goods has passed to the buyer, the seller is entitled to recover.

(a) any loss caused to him by the buyer's refusal or neglect to take delivery.

(b) any reasonable charge for the care and custody of the goods."

The provisions of Indian contract Act contained under section 73 will be equally applicable for determining the account of damges.

THOMSON VS. ROBINSON (1955, C.H. 177). In this case, T, a car dealer contracted to supply a motor car to R. R, refused to take delivery. It was found that supply of cars was in excess of demand at the time of breach of contract and thus there was no ready market for cars on the date of breach. It was held that T was entitled to recover damages for the loss of profit in the bargain.

According to section 60 of this Act, "where the buyer repudiates the contract before the date of delivery, the seller may either treat the contract as continue and wait till the date of delivery or he may treat the contract as rescinded and sue for damage for the breach."

(iii) ***Suit for interest:*** when in a contract of sale, the seller tenders delivery of goods to the buyer and the buyer wrongfully refuses or neglect to accept and pay the price, the seller has right to claim reasonable interest on the amount of the price. The interest may be calculated from the date of tender of delivery of goods or from the date on which the price was payable. In the absence of specific agreement, the court may award interest at such rate as it think reasonable and fit on the amount of the price.

RIGHTS OF THE BUYER

In case, the seller makes breach of contract, the buyer will be considered as an aggrieved party. He has the following rights against the seller:

(i) Suit for Damage: Section 57

Where the buyer is ready and willing to accept delivery of goods, but the seller wrongfully refuses or neglects it, the buyer may sue upon the seller to claim damages for non-delivery of the goods.

(ii) Suit for Specific Performance: Section 58

In a contract of sale of specific goods, if the seller fails to deliver the goods, the buyer may file a suit for specific performance. But the court will pass such order only in those cases where the damages are not a suitable remedy as such that the goods to be supplied were of unique nature etc.

Example: A made a contract of sale for selling rare piece of painting to B for Rs. 10,000. Later on A refused to deliver that painting piece. On account of breach of contract, the loss suffered by B can not be measured in terms of money, thus damage is not a adequate remedy. B can claim order of specific performance.

(iii) Suit for Breach of Warranty: Section 59

In case the seller makes breach of warranty, or the buyer treats breach of condition as a breach of warranty, the buyer can claim damage for the loss suffered by him. However, in case of breach of warranty, the buyer has no right to reject the goods.

(iv) Repudiation of a Contract: Section 60

Where the seller repudiates the contract before the date of delivery, the buyer may either treat the contract as continue and wait till the date of delivery or he may treat the contract as rescinded and can proceed against the seller for the damages.

(v) Suit for Recovery of the Price with Interest Section 61

In case, the buyer has paid the price to the seller, on due and date, the seller fails to deliver the goods. The buyer has right to file a suit for the recovery of the price along with interest on the amount of price. The interest will be calculated from the date on which the price was paid by the buyer.

AUCTION SALE

One of the very popular way of selling the goods is to sell them by auction. A sale by auction is a public sale, where upon, people are invited to compete for the purchase of property by successive offers of higher amount. The offer of the price is known as 'bid' and the person offering the price is known as 'bidder'.

Auction sale may be arranged either by the seller himself or he may appoint some one as 'auctioneer' to sell the goods on his behalf. The auctioneer will act as an agent on behalf of the owner.

In order to sell the goods in auction, the auctioneer makes wide publicity of time, date and place of the sale. The prospective bidders are provided an opportunity to inspect the goods. Since the auctioneer invites the public to make an offer, he is not bound to sell the goods at time, date and place as mentioned in the advertisement. In case, the auctioneer postpones the sale, prospective bidders have no right to sue upon him.

According to the usual practice, auction sale programe is duly advertised and printed catalogue of the goods along with the conditions of sale are circulated among the prospective bidders. At appointed time and place the auctioneer invites, bidder to offer the price. He announces the acceptance of the last bid by a tap with his hammer or by any other approved method.

Rules regarding Auction Sale

(i) Where the goods are put up for sale in lots, each lot is prima facie deemed to be subject matter of a separate contract of sale.

(ii) The sale is complete when the auctioneer announces its completion by fall of the hammer or by any other approved method.

(iii) As soon as the auctioneer announces the completion of sale, property in goods passes immediately to the buyer.

(iv) Before the completion of sale, any bidder may withdraw his offer.

(v) A right to bid may be reserved expressly either by the seller or on his behalf by any person. It may be done for protecting the interest of the seller.

(vi) It is very usual to announce a 'reserve price' by the auctioneer. It is a price below which, the auctioneer will not sell.

(vii) In case the seller makes use of pretended bidding to raise the price, the sale is voidable at the option of the buyer.

(viii) Damping is an unlawful act, because it intends to discourage the bidders from bidding. This is done by printing out defects in the goods or scaring prospective bidders away so that they may not participate in the auction sale.

(ix) The seller can appoint only one 'puffer'. He is the person employed by the seller for the purpose of raising the price but he has no intention to buy the goods.

Review Questions

1. Define 'unpaid seller'. What are his rights?
2. Explain the rights of an unpaid seller (a) as against the goods (b) as against the buyer.
3. 'Right of stoppage in transit is an extension of right of lien'. Comment.
4. Distinguish between right of lien and right of stoppage of goods in transit.
5. Discuss the situation when the transit ends.
6. Explain the right to resell the goods by unpaid seller and discuss the situations under which resale in valid.
7. Explain the effects of sub-sale or pledge on unpaid seller's right of lien and stoppage in transit.
8. What is auction sale? Discuss various rules regarding auction sale.
9. Comment on the following:
   (a) Seller becomes an unpaid seller only on account of non-payment of the price.
   (b) Right of lien is possessory in nature.

Practical Problems

1. A sold a machine part to B without any stipulation to deliver the goods until the price is paid. Advise A.
2. Ram sells the goods to Shyam. Shyam makes payment of the price by cheque. Before Shyam could obtain delivery of goods, his cheque is dishonored by the bank. Ram therefore refuses to deliver the goods until payment is made. Is Ram's action Justified. (Yes)
3. Sohan sells one hundred bags of cement to Mohan of calcutta. He sends the goods by railways. The railway receipt duly made in favour of Mohan was sent to him. On the arrival of the goods in calcutta, Mohan asked the railways to carry them to Durgapur. In the meantime Mohan became insolvent. Sohan asks railways to stop the goods. Will he succeed? (No)

4. A sells the goods to B worth Rs. 5000 on credit. The goods were consigned to him by rail. B assigns railway receipt to C to borrow Rs. 2000 on the security of that receipt. Before the goods reach the appointed destination, B becomes insolvent. A gives notice to stop the goods in transit, but C claims them. Will A succeed in stopping the goods. (Yes, subject to condition of assignment)
5. Roshan sells 50 bags of wheat to Rajesh. The wheat bags are lying in the godown of Roshan. It is agreed that Rajesh shall get one month's credit for payment. Rajesh allowed wheat bags to remain in the godown of Roshan. Before the expiry of one months credit Rajesh becomes insolvent. Can Roshan refuse to deliver the wheat to the official assignee? (Yes).
6. Amar of Delhi places an order with Basant of Bombay to deliver some goods to him at Delhi. Basant sent goods by railways. When the goods reach Delhi, the railway official informs Amar that goods are lying at station, at the risk of Amar. Meanwhile Amar becomes insolvent. Can Basant stop the goods in transit. (No).
7. A participated in an auction sale and made a bid of Rs. 1000 for a second hand typewriter. But he withdraws his bid, before the fall of hammer. As per the condition of auction sale which, A knows, that bidding once made will not allow to be withdrawn. The auctioneer sued upon A for Rs. 1000 as his being the highest bid. Examine the case and advise A.
8. K sold some furniture to M by an auction. M, gave a cheque for the price and took the delivery of that furniture. One of the clause of the agreement was that property in goods will not pass to the buyer until the cheque was honoured. M sold the furniture to N. K, wants to take back the furniture from N. Will he succeed? Advise him.
9. Ashok made a bid for a steel almirah in an auction sale but withdrew the bid before the fall of hammer. Can Ashok is entitled to do it? (Yes)
10. A railway company is in possession of the goods as a carrier, when an unpaid seller gives notice of stoppage in transit. The buyer of the goods already owes some money to the railway coy. Can the railway company exercise right of lien over the goods in violation of the right of stoppage in transit of the seller. (No).

■■■

Part **3**

Limited Liability Act, 2008

Chapter **19**

Introduction and Preliminary

Learning Objectives

- Examine the rationale of LLP.
- Develop conceptual clarity about LLP.
- Remember salient feature of LLP Act.
- Develop clarity about various terms given in the LLP Act.

INTRODUCTION

There are several forms of business organisation. Among these, the form of partnership and Joint Stock Company have been very popular. In spite of having many inadequacies and serious drawbacks these two forms have remained in prominence till today.

In the form of partnership unlimited liability of partners has been considered as serious drawback. It is because for the act of managing partner or partners, the private property of all partners may be at risk for paying out debts in excess of assets of the partnership firm. Similarly in the form of Joint stock company though the liability of the members is limited, but due to an excessive interference of the law has made this form more rigid and unsuitable for the needs of modern business.

It is therefore, to boost the economic development of the country and to encourage enterpreneurship in modern business, need to introduce more suitable form of organisation was well felt. As a result of it, new form of partnership named as Limited Liability Partnership (LLP) has been introduced.

LLP is a body corporate brought into existence by fulfilling prescribed legal formalities given in the LLP Act, 2008. It has separate legal existence which is perpetual in nature. It can be formed with at least two designated partners, one of them must be resident in India and they have limited liability.

For the formation and regulation of LLP and to deal with matters connected therewith Limited Liability Partnership Act, 2008 (6 of 2009) has been enacted. It has received assent of the President of India on 7-1-2009 and published in the Gazettee of India Ext. Pt II S 1, dated 9-1-2009.

This Act has 81 Sections, 4 Schedules and 41 Rules (LLP Rules 2009).

Limited Liability Act, 2008 has been enacted with the following statement of objects and reasons.

Statement of objects and Reasons :

1. **Statement of Objects and Reasons:** With the growth of the Indian economy, the role played by its entrepreneurs as well as its technical and professional manpower has been acknowledged internationally. It is felt opportune that entrepreneurship, knowledge and risk capital combine to provide a further impetus to India's economic growth. In this background, a need has been felt for a new corporate form that would provide an alternative to the traditional partnership, with unlimited personal liability on the one hand, and the statute-based governance structure of the limited liability company on the other, in order to enable professional expertise and entrepreneurial initiative to combine, organise and operate in flexible, innovative and efficient manner.
2. **The Limited Liability Partnership (LLP)** is viewed as an alternative corporate business vehicle that provides the benefits of limited liability but allows its members the flexibility of organising their internal structure as a partnership based on a mutually arrived agreement. The LLP form would enable entrepreneurs, professionals and enterprises providing services of any kind or engaged in scientific and technical disciplines, to form commercially efficient vehicles suited to their requirements. Owing to flexibility in its structure and operation, the LLP would also be a suitable vehicle for small enterprises and for investment by venture capital.
3. Keeping in mind the need of the day, the Government had introduced the Limited Liability Partnership Bill, 2006 in the Rajya Sabha on the 15th December, 2006. It was referred to the Department Related

Parliamentary Standing Committee on Finance for examination and report. The Hon'ble Committee presented its 58th Report to the Lok Sabha on 27th November, 2007 and also laid the said Report in the Rajya Sabha on the same day. The Hon'ble Committee made several recommendations which were examined and considered by the Government. Most of the recommendations made by the Hon'ble Committee have been accepted by the Government. Based on the recommendations of the Hon'ble Committee, extensive changes were found to be necessary in the Bill. Hence, it is proposed to withdraw the Limited Liability Partnership Bill, 2006 and introduce a fresh Bill incorporating the changes.

Salient Features of LLP Act, 2008

The salient features of the Act are as follows :

1. LLP shall be a body corporate (association of two or more persons) brought in to existence by fulfilling legal formaties given in the Act. for carrying on lawful business with a profit motive. It has separate legal existence and perpetual succession.
2. The rights and duties of partners of LLP shall be defined and governed by a agreement between partners or LLP and partners. In the absence of any such agreement the provisions of this Act (Schedule 1) will apply.
3. The liability of LLP firm shall be limited to the full extent of its assets in business. But the liability of the partners shall be limited to the extent of their agreed contribution.

   No partner would be liable for the independent and unauthorised actions of other partners and for their misconduct. The liability of LLP and partners who have acted with intent to defraud creditors or for any fraudulent purpose shall be unlimited for all or any of the debt or other liability of the LLP.
4. Every LLP has to have at least two individuals as Designated Partners and of whom at least one shall be resident in India. The duties and obligations of Designated partners shall be defined and provided by the law.
5. Every LLP shall be under legal obligation to maintain Annual accounts which reflect true and fair view of its state of affairs. A statement of audited accounts and solvency shall be filed by every LLP with the Registrar every year. The Central Government may exempt any class of LLP from the requirement of auditing.

6. The Central Government is empowered for making an appointment of competent person as inspector for investigating the affairs of any LLP.
7. The compromise or arrangement including merger and amalgamation of LLP shall be made in accordance with the provisions of this Act.
8. A firm, private company or an unlisted public company would be allowed to be converted in to LLP. According to the provisions of this Act, from the date of registration of LLP, all assets including tangible and intangible, movable or immovable, in the firm or company along with the entire undertaking shall be transferred to LLP and a firm or company shall be deemed to be dissolved.
9. The LLP may be wound up either voluntarily or by the Tribunal to be established under the Company Act, 1956. Till the Tribunal is established, the power to dissolve LLP had been given to the High Court.
10. The Central Government is empowered to apply the provisions of Company Act, 1956 on LLP by making notification.
11. The Indian Partnership Act, 1932 shall not be applicable on LLPs.

PRELIMINARY

Short Title, Extent and Commencement of the Act (Sec-1). This Act may be called, The Limited Liability Partnership Act, 2008. It extends to the whole of India. It shall come in to force on such date, specified by the Central Government through notification in the Official Gazette. However different dates may be appointed for different provisions of this Act to be applied on.

Definitions – (Sect – 2)

(*a*) **"Address"**, of a partner of Limited Liability partnership means —

(*i*) if he is an individual, his usual residential address; and

(*ii*) if a body corporate, the address of its registered office.

(*b*) **"Advocate"** means an advocate as defined in the Advocate Act, 1961.

(*c*) **"Appellate Tribunal"**, means the National Company Law Appellate Tribunal, constituted under the provisions of the Company Act, 1956.

(*d*) **"Body Corporate"** means a company as defined in section 3 of the Company Act, 1956 and includes

(*i*) LLP registered under this Act.

(*ii*) LLP incorporated outside India.

(*iii*) Company incorporated outside India.

It does not include corporation sole, cooperative society.

(*e*) **"Business"** includes every trade, profession, service and occupation.

(*f*) **"Chartered Accountant"** means a Chartered accountant as defined in the Chartered Account Act, 1949 who has obtained a certificate of practice under the relevant provisions of this Act.

(*g*) **"Company Secretary"** means a company secretary as defined in the company Secretaries Act, 1980 and who has obtained a certificate of practice under the provisions of this Act.

(*h*) **"Cost Accountant"** means a cost accountant as defined in the cost and works Accountant Act, 1959 and who has obtained certificate of practice under the provisions of this Act.

(*i*) **"Designated Partner"** means any partner designated as such under the provisions of LLP Act.

(*j*) **"Court"** means the court having Juridication as per the provisions of LLP Act with respect to any offence under this act.

(*k*) **"Entity"** means any body corporate and includes a firm setup under Indian partnership Act 1932.

(*l*) **"Financial Year"** in relation to LLP, means the period from 1st day of April of a year to the 31st day of March of the following year.

(*m*) **"Foreign Limited Liability Partnership"** means a limited liability partnership formed incorporated or registered outside India, which establishes place of business within India.

(*n*) **"Limited Liability Partnership,"** means a partnership formed and registered under this Act.

(*o*) **"Limited Liability Partnership Agreement"** means any written agreement between the partners of limited liability partnership and its partners which determines the mutual rights and duties of partners and their rights and duties in relation to that limited liability partnership.

(*p*) **"Name"** in relation to a partner of a limited liability partnership means—

(*a*) in case of an individual, his forename, middle name and surname;

(*b*) in case of body corporate, its registered name.

(*q*) **"Partner"**, in relation to limited liability partnership, means any person who becomes a partner in accordance with an agreement of limited liability partnership.

(*r*) **"Prescribed"** means prescribed by rules made under this Act.

(*s*) **"Registrar"** means a Registrar or an additional, a joint, a deputy or an assistant Registrar having the duty of registering companies under the Companies Act, 1956.

(*t*) **"Schedule"** means schedule to this Act.

(*u*) **"Tribunal"**, means the National Company Law Tribunal constituted under the provision of Companies Act, 1956.

In addition, words and expression used but not defined in this Act will carry the meaning assigned to them in the Companies Act, 1956.

Review Questions

1. What do you mean by limited liability partnership how does it differ from traditional partnership?
2. Describe the statement of objects and reason of LLP Act, 2008.
3. Explain the need for enacting LLP Act, 2008.
4. Discuss the salient features of limited liability partnership Act.
5. Write notes on: (*a*) Address (*b*) Body Corporate (*c*) Foreign limited liability partnership. (*d*) Tribunal (*e*) Limited liability partnership agreement.

■■■

Chapter **20**

Nature of Limited Liability Partnership

Learning Objectives

- Understand basic nature of LLP.
- Distinguish between LLP and traditional partnership.
- Examine legal position of Designated Partner.

INTRODUCTION

Limited liability partnership is an alternative form of business organisation. It has distinct features of limited liability of partners, separate legal existence and perpetual succession of like a company. This form of organisation can profitably be used even for conducting a business at small scale. It provides perfect combination of professional expertise, flexibility of structure and operation and risk taking capability of partners.

The basic nature of limited liability partnership can be well understood on the basis of following special features attached to it.

1. **Limited liability partnership is a body corporate (Section 3):** A limited liability partnership is a body corporate. It is brought into existence by fulfilling legal formalities prescribed under this Act. Once it is formed and incorporate it acquires legal entity which is separate from that of its partners. Any change in the partners shall not affect the existence, rights and liabilities of the limited liability partnership. As a result, it enjoys perpetual succession.

2. **Non-applicability of Indian Partnership Act, 1932 (Section 4):** Unless and until it is provided so, the provisions of Indian partnership Act, 1932 shall not apply to limited liability partnership.
3. **Partners (Section 5):** This section provides that any individual or a body corporate may be a partners in a limited liability partnership. It is also provides that an individual shall not be capable of becoming a partner in LLP if:
   (*a*) he has been found to be of unsound mind by a competent court.
   (*b*) he is an undischarged insolvent. It means he has not obtained order of discharge, on the completion of insolvency proceedings.
   (*c*) he has applied to be adjudicated as as insolvent and his application is pending
4. **Minimum number of partners (Section 6):** According to this section, every limited liability partnership shall have at least two partners. If at any time the number of partners of limited liability partnership is reduced below two and the business is carried on for more than 6 months, the person who is the only partner during that period having knowledge of such situation shall be liable personally for the obligations of LLP incurred during that period.
5. **Designated partners (Section 7):** Every limited liability partnership must have at least two designated partners who are individuals and at least one of them shall be resident in India.

   The above section further provides that in case of limited liability partnership in which all the partners are bodies corporate or one or more partners are individuals and bodies corporate, so at least two individuals who are partners of such LLP or nominees of such bodies corporate shall act as designated partners.

   According to the explanation, given for the purpose of the above section, the term 'resident in India' means a person who has stayed in India for a period of not less than one hundred and eighty two days during the immediately preceding one year.

   According to subsection (2) if the incorporation document specifies that who are to be designated partners on incorporation or such document states that each of the partners is to be designated partner from time to time, every such person shall be a designated partner.

   Any partner may become designated partner by and in accordance with LLP agreement and a partner may also cease to be a designated partner in accordance with that agreement.

   For becoming designated partner in limited liability partnership, an individual shall have to give his consent to act as designated partner in the form and manner as may be prescribed by the rules. With in 30 days of such appointment, the Registrar has to be informed of the particulars of individuals who have consented to act as designated partners.

An individual who is eligible to be designated partner shall satisfy prescribed conditions and requirements.

According to LLP Rule 9(1) 2009, a person shall not be capable of being appointed as designated partner of LLP if he —

(*a*) has, at any time with in preceding 5 years been adjudged insolvent; or

(*b*) has suspended, with in preceding 5 years payment to his creditors or has not made composition with them, or

(*c*) has been convicted by the court for any offence involving moral turpitude and has been imprisoned for not less than 6 months; or

(*d*) has been convicted by the court for an offence involving section 30 of this Act. The Central Government is empowered to remove the disqualification incurrent by a person by making notification in 'Official Gazette.'

Every designated partner of a limited liability partnership shall obtain Designated Partner Identification Number (DPIN) from the Central Government. For this purpose, the relevant provisions of companies Act, 1956 applicable on director's identification number will apply.

6. **Liabilities of designated partners (Section 8):** Unless expressly provided otherwise in this Act every designated partner shall be liable

(*a*) for the doing of all acts, matters and things which are required to be done by limited liability partnership for complying with the provisions of this act which includes filing of document, returns statements and the like report pursuant to the provisions of this Act and also as may specified in LLP agreement.

(*b*) to all penalties which are imposed on limited liability partnership for the contravention of those provisions of this Act.

7. **Changes in designated partners (Section 9):** According to this section, in case of vacancy of designated partner, the limited liability partnership has to appoint designated partner with in 30 days of a vacancy arising for any reason. In respect of each such new designated partner the provisions of section 7(4) and (5) shall apply.

In case, no designated partner is appointed or if at any time, there is only one designated partner, each partner of the LLP shall be deemed to be a designated partner.

8. **Punishment for not complying the provisions of this Act (Section 10):** This section provides punishment for LLP and its partners for contravention of section 7, 8 and 9. According to this section, if LLP fails to appoint designated partners under section 7 and subsection (1) of

this Act, then the LLP and its every partners shall be punishable with a minimum fine of ten thousand rupees which may extend to five lakh rupees.

In similar way if the LLP does not meet conditions and requirement prescribed for the appointment of designated partner in this Act and does not comply with other requirements regarding designated partners given under section 8 and 9, then the LLP and its every partner shall be punishable with a minimum fine of ten thousand rupees which may extend to one lakh rupees.

Review Questions

1. Discuss the nature of limited liability partnership given in this Act.
2. Explain the legal position, liability and change in the designated partners.

■■■

Chapter **21**

Incorporation of Limited Liability Partnership

Learning Objectives

- Understand how LLP is formed.
- Remember the contents of incorporation document.
- Examine incorporation by registration and effect of registration.
- Examine provisions regarding name, its registration and change in name.

INTRODUCTION

To get the status of body corporate and legal existence, the LLP has to be registered and incorporated under this Act. For incorporating the LLP the following legal formalities prescribed in this Act are to be fulfilled.

Incorporation Document (Section 11) Sub sect.(1) According to this rection for a limited laibility partnership to be incorporated the following legal requirements regarding incorporation document are to be fulfilled.

(*a*) two or more persons those who are intended and associated for carrying an lawful business with profit motive shall subscribe their names to a incorporation document.

(*b*) the incorporation document shall be filed in the manner and with such fees as may be prescribed with the Registrar of the state in which registered office of LLP is to be situated.

(*c*) Along with incorporation document the statement in prescribed form either by Advocate, or a company Secretary or Chartered Accountant or a Cost Accountant who is engaged in the formation of LLP or by any one who subscribed his name to the incorporation document declaring that rules regarding incorporation given in this Act have been complied with, will also be filed with the Registrar.

Contents of incorporation Document: According to subsection (2) of section 11, the incorporation document must contain the following information about LLP;

(*a*) the incorporation document must be in the form as prescribed under this Act.

(*b*) it must contain name of limited liability partnership.

(*c*) it must state the proposed business of LLP.

(*d*) it must state address of registered office of LLP.

(*e*) it has to state the names and addresses of all persons who are to be partners on incorporation.

(*f*) it must state names and addresses of a person who are to be designated partners.

(*g*) it must contain such other information concerning to the proposed limited liability partnership as may be prescribed under this Act.

In addition to contents to be provided in the incorporation document and the form and manner in which it shall be filed with the Registrar the above clause also makes provision of penalty.

According to subsection (3) of Section 11 of this Act, if a person makes a statement specified in subsection (1) of section 11 which he knows to be false or does not believe to be true, he is punishable with imprisonment for a term which may extend to two years and fine with a minimum of ten thousand rupees which may extend to five lakh rupees.

Incorporation by Registration (Section 12)

This section deals with the registration of incorporation documents and issue of certificate of incorporation of the limited liability partnership by the Registrar.

According to this section, when the requirement for incorporation of LLP prescribed under section 11 this Act are fulfilled, the Registrar has to retain incorporation documents get it registered with in 14 days and issue a certificate that the LLP is incorporated by the name specified in the documents.

The Registrar may accept the statement under section 11 as sufficient evidence that the requirement of registration has been complied with.

The certificate issued by the Registrar shall be a conclusive evidence that the limited liability partnership is incorporated by the name specified on the certificate.

Registered Office of LLP and Change in it (Section 13)

This section deals with registered office of LLP, change in it and the manner in which all communications and notices will be served to LLP and its partners.

According to this section, every LLP must have a registered office, and all communications and notices may be addressed and received in the registered office.

A document may be served on LLP or a partner or designated partners of LLP by sending it by post under certificate of posting or by registered post or in any other manner as may be prescribed. Such service may be made either in the address of registered office or at any other place and manner specifically declared by limited liability partnership.

The LLP may change the place of its registered office. The notice of such change must be filed with the Registrar in the prescribed form and manner. The change in the address of registered office will become effective from the date of filing it.

In case the limited liability partnership does not comply with the above section the LLP and its every partner shall be punishable with fine minimum of two thousand rupees which may extend twenty five thousand rupees.

Effect of Registration (Section 14)

Once the limited liability partnership gets registered, it acquires legal existent which is separate from its partners and also gets the following rights:

(*a*) it can file suit in the court of law and can also be sued upon.

(*b*) it can acquire, own, hold, develop or dispose of movable, immovable, tangible or intangible properties.

(*c*) it can have its common seal if it decides so.

(*d*) it can do and suffer such acts and things as other bodies corporate lawfully do and suffer.

Name (Section 15)

This section deals with the name of limited liability partnership and put an obligation on the LLP for having particular name which is not undesirable or resembling with the name of other bodies corporate.

According to this section, every limited liability partnership must have either the word 'limited liability partnership' or LLP as the last word of its name.

The limited liability partnership will not be allowed to get registered by a name which in the opinion of the Central Government is undesirable or identical or resembling to that of other partnership firms bodies corporate or registered trade mark of any other person for registration under the trade marks Act, 1999.

Reservation of Name (Section 16)

This section deals with an application for reserving proposed name of LLP or the name which LLP wants to have after change of its existing name.

According to this section, a person may file an application with the Registrar for the reservation of the name mentioned in the application as the name of proposed LLP or the name to which a LLP proposed to change its name.

On receipt of such application and payment of prescribed fees, the Registrar, if he is satisfied, may reserve the name for a period of three months from the date of intimation by the Registrar.

An application for the reservation of the name is to be made in such form and manner and accompanied by such fees as may be prescribed by this Act.

The Central Government is empowered to make rules regarding form, manner and fees payable on such application which may be followed by the Registrar.

Change of Name of LLP (Section 17)

According to this section, if the limited liability partnership has been registered with a name which is undesirable or closely resembling with the name of other LLP or bodies corporate or other names as likely to be mistaken for it, the Central Government is empowered to give direction to LLP for rectifying its name.

In case the LLP fails to comply with the directions of the Central Government with in three months it shall be liable for a fine of not less than ten thousand rupees which may extend to five lakh rupee.

The designated partner will also be liable to a fine minimum of ten thousand rupees which may extend to one lakh rupee.

Application for Direction to Change Name in Certain Circumstances (Section 18)

According to this section, any entity which already has a name similar to the name of limited liability partnership which has been incorporated subsequently after that entity; such entity may apply to the Registrar to give direction to limited liability partnership on the ground specified under section 17 of this Act, to change its name.

The Registrar shall consider any application to give direction to a limited liability partnership provided the Registrar receives an application with in 24 months from the date of registration of the limited liability partnership under that name.

Change of Registered Name (Section 19)

Any limited liability partnership may change its name with which it has been registered by filing a notice of such change with the Registrar.

A notice of such change is to be filed in such a form and manner and on payment of fees as may be prescribed by this Act.

Penalty for Improper use of words limited liability partnership or LLP (Section 20)

According to this section, if any person carries on business and uses the word limited liability partnership or LLP without getting registered as LLP under this Act, he shall be punished with a minimum fine of fifty thousand rupees which may extend to five lakh rupees.

Publication of Name and Limited Liability (Section 21)

According to this section, every limited liability partnership will ensure that its invoices, official correspondence and publications bear on it, the name, address of registered office, registration number and the statement that it is registered with limited liability.

In case the limited liability partnership does not comply with this provision, it shall be punishable with fine minimum of two thousand rupees which may extend to twenty five thousand rupees.

Review Questions

1. Discuss the procedure of getting a group of people incorporated as limited liability partnership.
2. Explain the contents of incorporation document.
3. Discuss the effect of registration of LLP.
4. Explain the provisions regarding change of name of LLP.
5. Discuss the legal provisions of this Act regarding the name of LLP and its reservation.
6. Discuss the procedure of changing registered office of LLP.

■■■

Chapter **22**

Partner's Relations and Extent and Limitation of Liability of LLP and Partners

Learning Objectives

- Know that how a person becomes partner in LLP.
- Get clarity about partner relationship.
- Examine provisions regarding cessation of partner.
- Remember the extent of partners liability.

INTRODUCTION

A limited liability partnership is an upgraded and improved version of traditional partnership. Basically it is also an association of two or more persons of doing some business with profit motive. Thus, those who form such association and get it registered under this Act are known as partners.

They have mutual rights and duties towards each other and towards limited liability partnership. Generally these rights and duties are determined and governed by LLP agreement made by the partners. In absence of such agreement, their mutual rights and duties shall be determined by the rules as set out in the 'First Schedule' of this Act.

This chapter deals with an eligibility of partners, their relationship, when they cease to be a partner and registration of change in partners.

Eligibility to be a Partner (Section 22)

According to this section, the persons who have subscribed their names to the incorporation documents shall be treated as its partners on the incorporation and registration of limited liability partnership.

In addition to it, any other person may become a partner of the limited liability partnership by and in accordance with the limited liability partnership agreement.

Relationship of Partners (Section 23)

According to this section, mutual rights and duties of a partners of limited liability partnership and mutual rights and duties of LLP and its partners shall be determined by an agreement entered into between the partners or between LLP and its partners. As stated earlier in absence of such agreement rules given in the 'First Schedule' of this Act will apply.

The limited liability partnership agreement and any change in it shall be filed with the Registrar in such a form, manner and fees payable as may be prescribed. The Central Government is empowered to prescribed rules regarding form, manner and fees payable.

An agreement made in writing before the incorporation of limited liability partnership, between the persons subscribing their names to incorporation document may impose an obligation or LLP, provided such agreement is ratified by all partners after the incorporation of limited liability partnership.

In the absence of agreement as to any matter, mutual sights and duties of partners and mutual rights and duties of LLP and its partners shall be determined by the provisions relating to that matter as set out in the 'First Schedule' of this Act.

Cessation of Partnership Interest (Section 24)

This section states that a person may cease to be a partner of limited liability partnership in accordance with an agreement with the other partners.

In the absence of an agreement he may cease to be a partner by giving notice in writing to the other partners at least thirty days before of his intention to resign as partner.

A person ceases to be a partner of limited liability partnership under the following situation:

(*a*) a death of a person or dissolution of limited liability partnership.

(*b*) if he becomes of unsound mind.

(*c*) if he has applied to be adjudged as an insolvent or has been declared as an insolvent.

Where a person ceases to be a partner of limited liability partnership, he will be referred as a 'former partner'. In relation to any person, who is dealing with limited liability partnership the 'former partner' will be considered as a partner of LLP unless the person who is dealing has a notice that the former partner has ceased to be a partner of LLP or notice of this fact has been delivered to the Registrar.

In case a person ceases to be a partner of limited liability partnership, he will not automatically be discharged from his obligation to LLP or to the other partners or to any other person which he has incurred while being a partner.

Unless otherwise provided in LLP agreement the former partner or a person who is legally entitled to his share on the death or insolvency of the former partner is entitled to receive from limited liability partnership —

(*a*) an amount equal to the capital contribution made by the former partner to limited liability partnership.

(*b*) his right to share in the accumulated profits of limited liability partnership after deduction of accumulated losses determined at the date when former partner ceases to be a partner.

A former partner on a person entitled to his share on his death or insolvency shall not have any right to interfere in the management of limited liability partnership.

Registration of Change in Partners (Section 25)

According to this section, every partner shall inform the limited liability partnership of any change in his name or address within a period of 15 days of such change.

A limited liability partnership shall file a notice with the Registrar with in thirty days from the date he ceases to be a partner or he makes any change in his name or address.

A notice filed with the Registrar must be signed by designated partner of limited liability partnership and must be in such form and accompanied by such fees as may be prescribed.

In case of incoming partner, statement made by him must contain his consent to be a partner and must be duty signed by him and authenticated in a manner as may be prescribed.

Where a limited liability partnership fails to file a notice with registrar regarding his being ceases to be a partner or about change in his name and address, the LLP and every designated partner of it shall be punishable with a minimum fine of two thousand rupees which may extend to twenty five thousand rupees.

Where a partner fails to inform limited liability partnership about the change in his name and address with in prescribed time period, he shall be punishable with a minimum fine of two thousand rupees which may extend to twenty five thousand rupees.

Any person ceases to be a partner of limited liability partnership may himself file notice with the Registrar if he has reasonable cause to believe that limited liability partnership may not file such notice. The Registrar shall obtain confirmation from limited liability partnership to this effect. In case no confirmation is given by LLP the Registrar shall register the notice made by a person ceasing to be a partner.

Extent and limitation of liability of limited liability partnership and partners:

Partner as Agent (Section 26)

This section states that every partner of limited liability partnership, for the purpose of business is the agent of limited liability partnership but not of other partners of LLP.

Extent of Liability of LLP (Section 27)

The limited liability partnership shall not be bound by any act done by a partner for which he had no authority and the person with whom he is dealing also knows that partner has no authority for doing such act.

The limited liability partnership will be liable in case the partner of LLP becomes liable to any person as a result of warongful act or omission on the part of such person in the course of business of limited liability partnership or with its authority.

An obligation of limited liability partnership arising out of a contract or otherwise will be solely the obligation of limited liability partnership.

The liabilities of limited liability partnership shall be met or paid out of the properties of the limited liability partnership.

Extent of Liability of Partner (Section 28)

According to this section, partner of LLP is not personally liable directly or indirectly for an obligation of limited liability partnership whether arising out of a contract or otherwise.

A partner will be personally liable for his own wrongful act or omission but shall not be personally liable for the wrongful act or omission of any other partner of limited liability partnership.

Holding Out (Section 29)

According to this section, any person who represents himself to be a partner of limited liability partnership either by the words of mouth or in writing or by his conduct will be liable to such other person who on the faith of such representation gives credit to the limited liability partnership. It is immaterial whether the person so representing or represented to be a partner does or does not know that the representation has induced the other person to give credit to limited liability partnership. The limited liability partnership also becomes liable to the extent of credit received or benefit derived by it on such representation.

In case the partner dies, but the business is continued in the name of same limited liability partnership, the continued use of that name or the name of deceased partner shall not make his legal representation or his estate liable for any act of LLP done after the death of partner.

Unlimited Liability in Case of Fraud (Section 30)

This section imposes unlimited liability on the limited liability partnership and its partners. According to this section, the limited liability partnership and its partners will have unlimited liability for those acts which they are intended to carry out to defraud creditors or any other person or do such acts for fraudulent purpose. For all such acts done by the partner, the limited liability partnership is liable to the same extent as the partner unless it is established by the LLP that such act was done without a knowledge or authority of limited liability partnership.

Where any business is carried on with an intent to defraud creditors or for other fraudutent purpose knowingly, the persons carrying on business in that manner are punishable with imprisonment extending to two years and minimum fine of fifty thousand rupees which may extend to five lakh rupee.

When the limited liability partnership, or any of its partner, designated partner or employee has conducted the affairs of LLP in a fraudulent manner. Then in addition to any criminal liability under any law being in force, such partner, designated partner or employee shall be liable to pay compensation to any person who has suffered any loss or damage due to such conduct.

But limited liability partnership shall not be liable if the partner, designated partner or the employee has acted fraudulently without knowledge of LLP.

Whistle Blowing (Section 31)

The court of Tribunal may reduce or waive any penalty leviable against any partner or employee of limited liability partnership if it is satisfied that —

(*a*) such partner or employee of a limited liability partnership has provided useful information during investigation of such limited liability partnership; or

(*b*) when any information given by any partner or employee leads to limited liability partnership or any partner or employee of such LLP being convicted under this Act or under any other Act.

No such partner or employee of any limited liability partnership or employee of any limited liability partnership will be discharged denoted, suspended, threatened, harassed or in any other manner discriminated against the term and condition of LLP agreement or employment simply because he has provided information to the court or Tribunal.

Review Questions

1. When a partner of limited liability partnership may cease to be a partner? Discuss his rights and obligations.
2. Explain the legal provisions regarding registration of change in the name and address of the partner.
3. Discuss the extent of liability of limited liability partnership and its partner.
4. Explain the liability of limited liability partnership and its partner in case of fraud.
5. Write notes on (*a*) Holding out partner (*b*) Whistle blowing (*c*) Relationship of partners.

■■■

Chapter **23**

Contribution and Financial Disclosure

Learning Objectives

- Get Clarity regarding the form and obligation of contribution.
- Examine liability of LLP for maintaining accounts and filing returns.

INTRODUCTION

Limited liability partnership is also a joint venture. The partners invest capital and make other contributions in the business of partnership. The first two section of this Act deal with form and obligation of a partner for making contribution. And remaining other sections of this Act prescribe the provisions to be followed by limited liability partnership for maintaining books and account and filing annual returns.

Form of Contribution (Section 32)

This section states that a contribution of a partner may consists of tangible, intangible, movable or immovable property or other benefits including money, promissary notes, agreement to contribute cash or property and contract of services performed or to be performed for the limited liability partnership.

The monetary value of contribution made by each partner shall be accounted for and disclosed in the accounts of limited liability partnership in the manner as may be prescribed.

Obligation to Contribute (Section 33)

This section seeks to provide that the obligation of a partner to contribute money or other property or other benefits or to perform services for a limited liability partnership shall be as per the LLP agreement.

A creditor of limited liability partnership who extends credit or otherwise acts in reliance on an obligation may enforce the original obligation against any partner of LLP without notice of any subsequent compromise between partners.

FINANCIAL DISCLOSURES

Maintenance of Books of Accounts other Records and Audit (Section 34)

The limited liability partnership has a obligation to maintain such proper books of account relating to its affairs for each year, as may be prescribed on cash basis or accrual basis and according to double entry system of accounting. These accounts will be maintained and kept at its registered office for such period as may be prescribed.

Every limited liability partnership has to prepare statement of Accounts and solvency with in a period of six months from the end of each financial year as on the last day of financial year in such form as may be prescribed. These statements must be signed by designated partners of limited liability partnership.

Every limited liability partnership has to file Statement of Accounts and Solvency with the Registrar every year with in prescribed time, in such form and manner and accompanied by such fees as may be prescribed.

The accounts of limited liability partnership shall be audited in accordance with such rules as may be prescribed. The Central Government is empowered to exempt any class of limited liability partnership from the requirement of this section.

It can be done by making notification to this effect in the 'Official Gazette'.

Any limited liability partnership which fails to comply the provisions of this section shall be punishable with a minimum fine of twenty-five thousand rupees (Rs. 25,000) which may extend to five lakh rupee (Rs. 5,00,000). In addition every designated partner of such LLP shall also be punishable with a minimum five of ten thousand rupees (Rs. 10,000) which may extend to one lakh rupee (Rs. 1,00,000).

Annual Return (Section 35)

Every limited liability partnership has to file an annual return duly authenticated, with the Registrar with in 60 days of closure of its financial year. It shall be filed in such form, manner and fees as may be prescribed.

Any limited liability partnership which fails to comply with the provisions of this section shall be punishable with a minimum fine of twenty-five thousand rupee (Rs. 25,000) which may extend to five lakh rupee (Rs. 5,00,000).

The designated partner of such defaulting LLP shall also be punishable with a minimum fine of ten thousand rupees (Rs. 10,000) which may extend to one lakh rupees (Rs. 1,00,000).

Inspection of Documents Kept by Registrar (Section 36)

According to this section, the incorporation document names of partners and changes in the names if any, statement of Account, solvency and annual return are filed by limited liability partnership with the Registrar. These documents are to be made available for inspection by any person in such a manner and a payment of such fees as may be prescribed. The Central Government is empowered to prescribe such rules regarding the manner and amount of fees for such inspection.

Penalty for False Statement (Section 37)

According to this section, if any person makes any statement knowing it to be false or false in any material particularly in any return, document statement or omits any material fact knowingly shall be punishable with

- Imprisonment for a term which may extend to two years, and
- Minimum fine of one lakh rupee (Rs. 1,00,000) which may extend to five lakh rupee (Rs. 5,00,000).

Power of Registrar to Obtain Information (Section 38)

This section empowers the Registrar to obtain such information which he considers necessary for the purpose of carrying out the provisions of this Act. The Registrar may call up on and seek such information from any person including present or former partners or designated partner or employee of a limited liability partnership. The Registrar may ask them to answer any question make any declaration or furnish any details or particulars in writing with in reasonable period of time.

The Registrar has got a power to summon any person referred above to appear before him or before an inspector or any public officer to answer the question or to make declaration or furnish details or particular as the case may be if:

(*a*) that person does not answer questions or make declaration or supply information with in this time given by the Registrar, or

(*b*) the Registrar is not satisfied with the reply or declaration or details supplied by that person.

Any person who fails to comply with any summon or a requisition of the Registrar under this section, with out, lawful excuse, shall be punishable with a minimum fine of two thousand rupees (Rs. 2,000) which may extend to twenty-five thousand rupees (Rs. 25,000).

Compounding of an Offence (Section 39)

This section empowers the Central Government for compounding any offence which is punishable with a fine only. The Central Government may compound the offence by collecting a sum not exceeding maximum fine prescribed for the offence from the person who is reasonably suspected of having committed the offence.

Destruction of Old Records (Section 40)

The Registrar may destroy any document filed or registered with him in physical or electronic form by the limited liability partnership. This section empowers the Central Government to prescribe the rules and the manner in which the Registrar may destroy documents filed or registered with him.

Enforcement of Duty to Make Returns etc. (Section 41)

If any limited liability partnership in default with:

(*a*) any provisions of this Act or of any other law which requires the filing of any return, account or other document or giving of any notice to him of any matter; or

(*b*) any request of the Registrar to amend or complete and resubmit any document or to submit fresh document;

and fails to make good, the default with in 14 days after the service of notice on the limited liability partnership. The Tribunal may on application made by the Registrar pass such an order directing that limited liability partnership or its designated partners or its partners to make good the default with in the period of time prescribed in the order.

Such order may also provide that the cost of application and any other incidental to it shall be borne by that limited liability partnership.

Assignment and Transfer of Partner's Rights (Section 42)

This section states that the rights of partners to a share of the profit and losses of the limited liability partnership and to receive distribution in accordance with LLP agreement are transferable either wholly or in part.

The transfer of any right by any partner does not automaticaly cause disassociation of the partner or dissolution or winding up of limited liability partnership.

Such transfer of rights does not by itself make transferee or assignee entitled to participate in the management or conduct of activities of limited liability partnership. Similarly he shall have no access to information concerning the transactions of LLP.

Review Questions

1. Discuss the legal provision of this Act regarding form of the obligation of contribution made by the partner of LLP.
2. Discuss the liability of LLP with regard to maintenance of account and filing of return with the Registrar.
3. Discuss the right of Registrar for obtaining information from LLP or its partner or employee.
4. How does the Registrar enforces LLP for making returns.

■■■

Chapter **24**

Investigation

Learning Objectives

- Understand, the concept of investigation.
- Examine the powers of inspector
- Remember the provisions regarding expenses of investigation.

INTRODUCTION

Under this Act, the Central Government has got a power to investigate in to the affairs and working of limited liability partnership. It can be done by appointing an inspector who enjoys powerful legal position to call for evidences, document, to seige documents related to the working of LLP. It is only on the basis of report submitted by the inspector the Central Government can prosecute that person who is found guilty of having committed an offence.

This chapter deals with an appointment of inspector, his power, submission of report and prosecution of the person for an offence.

Investigation of the Affairs of Limited Liability Partnership (Section 43)

According to this section, the Central Government is empowered to appoint one or more competent person as inspectors for investigating affairs of LLP and submit report in a manner as may be prescribed. The Central Government may appoint such inspector under the following situations:

(*a*) where the tribunal either 'suo motu' or on the basis of application made by at least (1/5) one fifth of the total number of partners of limited liability partnership of LLP should be investigated.

(*b*) any court, by order declares that the affairs of LLP ought to be investigated.

In addition to these, the appointment of inspectors may be made under the following situation:

(*a*) if at least one fifth (1/5) of the total number of partners of LLP make an application along with supporting documents and amount of security as may be prescribed.

(*b*) if the limited liability partnership makes an application along with supporting evidences and prescribed amount of security.

(*c*) if in the opinion of the Central Government the following circumstances exist.

(*i*) The business of limited liability partnership has been conducted with an intent to defraud its creditors partners or any other persons or for unlawful purpose or in a manner which is oppressive to some or any of its partners or LLP was formed for any fraudulent or unlawful purpose.

(*ii*) The affairs of limited liability partnership are not being conducted in accordance with the provisions of this Act.

(*iii*) On receipt of report of Registrar or any other investigating or regulatory authority which shows sufficient reasons that the affairs of the limited liability partnership ought to be investigated.

Application by Partners for Investigation (Section 44)

This section provides that an application made by at least one-fifth of total number of partners of LLP to the Tribunal for getting affairs of limited ability partnership investigated must be supported by required evidences. These evidences must be sufficient to show that the applicants have good reasons for requiring investigation.

The Central Government may ask the applicants before appointing the inspector to deposit the amount of security for the payment of cost of investigation.

Firm, Body Corporate or Association not be to Appointed as Inspector (Section 45)

According to this section, no firm, body corporate or association shall be appointed as an inspector.

Power of Inspectors (Section 46)

This section provides that if the inspector appointed by the Central Government to investigate affairs of LLP thinks it necessary, he can investigate into the affairs of:

(*a*) an entity associated with the LLP in the past or presently.

(*b*) present or former partners of LLP.

(*c*) present or former designated partner of LLP.

The inspector has also power to report on the affairs of the above parties that the results of his investigation are relevant to the investigation of limited liability partnership.

However before granting an approval to the inspector for investigating the affairs of other associated entities partners and designate partners, the Central Government shall provide them reasonable opportunity to show cause why such approval should not be accorded.

Production of Documents and Evidences (Section 47)

According to this section, the designated partners and partners of limited liability partnership are under obligation:

(*a*) to preserve and to produce before an inspector or any other person authorised by him.

(*b*) to furnish any information which is his duty under this section.

(*c*) to appear before the inspector personally when he is required to do so,

(*d*) to sign the notes of any examination conducted by the inspector.

He shall be punishable with a minimum fine of two thousand rupees (Rs. 2,000) which may extend to twenty five thousand rupees (Rs. 25,000) and with an further five of not less than fifty rupees(Rs. 50) which may extend to five hundred rupees (Rs. 500) for every day after the first day after which default continues.

The inspector is also empowered to make examination of the person on oath and to take down notes of such examination in writing duly signed by the person who was examined. The copy of such notes shall be given to that person and thereafter be used as an evidence by the inspector.

Seizure of Document by Inspector (Section 48)

This section empowers the inspector to seize books and papers related to limited liability partnership, or other entity or partner or designated partner of LLP. He can exercise this power provided, he has reasonable ground to believe that such books and papers may be destroyed mutilated, altered, falsified or secreted. For the seizure of accounts and papers he has to make an application to the judicial magistrate of first class or Metropolitan Magistrate having Juridiction.

After considering the application and hearing the inspector, the Judicial Magistrate, if necessary, may authorise the inspector —

(*a*) to enter the place or places where such books and papers are kept.

(*b*) to search that or those places in the manner as may be prescribed in the order.

(*c*) to seize books and papers which the inspector considers necessary for the purpose of his investigation.

The inspector shall keep books and paper so seized, in his custody till the end of investigation, if necessary thereafter such books and papers shall be returned to the concerned entity or person and the Magistrate will be informed of such return. However the books and papers shall not be kept seized for a continuous period of more than six months. The inspector may put identification marks on those books and papers before returning them to the parties concerned.

The inspector is required to make every search or seizure under this section for the purpose of investigation in accordance with the provisions of The Code of Criminal Procedure 1973.

Inspectors Report (Section 49)

According to this section, on the direction of the Central Government the inspector shall make interim reports to the Government on the completion of investigation. He shall make final report to The Central Government in writing or printed form as may be directed by the Government.

The Central Government:

(*a*) shall forward copy of any report (other than interim report) made by the inspector to the limited liability partnership at its registered office and also to any other entity or persons related to the report.

(*b*) may also furnish a copy of such report on request and on payment of required fees to any person or entity related to or affected by the report.

Prosecution (Section 50)

This section provides that on the basis of the report of investigation made by the inspector if the Central Government forms the opinion that any person in relation to LLP or other entity whose affairs have been investigated is found guilty of any offence. Such person may be prosecuted by the Central Government. In this regard, all partners, designated partners and other employees and agents of LLP or other entity will have to provide all assistance to the Central Government for prosecuting the guilty person.

Application for Winding up of Limited Liability Partnership (Section 51)

According to this section, the Central Government or any person authorised by it, may file a petition to the Tribunal for the winding up of limited liability partnership under the following grounds:

(*a*) if it appears to the Central Government from the report made by inspector that the LLP is liable to be wound up under this Act or other law in force.

(*b*) the business of LLP is conducted with an intend to defraud its creditors, partners or any other persons.

(*c*) business of LLP is conducted in a manner which is oppressive to some or any of its partners.

(*d*) the LLP was formed for any fraudulent or unlawful purpose.

(*e*) the affairs of LLP are not being conducted in accordance with the provisions of this Act.

(*f*) it is just and equitable that the LLP should be wound up

Proceedings for Recovery of Damages or Property (Section 52)

According to this section, if from the report of inspector it appears to the Central Government the proceeding ought to be brought in public interest, by limited liability partnership or other entity whose affairs have been investigated —

(*a*) for the recovery of damages in respect of any fraud, misfeasance or misconduct regarding promotion or formation or the management of the affairs of such LLP or other entity; or

(*b*) for the recovery of any property of such LLP or other entity which has been misapplied or wrongfully retained,

the Central Government may itself bring proceedings for that purpose.

Expenses of Investigation (Section 53)

According to this section, the expenses of and incidental to an investigation by an inspector, at first instance shall be defrayed by the Central Government. However the following persons shall to the extent, mentioned here would be liable to reimburse such expenses —

(*a*) any person who is convicted on prosecution or who is ordered to pay damages or restore any property brought in the proceedings under section 52 is liable to pay expenses to that extent specified by the court convicting that person.

(*b*) any other entity in whose name proceedings are brought shall be liable to the extent of amount or value of any property recovered by it as a result of proceedings.

(*c*) in the absence of any prosecution, the expenses would be borne by:

(*i*) any entity partner, designated partner or any other person dealt with by the report is liable to reimburse for whole of the expenses unless the Central Government, otherwise directs.

(*ii*) the applicant for the investigation where the inspector was appointed under section 43 (1) and clause (*a*), shall be liable to such extent as the Central Government may direct.

Any amount for which LLP or other entity will be liable under section 53 (1) and clause (*b*) shall be a first charge on the sums or property mentioned in that clause.

The amount of expenses for which LLP or other entity or a partners, designated partner or any other person is liable under 53 (1) (*c*) (*i*) clause, to reimburse the Central Government are to be recovered as arrears of land revenue.

For the purpose of this section, any cost or expenses incurred by the Central Government in connection with the proceedings brought under section 52 are to be treated as expenses of the investigation giving rise to the proceedings.

A copy of the report of the inspector authenticated in the prescribed manner is to be admissible as evidence in any legal proceedings in relation to any matter contained in the report.

REVIEW QUESTIONS

1. Discuss the circumstances under which the Central Government appoints an inspector to investigate into the affairs of LLP.
2. Explain the powers of an inspector appointed to investigate the affairs of LLP.
3. What do you means by seizure of document. Discuss the legal provisions related to it.

4. Who is to bear the expenses of investigation. Explain the provisions regarding reimbursement of expenses.
5. Explain legal provisions of this Act regarding winding up of LLP and proceedings for recovery of damages or property.
6. Write notes on:
   (*a*) Inspectors report
   (*b*) Prosecution
   (*c*) Production of documents and evidences.

■■■

Chapter 25

Conversion into Limited Liability Partnership

Learning Objectives

- Develop clarity about conversion of firm in to LLP.
- Examine provisions regarding conversion of private company and conversion of unlisted log in to LLP.
- Remember legal provisions regarding foreign limited liability partnership.

INTRODUCTION

This form of organisation has distinct features and greater amount of flexibility with regard to management of business and structure and operation. Therefore, the other forms such as traditional partnership firm, private and public companies may also get converted in to limited liability partnership. This chapter deals with the legal provision relating to such conversions.

Conversion from Firm into Limited Liability Partnership (Section 55)

A firm may convert in to limited liability partnership in accordance with the provisions of this chapter and the 'Second Schedule' of this Act.

Conversion from Private Company into Limited Liability Partnership (Section 56)

A private company may convert in to limited liability partnership in accordance with the provisions of this chapter and the 'Third Schedule'.

Conversion form Unlisted Public Company into Limited Liability Partnership (Section 57)

This section provides that the unlisted public company may convert into limited liability partnership in accordances with the provisions of this chapter and the 'Forth Schedule'.

Registration and Effect of Conversion (Section 58)

The Registrar on being satisfied that a firm, private company or an unlisted public company has complied with the provisions of the Schedule as applicable on it, provisions of this Act and rules made thereunder, may register the documents submitted to it. Thereafter, the Registrar will issue the certificate of registration in the form as Registrar may determine. This certificate will state that the limited liability partnership on and from the date specified in the certificate, is registered.

The limited liability partnership, with in fifteen days from the date of registration, shall inform the concerned Registrar of Firms or Registrar of companies as the case may be with which it was registered under partnership Act 1932 or Companies Act 1956. The LLP will give information about the conversion and other particulars in such form and manner as may be prescribed.

Upon such conversion the partners of the firm, the shareholders of private company or unlisted public company and limited liability partnership to which such firm or company has converted and the partners of LLP shall be bound by the provisions of the Second Schedule, the Third Schedule or the Fourth Schedule as the case may be applicable to them.

Upon the conversion, on and from the date of certificate of registration the effect of conversion shall be as specified in the Second, Third and Fourth Schedules, as the case may be.

Such conversion will also produce the following effects on and from the date of registration:

(*a*) there shall be limited liability partnership by the name specified in the certificate of registration.

(*b*) all tangible, intangible, movable, immovable property, all assets, interest, rights privileges, liabilities and obligations and the whole of the undertaking of the firm or company so converted shall be transferred to LLP without further act or deed.

(*c*) the firm or company shall be deemed to be dissolved and removed from the records of the Registrar of firms or the Registrar of the Company.

Foreign Limited Liability Partnership (Section 59)

The limited liability partnership which is formed, incorporated or registered outside India which establishes place of business in India, is known as foreign limited liability partnership.

The Central Government is empowered to make rules for provisions in relation to establishment of place of business for foreign limited liability partnership within India and carrying on their business therein by applying or incorporating with appropriate modification provisions of the companies Act 1956.

1. A foreign limited liability partnership shall, within thirty days of establishing a place of business in India, file with the Registrar of firms 27—

   (*a*) a copy of the certificate of incorporation or registration and other instrument(s) constituting or defining the constitution of the limited liability partnership;

   (*b*) the full address of the registered or principal office of the limited liability partnership in the country of its incorporation;

   (*c*) the full address of the office of the limited liability partnership in India which is to be deemed as its principal place of business in India; and

   (*d*) list of partners and designated partners, if any, and the names and addresses of two or more persons resident in India, authorised to accept on behalf of the limited liability partnership, service of process and any notices or other documents required to be served on the limited liability partnership.

2.(*i*). If the limited liability partnership is incorporated in any country which is a part of the Commonwealth, the copies of the documents referred to in sub-rule (1) shall be certified as true copies—

   (*a*) by an official of the Government to whose custody the original is committed; or (*b*) by a Notary (Public) in that Part of the Commonwealth; or

(*c*) by an officer of the limited liability partnership, on oath before a person having authority to administer an oath in that part of the Commonwealth.

(*ii*) If the Limited Liability Partnership is incorporated in a country that falls outside the Commonwealth but is a party to the Hague Apostile Convention, 1961—

(*a*) the copies of the documents referred to in sub-rule (1) shall be certified by an official of the Government to whose custody the original is committed and be duly apostillised in accordance with Hague Convention;

(*b*) a list of the partners and designated partners of the LLP, if any, the name and address of persons resident in India, authorised to accept notice on behalf of the Limited Liability Partnership shall be duly notarised and be apostillised in the country of their origin in accordance with Hague Convention.

(*iii*) If the limited liability partnership is incorporated in a country outside the Commonwealth and is not a party to the Hague Convention, the copy of the incorporation documents referred in sub-rule (1) shall be certified—

(*a*) by an official of the Government to whose custody the original is committed; or

(*b*) a Notary (Public) of such country; or

(*c*) by an officer of the limited liability partnership.

(*iv*) The signature or seal of the official referred to in sub-clause (*a*) of clause (*iii*) or the certificate of the Notary (Public) referred to in sub-clause (*b*) of that clause shall be authenticated by a Diplomatic or Consular Officer empowered in this behalf under section 3 of the Diplomatic and Consular Officers (Oaths and Fees) Act, 1948 (40 of 1948), or where there is no such officer, by any of the officials mentioned in section 6 of the Commissioners of Oaths Act, 1889 (52 and 53 Vic. C. 10) or in any Act amending the same.

(*v*) The certificate of the officer of the limited liability partnership referred to in sub-clause (*c*) of clause (*iii*) shall be signed before a person having authority to administer an oath as provided under section 3 of the

Diplomatic; and Consular Officers (Oaths and Fees) Act, 1948 (40 of 1948), or as the case may be, by section 3 of the Commissioners of Oaths Act, 1889 (52 and 53 Vic. C. 10) the status of the person administering the oath in the latter case being authenticated by any official specified in section 6 of the Commissioners Oaths Act, 1889 (52 and 53 Vic. C. 10) or in any Act amending the same.

3.(*i*) If any alteration is made or occurs in—

(*a*) the instrument constituting or defining the constitution of a limited liability partnership incorporated or registered outside India;

(*b*) the registered or principal office of a limited liability partnership incorporated or registered outside India; or

(*c*) the partner or designated partner, if any, of a limited liability partnership incorporated or registered outside India,

the foreign limited liability partnership shall file in Form 28 such alterations with the Registrar within sixty days of the close of the financial year.

(*ii*) If any alteration is made or occurs in—

(*a*) the certificate of incorporation or registration of limited liability partnership incorporated or registered outside India;

(*b*) the name or address of any of the persons authorised to accept service on behalf of a foreign limited liability partnership in India; or

(*c*) the principal place of business of foreign limited liability partnership in India,

the foreign limited liability partnership shall file in Form 29 such alterations with the Registrar within thirty days from the date on which the alteration was made or occurred.

4. Every foreign limited liability partnership shall file with the Registrar the Statement of Account and Solvency in Form 8 in accordance with provisions of rule 24 duly signed by the authorised representatives within a period of 30 days from the end of six months of the financial year.

5.(*i*) If any document as is mentioned in sub-rule (1) or (3) is not in the English language, there shall be annexed to it a certified translation thereof.

(*ii*) The translation of documents into English required to be filed with the Registrar in pursuance of sub-rule (1) or (3) shall be certified to be correct in the manner as provided in clause *(iii)* or clause *(iv)* of this sub-rule, as the case maybe.

(*iii*) Where any translation is made outside India, it shall be authenticated in the manner specified in sub-rule (2).

(*iv*) Where such translation is made within India, it shall be authenticated—

(*a*) by an Advocate, Chartered Accountant, Company Secretary or Cost Accountant; or

(*b*) by an affidavit of a person who, in the opinion of the Registrar has adequate knowledge of the language of the original and of English.

6. Every foreign limited liability partnership shall cause the name of the foreign limited liability partnership and of the country in which the limited liability partnership is incorporated, to be stated in legible English characters in all invoices, official correspondence and publications of the limited liability partnership.

7. (*a*) Where any such limited liability partnership makes default in delivering to the Registrar the names and addresses of persons resident in India who are authorised to accept on behalf of the limited liability partnership service of process, notices or other documents; or

(*b*) if at any time all the persons whose names and addresses have been so delivered are dead or have ceased so to reside, or refuse to accept service on behalf of the limited liability partnership or for any reason, cannot be served, a document may be served on the limited liability partnership by leaving it at, or sending it by post to, any place of business established by the limited liability partnership in India.

8. If any foreign limited liability partnership ceases to have a place of business in India, it shall give notice to the Registrar in Form 29 within 30 days of its intention to close the place of business and as from the date on which notice is so given, the obligation of the limited liability partnership to file any document to the Registrar shall cease, provided it has no other place of business in India and it has filed all the documents due for filing as on the date of the notice.

9. Every document which is required to be filed by any foreign limited liability partnership shall be filed in the electronic form to the Registrar having jurisdiction over New Delhi, through the portal maintained by the Ministry of Corporate Affairs on its website www.mca.gov.in.

10. The Registrar shall, on registration of Form 27, issue a certificate for establishment of place of business in India by the foreign limited liability partnership in Form 30.

11. There shall be paid to Registrar for filing or delivery or registering any form or document required by this Chapter the fee as mentioned in Annexure "A".

■■■

Chapter **26**

Compromise, Arrangement or Reconstruction and Winding up of LLP

Learning Objectives

- Get clarity about the concept of compromise or arrangement.
- Remember the provisions for facilitating reconstruction or amalgamation.
- Examine legal provisions regarding winding up of LLP.

INTRODUCTION

Where a compromise or arrangement is proposed between LLP and its creditors or between the LLP and its partners, an application can be made to the Tribunal. The application can be made by the LLP or any of its partners or creditors. If the LLP is in winding up, the liquidator can apply. The Tribunal can order a meeting of the creditors or of partners to be called, held and conducted in such manner as the Tribunal may prescribe. [S. 60(1)]

If a majority representing three-fourths in value of the creditors or partners at the meeting agrees to any arrangement or compromise, the Tribunal may sanction the scheme and pass an order to that effect. The order becomes binding on all the creditors or partners or the liquidator and contributories of the LLP.

The Tribunal is not to sanction the scheme unless satisfied that the LLP or the applicant has disclosed to the Tribunal, by affidavit or otherwise, all materials facts relating to the LLP including the latest financial position and the pendency of any investigation proceedings in relation to the LLP. [S. 60(2)]

The order has to be filed by the LLP with the Registrar within 30 days from its date. It becomes effective only on such filing. [S. 60(3)][1]

The Tribunal may, after filing of an application, stay the commencement or continuation of any suit or proceeding against the LLP on such terms as the Tribunal considers fit until the application is finally disposed of.

Power of Tribunal to Enforce Compromise or Arrangement [S. 61]

Where the Tribunal has sanctioned a scheme of compromise or arrangement, it:

(*a*) is to have power to supervise the carrying out of the compromise or an arrangement; and

(*b*) may give such directions or make such modifications in the scheme as it may consider necessary for proper working of the scheme. [sub-s (1)]

If the Tribunal is satisfied that the scheme sanctioned by it cannot be worked out satisfactorily with or without modifications, either of its own motion or on the application of an interested person, make an order for winding up of the LLP. Such order is deemed to be an order made under Section 64 of the Act. [sub-s (2)]

Provisions for Facilitating Reconstruction or Amalgamation [S. 62]

Where an application is made to the Tribunal under Section 60 for sanctioning a scheme of compromise or arrangement and it is shown that the compromise or arrangement has been proposed for the purposes of the scheme of reconstruction and under the scheme of the whole or any part of the undertaking, property or liabilities of an LLP (transferor LLP) is to be transferred to another LLP (transferee LLP), the Tribunal may by order

1. Any default in the respect would render the LLP and its designated partner liable to a fine which may extend to one laks rupees. [sub-s (4)]

sanctioning the scheme or by a subsequent order, make provisions for all or any of the following matters, namely:

(*i*) the transfer to the transferee LLP of the whole or any part of the undertaking, property or liabilities of the transferor LLP;

(*ii*) the continuation by or against the transferee LLP of any legal proceedings by or against the transferor LLP;

(*iii*) the dissolution, without winding up of the transferor LLP;

(*iv*) the provision to be made for any person who dissented from the scheme;

(*v*) such incidental, consequential and supplemental matters as are necessary to secure that the scheme is fully and effectively carried out.

A scheme is not to be sanctioned unless the Tribunal has received a report from a Registrar that the affairs of the LLP have not been conducted in a manner prejudicial to the interests of its partners or public interest.

An order for dissolution of the transferor LLP is not to be made unless the Official Liquidator has scrutinised the books and papers of the LLP and made a report to the Tribunal that the affairs of the LLP have not been carried out in a manner prejudicial to the interests of its partners or public interest. [sub-s (1)]

Where an order provides for the transfer of any property or liabilities then by virtue of the order the property has to be transferred to and vest in the LLP. The liabilities are to become the liabilities of the transferee LLP. The Tribunal may order that a charge, if any, on the properties of transferor LLP is to cease to the extent necessary under the scheme. [sub-s (2)]

Within 30 days of the order, the LLP in reference to which the order has been made is to file a certified copy of the order for registration. [sub-s (3)][2]

The Explanation to the section clarifies that the word property as used in the section includes property, rights and powers of every description and the word "liabilities" includes duties of every description.

2. A default in complying with the requirement of filing, the LLP and every designated partner becomes punishable with a fine extending up to fifty thousand rupees.

WINDING UP OF LLP

The winding up of a limited liability partnership may be either voluntary or by the Tribunal. The LLP so wound up may be dissolved. [S. 63]

Circumstances in which LLP may be wound up by Tribunal [S. 64]

An LLP may be wound up by the Tribunal in the following cases:

(*a*) where an LLP decides that it may be wound up by the Tribunal;

(*b*) where for a period of more than six months, the number of partners is reduced to below two;

(*c*) if the LLP is unable to pay its debts;

(*d*) if the LLP has acted against the interest of the sovereignty and integrity of India, the security of State or public order;

(*e*) if the LLP has made a default in filing with the Registrar the Statement of Account and Solvency or Annual Return for any five consecutive financial years; or

(*f*) if the Tribunal is of the opinion that it is just and equitable that the LLP be wound up.

The Central Government may make rules for provisions in relation to winding up and dissolution of LLPs. [S. 65].

■■■

Chapter 27

Miscellaneous

Business Transactions of Partner with Limited Liability Partnership [S. 66]

A partner may lend money to the LLP and also transact any other business with it. He will have the same rights and obligations with respect to the loan or other transactions as a person who is not a partner.

Applications of Provisions of the Companies Act [S. 67]

The Central Government may, by notification in the Official Gazette, direct that any of the provisions of the Companies Act, 1956 specified in the notification are to apply to an LLP; or apply to any LLP with such exception, modification and adaptation as may be specified in the notification.

A copy of every such proposed notification is to be laid in draft before each House of Parliament, while it is in session for a total period of 30 days which may be comprised in one session or in two or more successive sessions. Parliamentary approval is necessary for issue of any such notification.

Electronic Filing of Documents [S. 68]

Documents required to be filed, recorded or registered have to follow the manner of filing etc., and subject to such conditions as may be prescribed.

The copy of an electronically filed document which is supplied or issued by the Registrar and certified through affixing digital signature as per the Information Technology Act, 2000 is to be a true copy of or extract from such document, and in any proceedings to be admissible in evidence as of equal validity with the original document.

Any information supplied by the Registrar that is certified by him through affixing digital signature is to be a true extract from any document filed with or submitted to the Registrar and is admissible in evidence in any proceedings and is to be presumed to be a true extract from such document unless any evidence to the contrary is adduced.

Payment of Additional Fee [S. 69]

Late filing of documents is allowed within 300 days from the date within which it should have been filed on payment of additional fee of Rs 100 for every day of delay in addition to any fee as is payable for filing such document or return. Filing after 300 days is also allowed on payment of fee and additional fee as specified in the section. Such double late filing is not to prejudice any other action or liability under the Act.

Enhanced Punishment [S. 70]

Where any LLP or any partner or designated partner of the LLP commits any offence second time or any subsequent offence, he is punishable with imprisonment as provided. But in the case of offences for which fine is prescribed either alongwith or exclusive of imprisonment, the fine amount would be twice the amount of fine prescribed for such offence.

Application of Other Laws not Barred [S. 71]

The provisions of the LLP Act are in addition to and not in derogation of the provisions of any other law for the time being in force.

Jurisdiction of Tribunal and Appellate Tribunal [S. 72]

The Tribunal can exercise such powers and perform such functions as have been or may be conferred on it by or under the Act or any other law for the time being in force. Any person aggrieved by an order or decision of the Tribunal may prefer an appeal to the Appellate Tribunal. The provisions of Sections 10-FQ to 10-FZA, 10-G, 10-GD, 10-GE and 10-GF of the Companies Act, 1956 are to be applicable in respect of such appeals.

Penalty for Non-compliance of Tribunal's Order [S. 73]

Non-compliance with Tribunal's order under the Act is punishable with imprisonment which may extend to six months. There is also the liability of fine which is not to be less than Rs 50,000.

General Penalties [S. 74]

A person guilty of offence under the Act for which no punishment is expressly provided is to be liable to a fine which may extend to five lakh rupee but which is not to be less than Rs. 5000. There will also be a further fine up to Rs. 50 extending for everyday for which the default continues.

Power of Registrar to Strike off Defunct LLP [S. 75]

Where the Registrar has a reasonable cause to believe that an LLP is not carrying on business or its operation in accordance with the provisions of the Act, the name of such LLP may be struck off from the register in the prescribed manner. The Registrar has to give the LLP a reasonable opportunity to be heard before taking the drastic step.

Offences by LLPs [S. 76]

Where an offence under the Act committed by an LLP is proved to have been committed with the consent or connivance of a partner or designated partner or is attributable to any neglect on the part of a partner or designated partner, then such partner or designated partner as well as the LLP are to be regarded as guilty of the offence and liable to be proceeded against and punished accordingly.

Jurisdiction of Court [S. 77]

The Judicial Magistrate of the First Class or the Metropolitan Magistrate has been conferred with the jurisdiction to try any offence under the Act and shall have power to impose punishment in respect of the offence. The section opens with the words: "Notwithstanding any provision to the contrary in any Act for the time being in force".

Power to Alter Schedules [S. 78]

The Central Government may, by notification in the Official Gazette, alter any of the provisions contained in any of the Schedules to the Act. Any alteration thus notified is to have the effect as if enacted in the Act. It is to come into force on the date of notification unless some other date is specified.

As soon as it may be any such alteration has to be laid before each House of Parliament while it is in session for a total period of 30 days.

Power to Make Rules [S. 79]

1. The Central Government may, by notification in the Official Gazette, make rules for carrying out the provisions of this Act.
2. In particular, and without prejudice to the generality of the foregoing power, such rules may provide for all or any of the following matters, namely:
   (*a*) form and manner of prior consent to be given by designated partner under Sub-section (3) of Section 7;
   (*b*) the form and the manner of particulars of every individual agreeing to act as a designated partner of limited liability partnership under Sub-section (4) of Section (7);
   (*c*) the conditions and requirements relating to the eligibility of an individual to become a designated partner under Sub-section (5) of Section 7;
   (*d*) the manner of filing the incorporation document and payment of fees payable thereof under clause (b) of Sub-section (1) of Section 11;
   (*e*) the form statement to be filed under cause (c) of Sub-section (1) of Section 11;
   (*f*) the form of incorporation document under clause (a) of Sub-section (2) of Section 11;
   (*g*) the information to be contained in the incorporation document concerning the proposed limited liability partnership under clause (g) of Sub-section (2) of Section 11;
   (*h*) the manner of serving the documents on a limited liability partnership or a partner or a designated partner and the form and manner in which any other address may be declared by a limited liability partnership under Sub-section (2) of Section 13;
   (*i*) the form and manner of notice to the Registrar and the conditions in respect of change of registered office under Sub-section (3) of Section 13;
   (*j*) the form and manner of application and amount of fee payable to the Registrar under Sub-section (1) of Section 16;
   (*k*) the manner in which names will be reserved by the Registrar under Sub-section (2) of Section 16;
   (*l*) the manner in which an application may be made by an entity under Sub-section (1) of Section 18;

(*m*) the form and manner of notice of change of name of limited liability partnership and the amount of fee payable under Section 19;

(*n*) the form and manner of the limited liability partnership agreement and the changes made therein and the amount of fee payable under Sub-section (2) of Section 23;

(*o*) the form of notice, the amount of fee payable and the manner of authentication of the statement under clauses (a), (b) and (c) of Sub-section (3) of Section 25;

(*p*) the manner of accounting and disclosure of monetary value of contribution of a partner under Sub-section (2) of Section 32;

(*q*) the books of account and the period of their maintenance under Sub-section (1) of Section 34;

(*r*) the form of Statement of Account and Solvency under Sub-section (2) of Section 34;

(*s*) the form, manner, fee and time of filing of Statement of Account and Solvency under Sub-section (3) of Section 34;

(*t*) the audit of accounts of a limited liability partnership under Sub-section (4) of Section 34;

(*u*) the form and manner of annual return and fee payable under Sub-section (1) of Section 35;

(*v*) the manner and amount of fee payable for inspection of incorporation document, names of partners and changes made therein, Statement of Account and Solvency and Annual Return under Section 36;

(*w*) the destruction of documents by Registrar in any form under Section 40;

(*x*) the amount required as security under clause (a) of Sub-section (3) of Section 43;

(*y*) the amount of security to be given under Section 44;

(*z*) the fee payable for furnishing a copy under clause (b) of Sub-section (2) of Section 49;

(*za*) the manner of authentication of report of inspector under Section 54;

(*zb*) the form and manner of particulars about conversion under the *proviso* to Sub-section (1) of Section 58;

(*zc*) in relation to establishment of place of business and carrying on business in India by foreign limited liability partnerships and regulatory mechanism and composition under Section 59;

(*zd*) the manner of calling, holding and conducting meeting under Sub-section (1) of Section 60;

(*ze*) in relation to winding up and dissolution of limited liability partnerships under Section 65;

(*zf*) the manner and conditions for filing document electronically under Sub-section (1) of Section 68;

(*zg*) the manner for striking off the names of limited liability partnerships from the register under Section 75;

(*zh*) the form and manner of statement containing particulars and amount of fee payable under sub-paragraph (a) of Paragraph 4 of the Second Schedule;

(*zi*) the form and manner of particulars about conversion under the *proviso* to Paragraph 5 of the Second Schedule;

(*zj*) the form and manner of the statement and the amount of fee payable under sub-paragraph (a) of Paragraph 3 of the Third Schedule; and

(*zk*) the form and manner of particulars about conversion under the *proviso* to Paragraph 4 of the Third Schedule;

(*zl*) the form and manner of the statement and amount of fee payable under sub-paragraph (a) of Paragraph 4 of the Fourth Schedule; and

(*zm*) the form and manner of particulars about conversion under the *proviso* to Paragraph 5 of the Fourth Schedule.

3. Every rule made under this Act by the Central Government shall be laid, as soon as may be after it is made, before each House of Parliament, while it is in session, for a total period of 30 days which may be comprised in one session or in two or more successive sessions, and if, before the expiry of the session immediately following the session or the successive sessions aforesaid, both Houses agree in making any modification in the rule, or both Houses agree that the rule should not be made, the rule shall thereafter have effect only in such modified form or be of no effect, as the case may be; so that any such modification or annulment shall be without prejudice to the validity or anything previously done under that rule.

Power to Remove Difficulties [S. 80]

1. If any difficulty arises in giving effect to the provisions of this Act, the Central Government may, by order published in the Official Gazette,

make such provisions, not inconsistent with the provisions of this Act as may appear to it to be necessary removing the difficulty:

Provided that no such order shall be made under this section after the expiry of a period of two years from the commencement of this Act.

2. Every order made under this section shall be laid, as soon as may be, after it is made, before each House of Parliament.

Transitional Provisions [S. 81]

Until the Tribunal and the Appellate Tribunal are constituted under the provisions of the Companies Act, 1956 the LLP Act would apply with the following modifications:

(*a*) for the word "Tribunal" occurring in Section 41, Section 43 and Section 44, the words "Company Law Board" are to be substituted;

(*b*) for the word "Tribunal" occurring in Section 51 and Sections 60 to 64, the words "High Court" are to be substituted.

(*c*) for the words "Appellate Tribunal" occurring in Section 72(2), the words "High Court" are to be substituted.

The First Schedule [See Section 23(4)]

Provisions regarding matters relating to mutual rights and duties of partners and limited liability partnership and its partners applicable in the absence of any agreement on such matters

1. The mutual rights and duties of the partners and the mutual rights and duties of the limited liability partnership and its partners shall be determined, subject to the terms of any limited liability partnership agreement or in the absence of any such agreement on any matter, by the provisions in this Schedule.
2. All the partners of a limited liability partnership are entitled to share equally in the capital, profits and losses of the limited liability partnership.
3. The limited liability partnership shall indemnify each partner in respect of payments made and personal liabilities incurred by him:

   (*a*) in the ordinary and proper conduct of the business of the limited liability partnership; or

   (*b*) in or about anything necessarily done for the preservation of the business or property of the limited liability partnership.
4. Every partner shall indemnify the limited liability partnership for any loss caused to it by his fraud in the conduct of the business of the limited liability partnership.

5. Every partner may take part in the management of the limited liability partnership.
6. No partner shall be entitled to remuneration for acting in the business or management of the limited liability partnership.
7. No person may be introduced as a partner without the consent of all the existing partners.
8. Any matter or issue relating to the limited liability partnership shall be decided by a resolution passed by a majority in number of the partners, and for this purpose, each partner shall have one vote. However, no change may be made in the nature of business of the limited liability partnership without the consent of all the partners.
9. Every limited liability partnership shall ensure that decisions taken by it are recorded in the minutes within thirty days of taking such decisions and are kept and maintained at the registered office of the limited liability partnership.
10. Each partner shall render true accounts and full information of all things affecting the limited liability partnership to any partner or his legal representatives.
11. If a partner, without the consent of the limited liability partnership, carries on any business of the same nature as and competing with the limited liability partnership, he must account for and pay over to the limited liability partnership all profits made by him in that business.
12. Every partner shall account to the limited liability partnership for any benefit derived by him without the consent of the limited liability partnership from any transaction concerning the limited liability partnership, or from any use by him of the property, name or any business connection of the limited liability partnership. .
13. No majority of the partners can expel any partner unless a power to do so has been conferred by express agreement between the partners.
14. All disputes between the partners arising out of the limited liability partnership agreement which cannot be resolved in terms of such agreement shall be referred for arbitration as per the provisions of the Arbitration and Conciliation Act, 1996 (26 of 1996).

The Second Schedule [See Section 55]

Conversion from firm Into limited liability partnership

1. Interpretation—In this Schedule, unless the context otherwise requires:
   (*a*) "firm" means a firm as defined in Section 4 of the Indian Partnership Act, 1932 (9 of 1932);

(*b*) "convert", in relation to a firm converting into a limited liability partnership, means a transfer of the property, assets, interests, rights, privileges, liabilities, obligations and the undertaking of the firm to the limited liability partnership in accordance with this Schedule.

2. Conversion from firm into limited liability partnership:

(*a*) A firm may convert into a limited liability partnership by complying with the requirements as to the conversion set out in this Schedule.

(*b*) Upon such conversion, the partners of the firm shall be bound by the provisions of this Schedule that are applicable to them.

3. Eligibility for conversion—A firm may apply to convert into a limited liability partnership in accordance with this Schedule if and only if the partners of the limited liability partnership into which the firm is to be converted, comprise, all the partners of the firm and no one else.

4. Statements to be filed—A firm may apply to convert into a limited liability partnership by filing with the Registrar:

(*a*) a statement by all of its partners in such form and manner and accompanied by such fee as the Central Government may prescribe, containing the following particulars namely:

(*i*) the name and registration number, if applicable, of the firm; and

(*ii*) the date on which the firm was registered under the Indian Partnership Act, 1932 (9 of 1932) or under any other law, if applicable; and

(*b*) incorporation document and statement referred to in Section 11.

5. Registration of conversion—On receiving the documents referred in Paragraph 4, the Registrar shall subject to the provisions of this Act, register the documents and issue a certificate of registration in such form as the Registrar may determine stating that the limited liability partnership is, on and from the date specified in the certificate, registered under this Act:

Provided that the limited liability partnership shall, within fifteen days of the date of registration, inform, the concerned Registrar of Firms with which it was registered under the provisions of the Indian Partnership Act, 1932 (9 of 1932) about the conversion and of the particulars of the limited liability partnership in such form and manner as the Central Government may prescribe.

6. Registrar may refuse to register.
   1. Nothing in this Schedule shall be construed as to require the Registrar to register any limited liability partnership if he is not satisfied with the particulars or other information furnished under the provisions of this Act.

      Provided that an appeal may be made before the Tribunal in case of refusal of registration by the Registrar:

      [23] [Provided further that until the Tribunal is constituted under the Companies Act, 1956, the appeal under this sub-paragraph may be made before the Company Law Board].
   2. The Registrar may, in any particular case, require the documents referred to in Paragraph 4 to be verified in such manner, as he considers fit.
7. Effect of registration—On and from the date of registration specified in the certificate of registration issued under Paragraph 5:
   (*a*) there shall be a limited liability partnership by the name specified in the certificate of registration registered under this Act;

   (*b*) all tangible (movable and immovable) property as well as intangible property vested in the firm, all assets, interests, rights, privileges, liabilities, obligations relating to the firm and the whole of the undertaking of the firm shall be transferred to and shall vest in the limited liability partnership without further assurance, act or deed; and

   (*c*) the firm shall be deemed to be dissolved and if earlier registered under the Indian Partnership Act, 1932 (9 of 1932) removed from the records maintained under that Act.
8. Registration in relation to property—If any property to which sub-paragraph *(b)* of Paragraph 7 applies is registered with any authority, the limited liability partnership shall, as soon as practicable after the date of registration, take all necessary steps as required by the relevant authority to notify the authority of the conversion and of the particulars of the limited liability partnership in such medium and form as the authority may specify.

23. Ins. by G. S. R. 386 (E), dt. 4-6-2009 (w.e.f. 4-6-2009)

9. Pending proceedings—All proceedings by or against the firm which are pending in any Court or Tribunal or before any authority on the date of registration may be continued, completed and enforced by or against the limited liability partnership.
10. Continuance of conviction, ruling, order or judgment—Any conviction, ruling, order or judgment of any Court, Tribunal or other authority in favour of or against the firm may be enforced by or against the limited liability partnership.
11. Existing agreements—Every agreement to which the firm was a party immediately before the date of registration, whether or not of such nature that the rights and liabilities thereunder could be assigned, shall have effect as from that date as if:
    (*a*) the limited liability partnership were a party to such an agreement instead of the firm; and
    (*b*) for any reference to the firm, there were substituted in respect of anything to be done on or after the date of registration a reference to the limited liability partnership.
12. Existing contracts, etc—All deeds, contracts, schemes, bonds, agreements, applications, instruments and arrangements subsisting immediately before the date of registration relating to the firm or to which the firm is a party, shall continue in force on and after that date as if they relate to the limited liability partnership and shall be enforceable by or against the limited liability partnership as if the limited liability partnership were named therein or were a party thereto instead of the firm.
13. Continuance of employment—Every contract of employment to which Paragraph 11 or Paragraph 12 applies shall continue to be in force on or after the date of registration as if the limited liability partnership were the employer thereunder instead of the firm.
14. Existence appointment, authority or power—
    1. Every appointment of the firm in any role or capacity which is in force immediately before the date of registration shall take effect and operate from that date as if the limited liability partnership were appointed.
    2. Any authority or power conferred on the firm which is in force immediately before the date of registration shall take effect and operate from that date as if it were conferred on the limited liability partnership.

15. Application of Paragraphs 7 to 14—The provisions of Paragraphs 7 to 14 (both inclusive) shall apply to any approval, permit or licence issued to the firm under any other Act which is in force immediately before the date of registration of the limited liability partnership, subject to the provisions of such other Act under which such approval, permit or licence has been issued.

16. Partner liable for liabilities and obligations of firm before conversion—

    1. Notwithstanding anything in Paragraph 7 to 14 (both inclusive), every partner of a firm that has converted into a limited liability partnership shall continue to be personally liable (jointly and severally with the limited liability partnership) for the liabilities and obligations of the firm which were incurred prior to the conversion or which arose from any contract entered into prior to the conversion.

    2. If any such partner discharges any liability or obligation referred to in sub-paragraph (1), he shall be entitled (subject to any agreement with the limited liability partnership to the contrary) to be fully indemnified by the limited liability partnership in respect of such liability or obligation.

17 Notice of conversion in correspondence—

   1. The limited liability partnership shall ensure that for a period of twelve months commencing not later than fourteen days after the date of registration, every official correspondence of the limited liability partnership bears the following:

      (*a*) a statement that it was, as from the date of registration, converted from a firm into a limited liability partnership; and

      (*b*) the name and registration number, if applicable, of the firm from which it was converted.

   2. Any limited liability partnership which contravenes the provisions of sub-paragraph (1) shall be punishable with fine which shall not be less than ten thousand rupees but which may extend to one lakh rupees and with a further fine which shall not be less than fifty rupees but which may extend to five hundred rupees for everyday after the first day after which the default continues.

The Third Schedule [See Section 56]

Conversion from private company into limited liability partnership

1. Interpretation—In this Schedule unless the context otherwise requires:
   - (*a*) "company" means a private company as defined in clause *(iii)* of Sub-section (1) of Section 3 of the Companies Act, 1956 (1 of 1956);
   - (*b*) "convert", in relation to a private company converting into a limited liability partnership, means a transfer of the property, assets, interests, rights, privileges, liabilities, obligations and the undertaking of the private company to the limited liability partnership in accordance with this Schedule.

2. Eligibility for conversion of private companies into limited liability partnership—(1) A company may convert into a limited liability partnership by complying with the requirements as to the conversion set out in this Schedule.
   2. A company may apply to convert into a limited liability partnership in accordance with this Schedule if and only if:
      - (*a*) there is no security interest in its assets subsisting or in force at the time of application; and
      - (*b*) the partners of the limited liability partnership to which it converts comprise all the shareholders of the company and no one else.
   3. Upon such conversion, the company, its shareholders, the limited liability partnership into which the company has converted and the partners of that limited liability partnership shall be bound by the provisions of this Schedule that are applicable to them.

3. Statements to be filed—A company may apply to convert into a limited liability partnership by filing with the Registrar:
   - (*a*) a statement by all its shareholders in such form and manner to be accompanied by such fees as the Central Government may prescribe, containing the following particulars, namely:
     - (*i*) the name and registration number of the company;
     - (*ii*) the date on which the company was incorporated; and
   - (*b*) incorporation document and statement referred to in Section 11.

4. Registration of conversion—On receiving the documents referred to in Paragraph 3, the Registrar shall, subject to the provisions of this Act and the rules made thereunder, register the documents and issue a certificate

of registration in such form as the Registrar may determine stating that the limited liability partnership is, on and from the date specified in the certificate, registered under this Act.

Provided that the limited liability partnership shall, within fifteen days of the date of registration, inform the concerned Registrar of Companies with which it was registered under the provisions of the Companies Act, 1956 (1 of 1956) about the conversion and of the particulars of the limited liability partnership in such form and manner as the Central Government may prescribe.

5. Registrar may refuse to register—

   1. Nothing in this Schedule shall be constructed as to require the Registrar to register any limited liability partnership if he is not satisfied with the particulars or other information furnished under the provisions of this Act.

      Provided that an appeal may be made before the Tribunal in case of refusal of registration by the Registrar:

      [24][Provided further that until the Tribunal is constituted under the Companies Act, 1956, the appeal under this sub-paragraph may be made before the Company Law Board].

   2. The Registrar may, in any particular case, require the documents referred to in Paragraph 3 to be verified in such manner, as he considers fit.

6. Effect of registration—On and from the date of registration specified in the certificate of registration issued under Paragraph 4:

   (*a*) there shall be a limited liability partnership by the name specified in the certificate of registration registered under this Act;

   (*b*) all tangible (movable and immovable) and intangible property vested in the company, all assets, interests, rights, privileges, liabilities, obligations relating to the company and the whole of the undertaking of the company shall be transferred to and shall vest in the limited liability partnership without further assurance, act or deed; and

   (*c*) the company shall be deemed to be dissolved and removed from the records of the Registrar of Companies.

7. Registration in relation to property—If any property to which clause (*b*) of Paragraph 6 applies is registered with any authority, the limited

24. Ins. by G. S. R. 386 (E), dt. 4-6-2009 (w.e.f. 4-6-2009)

liability partnership shall, as soon as practicable, after the date of registration, take all necessary steps as required by the relevant authority to notify the authority of the conversion and of the particulars of the limited liability partnership in such form and manner as the authority may determine.

8. Pending proceedings—All proceedings by or against the company which are pending before any Court, Tribunal or other authority on the date of registration may be continued, completed and enforced by or against the limited liability partnership.

9. Continuance of conviction, ruling, order or judgment—Any conviction, ruling, order or judgment of any Court, Tribunal or other authority in favour of or against the company may be enforced by or against the limited liability partnership.

10. Existing agreements—Every agreement to which the company was a party immediately before the date of registration, whether or not of such nature that the rights and liabilities thereunder could be assigned, shall have effect as from that date as if:

    (*a*) the limited liability partnership was a party to such an agreement instead of the company;

    (*b*) for any reference to the company, there were substituted in respect of anything to be done on or after the date of registration a reference to the limited liability partnership.

11. Existing contracts, etc.—All deeds, contracts, schemes, bonds, agreements, applications, instruments and agreements subsisting immediately before the date of registration relating to the company or to which the company is a party shall continue in force on and after that date as if they relate to the limited liability partnership and shall be enforceable by against the limited liability partnership as if the limited liability partnership were named therein or were a party thereto instead of the company.

12. Continuance of employment—Every contract of employment to which Paragraph 10 or Paragraph 11 applies shall continue in force on or after the date of registration as if the limited liability partnership were the employer thereunder instead of the company.

13. Existing appointment, authority or power—(1) Every appointment of the company in any role or capacity which is in force immediately before the date of registration shall take effect and operate from that date as if the limited liability partnership were appointed.

2. Any authority or power conferred on the company which is in force immediately before the date of registration shall take effect and operate from that date as if it were conferred on the limited liability partnership.

14. Application of Paragraphs 6 to 13—The provisions of Paragraphs 6 to 13 (both inclusive) shall apply to any approval, permit or licence issued to the company under any other Act which is in force immediately before the date of registration of the limited liability partnership, subject to the provisions of such other Act under which such approval, permit or licence has been issued.

15. Notice of conversion in correspondence—(1) The limited liability partnership shall ensure that for a period of twelve months commencing not later than fourteen days after the date of registration, every official correspondence of the limited liability partnership bears the following, namely:

   (*a*) a statement that it was, as from the date of registration, converted from a company into a limited liability partnership; and

   (*b*) the name and registration number of the company from which it was converted;

2. Any limited liability partnership which contravenes the provisions of sub-paragraph (1) shall be punishable with fine which shall not be less than ten thousand rupees but which may extend to one lakh rupees and with a further fine which shall not be less than fifty rupees but which may extend to five hundred rupees for every day after the first day after which the default continues.

The Fourth Schedule [See Section 57]

Conversion from unlisted public company into limited liability partnership

1. Interpretation—(1) In this Schedule, unless the context otherwise requires:

   (*a*) "company" means an unlisted public company;

   (*b*) "convert", in relation to a company converting into a limited liability partnership, means a transfer of the property, assets, interests, rights, privileges, liabilities, obligations and the undertaking of the company to the limited liability partnership in accordance with the provisions of this Schedule;

(*c*) "listed company" means a listed company as defined in the Securities Exchange Board of India (Disclosure and Investor Protection) Guidelines, 2000 issued by the Securities and Exchange Board of India under Section 11 of the Securities and Exchange Board of India Act, 1992 (15 of 1992);

(*d*) "unlisted public company" means a company which is not a listed company.

2. Conversion of company into a limited liability partnership—(1) A company may convert into a limited liability partnership by complying with the requirements as to the conversion set out in this Schedule.

2. Upon such conversion, the company, its shareholders, the limited liability partnership into which the company has converted and the partners of that limited liability partnership shall be bound by the provisions of this Schedule that are applicable to them.

3 Eligibility for conversion—A company may apply to convert into a limited liability partnership in accordance with the provisions of this Schedule if and only if:

(*a*) there is no security interest in its assets subsisting or in force at the time of application; and

(*b*) the partners of the limited liability partnership to which it converts comprise all the shareholders of the company and no one else.

4. Statements to be filed—A company may apply to convert into a limited liability partnership by filing with the Registrar:

(*a*) a statement by all its shareholders in such form and manner to be accompanied by such fee as the Central Government may prescribe containing the following particulars, namely:

(*i*) the name and registration number of the company;

(*ii*) the date on which the company was incorporated; and

(*b*) incorporation document and statement referred to in Section 11.

5. Registration of conversion—On receiving the documents referred to in Paragraph 4, the Registrar shall, subject to the provisions of this Act, and the rules made thereunder, register the documents and issue a certificate of registration in such form as the Registrar may determine stating that the limited liability partnership is, on and from the date specified in the certificate, registered under this Act: Provided that the limited liability partnership shall, within fifteen days of the date of registration inform

the concerned Registrar of Companies with which it was registered under the provisions of the Companies Act, 1956 (1 of 1956) about the conversion and of the particulars of the limited liability partnership in such form and manner as the Central Government may prescribe.

6. Registrar may refuse to register—(1) Nothing in this Schedule shall be constructed as to require the Registrar to register any limited liability partnership if he is not satisfied with the particulars or other information furnished under the provisions of this Act:

   Provided that an appeal may be made before the Tribunal in case of refusal of registration by the Registrar:

   [25][Provided further that until the Tribunal is constituted under the Companies Act, 1956, the appeal under this sub-paragraph may be made before the Company Law Board].

   2. The Registrar may, in any particular case, require the documents referred to in Paragraph 4 to be verified in such manner, as he considers fit.

7. Effect of registration—On and from the date of registration specified in the certificate of registration issued under Paragraph 5:

   (*a*) there shall be a limited liability partnership by the name specified in the certificate of registration registered under this Act;

   (*b*) all tangible (movable or immovable) and intangible property vested in the company, all assets, interests, rights, privileges, liabilities, obligations relating to the company and the whole of the undertaking of the company shall be transferred to and shall vest in the limited liability partnership without further assurance, act or deed; and

   (*c*) the company shall be deemed to be dissolved and removed from the records of the Registrar of Companies.

8. Registration in relation to property—If any property to which clause (*b*) of Paragraph 7 applies is registered with any authority, the limited liability partnership shall, as soon as practicable, after the date of registration, take all necessary steps as required by the relevant authority to notify the authority of the conversion and of the particulars of the limited liability partnership in such form and manner as the authority may determine.

25. Ins. by G. S. R. 386 (E), dt. 4-6-2009 (w.e.f. 4-6-2009)

9. Pending proceedings—All proceedings by or against the company which are pending in any Court or Tribunal or before an authority on the date of registration may be continued, completed and enforced by or against the limited liability partnership.

10. Continuance of conviction, ruling, order or judgment—Any conviction, ruling, order or judgment of any Court, Tribunal or other authority in favour of or against the company may be enforced by or against the limited liability partnership.

11. Existing agreements—Every agreement to which the company was a party immediately before the date of registration, whether or not of such nature that the rights and liabilities thereunder could be assigned, shall have effect as from the date as if that:

    (*a*) the limited liability partnership were a party to such an agreement instead of the company; and

    (*b*) for any reference to the company, there were substituted in respect of anything to be done on or after the date of registration a reference to the limited liability partnership.

12. Existing contracts, etc.—All deeds, contracts, schemes, bonds, agreements, applications, instruments and arrangements subsisting immediately before the date of registration relating to the company or to which the company is a party shall continue in force on and after that date as if they relate to the limited liability partnership and shall be enforceable by or against the limited liability partnership as if the limited liability partnership were named therein or were a party thereto instead of the company.

13. Continuance of employment—Every contract of employment to which Paragraph 11 or Paragraph 12 applies shall continue in force on or after the date of registration as if the limited liability partnership were the employer thereunder instead of the company.

14. Existing appointment, authority or power—(1) Every appointment of the company in any role or capacity which is in force immediately before the date of registration shall take effect and operate from that date as if the limited liability partnership were appointed.

    2. Any authority or power conferred on the company which is in force immediately before the date of registration shall take effect and operate from that date as if it were conferred on the limited liability partnership.

15. Application of Paragraphs 7 to 14—The provisions of Paragraphs 7 to 14 (both inclusive) shall apply to any approval, permit or licence issued to the company under any other Act which is in force immediately before the date of registration of the limited liability partnership, subject to the provisions of such other Act under which such approval, permit or licence has been issued.

16. Notice of conversion in correspondence—

    1. The limited liability partnership shall ensure that for a period of twelve months commencing not later than fourteen days after the date of registration, every official correspondence of the limited liability partnership bears the following namely:

        (*a*) a statement that it was, as from the date of registration, converted from company into a limited liability partnership; and

        (*b*) the name and registration number of the company from which it was converted.

    2. Any limited liability partnership which contravenes the provisions of sub-paragraph (1) shall be punishable with fine which shall not be less than ten thousand rupees but which may extend to one lakh rupees and with a further fine which shall not be less than fifty rupees but which may extend to five hundred rupees for everyday after the first day after which the default continues.

■■■

Part **4**

IT Act 2000

Chapter **28**

Introduction and Application of IT Act

Learning Objectives

- Examine necessity of IT Act and find out areas of its non-application.
- Analyse the various objects of IT Act.
- Get a conceptual clarity of the various terms, which are used in this Act.
- Get an idea about computer, computer system, computer network and computer resource.

INTRODUCTION

In the recent years, there has been tremendous development in the sector of information technology. Its worldwide use and applications have greatly affected business practices and stage governance. On one hand business transactions within the country as well as amongst the various countries are being conducted and settled by using electronic devices and procedures. On the other, it has paved the way for e-Governance (Electronic governance).

In other words, information technology is being equally used by the states for conducting various operations and activities which are related to social, economic and political systems of the countries.

The use of information technology has in fact facilitated inexpensive and rapid communication, on line trading of goods and services, electronic transfer of funds and transmission and exchange of information amongst the various organisations.

In fact, paper based records of information is being replaced by electronically stored, processed and transmitted records. High degree of precision, lesser cost and high speed of conducting transactions are well known features associated with the use of this technology.

NEED OF THE ACT

In order to use electronic devices and procedures in the area of business and state governance, a suitable legal framework consisting of 'cyber laws' and other regulatory measures is required to be built. With the help of such legal framework, the use of this technology particularly in the business will gain worldwide acceptability and recognition. Similarly by using suitable legal measures, internet use may be made more popular and reliable.

INFORMATION TECHNOLOGY ACT 2000

This is the cyber law, first of its kind in India. It was enacted in the Parliament with the consent of the Indian President on 9th June 2000. This act is based on the model law on Electronic Commerce prepared and adopted by the United Nations Commission on International Trade Law in 1997. The General assembly of United Nations also recommended that all states should give favourable consideration to this 'Model Law on e-Commerce' at the time of enacting suitable piece of legislation for their country. It will bring uniformity with regard to the provisions applicable on e-Commerce and e-Governance.

To make an effective application of this law; it was also recommended that the state should also revise and amend other laws which are related to this law. In our country, Indian Penal Code, Indian Evidence Act 1872, Banker's Books Evidence Act 1891, and Reserve Bank of India Act 1934 may be suitably amended for facilitating an application of Information Technology Act.

In India, Information Technology Act was passed by Parliament and received the assent of the President of India on 9th june 2000. This Act may be called the Information Technology Act 2000.

This act provides legal recognition for transactions carried out by means of electronic data interchange and other means of electronic communication, commonly referred to as 'electronic commerce', which involves the use of alternatives paper based method of communication and storage of information, to facilitate electronic filing of documents with the Govt. agencies and it provides to further to amend Indian Penal Code, Indian Evidence Act 1872, Banker's Books Evidence Act 1891 and Reserve Bank of India Act 1934 and for matters connected there with or incidental thereto

On the basis of above contents, it becomes clear that Information Technology Act 2000 provides.

(i) Legal recognition of business transactions which are related to Electronic-Commerce.

(ii) Electronic filing of documents with Govt. agencies and promote 'Electronic-Governance'.

(iii) Suitable amendments in the various existing Acts mentioned above, which are related to various previsions of this Act.

This Act shall extend to the whole of India. It also applies to any offence or contravention committed thereunder, by any person, outside India.

This Act shall not apply to:

(i) A negotiable instrument as defined in Section 13 of the Negotiable Instrument Act 1881

(ii) A 'power of attorney', as defined in Section 1A of the Power of Attorney Act 1882

(iii) A 'trust' as defined in Section 3 of the Indian Trust Act 1882.

(iv) A 'will' as defined in Section 2, clause (h) of the Indian Succession Act 1925.

(v) Any contract for the sale or conveyance of immovable property or any interests in such property.

(vi) Any such class of documents or transactions as may be notified by the Central Government in the Official Gazette.

OBJECTS OF THE ACT

Information Technology Act contains 94 sections mainly to deal with electronic-commerce, electronic-governance, digital signature, role of certifying authorities and their regulation and cyber offences and penalties provided for. The Act aims at to achieve following objectives:

(i) To facilitate and promote electronic commerce and provide legal recognition to all transactions made through electronic devices and procedures.

(ii) To facilitate electronic-governance by providing suitable electronic devices and procedures for performing various operations and activities related to state governance.

(iii) To provide legal recognition to digital signature at par with paper based signature.

(iv) To regulate and control the functioning of various agencies dealing with electronic transactions such as certifying authorities, controller of certifying authorities and controller, etc.

(v) To check and prevent cyber offences of various nature and prescribe suitable penalties for them.

(vi) To recognise electronic transactions and records at par with paper based documentation and records.

(vii) To provide legal framework with in which electronic devices and procedures can be effectively used in a every walk of like.

(viii) To bring uniformity with regard to the use and application of electronic devices and procedures for various purposes by international community.

DEFINITIONS OF IMPORTANT TERMES

Section 2 of the IT Act provides definitions of various terms or expressions which are commonly used in this Act. These definitions are as follows:

(i) ***Access:*** In order to work upon an electronic devices one must have access to that device.

Thus an 'Access' means "gaining entry in to, instructing or communicating the logical arithmetical or memory function resources of a computer, computer system or computer network".

It is therefore, an unauthorised access or use of the device with out access will lead to an offence.

(ii) ***Addressee:*** "means a person who is intended by the originator to receive the electronic record, but does not include any intermediary".

In order to transfer or communicate information or record through electronic device two ends are needed. At one point there is a originator who originates and transfers information and at other point some one to receive it, he is known as addressee.

(iii) ***Adjudicating Officer*:** "means an adjudicating officer appointed under section 46 (1) of this Act".

Thus such officer is appointed by the Central Government for adjudging whether any person has committed any cyber offence under this Act.

(iv) ***Affixing digital signature:*** "means adoption of any methodology or procedure by a person for the purpose of authenticating an electronic record by means of digital signature".

Thus any person may transmit any information through electronic device. In order to authenticate information and to ensure that the information is same as being transmitted by the originator, digital signature method is used. It verifies identity of originator and authenticity of the information by electronic method.

(v) ***Asymmetric crypto system:*** **"**means a system of a secure key pair consisting of a private key for creating digital signature and public key to verify digital signature".

This system is also known as 'public key encryption'. It involves the use of private key and public key. Which are simply two mathematically related numbers. A private key which is used for creating digital signature transforms message or data in to coded form. And another key which is used for verifying digital signature brings coded data or message in to decoded form or original form.

(vi) ***Appropriate Government:*** "means as respect any matter".

(a) Enumerated in list II of seventh schedule to the constitution.

(b) Relating to any state law enacted under list III of the seventh schedule to the constitution.

The State Government and in any other case, the Central Government.

(vii) ***Certifying Authority:*** "means a person, who has been granted a licence to issue digital signature certificate under section 24".

The certifying authority has an important role in verifying and identifying the person seeking a certificate. And in certifying that a public key is associated with him.

(viii) ***Certification Practice Statement:*** "means a statement issued by certifying authority to specify the practices that the certifying authority employs in issuing digital signature certificate".

(ix) ***Computer:*** "means any electronic magnetic, optical or other high speed data processing device or system which performs logical, arithmetic and memory functions by manipulation of electronic, magnetic an optical impulses and includes all input, output, processing storage, computer software or communication facilities which are connected or related to the computer in a computer system or computer network".

Thus a computer is a

(a) Electronic device used for processing data.

(b) For processing data, it performs logical, mathematical and memory functions.

(c) It also include input, output, process, software and other communication facilities.

(x) ***Computer Network:*** "means inter-connection of one or more computer through"-

(a) The use of satellite, microwave, terrestrial line, or other communication media.

(b) Terminals or a complex consisting of two or more interconnected computers, whether or not the inter connection is continuously maintained.

(xi) ***Computer Resource:*** "means, computer, computer system computer network, data, computer data base or software".

(xii) ***Computer System:*** "means a device or collection of devices, including input and output support devices, excluding calculators which are not programmable and capable of being used in conjunction with external files, which contains computer programme, electronic instructions, input data and output data that performs logic, arithmetic, data storage and retrieval, communication control and other functions".

(xiii) ***Controller:*** "means the controller of certifying Authorities appointed under sub-section (1) of section 17".

(xiv) ***Cyber Appellate Tribunal:*** "means the cyber regulation appellate tribunal established under sub section (1) of section 48".

(xv) ***Data:*** "means a representation of information knowledge, facts, concepts, or instructions which are being prepared or have been prepared in a formalized manner and is intended to be processed or has been processed in a computer system or computer network or may be in any form (including computer printouts, magnetic or optical storage media, punch cards, punched tapes) or stored internally in the memory of the computer".

(xvi) ***Digital Signature:*** "means authentication of any electronic record by a subscriber by means of an electronic method or procedure in accordance with the provisions of section 3".

(xvii) ***Digital Signature Certificate:*** "means a Digital Signature Certificate issued under sub-section (4) of section 35".

(xviii) ***Electronic Form:*** with reference to information means any information generated, sent, received or stored in media, magnetic, optical, computer memory, micro film, computer generated micro fiche or similar device.

(xix) ***Electronic Gazette:*** means the Official Gazette published in the electronic form.

(xx) ***Electronic Record:*** means data, record or data generated, image or sound stored, received or sent in an electronic form or micro film or computer generated micro fiche.

(xxi) ***Function:*** in relation to a computer, includes logic, control, arithmetical process, deletion, storage and retrieval and communication or telecommunication from or within a computer.

(xxii) ***Information:*** includes data, text, images, sound, voice, codes, computer programmes, software and databases or micro film or computer generated micro fiche.

(xxiii) ***Intermediary:*** with respect to any particular electronic message means any person who on behalf of another person receives, stores or transmits that message or provides any service with respect to that message.

(xxiv) ***Key Pair:*** in an asymmetric crypto system, means a private key and its mathematically related public key, which are so related that the public key can verify a digital signature created by the private key.

(xxv) ***Law:*** includes any Act of Parliament or of a State Legislature, Ordinances promulgated by the President or a Governor, as the case may be. Regulations made by the President under article 240, Bills enacted as President's Act under sub-clause (a) of clause (1) of article 357 of the Constitution and includes rules, regulations, bye-laws and orders issued or made thereunder.

(xxvi) ***Licence:*** means a licence granted to a Certifying Authority under section 24.

(a) ***Originator:*** means a person who sends, generates, stores or transmits any electronic message or causes any electronic message to .be sent, generated, stored or transmitted to any other person but does not include an intermediary.

(b) ***Prescribed:*** means prescribed by rules made under this Act.

(c) ***Private key:*** means the key of a key pair used to create a digital signature.

(d) ***Public key:*** means the key of a key pair used to verify a digital signature and listed in the Digital Signature Certificate.

(e) ***Secure system:*** means computer hardware, software, and procedure that—

  (i) are reasonably secure from unauthorised access and misuse;

  (ii) provide a reasonable level of reliability and correct operation;

  (iii) are reasonably suited to performing the intended functions; and

  (iv) adhere to generally accepted security procedures;

(f) ***Security procedure:*** means the security procedure prescribed under section 16 by the Central Government;

(g) ***Subscriber:*** means a person in whose name the Digital Signature Certificate is issued.

(h) ***Verify:*** in relation to a digital signature, electronic record or public key, with its grammatical variations and cognate expressions means to determine whether—

  (i) the initial electronic record was affixed with the digital signature by the use of private key corresponding to the public key of the subscriber;

  (ii) the initial electronic record is retained intact or has been altered since such electronic record was so affixed with the digital signature.

Review Questions

1. What do you mean by Information Technology. Discuss its role in business and state governance.
2. Explain Information Technology Act 2000. Discuss the need of enacting this act.
3. Explain various objectives of Information Technology Act 2000.
4. Write a note on the applications of Information Technology Act 2000.
5. Define the following terms:

   (i) Addressee

   (ii) Computer

   (iii) Data

   (iv) Information

   (v) Digital signature

   (vi) Originator

   (vii) Certifying authority

   (viii) Computer system

   (ix) Computer network

   (x) Asymmetric crypto system.

■■■

Chapter 29

Digital Signature and Electronic Governance

Learning Objectives

- Get familiar with the concept of Digital Signature and find out its significance in business.
- Compare public key with private key.
- Analyse the system of making and using digital signature.
- Have a Conceptual Clarity about Electronic Governance and remember legal provisions which facilitate electronic-governance.

INTRODUCTION

While using paper based documents, it is easy for the originator or sender of a message or information to put his signature on it. By signing the documents, the identity of the sender is being certified and the information or the message gets authenticated.

But in an electronic message it is not possible to affix a handwritten signature while transmitting it. Therefore, Information Technology Act has recognised digital signature so that the transactions made through electronic device is authenticated and gets legal consequences. A digital signature plays a key role in authenticating electronic records. Therefore digital signature are considered at par with paper signature. Like paper signature, it can be used as a proof of a contract or transaction between two parties. This is so because the party initiating electronic transaction cannot deny the contents of a document originated and transmitted through electronic device.

Due to digital signature, on-line trading and internet contracts have been legally possible.

MEANING

According to section 2 (1) (d) 'affixing digital signatur' means, "the adoption for the purpose of authenticating or procedure by a person for the purpose of authenticating an electronic record by means of digital signature".

Thus digital signature means authentication of electronic record and transactions.

"According to the Information Technology Act, digital signature means, authentication of an electronic record in accordance with the provisions of section 3. Subscriber means, "a person in whose name the digital signature certificate is issued".

Digital signature is a data item that accompanies digitally encoded message which can be used to ascertain an identity of originator and integrity of message.

AUTHENTICATION OF ELECTRONIC RECORDS (SECTION 3)

(Creating and verifying digital signature).

"Any subscriber in whose name digital signature certificate is issued may authenticate an electronic record by affixing his digital signature. The authentication of an electronic record shall be affected by the use of 'asymmetric crypto system' and 'hash function' which envelop and transform the initial electronic record into another electronic record".

In other words, digital signature is technically a 'message digest'. It is created by processing the contents of a message through special algorithm. It means it involves the transformation of message into 'message digest' by using a technical process called 'hash function', encoding it and sending it with the message which is also encoded.

***Explanation*:** For the purpose of this section, 'hash function' means an algorithm mapping or translation of one sequence bits into another, generally smaller set known as "hash result', such that an electronic record yields the same 'hash result' every time the algorithm is executed with the same electronic record as its input making it computationally infeasible—

(a) To derive or reconstruct the original electronic record from the 'hash result' produced by the algorithm.

(b) That two electronic records can produce same 'hash result' using the algorithm.

***Algorithm*:** An algorithm is a set of mathematical instruction used for finding out answer to a mathematical problem. It may also be defined as a finite set of instructions that accomplish a particular task. Thus it is with the help of a special algorithm the contents of message are processed to yield a value which is known as 'has result'.

***Asymmetric crypto system*:** While transmitting information and making transactions through electronic device it is necessary to ensure that these are authentic and have not been tampered with by any intermediary in the process of transmission.

For this purpose, section 3 of this Act provides that authentication of electronic record is to be affected by the use of 'asymmetric crypto system'. This system involves the use of 'encryption' (coding of message) and 'decryption' (decoding of a message) methodologies and other software tools.

According to section 2 (1) (t) "asymmetric crypto system means a system of a secure key pair consisting of private key for creating digital signature and a public key to verify digital signature". These keys are like large passwords.

In asymmetric crypto system, each person will have two corresponding and matched keys-one called a 'private key' which is always kept secure with such person. And the others called 'public key' which the person shares with others and makes it available to them on specialised database called 'repositories' or through 'certifying authorities'.

These two keys public key and private key are used to encrypt and decrypt the massage respectively. The sender or originator of message procures public key of the intended receiver from 'repositories' and by using this key he encrypts the message. (Coded message). On receiving such coded message, the receiver or addressee use his private key (which is only with him) to decrypt (decode) the encrypted (coded) message.

The public key and private key of any person or organisation would be so mathematically linked that a messages encrypted using one key can only be decrypted by using corresponding other key. However, it is not possible to derive private key of a person from his public key.

***Verification*:** Any person by the use of public key of the subscriber can verify electronic record. The private key and public key are unique to the subscriber and constitute a functioning 'key pair'.

Difference between public key and private key.

	Public key	*Private key*
1. Use	Public key is used for encrypting (coding) the a message.	Private key is used for decrypting (decoding) a message.
2. Availability	Public key is freely available on 'repositories' on through certifying authorities.	Private key is available only with the sender of message. It is always kept secure with him.
3. Function	Public key is used to verify digital signature.	Private key is used for creating digital signature.

ELECTRONIC GOVERNANCE

An electronic device and procedures are also being used in the sphere of governance. To make its use more dependable, transparent and effective, the Information Technology Act has accorded legal recognition to electronic records, digital signatures, electronic form of dealing with Govt. offices and its agencies. Not only this, but also the retention of information in an electronic format has also been given legal recognition provided such information remains accessible and usable in future.

The Act also provides for the filing of any form or application, creation, retention of records, issue or grant of licence, receipt and payment in Govt. offices in electronic form. It has been primarily done with an object of facilitating electronic-governance.

The Act provides the following provisions to facilitate electronic-governance.

1. *Legal recognition of eleconic records*—(section 4)

Where any law provides that information or any other matter shall be in writing or in the typewritten or printed form, then, notwithstanding anything contained in such law, such requirement shall be deemed to have been satisfied if such information or matter is–

(a) rendered or made available in an electronic form; and
(b) accessible so as to be usable for a subsequent reference.

2. *Legal recognition of digital signatures*

Where any law provides that information or any other matter shall be authenticated by affixing the signature or any document shall be signed or bear the signature of any person (hen, notwithstanding anything contained in such law, such requirement shall be deemed to have been satisfied, if such information or matter is authenticated by means of digital signature affixed in such manner as may be prescribed by the Central Government.

***Explanation*—**For the purposes of this section, 'signed', with its grammatical variations and cognate expressions, shall, with reference to a person, means affixing of his hand written signature or any mark on any document and the expression 'signature' shall be construed accordingly.

3. *Use of electronic records and digital signatures in Government and its agencies*

(1) Where any law provides for—

(a) the filing of any form application or any other document with any office, authority, body or agency owned or controlled by the appropriate Government in a particular manner;
(b) the issue or grant of any licence, permit, sanction or approval by whatever name called in a particular manner;

(c) the receipt or payment of money in a particular manner, then, notwithstanding anything contained in any other law for the time being in force, such requirement shall be deemed to have been satisfied if such filing, issue, grant, receipt or payment, as the case may be, is effected by means of such electronic form as may be prescribed by the appropriate Government.

(2) The appropriate Government may, for the purposes of sub-section (1), by rules prescribe —

(a) the manner and format in which such electronic records shall be filed, created or issued;

(b) the manner or method of payment of any fee or charges for filing, creation or issue any electronic record under clause (a).

4. *Retention of electronic records*

(1) Where any law provides that documents, records or information shall be retained for any specific period, then, that requirement shall be deemed to have been satisfied if such documents, records or information are retained in the electronic form, if—

(a) the information contained therein remains accessible so as to be usable for a subsequent reference;

(b) the electronic record is retained in the format in which it was originally generated, sent or received or in a format which can be demonstrated to represent accurately the information originally generated, sent or received;

(c) the details which will facilitate the identification of the origin, destination, date and time of despatch or receipt of such electronic record are available in the electronic record:

Provided that this clause does not apply to any information which is automatically generated solely for the purpose of enabling an electronic record to be despatched or received.

(2) Nothing in this section shall apply to any law that expressly provides for the retention of documents, records or information in the form of electronic records.

5. *Publication of rule, regulation, etc., in Electronic Gazette*

Where any law provides that any rule, regulation, order, bye-law, notification or any other matter shall be published in the Official Gazette, then, such requirement shall be deemed to have been satisfied if such rule, regulation, order, bye-law, notification or any other matter is published in the Official Gazette or Electronic Gazette:

Provided that where any rule, regulation, order, bye-law, notification or any other matter is published in the Official Gazette or Electronic Gazette, the date of publication shall be deemed to be the date of the Gazette which was first published in any form.

6. Sections 6, 7 and 8 not to confer right to insist document should be accepted in electronic form

Nothing contained in sections 6, 7 and 8 shall confer a right upon any person to insist that any Ministry or Department of the Central Government or the State Government or any authority or body established by or under any law or controlled or funded by the Central or State Government should accept, issue, create, retain and preserve any document in the form of electronic records or effect any monetary transaction in the electronic form.

7. Power to make rules by Central Government in respect of digital signature

The Central Government may, for the purposes of this Act, by rules, prescribe—

- (a) the type of digital signature;
- (b) the manner and format in which the digital signature shall be affixed;
- (c) the manner or procedure which facilitates identification of the person affixing the digital signature;
- (d) control processes and procedures to ensure adequate integrity, security and confidentiality of electronic records or payments; and
- (e) any other matter which is necessary to give legal effect to digital signatures.

8. Attribution of electronic records

An electronic record shall be attributed to the originator—

- (a) if it was sent by the originator himself;
- (b) by a person who had the authority to act on behalf of the originator in respect of that electronic record; or
- (c) by an information system programmed by or on behalf of the originator to operate automatically.

9. Acknowledgment of receipt

(1) Where the originator has not agreed with the addressee that the acknowledgment of receipt of electronic record be given in a particular form or by a particular method, an acknowledgment may be given by—

- (a) any communication by the addressee, automated or otherwise; or
- (b) any conduct of the addressee, sufficient to indicate to the originator that the electronic record has been received.

(2) Where the originator has stipulated that the electronic record shall be binding only on receipt of an acknowledgment of such electronic record by him, then unless acknowledgment has been so received, the electronic record shall be deemed to have been never sent by the originator.

(3) Where the originator has not stipulated that the electronic record shall be binding only on receipt of such acknowledgment, and the acknowledgment has not been received by the originator within the time specified or agreed or, if no

time has been specified or agreed to within a reasonable time, then the originator may give notice to the addressee stating that no acknowledgment has been received by him and specifying a reasonable time by which the acknowledgment must be received by him and if no acknowledgment is received within the aforesaid time limit he may after giving notice to the addressee, treat the electronic record as though it has never been sent.

10. ***Time and place of despatch and receipt of electronic record***

(1) Save as otherwise agreed to between the originator and the addressee, the dispatch of an electronic record occurs when it enters a computer resource outside the control of the originator.

(2) Save as otherwise agreed between the originator and the addressee, the time of receipt of an electronic record shall be determined as follows, namely :—

- (a) if the addressee has designated a computer resource for the purpose of receiving electronic records,—
  - (i) receipt occurs at the time when the electronic, record enters the designated computer resource; or
  - (ii) if the electronic record is sent to a computer resource of the addressee that is not the designated computer resource, receipt occurs at the time when the electronic record is retrieved by the addressee;
- (b) if the addressee has not designated a computer resource along with specified timings, if any, receipt occurs when the electronic record enters the computer resource of the addressee.

(3) Save as otherwise agreed to between the originator and the addressee, an electronic record is deemed to be despatched at the place where the originator has his place of business, and is deemed to be received at the place where the addressee has his place of business.

(4) The provisions of sub-section (2) shall apply notwithstanding that the place where the computer resource is located may be different from the place where the electronic record is deemed to have been received under sub-section (3).

(5) For the purposes of this section, —

- (a) if the originator or the addressee has more than one place of business, the principal place of business, shall be the place of business;
- (b) if the originator or the addressee does not have a place of business, his usual place of residence shall be deemed to be the place of business;
- (c) 'usual place of residence', in relation to a body corporate, means the place where it is registered.

Review Questions

1. What is digital signature? How would you create and verify digital signature.
2. Define Asymmetric Crypto System and distinguish between 'Public key' and 'Private key'.
3. What do you mean by Electronic Governance? Discuss the various provisions of IT Act which Electronic Governance.
4. Write notes on:
    1. Digital Signature
    2. Electronic Governance
    3. Asymmetric Crypto System
    4. Provision regarding retention of electronic records in govt. offices.

■■■

Chapter **30**

Regulation of Certifying Authorities

Learning Objectives

- Examine the legal mechanism of regulation of certifying authorities.
- Remember the procedure of appointment and functions of controller and other officers.
- Examine the legal provisions of this Act regarding issue of licence used for issuing digital signature, its renewal, suspension and rejection.
- Get an idea about operational responsibility of certifying authority.
- Analyse the procedure of issue, suspension and revocation of digital signature certificate.

INTRODUCTION

To encourage the rapid growth of e-Commerce and e-Governance, an effective legal environment and mechanism is required. It is necessary to build and strengthen proper legal infrastructure of various authorities to regulate the devices and procedures such as issue and use of digital signature certificate, use of public and private keys, use of internet facilities and use of cyber space, etc.

With a view to regulate these, IT Act 2000, provides for an appointment, functions, powers and duties of the controller of certifying authorities. It also lays down procedure for issuing licence to scertifying authority who grants digital signature certificate and seeks compliance of relevant provisions of this Act. It also deals with suspension, revocation and renewal of licence issued to these authorities. The Act also provides legal provisions regarding operational responsibilities, powers and functions of certifying authorities.

In brief, the regulation of certifying authorities or digital infrastructure in India consists of

(a) Appointment of controller of certifying authority (C.C.A). The Central govt. has already appointed such controller for superwising and controlling overall functioning of certifying authorities.

(b) Certifying Authorities (C.A.). These authorities will get licence from the controller and will function under the supervision and directions of the controller. These authorities primarily deal with an issues and use of digital signature certificate.

A. Appointment of Controller and other Officers

(i) The Central Government may, by notification in the Official Gazette, appoint a Controller of Certifying Authorities for the purposes of this Act and may also by the same or subsequent notification appoint such number of Deputy Controllers and Assistant Controllers as it deems fit.

(ii) The Controller shall discharge his functions under this Act subject to the general control and directions of the Central Government.

(iii) The Deputy Controllers and Assistant Controllers shall perform the functions assigned to them by the Controller under the general superintendence and control of the Controller.

(iv) The qualifications, experience and terms and conditions of service of Controller, Deputy Controllers and Assistant Controllers shall be such as may be prescribed by the Central Government.

(v) The Head Office and Branch Office of the office of the Controller shall be at such places as the Central Government may specify, and these may be established at such places as the Central Government may think fit.

(vi) There shall be a seal of the Office of the Controller.

B. Functions of Controller

The Controller may perform all or any of the following functions, namely:-

(a) exercising supervision over the activities of the Certifying Authorities;

(b) certifying public keys of the Certifying Authorities;

(c) laying down the standards to be maintained by the Certifying Authorities;

(d) specifying the qualifications and experience which employees of the Certifying Authorities should possess;

(e) specifying the conditions subject to which the Certifying Authorities shall conduct their business;

(f) specifying the contents of written, printed or visual materials and advertisements that may be distributed or used in respect of a Digital Signature Certificate and the public key;

(g) specifying the form and content of a Digital Signature Certificate and the key,

(h) specifying the form and manner in which accounts shall be maintained by the Certifying Authorities;

(i) specifying the terms and conditions subject to which auditors may be appointed and the remuneration to be paid to them;

(j) facilitating the establishment of any electronic system by a Certifying Authority either solely or jointly with other Certifying Authorities and regulation of such systems;

(k) specifying the manner in which the Certifying Authorities shall conduct their dealings with the subscribers;

(I) resolving any conflict of interests between the Certifying Authorities and the subscribers;

(m) laying down the duties of the Certifying Authorities;

(n) maintaining a database containing the disclosure record of every Certifying Authority containing such particulars as may be specified by regulations, which shall be accessible to public.

C. Recognition of foreign Certifying Authorities

(1) Subject to such conditions and restrictions as may be specified by regulations, the Controller may with the previous approval of the Central Government, and by notification the Official Gazette, recognise any foreign Certifying Authority as a Certifying Authority for the purposes of this Act.

(2) Where any Certifying Authority is recognised under sub-section (1), the Digit Signature Certificate issued by such Certifying Authority shall be valid for the purposes of this Act.

(3) The Controller may, if he is satisfied that any Certifying Authority has contravened any of the conditions and restrictions subject to which it was granted recognition under subsection (1) he may, for reasons to be recorded in writing, by notification in the Official Gazette, revoke such recognition.

D. Controller to Act as Repository

(1) The Controller shall be the repository of all Digital Signature Certificates issued under this Act.

(2) The Controller shall–

   (a) make use of hardware, software and procedures that are secure .from intrusion and misuse;

   (b) observe such other standards as may be prescribed by the Central Government to ensure that the secrecy and security of the digital signatures are assured.

(3) The Controller shall maintain a computerised data base of all public keys in such a manner that such data base and the public keys are available to any member of the public.

E. Licence to Issue Digital Signature Certificates

(1) Subject to the provisions of sub-section (2), any person may make an application, to the Controller, for a licence to issue Digital Signature Certificates.

(2) No licence shall be issued under sub-section (1), unless the applicant fulfils such requirements with respect to qualification, expertise, manpower, financial resources and other infrastructure facilities, which are necessary to issue Digital Signature Certificates as may be prescribed by the Central Government

(3) A licence granted under this section shall–

(a) be valid for such period as may be prescribed by the Central Government.

(b) not be transferable or heritable.

(c) be subject to such terms and conditions as may be specified by the regulations.

I. Application for licence

(1) Every application for issue of a licence shall be in such form as may be prescribed by the Central Government.

(2) Every application for issue of a licence shall be accompanied by–

(a) a certification practice statement;

(b) a statement including the procedures with respect to identification of the applicant;

(c) payment of such fees, not exceeding twenty-five thousand rupees as may be prescribed by the Central Government;

(d) such other documents, as may be prescribed by the Central Government.

II. Renewal of licence

An application for renewal of a licence shall be–

(a) in such form;

(b) accompanied by such fees, not exceeding five thousand rupees,

as may be prescribed by the Central Government and shall be made not less than forty-five days before the date of expiry of the period of validity of the licence.

III. Procedure for grant or rejection of licence

The Controller may, on receipt of an application under sub-section (1) of section 21, after considering the documents accompanying the application and such other factors, as he deems fit, grant the licence or reject the application:

Provided that no application shall be rejected under this section unless the applicant has been given a reasonable opportunity of presenting his case.

IV. Suspension of licence

(1) The Controller may, if he is satisfied after making such inquiry, as he may think fit, that a Certifying Authority has–

(a) made a statement in, or in relation to, the application for the issue or renewal of the licence, which is incorrect or false in material particulars;

(b) failed to comply with the terms and conditions subject to which the licence was granted;

(c) failed to maintain the standards specified under clause (b) of sub-section (2) of section 20;

(d) contravened any provisions of this Act, rule, regulation or order made thereunder,

The controller may revoke the licence:

Provided that no licence shall be revoked unless the Certifying Authority has been given a reasonable opportunity of showing cause against the proposed revocation.

(2) The Controller may, if he has reasonable cause to believe that there is any ground for revoking a licence under sub-section (1), by order suspend such licence pending the completion of any inquiry ordered by him:

Provided that no licence shall be suspended for a period exceeding ten days unless the Certifying Authority has been given a reasonable opportunity of showing cause against the proposed suspension.

(3) No Certifying Authority whose licence has been suspended shall issue any Digital Signature Certificate during such suspension.

V. Notice of suspension or revocation of licence

(1) Where the licence of the Certifying Authority is suspended or revoked, the Controller shall publish notice of such suspension or revocation, as the case may be, in the database maintained by him.

(2) Where one or more repositories are specified, the Controller shall publish notices of such suspension or revocation, as the case may be, in all such repositories:

Provided that the data base containing the notice of such suspension or revocation, as the case may be, shall be made available through a web site which shall be accessible round the clock.

Provided further that the Controller may, if he considers necessary, publicise the contents of database in such electronic or other media, as he may consider appropriate.

F. Powers of Controller

The controller of Certifying Authorities has the following powers:

I. Power to delegate

The Controller may, in writing, authorise the Deputy Controller, Assistant Controller or any officer to exercise any of the powers of the Controller under this Chapter.

II. Power to investigate contraventions

(1) The Controller or any officer authorised by him in this behalf shall take up for investigation any contravention of the provisions of this Act, rules or regulations made thereunder.

(2) The Controller or any officer authorised by him in this behalf shall exercise the like powers which are conferred on Income-tax authorities under Chapter XIII of the Income-tax Act, 1961 and shall exercise such powers, subject to such limitations laid down under that Act.

III. Access to computers and data.

(1) Without prejudice to the provisions of sub-section (1) of section 69, the Controller or any person authorised by him shall, if he has reasonable cause to suspect that any contravention of the provisions of this Act, rules or regulations made thereunder has been committed, have access to any computer system, any apparatus, data or any other material connected with such system, for the purpose of searching or causing a search to be made for obtaining any information or data contained in or available to such computer system.

(2) For the purposes of sub-section (1), the Controller or any person authorised by him may, by order, direct any person incharge of, or otherwise concerned with the operation of, the computer system, data apparatus or material, to provide him with such reasonable technical and other assistance as he may consider necessary.

Certifying Authority

Certifying authority may be defined as an individual or body corporate who has been granted licence by the controller for issuing digital signature certificate. Such individual or body corporate possess required technical skills. In our country, National Information Centre (NIC) and Tata Consultancy Services (TCS) are the leading certifying authorities.

Operational Responsibilities of Certifying authorities

The certifying authorities have the following responsibilities:

1. *Every Certifying Authority shall–*

(a) make use of hardware, software and procedures that are secure from isntrusion and misuse.

(b) provide a reasonable level of reliability in its services which are reasonably suited to the performance of intended functions;

(c) adhere to security procedures to ensure that the secrecy and privacy of the digital signatures are assured; and

(d) observe such other standards as may be specified by regulations.

2. *Certifying Authority to ensure compliance of the Act, etc.*

Every Certifying Authority shall ensure that every person employed or otherwise engaged by it complies, in the course of his employment or engagement, with the provisions of this Act, rules, regulations and orders made thereunder.

3. *Display of licence*

Every Certifying Authority shall display its licence at a conspicuous place of the premises in which it carries on its business.

4. *Surrender of licence*

(1) Every Certifying Authority whose licence is suspended or revoked shall immediately after such suspension or revocation, surrender the licence to the Controller.

(2) Where any Certifying Authority fails to surrender a licence under sub-section (1), the person in whose favour a licence is issued, shall be guilty of an offence and shall be punished with imprisonment which may extend up to six months or a fine which may extend up to ten thousand rupees or with both.

5. *Disclosure*

(1) Every Certifying Authority shall disclose in the manner specified by regulations–

   (a) its Digital Signature Certificate which contains the public key corresponding to the private key used by that Certifying Authority to digitally sign another Digital Signature Certificate;

   (b) any certification practice statement relevant thereto;

   (c) notice of the revocation or suspension of its Certifying Authority certificate, if any; and

   (d) any other fact that materially and adversely affects either the reliability of a Digital Signature Certificate, which that Authority has issued, or the Authority's ability to perform its services.

(2) Wherein the opinion of the Certifying Authority any event has occurred or any situation has arisen which may materially and adversely affect the integrity of its computer system or the conditions subject to which a Digital Signature Certificate was granted, then, the Certifying Authority shall–
   (a) use reasonable efforts to notify any person who is likely to be affected by that occurrence; or
   (b) act in accordance with the procedure specified in its certification practice statement to deal with such event or situation.

DIGITAL SIGNATURE CERTIFICATES

The basic function of certifying authority is to issue digital signature certificate to the applicants. The following procedure is used for this purpose:

Procedure to Issue Digital Signature Certificate

(1) Any person may make an application to the Certifying Authority for the issue of a digital Signature Certificate in such form as may be prescribed by the Central Government.

(2) Every such application shall be accompanied by such fee not exceeding twenty-five thousand rupees as may be prescribed by the Central Government, to be paid to the Certifying Authority:

Provided that while prescribing fees under sub-section (2) different fees may be prescribed for 'different classes of applicants'.

(3) Every such application shall be accompanied by a certification practice statement or where there is no such statement, a statement containing such particulars, as may be specified by regulations.

(4) On receipt of an application under sub-section (1), the Certifying Authority may, after consideration of the certification practice statement or the other statement under sub-section (3) and after making such enquiries as it may deem fit, grant the Digital Signature Certificate or for reasons to be recorded in writing, reject the application:

Provided that no Digital Signature Certificate shall be granted unless the Certifying authority is satisfied that–

(a) the applicant holds the private key corresponding to the public key to be listed in the Digital Signature Certificate;

(b) the applicant holds a private key, which is capable of creating a digital signature;

(c) the public key to be listed in the certificate can be used to verify a digital signature affixed by the private key held by the applicant:

Provided further that no application shall be rejected unless the applicant has been given a reasonable opportunity of showing cause against the proposed rejection.

Representations upon Issuance of Digital Signature Certificate

A Certifying Authority while issuing a Digital Signature Certificate shall certify that—

(a) it has complied with the provisions of this Act and the rules and regulations made thereunder,

(b) it has published the Digital Signature Certificate or otherwise made it available to such person relying on it and the subscriber has accepted it;

(c) the subscriber holds the private key corresponding to the public key, listed in the Digital Signature Certificate;

(d) the subscriber's public key and private key constitute a functioning key pair,

(e) the information contained in the Digital Signature Certificate is accurate; and

(f) it has no knowledge of any material fact, which if it had been included in the Digital Signature Certificate would adversely affect the reliability of the representations made in clauses (a) to (d).

Suspension of Digital Signature Certificate

(1) Subject to the provisions of sub-section (2), the Certifying Authority which has issued a Digital Signature Certificate may suspend such Digital Signature Certificate,–

(a) on receipt of a request to that effect *from*–

(i) the subscriber listed into Digital Signature Certificate; or

(ii) any person duly authorised to act on behalf of that subscriber,

(b) if it is of opinion that the Digital Signature Certificate should be suspended in public interest

(2) A Digital Signature Certificate shall not be suspended for a period exceeding fifteen days unless the subscriber has been given an opportunity of being heard in the matter.

(3) On suspension of a Digital Signature Certificate under this section, the Certifying Authority shall communicate the same to the subscriber.

Revocation of Digital Signature Certificate

(1) A Certifying Authority may revoke a Digital Signature Certificate issued by it–

(a) where the subscriber or any other person authorised by him makes a request to that effect; or

(b) upon the death of the subscriber, or

(c) upon the dissolution of the firm or winding up of the company where the subscriber is a firm or a company.

(2) Subject to the provisions of sub-section (3) and without prejudice to the provisions of sub-section (1), a Certifying Authority may revoke a Digital Signature Certificate which has been issued by it at any time, if it is of opinion that–

(a) a material fact represented in the Digital Signature Certificate is false or has been concealed;

(b) a requirement for issuance of the Digital Signature Certificate was not satisfied;

(c) the Certifying Authority's private key or security system was compromised in a manner materially affecting the Digital Signature Certificate's reliability;

(d) the subscriber has been declared insolvent or dead or where a subscriber is a firm or a company, which has been dissolved, wound-up or otherwise ceased to exist.

(3) A Digital Signature Certificate shall not be revoked unless the subscriber has been given an opportunity of being heard in the matter.

(4) On revocation of a Digital Signature Certificate under this section, the Certifying Authority shall communicate the same to the subscriber.

Notice of Suspension or Revocation

(1) Where a Digital Signature Certificate is suspended or revoked under section 37 or section 38, the Certifying Authority shall publish a notice of such suspension or revocation, as the case may be, in the repository specified in the Digital Signature Certificate for publication of such notice.

(2) Where one or more repositories are specified, the Certifying Authority shall publish notices of such suspension or revocation, as the case may he. in all such repositories.

DUTIES OF SUBSCRIBERS

The individual or organisation who has been granted digital signature certificate in known as 'subscriber'. The subscriber has the following duties which are laid down under section 41 to 43 or this Act :

A. *Generating key pair*

Where any Digital Signature Certificate, the public key of which corresponds to the private key of that subscriber which is to be listed in the Digital Signature Certificate has been accepted by a subscriber, then, the subscriber shall generate the key pair by applying the security procedure.

B. *Acceptance of Digital Signature Certificate*

(1) A subscriber shall be deemed to have accepted a Digital Signature Certificate if he publishes or authorises the publication of a Digital Signature Certificate–

(a) to one or more persons;

(b) in a repository, or otherwise demonstrates his approval of the Digital Signature Certificate in any manner.

(2) By accepting a Digital Signature Certificate the subscriber certifies to all who reasonably rely on the information contained in the Digital Signature Certificate that–

(a) the subscriber holds the private key corresponding to the public key listed in the Digital Signature Certificate and is entitled to hold the same;

(b) all representations made by the subscriber to the Certifying Authority and all material relevant to the information contained in the Digital Signature Certificate are true;

(c) all information in the Digital Signature Certificate that is within the knowledge of the subscriber is true.

C. *Control of Private key*

(1) Every subscriber shall exercise reasonable care to retain control of the private key corresponding to the public key listed in his Digital Signature Certificate and take all steps to prevent its disclosure to a person not authorised to affix the digital signature of the subscriber.

(2) If the private key corresponding to the public key listed in the Digital Signature Certificate has been compromised, then, the subscriber shall communicate the same without any delay to the Certifying Authority in such manner as may be specified by the regulations.

Explanation—For the removal of doubts, it is hereby declared that the subscriber shall be liable till he has informed the Certifying Authority that the private key has been compromised.

Review Questions

1. What do you mean by controller of certifying authorities? Explain his functions.
2. Explain the procedure to be followed by the controller for issuing licence and suspending its use.
3. Discuss the various powers which are given to the controller under the provisions of IT Act.

4. What do you mean be certifying authorities? Discuss the operational responsibilities of such authorities.
5. Define digital signature certificate. Explain the procedure followed by the certifying authorities to issue digital signature certificate.
6. Who is a subscriber? Discuss his duties regarding digital signature certificate.
7. Explain the main provisions of the IT Act with respect to digital signature certificate.
8. Write notes on:
   (a) Digital signature certificate
   (b) Certifying authorities
   (c) Subscriber
   (d) Revocation of digital signature certificate

Chapter **31**

Cyber Contraventions, Adjudication and Offences

Learning Objectives

- Understand the basic concept of cyber contraventions and compare these with cyber offences.
- Analyse the penalty prescribed for cyber contraventions and get to know how these contraventions are adjudicated.
- Examine the necessity of having Cyber Regulations Appellate Tribunal.
- Analyse the various cyber offences and penalties prescribed for these offences.

INTRODUCTION

In spite of adequate security measures adopted by an owner of computer, computer system and computer network, its unauthorised and illegal use can not be checked completely. Any illegal act or unauthorised use of the computer system amounts to cyber crimes. The terms cyber crime includes both cyber contraventions and cyber offences. Under Information Technology Act, penalty is imposed on the person who commits such crime. He may be compelled to pay compensation to the affected party or may be awarded imprisonment as the case may be. The cyber crimes may be in the form of contravention or offence.

(i) ***Contraventions:*** A contravention is a mere violation or breach of cyber rules or procedures used in computer system or network such as to gain unauthorized access to computer system, introducing computer virus, disrupting the use of system etc. The person who is found guilty for such acts may be liable to pay damage as compensation to the affected person not exceeding rupees one crore. Section 43 to 47 of this Act deal with contraventions, penalties and their adjudication.

According to section 43 of this Act "if a person, without permission of the owner or any other person who is in-charge of a computer, computer system or computer network does any of the following act, he shall be guilty of a contravention of the Act"

(a) *Accessing or securing access to such computer, computer system or computer network.*

This contravention can be considered as something similar to the trespass of a person's property. The term 'access' defined in Sec. 2(1)(a) would mean gaining a possibility of instructing or communicating with the logical, arithmetical or memory resources of a computer. The access may be secured in an, actual physical sense or from a distance.

(b) *Downloading, copying or extracting any data, computer data base or information from such computer, computer system or computer network including information or data held or stored in any removable storage medium.*

This provision would cover situations similar to theft or violation of a person's copyrights.

(c) *Introducing or causing to be introduced all computer contaminant or computer virus into any computer, computer system or computer network.*

These two terms 'contaminant' and 'virus' have been used in the Act. Although these two differ in their technical meaning but not in their consequence. The terms have been defined later under explanations,

(d) *Damaging or causing to be damaged any computer, computer system or computer network, data, computer data base or any other programs residing in such computer, computer system or computer network.*

It may be noted that a similar activity may amount to an section. 6.

(e) *Disrupting or causing disruption to any computer, computer system or computer network.*

The disruption may be caused by doing anything stated in earlier provisions, such a introduction of virus, etc. or a damage to any computer resource, or it may be done in any other manner.

(f) *Denying or causing the denial of access to any person authorized to access any computer, computer system or computer network by any means.*

Such denials may be attempted by the person by flooding the internet networks with unnecessary traffic so as to disrupt their normal functioning. Such disruption prevents the authorised users from utilising the services of these internet service providers (ISPs). In addition to it, there may be other methods also to cause a denial of access to an authorised user to a computer resource,

(g) *Providing any assistance to any person to facilitate access to a computer, computer system or computer network in contravention of the provisions of this Act, rules or regulations made thereunder.*

This provision implies the owners and users of computer resources not to help any other person in gaining an access to a computer resource in violation of the provisions of this Act.

(h) *Charging the services availed of by a person to the account of another person by tempering with or manipulating any computer, computer system or computer network.*

Explanations—for the purpose of this section.

(i) ***Computer contaminant:*** means any set of computer instructions that are designed

(a) to modify, destroy, record, transmit data or program residing within a computer, computer system or computer network: or

(b) by any means to usurp the normal operation of the computer, computer system, or computer network.

(ii) ***Computer database:*** means a representation of information knowledge, facts, concepts or instruction in text, image, audio, video that are being prepared or have been prepared in a formalised manner or have been produced by a computer, computer system or computer network and are intended for use in a computer, computer system or computer network;

(iii) ***Computer virus:*** means by computer instruction, information, data or program that destroys, damages, degrades or adversely affects the performance of a computer resource or attaches itself to another computer resource and operates when a program, data or instruction is executed or some other event take place in that computer resource;

(iv) ***Damage:*** means to destroy, alter, delete, add, modify or rearrange any computer resource by any means.

PENALTY FOR THE ABOVE CONTRAVENTIONS

The person guilty of a contravention as described above shall be liable to pay damages by way of compensation not exceeding Rs. 1 crore to the person so affected.

Penalties for Certain other Contraventions

Sec. 44 has described certain other contraventions also and the penalty for each of them as follows:

(a) Failure to furnish any document, return or report to the Controller or the Certifying Authority when required to do so.

The penalty shall be a fine of an amount not exceeding Rs. 1,50,000 for each such failure.

(b) Failure to file any return or furnish any information books or other documents within the time specified thereunder in the regulations.

The penalty shall be a fine of a amount not exceeding Rs. 5,000 for every day during which such failure continues.

(c) Failure to maintain books of account or records as required under law.

The penalty shall be a fine of an amount not exceeding Rs. 10,000 for every day during which the failure continues.

Residuary Penalty

Sec. 45 of this Act provides for various other possible contraventions which may not have been included in the Act specifically. It states: "Whoever contravenes any rules or regulations made under this Act, for the contravention of which no penalty has been separately provided, shall be liable to pay a compensation not exceeding Rs. 25,000 to the person affected by such contravention or a penalty not exceeding Rs. 25,000.

ADJUDICATION ON CONTRAVENTIONS AND APPOINTMENT OF ADJUDICATING OFFICER

Section 46 of this Act provides that where a need arises to fond out whether any person has committed a contravention of any of the provisions of this Act or of any rule etc. made thereunder, the Central Government shall appoint an officer to be an adjudicating officer for holding an inquiry in the manner prescribed by the Central Government.

The adjudicating officer shall give to the accuse person a reasonable opportunity for making representation in the matter. If he is satisfied that the person has committed the contravention, he may impose such penalty or award such compensation as he thinks fit.

No person shall be appointed as an adjudicating officer unless of possesses such experiences in the file of Information Technology and legal or judicial experience as may be prescribed by the Central Government.

Where more than one adjudicating officers are appointed, the Central Government shall specify by order the matters and places with respect to which such officers shall exercise their jurisdiction.

Every adjudicating offer shall have the powers of a civil court which are conferred on the Cyber Appellate Tribunal.

Factors to be taken into account by the adjudicating officer

While determining the quantum of compensation under this Act for contraventions, the adjudicating officer shall give due consideration to the following factors:

(a) the amount of gain of unfair advantage, whenever quantifiable, made as a result of the default;
(b) the amount of loss caused to any person as a result of the default;
(c) the repetitive nature of the default.

THE CYBER REGULATION APPELLATE TRIBUNAL (CRAT)

A Certifying Authority or a subscriber may feel aggrieved by the order of the Controller of Certifying Authorities or of an Adjudicating officer and may like to appeal against the order. The Act provides for creation of a suitable machinery for the speedy disposal of such appeals, in the form of Cyber Regulations Appellate Tribunals (CRAT).

Establishment of Cyber Appellate Tribunal

According to Section 48 of this Act

(1) The Central Government shall establish one or more appellate tribunals to be known as the Cyber Regulation Appellate Tribunal.

(2) The Central Government shall also specify, in the notification, the matters and places in relation to which the Cyber Appellate Tribunal may exercise jurisdiction.

A Cyber Appellate Tribunal shall consist of one person only called the Presiding Officer of the Tribunal.

The Act has laid down detailed provisions regarding the qualifications, terms of office, salary, etc., vacancies, resignation and removal of the Presiding officers of the Tribunals.

Appeal to Cyber Appellate Tribunal

Section 57 of this Act provides for the rules relating to appeals before an Appellate Tribunal. These are as under

(i) Any person aggrieved by an order made by Controller or an adjudicating officer under this Act may make an appeal to a Cyber Appellate Tribunal having jurisdiction in the matter. However, there can be no appeal against an order made by an adjudicating with the consent of parties.

(ii) An appeal shall be filed within a period of 45 days from the date on which a copy of the order made to be challenged is received by the person aggrieved and it shall be in such form and be accompanied by such fee as may be prescribed.

The Tribunal may extend this time period if it is satisfied that there was sufficient cause for not filing it within that period.

(iii) The Tribunal may, after giving the parties to the appeal, an opportunity of being heard, pass such orders thereon as it thinks fit, confirming, modifying or setting aside the order appealed against.

(iv) The Tribunal shall send a copy of every order made by it to the parties to the appeal and to the concerned Controller or adjudicating officer.

(v) The appeal filed shall be dealt with as expeditiously as possible and endeavour shall be made to dispose of the appeal finally within six months from the data of receipt of the appeal.

Procedure and Powers of the Cyber Appellate Tribunal

Section. 58 of this Act lays down provision regarding the procedure to be followed by the Tribunal and the powers available in the discharge of its duties.

The Cyber Appellate Tribunal shall not be bound by the procedure laid down by the Code of Civil Procedure, 1908 but shall be guided by the principles of natural justice and shall have powers to regulate its own procedure including the place at which it shall have it sittings.

The Cyber Appellate Tribunal shall have, for the purpose of discharging its functions under this Act, the same powers as are vested in a civil under the Code of Civil Procedure, 1908, while trying a suit, in respect of the following maters,

(a) summoning and enforcing the attendance of any person and examining him on oath;
(b) requiring the discovery and production of documents or other electronic records;
(c) receiving evidence on affidavits;
(d) issuing commissions for the examination of witnesses or document;
(e) reviewing its decisions;
(f) dismissing an application for default or deciding it ex parte;
(g) any other mater which may be prescribed.

Civil Courts Barred

"No civil court shall have jurisdiction to entertain any suit or proceeding in respect of any matter which an adjudicating officer appointed under this Act or the Cyber Appellate Tribunal is empowered to determine" (Section 61).

Appeal to High Court

Any person aggrieved by any decision or order of the Cyber Appellate Tribunal may file an appeal to the High Court within 60 days from the date of communication of the decision or order to him on any question of fact or law arising out of such order.

The High Court may, if it is satisfied that the appellant was prevented by sufficient causes from filing the appeal within the said period, allow it to be filed within a further period not exceeding 60 days (Section 62).

Compounding of Contraventions

Section 63 provides for the possibility of a compromise between the Controller or Adjudicating officer and the accused person regarding the quantum of the penalty.

Any contravention under the Act by a person may, either before or after the institution of adjudication proceedings, be compounded by the Controller or by the adjudicating officer, as the case may be. But, the compromised amount shall not, in any case, exceed the maximum amount of the penalty which may be imposed under this Act for the contravention so compounded.

This facility will not be available to a person who commits the same or similar contravention within a period of three years from the data on which the first contravention, committed by him, was compounded.

Explanation—Any second or subsequent contravention committed after the expiry of a period of three years from the date on which contravention was previously compounded shall be deemed to be a first contravention.

Recovery of Penalty

According to Section 64, a penalty imposed under this Act, if it is not paid, shall be recovered as an arrear of land revenue and the licence or the Digital Signature Certificate, as the case may be, shall be suspended till the penalty is paid.

CYBER OFFENCES AND PENALTIES

Cyber Offence

The use of computer, computer system and computer network is subject to legal provisions of Information Technology Act. Where the person commits any act which is prohibited by law or which defects the provisions of this Act, it will amount to cyber offence. In other words, cyber offence implies direct violation of legal provisions of this Act. A criminal intention on the part of the person committing illegal act constitute an offence. He intends to commit such with a view to cause loss to another person.

Section 65 to 76 of this Act deal with the offences and provide for penalty of imprisonment or imposition of fine or both on the person committing such offences.

The Act has recognised the following offences and has prescribed a quantum of penalty for the person committing such offences.

1. *Tempering with computer source codes (Section 65)*

This offence takes place when a person tempers with the valuable computer programs of another person.

The provision states that a person shall be guilty of an offence if he knowingly or intentionally conceals, destroys or alters or intentionally or knowingly causes another to conceal, destroy or alter any computer source code used for a computer, computer program, computer system or computer network, when the computer source code is required to be kept or maintained by law for the time being in force.

Penalty. Such a person shall be punished with imprisonment up to three years, or with fine which may extend up to Rs. 2 lakh, or with both.

Explanation. For the purposes of this provision, "computer source code" means the listing of programs, Computer command, design and layout and program analysis of computer resource in any form.

2. *Hacking with Computer System (Section 66)*

This provision declares 'hacking' as a punishable offence.

This offence take place when a person with the intent to cause or knowing that he is likely to cause wrongful loss or damage to the public or any person destroys or deletes or alters any information residing in a computer resource or diminishes its value or utility or affects it injuriously by any means.

Penalty. Whosever commits hacking shall be punished with imprisonment up to three years, or with fine which may extend up Rs. 2 lakh or with both.

Originally, the term 'hacking' was used for the efforts of computer-savvy people to make experiments with computer operations to, explore and exploit the, maximum abilities of the computer hardware and software. In course of time, the term 'hacking' has become a technique of indulging in certain types of cyber crimes.

'Hacking' involves a planned attempt to penetrate the security systems of a computer network and, having gained this unauthorised access into the system, causes a distortion or damage to the contents and functioning of the system. The damage may be caused to the hardware or to the software of the system. This may be done from a distance or by gaining a physical closeness to the system.

3. *Publishing of Obscene Information (Section 67)*

This offence takes place when a person publishes or transmits or causes to be published in the electronic form, any material which is lascivious or appeals to the prurient interest or if its effect is such as to tend to deprave and corrupt persons who are likely to read, see or hear the matter contained or embodied in it.

Penalty. The guilty person shall be punished on first conviction with imprisonment for a term which may extend to five years and with fine which may extend to Rs. 1 lakh and in the event of a second or subsequent conviction with imprisonment for a term which may extend to ten years and also with fine which may extend for Rs. 2 lakh.

4. *Failure to Comply with Controller's Directions (Section 68)*

When the Controller directs Certifying Authority or any employee of such 'Authority' to take such measures or cease carrying on such activities which are necessary to ensure compliance with the provisions of this Act, the concerned person is bound to comply with term. Any failure to do so will be an offence.

Penalty. Any person who fails to comply with any such order shall be liable on conviction to imprisonment for a term not exceeding three years or to a fine not exceeding Rs. 2 lakh to both.

5. *Failure to decrypt information (Section 69)*

The controller may direct any agency of the Government to intercept any information transmitted through any computer resource of any person, if he is satisfied that it is necessary or expedient so do to in the broad national interest. The government agency under the direction may call upon the person to extend all facilities and technical assistance to decrypt the information. Any failure to do so by the person shall be an offence.

Penalty. The person guilty of such an offence shall be punished with an imprisonment for a term which may extend to seven years.

6. *Breaking into protected System (Section 70)*

A Government may find it essential to sometimes declare any computer, computer system or computer network to be a protected system. The Government may, in such case, authorize specific person only to access such protected system.

It would be an offence for any unauthorized person to secure access or attempt to secure access to a protected system in contravention of these provisions.

Penalty. The guilty person shall be punished with imprisonment for a term which may extend to ten years and shall also be liable to pay fine.

7. ***Misrepresentation before CCA (Section 71)***

This offence is committed when a person makes any misrepresentation to, or suppresses any material fact from, the Controller or the Certifying Authority for obtaining any licence or Digital Signature Certificate, as the case may be.

Penalty. The guilty person shall be punished with imprisonment for a term which may extend to two years, or with fine which may extend to Rs. 1 lakh or with both.

8. ***Breach of Confidentiality or Privacy (Section 72)***

Under the provisions of this Act, a person representing an authority may have the powers to secure access to any electronic record other information etc. of a person without his consent. If he, on obtaining this access to the information, discloses such electronic record or other information to any other person, it shall amount to an offence.

Penalty. The person guilty of this offence shall be punished with imprisonment for a term which may extend to two years, or with fine which may extend to Rs. 1 lakh or with both.

9. ***Publishing erroneous digital signature certificate (Section 73)***

It may happen that a Digital Signature Certificate gets issued even while some error hade crept in the whole process of issuing it. No person should make a public announcement of such an erroneous certificate knowingly. If it is done, it shall amount to an offence. Sec. 73 states as follows:

"No person shall publish a Digital Signature Certificate or otherwise make it available to any other per son with the knowledge that—

(a) the Certifying Authority listed in the certificate has not issued it; or

(b) the subscriber listed in the certificate has not accepted it; or

(c) the certificate has been revoked or suspended,

unless such publication is for the purpose of verifying a digital signature created prior to such suspension or revocation."

Penalty. Any person who contravenes this provision shall be punished with imprisonment for a term which may extend to two years, or with fine which may extend to Rs. 1 lakh or with both.

10. ***Publication for Fraudulent Purpose (Section 74)***

This offence takes place when a person knowingly creates, publishes or otherwise make available a Digital Signature Certificate for any fraudulent or unlawful purpose.

Penalty. He shall be punished with imprisonment for a term which may extend to two years, or with fine which may extend to Rs. 1 lakh or with both.

11. ***Failure to Surrender the License (Section 33)***

As was discussed in the previous chapter, when a Certifying Authority's licence has been revoked or suspended, the person in whose name the licence is issued must surrender it before the Controller.

***Penalty*.** On failure to do so, he shall be liable for imprisonment up to six months or a fine up to Rs. 10,000 or for both.

Other Rules

(i) Offence or contravention committed outside India. The provisions of this Act shall apply also to any offence or contravention committed outside India by any person irrespective of his nationality, if the act or conduct constituting the offence or contravention involves a computer, computer system or computer network located in India.

(ii) Order for confiscation. Any computer hardware, in respect of which, any provision of this Act has been or is being contravened, shall be liable to confiscation.

But, where it is established to the satisfaction of the court adjudicating the confiscation that the person in whose possession, power or control of any such computer hardware is found is not responsible for the contravention of the provisions of this Act, the court may, instead of making an order for confiscation, make such other order authorized by this Act against the person contravening of the provisions of this Act, as it may think fit.

(iii) Penalties of confiscation not to interfere with other punishment. No penalty imposed or confiscation made under this Act shall prevent the imposition of any other punishment to which the person affected thereby is liable under any other law for the time being in force.

REVIEW QUESTIONS

1. Define the term 'Cyber Contravention'. Explain various cyber contraventions which are mentioned under section 43 of this Act. `
2. Discuss the penalty for certain other contraventions laid down under section 44 of this Act.
3. How does adjudication on contravention take place? What factors would be taken into account by adjudicating offices for determining quantum of compensation.
4. How, 'Cyber Appellate Tribunal' is formal. Discuss various rules for making appeal to such tribunal and explain powers of the tribunal.
5. Define 'Cyber Offence'. Discuss various offences with penalty prescribed for such offences.
6. Write notes on:
   (a) Adjudication Officer
   (b) Cyber Appellate Tribunal
   (c) Compounding of Contraventions
   (d) Publishing Obscene Information

■■■

Question Paper-I

B. Com. (Hons.)/I/NS (2007)

Paper V—BUSINESS LAW

(Admission of 2004 and onwards)

(New Course)

Time : 3 *Hours* *Maximum Marks* : 55

Write your Roll No. on the top immediately on receipt of this question paper.

Note:— Answers may be written either in English or in Hindi; but the same medium should be used throughout the paper.

Attempt *All* questions.

All questions carry equal marks.

1. (*a*) State with reasons in brief whether the following statements are True or False: 6

(*i*) Communication of offer is complete when it comes to the knowledge of the offeree.

(*ii*) Parties to a contract of sale can get the price of goods fixed by third parties.

(*iii*) Digital signature is an electronic image of the hand written signature of a person.

(*b*) "Insufficiency of consideration is immaterial but an agreement without consideration is void." Comment on the statement giving suitable examples. 5

or

(*a*) State, with reasons in brief, whether the following statements are True or False: 6

(*i*) Offer can be revoked any time before the communication of its acceptance is complete as against the offeree.

(*ii*) Property in goods passes only when the goods are delivered.

(*iii*) A promissory note can be made payable to bearer.

(*b*) "The law of contract is not the whole law of agreements nor is it the whole law of obligations." Critically examine the statement giving suitable examples. 5

2. (*a*) What do you understand by competency to contract? Explain the position of persons of unsound mind in this respect. 6

(*b*) A executed a promissory note in favour of B while he was a minor. The promissory note was renewed by A in favour of B when he attained the age of majority. B sues A on the basis of the second promissory note. Will he succeed? Give reasons. 5

or

(*a*) "Undue influence is a subtle form of coercion." Comment. 6

(*b*) A owed a sum of Rs. 15,000 to B. The debt was barred by Limitation Act. A signed a written promise to pay Rs. 10,000 to B on account of this time barred debt. Can B claim Rs. 10,000 from A? Give reasons for your answer. 5

3. (*a*) Explain the nature and extent of surety's liability. 6

(*b*) A sold his business including goodwill to B for Rs. 8,00,000 by an agreement. The agreement provided that A shall not engage in similar business in the whole of India for next 8 years. Is this restraint valid? Explain with reasons. 5

or

(*a*) Sub-agent and substituted agent;

(*b*) Particular lien and general lien;

(*c*) Void agreement and illegal agreement. 11

4. (*a*) Distinguish between a 'condition' and a 'warranty'. When can a condition be treated as a warranty? 6

(*b*) A purchased a tweed coat. After wearing it he developed rashes on his skin due to his abnormally sensitive skin. But he did not disclose this fact to the seller. Can A return the coat? Decide with reasons. 5

or

(*a*) Define and explain the term 'goods' under the Sale of Goods Act. 6

(*b*) A is an oil merchant. He has 450 litres of oil in a tank. He enters into a contract with B to sell 300 litres of oil from the said tank. Before B could pay and take delivery, the entire 450 litres of oil perished in a fire, Is B liable to bear the loss of 300 litres of oil? Decide with reasons. 5

5. (*a*) Make a comparison between a Bill of Exchange and a Cheque. 6

(*b*) Explain the term 'subscriber' and his duties under the I.T. Act, 2000. 5

or

(*a*) What is crossing of cheque? Explain the effect of 'not negotiable crossing'. 6

(*b*) Distinguish between 'contraventions' and 'offences' as per I.T. Act, 2000. Is 'hacking with the computer system' and offence under the Act. 5

Question Paper-II

B.Com. (Hons.)/I/NS (2006)

Paper V—BUSINESS LAW

(Admission of 2004 and onwards)
(New Course)

Time : 3 Hours *Maximum Marks* : 55

Attempt *All* questions.
All questions carry equal marks.

1. (*a*) State, with reasons, in brief, whether the following statements are True or False:

 (*i*) A contract becomes void due to inadequate consideration.

 (*ii*) Actionable claim cannot be the subject-matter of contract of sale of goods.

 (*iii*) 'Public-key' means the key of a key-pair used to create a digital signature. 6

 (*b*) "Special conditions to the offer must be communicated to the other party at the time of formation of a contract." Critically examine this statement giving suitable examples. 5

or

 (*a*) State, with reasons in brief, whether the following statements are True or False:

 (*i*) The person who gives consideration must be benefited.

 (*ii*) 'Money' cannot be the subject-matter of contract of sale of goods.

 (*iii*) Anti-dated cheques are not recongnised under Negotiable Instrument Act. 6

 (*b*) "Agreements in restraint of trade are void." Critically examine this statement giving suitable examples. 5

2. (*a*) Explain the rules governing measurement of damages in the case of breach of contract. 6

 (*b*) 'A' intends to sell his horse to 'B'. A's horse is not sound, He prepares a forged certificate of fitness of the horse seemingly issued by a Veterinary

Doctor. He pastes the certificate on the door of the stable. 'B', without looking at the certificate, enters the stable and purchases the horse. Later on 'B' comes to know that horse is not sound. Can 'B' now cancel the contract on the basis of fraud of 'A'? Give reasons. 5

or

(*a*) Discuss the 'Novation' and 'Remission' as a mode of discharge of contract, giving suitable examples. 6

(*b*) A's ornaments are stolen from her house. After some time, the ornaments are recovered by the police. The police keep the ornaments in its safe custody. Subsequently, the same ornaments are stolen from the police-custody also. Now, 'A' files a suit against the police department for claiming damages. Will 'A' succeed? Give reasons. 5

3. (*a*) What is agency be ratification? State the requisites of a valid ratification. 6

(*b*) 'A' gives a guarantee to 'B' on 1-1-2006 for the supply of tea worth rupees ten thousand to 'C', payment of which is to be made on 1-3-2006. 'C' makes the payment on 1-2-2006 and again gets tea of the same amount on credit. However, 'C' fails to make the payment. Now 'B' files a suit against 'A' for claiming the price. Will be succeed? Give reasons. 5

or

(*a*) Explain, citing case law, the legal position of a 'Minor-promisor' the Indian Contract Act. Can a minor be a promisee?

(*b*) 'A' goes to a hotel for a dinner. He finds a mobile-phone near his table and deposits it with 'B', the hotel manager. In spite of vigorous efforts the owner of the mobile phon could not be traced. Now, 'A' requests 'B' to return the mobile phone to him, but 'B' refuses to doe so. Now, 'A' files a suit against 'B' for getting back to mobile phone. Will he succeed? Give reasons. 5

4. (*a*) Define the term 'Unpaid Seller' as per Sale of Goods Act. Explain the unpaid seller's right of lien over the goods. 6

(*b*) 'A', a customer, has not knowledge about hot water bottles. He goes to 'B', a chemist, and demands a hot water bottle from him. 'B' gives a bottle to him and states that it is meant for hot water. After a few days, while using the bottle, it bursts and injures A's wife. 'A' files a suit against 'B' for claiming damages for injuries caused to his wife. Will be succeed? Give reasons. 5

or

(*a*) "No seller of goods can convey to the buyer of goods a better title than what he himself possesses." Examine this statement and explain the exceptions to this rule, as per Sale of Goods Act. 6

(*b*) 'A' agrees to sell his new fridge to 'B' for rupees fifteen thousand payable partly in cash and partly in exchange of old fridge. Is it a valid contract of sale of goods? Give reasons. 5

5. (*a*) Define the term 'Holder in due course' as per Negotiable Instruments Act. Discuss any three privileges of a holder in due course, with suitable examples. 6

(*b*) State the object of Information Technology Act. 2000. What provision has been made in the Act against publishing of information which is obscene is electronic form? 6

or

(*a*) Define, the term 'endorsement' as per Negotiable Instruments Act. Explain with illustrations 'Full Endorsement', 'Partial Endorsement' and 'Sans Recourse Endorsement'. 6

(*b*) What do you understand by 'Digital ' as per Information Technology Act, 2000? What purpose does this certificate serve? 5

■■■